CREATION BY ROSALIND GILLESPIE

PRESBYTERIANS IN IRELAND

PRESBYTERIANS IN IRELAND

An Illustrated History

LAURENCE KIRKPATRICK

CONSULTANT EDITOR
CLAUDE COSTECALDE

PHOTOGRAPHY
GORDON GRAY
CHRIS HILL SCENIC IRELAND

PICTURE EDITOR AND DESIGN
WENDY DUNBAR

BOOKLINK

Contents

The Presbyteries

Throughout their existence several congregations have occasionally changed their name. For ease of reference the current name has been used throughout. Also, all ministers have been designated 'Rev' when Presbyterians ministers were originally known as 'Mr'.

ACHILL ISLAND SCENIC IRELAND

WILLIAM BUTLER YEATS FAMOUSLY CLAIMED THAT 'his' people, the Anglo-Irish, were 'no petty people', and their historian, JC Beckett, contended that 'Ireland, without them, would not only be a different, but a poorer country.' Irish Presbyterians, sometime identified with the Scots-Irish, could make similar claims.

Since the early seventeenth century there has been a significant Presbyterian presence in Ireland, chiefly in the north, in Ulster, as the result of waves of immigration from Scotland. If we are to understand modern Irish history we need to take into account their distinctive role in that history, beginning with their seventeenth-century colonisation of Ulster and their part in the crises of that colony in the 1640s and the 'conflict of the kings' of 1689–91.

In the eighteenth century their disabilities as dissenters and their economic hardships as tenant farmers drove many to emigrate to colonial America where they contributed to the development of American Presbyterianism and to the colonists' fight for independence from Britain. Inspired to some extent by their example some Ulster Presbyterians became involved in the United Irish movement for Irish independence from Britain which led to the rebellion of 1798.

After the failure of the rebellion, followed by the Act of Union between Great Britain and Ireland, a majority of Presbyterians saw their spiritual and material interests best safeguarded by the union with Britain, in face of the increasing identification of the causes of Irish nationalism and Roman Catholicism. Their opposition to the Irish Home Rule movement was a major cause of the partition of Ireland and the establishment of Northern Ireland in which they are the largest Protestant church. 'The stronghold of Ulster Protestantism', TW Moody has written, 'has always been the Presbyterian Church, rooted in the Scottish reformation and maintaining close and continuous contact with Scotland.'

This is an attractive illustrated history of the Irish Presbyterians, who they were, where they came from, their identity and ethos, their theological and political conflicts, their outstanding personalities, their congregations and churches, what they have done and are doing at home and abroad in their obedience to Christ and His gospel. Professor Laurence Kirkpatrick and the publishers are to be congratulated on the excellence of this publication which should be of great interest not only to Irish Presbyterians but to all students of Irish history – I commend it to a wide readership.

THE VERY REV DR FINLAY HOLMES

Carrickfergus
Painting by
Andrew Nicholl 1804–86

1
The earliest Presbyterians

THE BIRTH OF THE PRESBYTERIAN CHURCH IN IRELAND took place at Carrickfergus on 10 June 1642. However, Presbyterian people had lived in Ireland for some time before that event. Walter Travers, for example, was the first resident provost of Trinity College in Dublin (founded in 1592 by Royal Charter from Elizabeth I) from 1594–1601. Travers was a puritan theologian and one time chaplain to William Cecil, first Baron Burghley, and tutor to his son Robert Cecil. He had been educated at the University of Cambridge and then travelled to Geneva to visit Calvin's successor, Theodore Beza. Following his Presbyterian ordination in Antwerp at the hands of Thomas Cartright, he had lectured at the Temple Church in London from 1585 until Archbishop Whitgift forbade him to preach in March 1586. The first elected fellows of Trinity College, James Fullerton and James Hamilton, were also Presbyterians.

Hugh O'Neill, Earl of Tyrone
Left: Trinity College, Dublin

The influx of significant numbers of Scottish Presbyterians into Ulster was a direct consequence of the change from Tudor to Stuart monarchy in 1603. Elizabeth had conducted war in Ulster for the final nine years of her reign. This titanic struggle represented the decisive clash of Gaelic and Anglo cultures in determining who would hold ultimate authority in Ireland. On 18 March 1603, the English commander Mountjoy took the final surrender of the Gaelic chief O'Neill at Mellifont, successfully concealing from him the fact that Elizabeth had died only six days earlier.

Surrender of Hugh O'Neill, Earl of Tyrone to Lord Deputy Essex

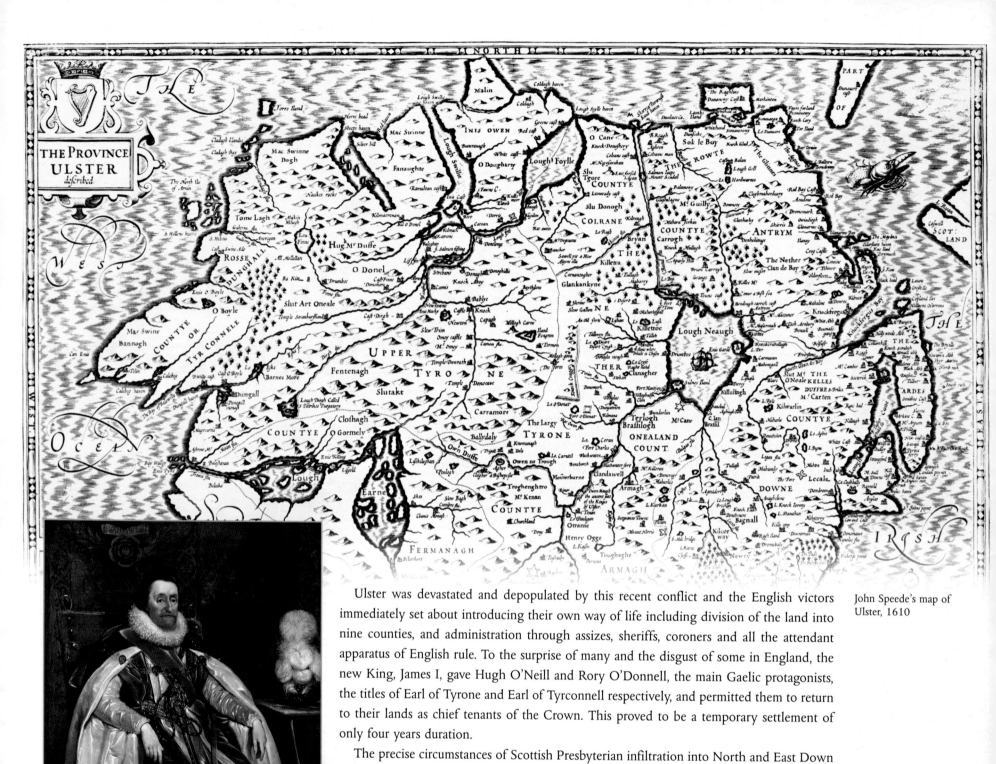

The Province Ulster described

John Speede's map of Ulster, 1610

James I of England and VI of Scotland
by Daniel Mytens

Ulster was devastated and depopulated by this recent conflict and the English victors immediately set about introducing their own way of life including division of the land into nine counties, and administration through assizes, sheriffs, coroners and all the attendant apparatus of English rule. To the surprise of many and the disgust of some in England, the new King, James I, gave Hugh O'Neill and Rory O'Donnell, the main Gaelic protagonists, the titles of Earl of Tyrone and Earl of Tyrconnell respectively, and permitted them to return to their lands as chief tenants of the Crown. This proved to be a temporary settlement of only four years duration.

The precise circumstances of Scottish Presbyterian infiltration into North and East Down was a combination of the unfortunate incarceration of a minor Gaelic chief, Conn MacNéill O'Neill – Lord of Upper Clandeboye and the Great Ards – in Carrickfergus Castle and the opportunism of the Scottish Presbyterian Hugh Montgomery, sixth Laird of Braidstone in Ayrshire. Conn found himself arrested for a foolish anti-English boast which he had uttered upon discovering that his shipment of Spanish wine was detained in Belfast. With Montgomery's help, Conn was assisted in escaping from the castle by lowering himself on a rope from the walls and then being transported to Largs. Montgomery, through the influence of his brother Rev George Montgomery in London, secured a royal pardon for Conn O'Neill on condition that another Scotsman with Irish connections, James Hamilton, also benefited. Hamilton was the son of a Presbyterian minister in Dunlop, Ayrshire and had been a schoolmaster in Glasgow and latterly bursar of Trinity College in Dublin.

Sir Arthur Chichester

In April 1605, and with the king's approval, O'Neill's lands were divided. Conn O'Neill retained sixty townlands: half of Upper Clandeboye centred upon Castlereagh. Hugh Montgomery received lands around Newtownards, Movilla and Greyabbey. James Hamilton received lands around Holywood, Bangor and Groomsport. Other Gaelic chieftains in Antrim and Down made land available for new English and Scottish settlers in return for secure titles to their remaining lands under English law. But it was Hugh Montgomery and James Hamilton who principally introduced Scottish settlers to their new lands from 1606. The king saw the introduction of new settlers as a means of civilizing former Gaelic territories. In 1606, Montgomery and Hamilton had less than thirty cabins on their lands but they brought smiths, masons and carpenters with the settlers to establish a new colony. Bumper harvests in 1606 and 1607 encouraged everyone in this new adventure. A survey in 1611 records that Newtown Ards had been established with over 100 houses *'peopled with Scottes'*, also Bangor and Holywood with eighty and twenty new houses respectively. Weekly markets were also sustained in Bangor, Holywood, Greyabbey and Castlereagh. A similar new colony was taking root in South Antrim on the lands of Sir Arthur Chichester, the new Lord Deputy since 1605.

Chichester monument in St Nicholas Church, Carrickfergus

The Plantation of Ulster

This process of colonisation in Ulster took a quantum leap forwards with the introduction of The Ulster Plantation following 'the flight of the Earls'. The gradual and inexorable increase of English control in the Earl of Tyrone's territories convinced O'Neill that he could never have a secure peace with the English. On 4 September 1607, O'Neill and other Gaelic chieftains, in a group of about 120 persons — the cream of Gaelic society — left their territories by ship from Rathmullan on the shore of Lough Swilly. The Gaelic exiles disembarked at Quillebeuf in France and travelled on to the

Flight of the Earls
Thomas Ryan

Spanish Netherlands. Although hoping for assistance from Spain in launching a mission to recover their former territories and freedom, they were to be disappointed. O'Neill eventually died in Rome in 1616. Meanwhile back in Ulster, Sir Cahir O'Doherty of Inishowen sparked a Gaelic revolt in the spring of 1608. He sacked Derry and Strabane. He also threatened to attack mid-Ulster, but was killed on 5 July 1608 near Kilmacrennan. Other clans, such as the O'Cahans and O'Hanlons, also revolted; they were ruthlessly put down.

In the wake of the flight of the Earls and O'Doherty's revolt, English policy now focused upon the possibility of a plantation of the former Gaelic lands in Ulster. The initial success of the

Ouer-throw of an Irish rebell, in a late battaile: Or The death of Sir Carey Adoughertie, who murdred Sir George Paulet in Ireland; and for his rebellion hath his head now standing ouer Newgate in Dublin.

Imprinted at London for I. Wright, and are to be fould at his shop neere Christ Church gate, 1608.

A contemporary pamphlet describing the suppppression of the O'Doherty Rebellion in 1608

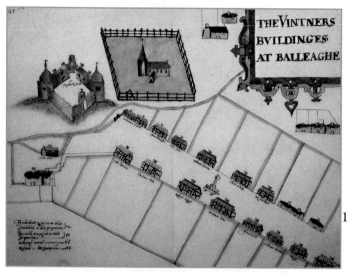

Sir Thomas Phillips 1622 'Survey of the
London Companies estates in County Lderry'
PUBLIC RECORD OFFICE OF NPRTHERN IRELAND

Montgomery and Hamilton colonies provided an encouraging model. By September
1609, a scheme had been drawn up, mainly upon the recommendations of Attorney-
General Sir John Davis, and the terms of the new scheme were published in London
in April 1610. Three groups of colonists were envisaged in a comprehensive
plantation plan which covered much of six counties: Armagh, Cavan, Coleraine (later
renamed Londonderry), Donegal, Fermanagh and Tyrone.

1 Undertakers had to be Scottish or English Protestants. These individuals could
   obtain land at an annual rent of £5.6.8 per 1,000 acres. They undertook to
   plant at least twenty-four Protestants from ten families minimum per 1,000
   acres and build a 'bawn' or defensive stone house in which they stored arms
   for the defence of their lands.

2 Servitors (army officers) could obtain similar grants but pay rent of £8
   per 1,000 acres if they did not plant English or Scottish
   tenants.

3 'Deserving Irish' could obtain land at an annual rent of
   £10.13.4 per 1,000 acres. A timescale was
   announced for arriving, building and
   commencing payment of rents but the story
   of this plantation is one of time slippage and
   partial compliance with the original plans.

The take up of the scheme never achieved
the required levels. A mere one hundred undertakers and fifty servitors came forward. The
government had to approach the merchants in the city of London for help. Of fifty-five
companies approached, only eighteen showed any interest in the plantation scheme.
Eventually all of County Coleraine and more besides was assigned to twelve leading London
companies. Surviving Ulster place-names such as Londonderry and Draperstown testify to

Bellaghy Bawn

Four surveyors from the London Companies

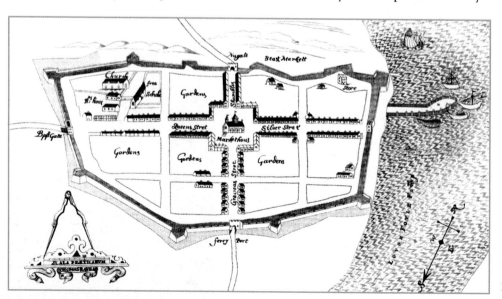

Plan of Londonderry

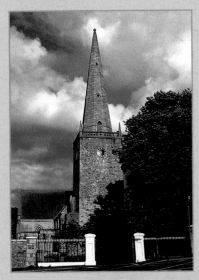

Bangor Abbey

Reverend Robert Blair
of Bangor
1593–1666

The window in Bangor Abbey recording Robert Blair's ministry

SCOTSMAN ROBERT BLAIR was, arguably, the leading Presbyterian minister in the earliest phase of Presbyterianism in Ireland, although his ministry in Ireland lasted only eleven years. On the invitation of James Hamilton, lately created Lord Clandeboye, Blair came to Ireland and was ordained in the parish of Bangor on 10 July 1623. Although ministering in the parish church, Robert Blair organised his ministry in Presbyterian fashion, appointing elders and deacons. He preached regularly, visited the twelve hundred souls under his care and, with other ministers, played a full role in the Antrim Meeting which arose out of the revival at Oldstone in 1625.

Robert Blair was connected by marriage to other ministers in Ulster. His first wife, Beatrix, was a sister of Janet, wife of Rev John Livingstone of Killinchy. His second wife, Catherine Montgomery, daughter of Viscount Montgomery of the Ards had two sisters, Isabel, wife of Rev Robert Cunningham of Holywood and Margaret, wife of Rev Robert Hamilton of Killyleagh.

With other Presbyterian ministers, Blair suffered at the hands of Bishop Echlin. After various legal proceedings, including Blair's personal appeal before King James I, Blair and other ministers were deposed and excommunicated in November 1634.

Blair was one of four Presbyterian ministers aboard the unsuccessful Eagle Wing voyage from Donaghadee to America in 1636. In July 1638, he became minister of the congregation in Ayr and later in St. Andrews. The Scottish Assembly sent him to Ulster in 1641 on a three month preaching mission based at Bangor and he expressed his sorrow at the depths of spiritual destitution he witnessed.

Following the Restoration in 1660, Blair was imprisoned for over three years at Musselburgh and later at Kirkcaldy. He spent his final years in retirement, dying on 27 August 1666.

these activities. The famous six metre thick walls of Londonderry were completed by the Irish Society in 1618 at a cost of £10,000. In that same year, according to Pynnar's Survey, there were ninety-two houses within the city providing accommodation for 102 families.

The coalescence of a number of factors at this time gave Presbyterianism a decisive foothold in Ulster. The new colonists came from England and Scotland and the fact that many of the latter were Presbyterian is obvious. The established Irish Church at that time was in very poor condition. There was a shortage of both preachers and buildings in Ulster, which had been until very recently the most Gaelic part of Ireland. James I preferred an Episcopal church system based upon bishops. When this was enforced in Scotland in 1610, Scottish Presbyterianism was under severe pressure and many Presbyterian ministers were compelled to resign from their charges for refusing to accept the imposition of Episcopalianism. They came to regard Ulster as a land of refuge. Some of the Bishops in the Irish Church were Scottish and were open to the possibility of installing Scottish Presbyterian ministers in their dioceses. Most notable in this practice were Bishop Robert Echlin of Down (1613–35) and Bishop Andrew Knox of Raphoe (1612–33) who knew at first hand of the theological training of their fellow Scots. These men participated alongside other ministers in services of ordination which they, as Bishops, could claim were legal services of Episcopal ordination, while the ordinands could equally claim that they were Presbyterian services of ordination – a practical and convenient accommodation which suited all concerned. Curious as it seems from a modern perspective, prior to 1613 about nineteen Presbyterian ministers came to Ulster and ministered in the Irish Episcopal Church. Rev Edward Brice was admitted to the charge of Broadisland (Ballycarry) in 1613. He is the earliest named Presbyterian minister in Ireland. This 'Prescopalian' period was to last for almost forty years and marks the period when Presbyterianism took permanent root in Ulster. A common Calvinistic theology, the sympathy and protection of Archbishop Ussher, and the patronage of Scottish landowners like James Hamilton and Hugh Clotworthy

Ruins of Brice Church at Broadisland, Ballycarry

The Earliest Presbyterian Ministers in Ireland

Edward Brice
Broadisland (Ballycarry) 1613–1636

William Dyal
Donaghenry (Stewartstown) 1614

Robert Cunningham
Holywood 1615–1636

Robert Hamilton
Killeshill (Tyrone) 1617–1623

John Ridge
Antrim 1619–1636

? Hubbard
Carrickfergus 1621–1623

James Glendinning
Coole (Carnmoney) pre-1622–1625
Oldstone 1625–1626

John Boyle
Killyleagh pre-1622

Robert Blair
Bangor 1623–1634

George Dunbar
Larne 1624–1634

James Hamilton
Ballywalter 1626–1636

Andrew Stewart
Donegore 1627–1634

Robert Cunningham
Killomard (Donegal) 1630–1645
Taughboyne (Ray) 1645–1654.

Henry Calvert
Oldstone 1630–1636

John Livingstone
Killinchy 1630–1636

Josias Welsh
Templepatrick pre 1630–1634

Robert Pont
Ramelton (Donegal) c1630–1639

John McClelland
Newtownards c1630–1636

David Kennedy
Newtownards 1638

Thomas Murray
Killyleagh pre 1640–1641

14

helped make this situation possible. It is clear from surviving records that most of these Scottish ministers did not use Anglican forms of service but rather dispensed with the liturgy and conducted worship according to their Presbyterian custom. They also established Kirk Sessions and maintained strict discipline among their people.

Several of these Presbyterian ministers were men of distinction, for example Robert Cunningham (Holywood from November 1615), Robert Blair (Bangor from July 1623), Andrew Stewart (Donegore from 1627) and Josias Welsh, a grandson of John Knox (Templepatrick from before 1630). The people among whom they ministered were not godly. On the contrary, they appear largely to have been poor and rough. Blair recorded,

'Although amongst those whom divine providence did send to Ireland there were several persons eminent for birth, education and parts, yet, for the most part were such as either poverty, scandalous lives or, at the best, adventurous seeking of better accommodation had forced thither, so that the security and thriving of religion was little seen … '

Rev Arthur Stewart ministered at Donegore Church 1627–34

The Sixmilewater Revival
The most noteworthy event in these early years of colonisation was the revival of 1625. It was centred in Oldstone near Antrim and has become known as the Sixmilewater Revival (after the river which flows through that area). Robert Blair heard Rev James Glendinning lecture in Carrickfergus and perceived that he was not really intellectually capable of maintaining a ministry in a town that was then the principal town in Ulster and the seat of English administration. Displaying a candid honesty, he spoke to Glendinning and advised him to relocate in a more rural region. Glendinning responded by moving to Oldstone, about three miles from Antrim. Glendinning's preaching style was akin to an Old Testament prophet – thundering the law of God and impressing upon his congregation the terrors of God as Judge. Increasing numbers of settlers were attracted to the services at Oldstone and many were broken by an overwhelming sense of their sinfulness. Unfortunately, Glendinning appears to have been unable to help these people find peace and salvation in Christ as Saviour. Neighbouring ministers came to help.

This work continued for several months and attracted increasing numbers of settlers. One local convert, Hugh Campbell, started a regular prayer meeting in his house on the last Friday of each month. This format of prayer and discussion became so popular that

Early Scots settlers
from a description by
Rev. Andrew Stewart, Donaghadee son of Rev Arthur Stewart, Donegore

'Thus, on all hands Atheism increased, and disregard of God – iniquity abounded, contention, fighting, murder, thieving, adultery, &c. – as among people who, as they had nothing within them to overawe them … And verily at this time the whole body of this people seemed ripe, and soon ripe for the manifestation, in a greater degree, of God's judgements or mercy than had been seen for a long time; for their carriage made them to be abhorred at home in their native land, insomuch that going for Ireland was looked on as a miserable mark of a deplorable person – yea, it was turned to a proverb, and one of the expressions of disdain that could be invented to tell a man that Ireland would be his hinder end. While thus it was, and when any man would have expected nothing but God's judgement to have followed the crew of sinners, behold the Lord visited them in admirable mercy, the like whereof had not been seen anywhere for many generations.'

Campbell's home could no longer accommodate all who wanted to attend. Rev John Ridge of Antrim suggested that his church building should be used, and as a result a regular monthly meeting developed on the first weekend of each month. Ministers arrived on Thursday and discussed matters of common interest together. Friday was a day of prayer and fasting and concluded with an evening service. Worship and teaching continued on Saturday with two morning and two afternoon services (one less in winter months) and the weekend concluded with a Sunday morning Communion Service followed by a Thanksgiving Service. The revival continued for several years with local ministers regularly participating in these meetings.

It has been suggested by subsequent Presbyterian commentators that these monthly meetings in Antrim served as a kind of 'proto-Presbytery' and there is undoubtedly some truth in the assertion. The saddest fact to emerge from the entire episode is that Rev James Glendinning, whose fiery preaching started the revival, played no further part in its activities. He was never invited to participate in the monthly Antrim meetings. He seems to have become quite unstable in his mind and was reported to have left the area to search for the seven churches of the book of Revelation. He did resurface in his native Scotland before 1630 and was eventually settled as minister of Row in Dumbartonshire. He was replaced in Oldstone by Josias Welsh.

Other Presbyterian ministers came to Ulster and participated in the Antrim meetings. The dominant custom was to follow the practice of the Presbyterian Church in Scotland. Presbyterian practice was for

Rev John Ridge ministered at Antrim Church, 1619–36, location of the Antrim Meeting.

the congregation to receive Communion while seated at specially erected tables in the aisles of the Church. In contrast, Anglican communion was served to the congregation as they came forward to kneel at the front of the Church. The Scottish Presbyterian ministers also oversaw the appointment of elders in their congregations to administer congregational discipline. Two native Irishmen who were converted at this time were Jeremiah O'Quinn, who became minister of Billy (Bushmills) in 1646, and Owen O'Connolly, who later served as a Presbyterian elder and warned the authorities of the impending attack upon Dublin castle in October 1641.

It has been estimated that in 1630 there were about thirty Scottish Presbyterian ministers preaching in the South Antrim and North Down area. Some operated as private chaplains to the wealthier settlers but others ministered in the fourteen or so congregations in the locality. This promising situation was not to remain stable for long. A number of factors construed to remove the vast majority of these ministers from their positions.

Communion in the aisles as practised still in Glascar Presbyterian Church

LLOYD TOAL

Eyewitness to the 1625 revival

by
Reverend Andrew Stewart as a young boy

'Indeed, the joy and spirit of that time in this place can't by words be well expressed. Then, those that feared the Lord spake often one to another, and the Lord hearkened and heard, and put them (as it were soon) among his jewels, if he had any jewels in any part of the earth. This is much to be observed when you consider what stuff he had to make them of, and when you think again that, without law or liberty sought or obtained of the rulers, Christ entered upon that work at his own hand, and strengthened his kingdom in Ireland by putting it in the hearts of a people who had been rebels all their lives long. When, therefore, the multitudes of wounded consciences were healed, they began to draw into holy communion, and met together privately for edification (a thing which in a lifeless generation is both neglected and reproved) . . .'

16

Charles I by an unknown artist

Death of Reverend Andrew Stewart

minister at Donegore 1627–34

Being called to the burial of that excellent man of God, Mr. Josiah Welsh (of Templepatrick), who was his neighbour minister, Mr. Stewart stood some time at the grave, as a sad observer of such a thing, and to some who were by said, 'Who knows who will be next?' but none answering, he said to them, 'I know,' and then turned away, and went home to Donegore on foot, and entering into the church, did bolt the doors, where he tarried some two hours; and, after going to his house, he fell asleep on his bed with an excess of grief, whence he never in health rose again, but was buried that day month (July 1634). When his wife returned, whom he had left with Mr. Welsh's widow, she inquired what he had been doing; to whom he said, 'I have been taking my leave of the church of Donegore, and I was there taking timber and stones to witness, that in my short time I had laboured to be faithful; and that, according to my light, I have revealed the whole counsel of God to the people.'

Presbyterian Persecution

King James died on 27 March 1625 and was succeeded by his son Charles. Charles I believed in the Divine right of kings. In other words that he, as king, had a right of absolute obedience from all his subjects. It was the policy of Charles I and his new archbishop, William Laud (appointed in 1633), to secure the triumph of Episcopacy over Presbyterianism throughout Charles' kingdoms which led to trouble in Ulster. Presbyterians were regarded by king and archbishop as stubborn schismatics who peddled dangerous theological and political views. In June 1630, at the height of the revival in Antrim, Blair and Livingstone travelled to Scotland and participated in a Communion Service at Kirk of Shotts. A revival started. It is reported that 500 people were converted through Livingstone's sermon on the Monday. Such religious enthusiasm was anathema to the Episcopal Church and complaints were made by James Law, bishop of Glasgow, and others to the Irish bishops to curtail these Irish ministers.

Robert Echlin, bishop of Down and Dromore, suspended Revs. Blair, Welsh, Dunbar and Livingstone from their positions, in September 1631. Although archbishop Ussher, who was sympathetic to the Presbyterian ministers, had their suspension lifted, they were again suspended on 4 May 1632 for refusing before Echlin to promise conformity to the Episcopal ceremonies. Blair had a personal audience in London with Charles I in which he pressed the unjustness of these suspensions. Although Charles did instruct that if the charges made against Blair and his fellow ministers proved false those responsible should be punished, nothing came of this because the king's instruction was addressed to the new Irish Lord Deputy, Sir Thomas Wentworth.

Wentworth was appointed Lord Deputy of Ireland in 1633 with a mission to raise funds for the royal coffers and enforce High Church conformity. He brought with him as his chaplain, John Bramhall, who became Bishop of Derry in 1634 and leader of the campaign to make the Irish Church conform to the model of the English Church. Despite receiving the king's letter in relation to Blair and his colleagues, Wentworth refused to lift their suspensions. Livingstone returned to Scotland but the other suspended ministers continued to preach in the open air to their people. Upon the intervention of Lord Castlestewart, himself a Presbyterian, Wentworth lifted the suspensions for six months in May 1634. Josias Welsh did not long enjoy his freedom for he died on 23 June 1634 from the effects of a cold which he had caught while undertaking open air preaching in Templepatrick. Rev Andrew Stewart of Donegore attended the funeral of his neighbour and friend and fell ill himself the next day and died in September.

Wentworth forced the timorous Bishop Echlin to renew the suspensions on Blair and Dunbar in November 1634. He also maintained a ruthless policy of forcing Irish bishops to secure conformity within their dioceses. The Antrim meeting was finally closed at that time with a solemn Communion Service. A convocation of the Irish Church met and

Thomas Wentworth, 1st Earl of Strafford, the King's able and loyal minister by Van Dyck
NATIONAL PORTRAIT GALLERY

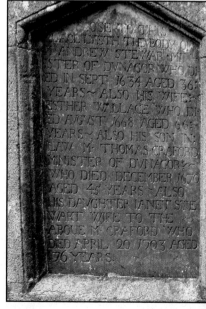

Andrew Stewart headstone

Old Holywood parish

Response of Reverend Robert Cunningham of Holywood

to deposition by Bishop Henry Leslie
12 August 1636

'I have now lived these twenty years amongst you in this kingdom, serving the Lord in his holy ministry, and thought so to have spent the rest of my days (which cannot be very long, for my body is very crazed) in the same employment. My doctrine and life for that time are known to most who are present here. I appeal to all their consciences if they can say anything against me in either of them. Yea, I have kept me close to the commission of my Lord; but now I am required to receive impositions upon my ministry, which are against my conscience. I rather lay down my ministry at the feet of my Lord and Saviour, Christ, of whom I did receive it, than to live with an evil conscience in the free liberty of it.'

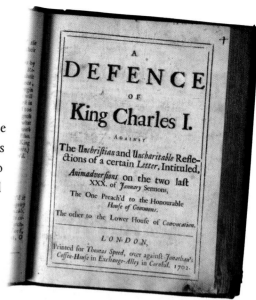

over 100 new canons were passed including the adoption of the Thirty-Nine Articles of the English Church. In 1635, Echlin was succeeded as bishop by Henry Leslie who proved to be no friend of the Presbyterians. In November 1635, he deposed Livingstone, having Melvin, the minister in Downpatrick, to pronounce a sentence of excommunication on him. In a visitation in 1636, he required all his clergy to sign documentation to the effect that they would abide by the new canons and conduct worship according to the strictest episcopal forms. While several clergy signed with reluctance, some refused for sake of conscience, including Edward Brice (Broadisland), Henry Calvert (Oldstone), Robert Cunningham (Holywood), James Hamilton (Ballywalter) and John Ridge (Antrim). They were summoned to attend a meeting in the Episcopal Church in Belfast on 10 August 1636.

The proceedings lasted three days. On the first day, 10 August, Bishop Leslie chose as his text Matthew 18:17, *'but if he neglect to hear the church, let him be unto thee as an heathen man and a publican.'* He then preached a sermon in which he stated his view that the only valid church was that in which bishops ruled – the Episcopal Church. He criticised those who believed they exercised valid ministries outside such a system. Such persons were, in Leslie's eyes, intruders who should not expect by *'their puff of preaching to blowe downe the godly orders of our church, as the walls of Jericho were beaten downe with sheepe's hornes.'* The five dissenting ministers were challenged to a public debate on these issues on the following day. They accepted and nominated James Hamilton of Ballywalter as their spokesperson. The debate attracted a large crowd of nobility, gentry and clergy, and Hamilton proved capable of rebutting the arguments of Leslie and Bramhall. After a lengthy debate, the Court was adjourned until the following day. On the third day, 12 August, Bishop Leslie pronounced a sentence of perpetual silence, within his diocese, upon the five dissenting ministers. Edward Brice, the first known Presbyterian minister in Ireland, died upon returning home! Robert Cunningham fled to Scotland where he died on 29 March 1637. Five weeks after his death he was summoned before the High Commission in Dublin and fined £20 for not appearing – though the Court was informed of his death. The officers of the Court then seized property from his widow to a value of £40 as security against payment of the original fine.

Clandestine Presbyterian meetings continued to be held in private homes and locations but it was clear to many of the ministers that their days of free and effective ministry were numbered. On 9 September

James Hamilton, Lord Clandeboye
NATIONAL TRUST

Stained glass window in First Bangor Presbyterian Church listing ministers, beginning with Robert Blair

18

Artist's impression of the Eagle Wing

1636, a group of 140 Presbyterians sailed from Groomsport, seeking freedom to live and worship according to their consciences in the 'New World.' Their ship weighed 150 tons and was called *Eagle Wing*. Among the passengers were four Presbyterian ministers, Blair (Bangor), Livingstone (Killinchy), Hamilton (Killeshill) and McClelland (Newtownards). Rev John Livingstone had written to John Winthrop, governor of Massachusetts, enquiring about prospects for Presbyterians in his lands. An offer was made: Winthrop's son visited Ulster in January 1635 and encouraged the emigrants to proceed with their plan. Despite sailing more than halfway to America, their ship was buffeted by severe storms and, interpreting this as a sign from God, they returned to Ireland, arriving on 3 November. The ministers were informed that warrants had been issued for their arrest and so made their way to Scotland, where they played a significant role in the struggle of the Presbyterian Church to resist the designs of King Charles and Archbishop Laud.

Livingstone became minister in Stranraer. He noted the faithfulness and tenacity of the Irish Presbyterians. On one famous Communion season in Stranraer, he records that a crowd of about 500 Irish Presbyterians travelled across the Irish Sea to receive Communion according to Presbyterian custom. He also baptised as many as twenty-eight children who accompanied them.

Meanwhile, Wentworth began a campaign of terrorizing Irish landlords. He examined the terms of their original grants and if he found anything defective he levied fines for the crown. The London Companies were fined £70,000 for non-compliance with some of the terms of their original grants in County Londonderry. The whole province of Connaught was seized and landowners permitted to purchase back only two-thirds of their original holdings. Needless to say, Thomas Wentworth was not a popular man in many quarters.

Once again, affairs in Scotland impinged upon Ulster. Laud introduced a new prayer book for the Church of Scotland which sparked rioting in Edinburgh. According to popular tradition, the new prayer book was first used in St Giles Cathedral in Edinburgh on 23 July 1637. One woman, Janet Geddis, disrupted the service and flung her stool at the pulpit in protest. A local riot ensued and soon developed into a national protest. It is interesting to note that Janet Geddis was a sister of

Groomsport Harbour

Robert Blair's first wife, Beatrix.

Scottish opposition to Laud's policy of imposing Anglicanism upon Scotland hardened. In February 1638, a National Covenant was drawn up and signatories sought. This Covenant was a declaration to defend 'true religion' as established by the Reformation in Scotland. The Scottish General Assembly pledged loyalty to the king but

Reverend John Livingstone
1603–72

JOHN LIVINGSTONE was born in 1603. He followed his father and grandfather in becoming a Presbyterian minister. One of his first sermons was preached in the church at Shotts on 21 June 1630. It lasted for one-and-a-half hours and about 500 individuals were converted at this service! Yet within days his confidence was at an all time low and he resolved not to preach again for some time.

That summer, he received a written invitation from Lord Clandeboye to come to Ulster and serve as minister in Killinchy. He accepted and was ordained by Bishop Andrew Knox of Raphoe and other ministers on 29 August 1630. For most of his ministry in Ulster Livingstone was persecuted by the episcopal authorities. He was finally deposed by Bishop Leslie in November 1636. Livingstone was one of four ministers on the abortive Eagle Wing expedition in September 1636.

From 5 July 1638, he ministered in Stranraer for twelve years. He also visited Ulster on several occasions (five visits of three months between 1642 and 1648) and helped to establish the fledgling Irish Presbyterian Church.

Upon the restoration of Charles II in 1660, Livingstone was banished from the kingdom. He travelled to Rotterdam where he died on 9 August 1672.

St Giles Cathedral,
Edinburgh

at the same time defied his form of church government. Charles interpreted this as rebellion and, when he tried to crush Scotland by force, he started the chain of events which was to lead to civil war and ultimately his own execution. Many of the Ulster Scots had a natural sympathy with the Scottish Covenanters and several ministers came to Ulster seeking, and readily gaining, new signatures. Wentworth moved the majority of the Irish army (over 9,000 soldiers) to Ulster to act as a deterrent to any who might contemplate any disruptive actions.

The most infamous aspect of Wentworth's policy at that time was the imposition of the 'Black Oath'. All Scots in Ulster over the age of sixteen years were required to swear this oath promising obedience to all the king's commands. It was in effect an oath designed to supersede all other covenants or oaths. Church of Ireland ministers and church wardens compiled lists of all Scots who were resident within their dioceses so that the oath could be

Janet Geddis protesting at the introduction of Laud's prayer book, 23 July, 1637

administered before a magistrate. Many Presbyterians refused to take this oath and fled to Scotland, abandoning their new settlements. So many Scots settlers fled that Chichester complained to Wentworth that 'these parts are left miserably poor and the country going to waste.' To refuse compliance and remain was to risk harsh punishment. Margaret Pont, daughter of Sir William Stewart and wife of Rev Robert Pont of Donegal, was imprisoned and fined £10,000 by the Court of Castle Chamber. This punishment was meted out despite the fact that Margaret's father was one of the leading Scottish landowners in Ulster. Her husband had fled to Scotland.

Events changed dramatically in 1641. The growing power of the Commons in Westminster and the king's defeat in Scotland led to the impeachment of Wentworth, the Earl of Strafford since 1640. The Lord Lieutenant had made countless enemies in the previous seven years. The London Companies and the Ulster Presbyterians, among others, had their revenge. Sir John Clotworthy of Antrim presented a lengthy petition on behalf of the persecuted Ulster settlers. His petition spoke of the banishment of their *'learned and conscionable'* ministers and their replacement by *'illiterate hirelings'*. Both Wentworth, in May 1641, and Laud, in January 1645, were executed.

In November 1641, the Gaelic Irish rose in rebellion against the settlers and this led to a period of unrest in Ireland that lasted for several years. Rory O'More of County Armagh led the conspiracy from February 1641. Returning army officers who had experience of fighting in Europe were added to the plot. Final plans had been laid on 5 October in the house of Turlough O'Neill at Lough Ross in County Monaghan. Dublin Castle was to be taken on 23 October and Sir Phelim O'Neill would lead a simultaneous attack in Ulster.

The National Covenant

II Kings 11:17 'And Jehoiada made a covenant between the Lord and the king and the people, that they should be the Lord's people; between the king also and the people.'

CHARLES I saw himself as the divinely appointed leader of society with the right to expect complete obedience from his subjects in all matters. As king of a united kingdom, Charles wanted to bring the Scottish Church into conformity with the English Church. To achieve this, he created Scottish bishops and, in July 1637, forced Archbishop Laud's English-style prayer book upon the Kirk.

The Scottish nobles resented the intrusion of bishops into government. Ministers and ordinary Presbyterians resented what they judged to be unfair dictatorship in the affairs of their church. The National Covenant was drawn up in February 1638 as a protest and statement of what Scottish Presbyterians believed. The Covenant demanded a Scottish Parliament and General Assembly free from the king's interference. Essentially, this document was regarded as a contract between the people and God, signed by nobles, ministers and thousands of ordinary people pledging themselves to religious liberty and stating what they would and would not agree to in matters of Church and State.

Scottish ministers travelled throughout Ulster gaining signatures to the National Covenant. On 4 April 1644, General Munro and his army at Carrickfergus signed the Covenant. Before the end of that month the people of Derry had also signed, in defiance of their mayor and governor. By June most other centres had also signed, with the exception of Lisburn and Newry. To counter this, Wentworth introduced the 'Black Oath' that all Scots settlers in Ulster were required to take, and by which they promised to obey all the king's commands.

Dublin Castle

The plot was betrayed on the evening of Friday 22 October by Hugh MacMahon who was drinking in Winetavern Street in Dublin with his foster brother Owen O'Connolly. O'Connolly was a native Irishman who had become a Presbyterian and was employed by Sir John Clotworthy. In fact, O'Connolly, a convert from the 1625 revival, was an elder in a Presbyterian congregation. A warning about the forthcoming insurrection was conveyed to the authorities and the leading conspirators were immediately imprisoned in Dublin Castle. However, the uprising in Ulster proceeded according to plan.

The 1641 Uprising

Sir Phelim and his men captured Lord Caulfield and the Charlemont garrison. Similar success followed at Dungannon, Mountjoy, Newry, Lurgan, Cavan and Armagh. Only rapid action by local settlers saved Lisburn, Belfast, Carrickfergus, Larne, Enniskillen, Coleraine and Derry. Success for the insurgents depended upon the Gaelic peasantry and once the initial uprising was complete, the hungry masses attacked the settlers without mercy. The resultant massacres have long been etched into the Ulster Protestant psyche. Perhaps the most infamous incident occurred in Portadown where Manus Roe O'Cahan drove about eighty men, women and children off a bridge and into the River Bann where they were drowned or shot. Mrs Anna Murray of Killyleagh witnessed the crucifixion of her husband, a minister, and the dismemberment of her two sons by insurgents. A party of about sixty old men, women and children were murdered by the O'Hara's near Carrickfergus. By way of revenge about thirty Roman Catholics were killed in Islandmagee. How often in Irish history has atrocity bred atrocity?

Over thirty manuscript volumes of sworn statements by survivors of the 1641 uprising repose in the library of Trinity College in Dublin. Undoubtedly, many of the incidents contained therein are embroidered or fabricated but equally certainly many of the incidents related actually occurred. Estimates of Protestant deaths in this uprising have varied from 10,000 to 100,000. Exact figures are unknown but recent studies suggest that perhaps 4,000 Protestants were murdered and a further 8,000 died of exposure and hunger, being stripped and abandoned in the hostile countryside. Certainly, the Ulster slaughter in the winter of 1641–2 represents the worst civilian loss of life in the history of the British Isles. The Presbyterians would appear to have suffered less than Anglicans in this uprising. Many of them, ministers and people, had already returned to Scotland. Livingstone, now minister in Stranraer, told of many refugees flooding into his parish at that time.

Traditional explanations of the cause of this uprising have cited the disaffected natives who lost their lands in the Ulster Plantation scheme of 1611. Having bided their time with mounting frustration at the injustice of

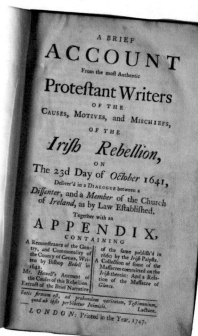

English policy, they mobilised in October 1641 in an attempt to seize back their lands. However, there are a number of factors which undermine this explanation. In 1641, the Ulster Plantation was thirty years old. Many native Irish had been absorbed into the plantation scheme and in fact several of those who rebelled in 1641 had been beneficiaries of the scheme. More likely, it was the repressive policies of Wentworth, combined with the poor harvests of 1629–33, which had driven the native Irish to a point of desperation resulting in an armed insurrection. Wentworth had questioned land occupation and put a 'financial squeeze' on many natives, driving them to borrow money and sell land to remain solvent. Also, he had oppressed Roman Catholics and Dissenters alike in an attempt to make the Acts of Uniformity and Supremacy a reality. Thirdly, he had gathered his own close group of advisors around him without regard for Irish customs and manners, thereby further alienating the native Irish. Given this background, the uprising of 1641 does not represent an attempt to overthrow government so much as an attempt by the native Irish to reorganise their constitutional position with rights guaranteed under common law.

Charles I was in Scotland when the rebellion broke out in October 1641. In early 1642, the rebellion spread throughout Ireland with the support of the Old English (those English who had come to Ireland with the Normans and had retained their Roman Catholicism). As the Westminster Parliament was already in dispute with the king, it was reluctant to raise an English army to be placed at his disposal. There was no guarantee that he would not use it against the Scots. The solution was to raise a Scottish army and ship it to Ulster to put down the rebellion. Eventually, an army of 10,000 men was dispatched under Major-General Robert Munro and the bulk of his men arrived in Carrickfergus on 15 April 1642. The Presbyterian Church was about to be planted in Irish soil.

Atrocities associated with the Irish rising of 1641. Propaganda exaggerated the humiliation undergone by Protestants.

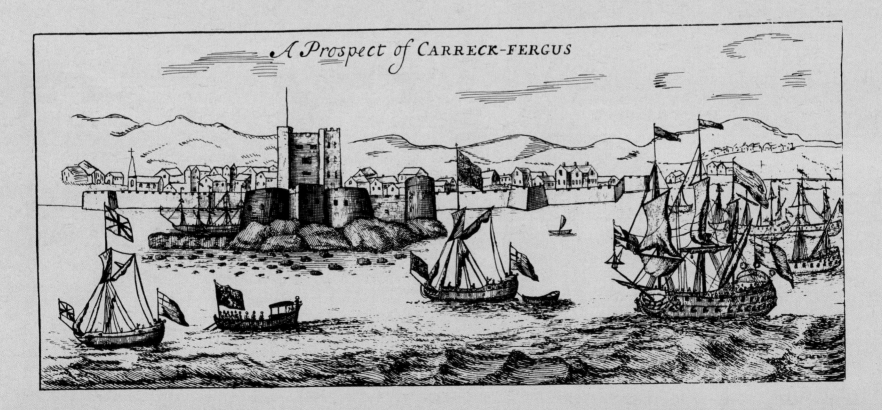

The Giant's Causeway
SCENIC IRELAND

2
Irish
Presbyterians
1642–1685

THE IRISH PRESBYTERIAN CHURCH was born at Carrickfergus on Friday 10 June 1642 amidst circumstances of uncertainty and war. The native uprising which erupted in October 1641 posed a serious threat to English authority in Ireland. Such a challenge required a decisive response from Westminster, but at that very moment King and Parliament were locked in a bitter conflict, which resulted in civil war in August 1642. The partial success of the rebels bought time for an English response. Eventually, a Scottish army, under the command of Major-General Robert Munro, was sent to Ulster to quell the uprising. Munro landed at Carrickfergus on 3 April 1642 and the bulk of his army shortly afterwards.

Carrickfergus Castle

Munro was a hardened veteran of the Thirty Years War and began a tough and uncompromising campaign of reprisals against the native Irish by butchering any rebels who crossed his path. He slaughtered captives at Kilwarlin Wood, Loughbrickland and Newry, where his soldiers shot and hanged sixty men. Eighteen women and two priests met a similar fate.

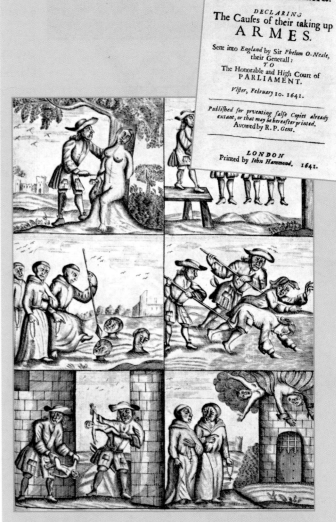

In 1641, there were reports of horrifying tales of murder and torture of Protestants all over Ireland as shown in these propaganda woodcuts.

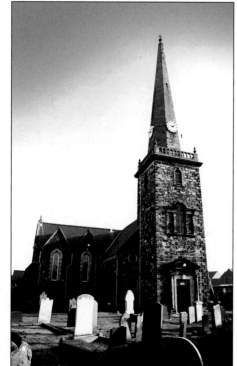

St Nicholas Church can be seen in this early seventeenth-century map of Carrickfergus and as it is today.

Dunluce Castle, seat of the Earl of Antrim

Munro's army consisted of about ten regiments and was accompanied by Scottish Presbyterian ministers acting as chaplains. In addition, Rev John Livingstone, previously of Killinchy, was sent by order of the Council of Scotland to accompany the army for three months. Livingstone stayed for six weeks in Carrickfergus and a further six weeks in Antrim with Sir John Clotworthy and his regiment. He preached in both towns and in several neighbouring localities. Interestingly, one of the first people to greet Livingstone when he arrived in Ulster in 1642 was Rev James Melvin who had pronounced Bishop Leslie's sentence of excommunication upon him six years earlier. Melvin asked for Livingstone's forgiveness.

The First Presbytery

Upon returning to Carrickfergus from Newry on 14 May, elderships were established within each of the four regiments quartered in Carrickfergus: Argyle's, Eglinton's, Glencairn's and Home's, with the agreement of Munro and his commanders. The ministers were therefore in a position to meet as a Presbytery, in accordance with the discipline of the Church of Scotland. This they did and the first Presbytery meeting on Irish soil took place in Carrickfergus on Friday 10 June 1642. In attendance were five ministers and four ruling elders. The ministers were: Revs Hugh Cunningham (Glencairn's regiment), John Baird (Campbell's regiment), Thomas Peebles (Eglinton's regiment), John Scott (Glencairn's regiment) and John Aird (Home's regiment). Rev James Simpson was at Newry with Sinclair's regiment and Rev John Livingstone was at Antrim with Clotworthy's regiment. Rev John Baird was appointed Moderator and preached on Psalm 51:18, 'Do good in thy good pleasure unto Zion, build Thou the walls of Jerusalem.' Rev Hugh Peebles was elected Clerk of the Presbytery.

The location of this meeting is unknown but could have been in the castle or St. Nicholas church in the town. John Livingstone recorded something of the business conducted at that first meeting. All present produced their letters of appointment and therefore entitlement to sit in Presbytery. They agreed to approach commanders of the other regiments in order to appoint Kirk Sessions and encouraged each chaplain to commence examination and catechetical instruction within their respective regiments. They also agreed to meet regularly, initially weekly, and open each meeting by conducting devotional meditations on portions of the prophecy of Isaiah. At the close of this first meeting, they appointed a fast to be held the following week. As Clerk, Rev Hugh Peebles wrote to Lords Clandeboye and Montgomery, whose regiments were attended by two non-ordained Presbyterian ministers, requesting their lordships permission for their chaplains to attend and participate in the new Presbytery. Both Clandeboye and Montgomery replied favourably.

Some further information should perhaps be given here concerning the five ministers who constituted the first Irish Presbytery. Rev Hugh Cunningham was installed in Ray in Donegal in 1647, but soon was forced to return to Scotland where he served as minister at Mearns (1649–51) and Erskine (1651). He returned to Ray about 1657 only

Ballymoney Parish Old Church Tower

The stones of this ruin testify to the vagaries of Irish church history. Its origins lie in the 14th century when it was within the control of the Diocese of Connor. The church here was served by a succession of priests until 1530 when it fell into a state of disrepair, the congregation having removed to Kilmoyle, outside the town. Following the Reformation the site came under the authority of the Church of Ireland and was linked with a church at Tullygore. In a 1622 visitation it is described as 'decayed' and 'the walls fallen to the ground'. Sir Randall MacDonnell, a Roman Catholic, assumed responsibility for this locality and introduced Scottish Presbyterian settlers to Ballymoney. MacDonnell repaired the church at Ballymoney for the use of these settlers. A surviving stone slab on the interior wall of the tower states, 'This church was built to the Glory of God 1637'. The original stone of the medieval structure is discernable with the red Bann brick from Agivey which was used in the renovations of 1637. As a result of the Uprising in 1641 many of the settlers withdrew to the safety of Coleraine and the church was destroyed in 1642. Presbyterian minister Rev James Ker was ordained in the rebuilt parish church in 1646. Like many other Presbyterian ministers, Ker was ejected in 1661 for refusal to conform to Episcopal requirements. The local Presbyterians then built their own church and the Church of Ireland resumed control of the original church. In 1780 it was decided that a new parish church should be built as the original was in need of expensive renovations. This new church was opened in 1782 and the old church and tower was allowed to fall into ruin. In the 1840s a new road was cut through the graveyard, leaving the old building on one side of the road and the new church on the other. When the Church of Ireland was disestablished in 1869 it lost all buildings separated from churches then in use. The Ballymoney tower then became the property of 'the poor law guardians'. When Ballymoney became a Borough Council in 1977 the old tower was the oldest building the town and was incorporated in the town coat of arms. It has recently been renovated and floodlit with money from the Council and Heritage Lottery Fund.

Ballymoney old church tower, donated to the Presbyterian church by the Earl of Antrim. The church was previously Church of Ireland.

General Petition
30 July 1642

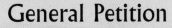
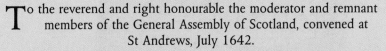

To the reverend and right honourable the moderator and remnant members of the General Assembly of Scotland, convened at St Andrews, July 1642.

The humble petition of the most part of the Scottish nation in the North of Ireland, in their own names, and the name of the rest of the Protestants there, humbly sheweth —

That where your petitioners, by the great blessing of the Lord, enjoyed for a little while a peaceable and fruitful ministry of the Gospel; yet, through our own abuse of so rich a mercy, and through the tyranny of the prelates, we have been a long time spoiled of our ministers (a yoke to many of us heavier than death), who, being chased into Scotland, were not altogether un-useful in the day of your need: and we having been since oppressed and scattered, as sheep who have no shepherd, now at last the wise and righteous hand of the Lord, by the sword of the rebels, hath bereft us of our friends, and spoiled us of our goods.

Neither know we what hand to turn us to for help, but to the land so far obliged by the Lord's late rare mercies, and so far enriched to furnish help of that kind, – a land whence many of us drew our blood and breath, and where (pardon the necessary boldness) some of our own ministers now are, who were so violently plucked from us, so sore against both their own and our wills: – yea. The land that so tenderly in their bosoms received our poor outcasts, and that hath already sent us so rich a supply of able and prosperous soldiers to revenge our wrong.

Therefore, although we know that your zeal and brotherly affection would urge you to take notice without our advertisement, yet give us leave in the bowels of our Lord Jesus Christ, to intreat, ... crying to you that ye would come over and help us, being the servants of the God of your fathers, and claiming interest with you in a common covenant, that, according to the good hand of God upon us, ye may send us ministers for the house of our God. We do not take upon us to prescribe to you the way or the number; but, in the view of all, the finger of the Lord points at these, whom, though persecution of the prelates drew from us, yet our interest in them could not be taken away; wherein we trust, in regard of several of them, called home by death, your bounty will superadd some able men of your own, that may help to lay the foundation of God's house, according to the pattern. But for these, so unjustly reft from us, not only our necessity, but equity pleads, that either you would send them all over, which were a work to be paralleled to the glories of the primitive times, or, at least, that you would declare them transportable, that when invitators shall be sent to any of them, wherein they may discern a call from God, there may be no difficulty in their loosing from thence, but they may come back to perfect what they began, and may get praise and fame in the land, where they were put to shame. ... But now seeing you abound in all things, and have formally given so ample a proof of your large bestowing on churches abroad in Germany and France, and knowing that you are not wearied in well-doing, we confidently promise to ourselves in your name, that you will abound in this grace also, following the example of our Lord and the primitive Churches who always sent out disciples in pairs. But if herein our hopes shall fail us, we shall not know whether to wish that we had died with our brethren by the enemies' hands, for we shall be if it were said unto us – 'Go, serve other gods.' Yet looking for another kind of answer at your hands – for in this you are to us an angel of God – we have sent these bearers, M. John Gordon and M. Hugh Campbell, our brethren, who may more particularly inform you of our case. ...

'Your most instant and earnest suppliants.'

to be deposed by Bishop Leslie of Raphoe in 1661. He died prior to 21 July 1661. Rev John Baird, the first Moderator of the Army Presbytery, was appointed to preach in Belfast every third Sunday, doubtless to counteract the only Episcopal preacher in the town, Rev Black. In 1646, Baird was installed as the first minister in Derrykeighan (now Dervock) but soon returned to Scotland. Rev Thomas Peebles served as the first Clerk of Presbytery for over thirty years. He was ordained into a charge with responsibility over Dundonald and Holywood in 1645. He resigned Dundonald in 1651 but retained Holywood. Peebles was deposed for Non-conformity in 1661 but continued to minister until his death in 1670. There is no record of either Rev John Scott or Rev John Aird settling in Ireland and it is likely that both gentlemen returned to Scotland.

The Earliest Presbyterian Congregations
This Irish Presbytery did not limit itself to ministry among the various army regiments. Applications for new additions were invited from surrounding localities where Presbyterian people were numerous. Soon requests came in from neighbouring areas where the people wished to be affiliated with this new Presbyterian cause. The Presbytery responded by encouraging people to elect their own Kirk Sessions and then to take steps to secure the services of suitable ministers. Preaching was supplied to several localities including, in County Antrim, Carrickfergus, Larne, Cairncastle, Ballymena, Antrim, Templepatrick and Belfast, and, in County Down, Holywood, Bangor, Donaghadee, Ballywalter, Portaferry, Killyleagh, Comber and Newtownards. These locations give the distinct appearance of a northern and southern circuit.

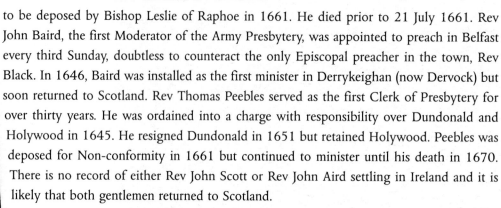

Gilbert Ramsey is buried at Bangor Abbey.

The demands for preaching far outweighed the supply and soon appeals for ministers were conveyed to the Scottish General Assembly, meeting in St Andrews on the last Wednesday of July in 1642. For example, petitions were presented from Bangor and Ballywalter, signed by sixty-three and forty-one heads of families respectively, and requesting the restoration of Revs Robert Blair and James Hamilton to their former parishes. The Presbyterians of Counties Antrim and Down drew up a General Petition, signed by 225 heads of families, requesting the General Assembly to help them. One of the Ulster Presbyterians who presented this Petition to the Scottish Assembly was Hugh Campbell – one wonders if it was the same individual who had opened his home in Antrim for prayer at the time of the Sixmilewater Revival?

The request from the Irish brethren was heard sympathetically in St. Andrews, but the Scottish Church was itself short of capable ministers and so could not spare any to settle permanently in Ulster. Instead, they commissioned six of their number to travel to Ulster for a three-month term. Four of this group of ministers were very familiar with these parts: Robert Blair, James Hamilton, John McClelland and John Livingstone. Of the others, Gilbert Ramsey stayed, being ordained in Bangor in 1646, though deposed for Non-conformity in 1657. He was later imprisoned in Carlingford

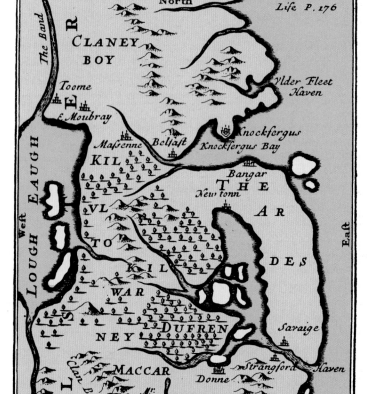

Seventeenth-century map of Antrim and Down

Castle in 1663 and died in 1670. Nothing is known of the sixth commissioner, Ballie, and he may not have travelled for some reason. In their travels, these ministers covered the greater parts of Antrim and Down. Slowly, the new church grew. James Baty, who had been acting for a time as a chaplain in Lord Clandeboye's regiment, was ordained and installed in Ballywalter by Rev James Hamilton. John Drysdale, who had also been acting as chaplain to Lord Clandeboye's regiment, was ordained and installed in Portaferry in December 1642 with Rev Robert Blair presiding. Several Episcopal clergymen abandoned their former practices and also joined the growing Presbytery, for example, Rev Thomas Vesey who had taken shelter in Coleraine during the massacres of 1641 and stayed as minister from that year.

Together these ministers developed and nourished an infant Irish Presbyterian Church. Discipline was introduced. Individuals who had taken the Black Oath, who had conformed to prelacy, or lived immoral lives, were not admitted to Communion until they professed their repentance publicly. Kirk Sessions operated as local courts. For instance, on 17 April 1648, Joyce Baylie and Oina O'Donnally were required to dress in white sheets and stand before the congregation of Templepatrick and make a full confession of their sins. Harsh as these measures appear to modern Christians, it is perhaps worth pondering the fact that at least such a system had the merit of scotching local gossip and enabling a community to deal with 'local sin' and move on.

Meanwhile, in England, King and Parliament came to blows in August 1642. Between the autumn of 1642 and the summer of 1646 there was serious fighting in and between

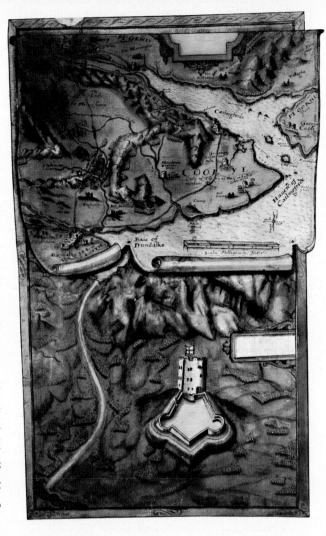

Map of Carlingford Castle by Richard Bartlett
NATIONAL LIBRARY OF IRELAND

The Execution of Charles I
ON LOAN TO THE NATIONAL PORTRAIT GALLERY OF SCOTLAND FROM THE COLLECTION OF LORD DALMENY

Presbyterian Ministers in the 1640s

NAME	YEAR	LOCATION
James Baty	1642	Ballywalter
John Drysdale	1642	Portaferry
James Simpson	1642	Newry
John Adamson	1644	North West area
Thomas Peebles	1645	Dundonald & Holywood
David Buttle	1645	Ballymena
Archibald Ferguson	1645	Antrim
Patrick Adair	1646	Cairncastle
John Baird	1646	Dervock
Robert Cunningham	1646	Broadisland (Ballycarry)
James Gordon	1646	Comber
John Greg	1646	Carrickfergus
Thomas Hall	1646	Larne
Anthony Kennedy	1646	Templepatrick
Thomas Kennedy	1646	Donaghmore (Carland) Co Tyrone
James Ker	1646	Ballymoney
Jeremiah O'Quinn	1646	Billy (Bushmills)
Gilbert Ramsey	1646	Bangor
Anthony Shaw	1646	Belfast
Hugh Cunningham	1647	Ray (Donegal)
David Gamble	1647	Laggan (North West)
William Semple	1648	Letterkenny
Fergus Alexander	1649	Greyabbey
Henry Main	1649	Islandmagee
William Richardson	1649	Killyleagh
Andrew Stewart	1649	Donaghadee
James Cunningham	1650	Antrim

ARDENS SED VIRENS

28

England, Scotland and Ireland. Oliver Cromwell and his new 'model army' proved too strong for Charles and his supporters. In short, the Parliamentarians emerged victorious because they won the main battles: Marston Moor on 2 July 1644 and Naseby on 14 June 1645. By the summer of 1646, Charles was bereft of soldiers and finances. He surrendered to the Scots and hoped to exploit differences among his enemies. Eventually, he was beheaded before the Banqueting Hall at Whitehall on 30 January 1649, 'in the forty-ninth year of his age, and the twenty-fourth of his reign'.

The Scottish Assembly in 1643 approved 'The Solemn League and Covenant', which represented a declaration of intent to remove prelacy and popery from Britain and Ireland. It also expressed the wish to reform the Church according to the Word of God and the example of the best Reformed Churches. This Covenant was also approved by the Scottish and English Parliaments. It is probably not an oversimplification to say that the Scots emphasised the religious aspects of the Covenant while the English emphasised the political aspects of the same Covenant.

The Westminster Assembly

The English House of Commons convened an Assembly of Divines at Westminster, which began deliberations on 1 July 1643. This English Assembly produced several important documents, the Westminster Confession of Faith, the Larger and Shorter Catechisms, the Directory for the Public Worship of God, the Form of Presbyterial Church Government and the Directory for Ordination. The Scottish Church adopted these documents as the subordinate standards, after Scripture, of their Church. The Irish Presbytery followed suit. Furthermore, on 1 April 1644, the Ulster Presbytery agreed that the Covenant should be administered to Munro's army. In practice, many individuals also subscribed to the Covenant. According to strict Presbyterian discipline, those who had taken Wentworth's 'Black Oath' had first to publicly repent before signing the Covenant. In this manner, for example, over 400 people signed the Covenant in Carrickfergus.

In the areas of Ulster where the Covenant was administered to the army, thousands of Presbyterian settlers also signed their names. Possibly, the ministers understood the Covenant as an undertaking to commence a great spiritual crusade in their locality while the people understood it more in terms of a common bond among settlers living in dangerous times. It is reckoned that, in addition to the army regiments, about 16,000 people signed the Covenant in Ulster.

The Presbyterian system continued to expand, especially in Antrim and Down throughout the 1640s. Although it was reported in 1644 that there were twenty-four desolate congregations in danger of perishing and only two ministers under care of the Presbytery, by 1647 there were about twenty congregations with their own ministers, all worshipping after the Presbyterian fashion. These were not easy times. Three ministers —

The humble ADVICE OF THE ASSEMBLY OF Divines,

Now by Authority of PARLIAMENT sitting at Westminster,

Concerning a Confession of Faith, with the Quotations and Texts of Scripture annexed. Presented by them lately to both Houses of PARLIAMENT.

A certain number of Copies are Ordered to be Printed only for the use of the Members of both Houses and of the Assembly of Divines, to the end that they may advise thereupon.

LONDON,
Printed for the Company of STATIONERS.

Westminster Confession of faith

Detail from a stained-glass window in San Francisco Theological Seminary depicting the story of the Presbyterian Church (USA)

A DIRECTORY FOR The Publique VVorship of GOD,

Throughout the Three KINGDOMS OF England, Scotland, and Ireland.

Together with an Ordinance of Parliament for the taking away of the Book of COMMON-PRAYER:

AND

For establishing and observing of this present DIRECTORY throughout the Kingdom of England, and Dominion of Wales.

Die Jovis, 13. Martii, 1644.

ORdered by the Lords and Commons assembled in Parliament, That this Ordinance and Directory bee forthwith Printed and Published:

Joh: Brown, Cleric. Parliamentorum.   H: Elsynge, Cler. Parl. D. Com.

LONDON:
Printed by G.M. and I.F. for the Company of STATIONERS. 1645.

Directory for Public Worship as approved by the Westminster Assembly

Hamilton, Watson and Weir – who had been administering the Covenant in Ulster in 1642, were captured en route to Scotland by Sir Alister MacDonald's frigate, *The Harp*, on 2 July 1644. They were held as hostages. David Watson and John Weir died in captivity and James Hamilton was eventually released after ten months imprisonment.

About September 1644, it was reported in the Army Presbytery that another Presbytery had been created in the area of Route, in North Antrim. After investigation, the Army Presbytery ruled that this Route Presbytery should 'be suppressed as an unlawful pretended Presbytery' on the grounds that several of its ministers had irregular or no calls from the people, there were no elders in this Presbytery, and some of the ministers were still clinging to Episcopal customs.

The introduction of the Solemn League and Covenant brought increasing confusion to Ireland. Much of the country was still in rebellion against the settlers, Major-General Munro and his Scottish army were loyal to the Parliamentarian cause and Ormond, commander in chief of the Crown forces, was loyal to Charles I. Although Sir Edward Chichester held Belfast for the king, Munro felt compelled to take it in the name of Parliament. In fact, this task was accomplished without bloodshed, when the Belfast garrison opened the city gates to him on Tuesday 14 May 1644.

Munro had so far failed to have a decisive battle with the Irish rebels under the leadership of Owen Roe O'Neill, nephew of the Great O'Neill. When the Scottish army first arrived in 1642 and marched as far south as Newry, O'Neill and his army had burned Armagh and retreated into his western territories. Finally, in early 1646, Munro pressed south with 6,000 men from his army, seeking O'Neill. The two armies met at Benburb on 5 June. Munro's men were exhausted after a march of twenty miles and their attack upon O'Neill's forces failed. With a loss of only seventy men, the Irish forces drove Munro's men back to the Blackwater and slaughtered between 2,000 and 3,000 of them. Hugh Montgomery, third Viscount of the Ards, was captured and Munro himself barely escaped with his life. However, O'Neill did not seize this opportunity to conquer Ulster. Instead, he retreated, marching south with his army. In consequence, no group in Ireland could dominate the other and the whole island endured a period of confusion and indecisive fighting. This was only brought to a halt by the activities of Oliver Cromwell in 1649–1650. One notable addition to the infant Irish Presbyterian Church was Rev Patrick Adair, who was installed in Cairncastle in 1646.

The Execution of Charles I

The news that Charles I had been beheaded on 30 January 1649 came as a shock to the Presbyterians in Ulster. The Ulster Presbytery met on Thursday 15 February 1649 in Belfast and replicated the verdict of the Scottish Assembly, condemning the king's execution. They composed a lengthy 'Representation' in which they spelt out their revulsion at the treatment of Charles. This document was read from pulpits by Presbyterian ministers on Sunday 25 February, and the people renewed the Solemn League and Covenant.

Interestingly, two ministers who were absent from the deliberations on 15 February,

Owen Roe O'Neill

Reverend Patrick Adair
1624–94

THE LIFE OF PATRICK ADAIR reads like an adventure by Robert Louis Stevenson. He was in fact one of the leading Presbyterian ministers in Ulster in the 17th century.

He was born in 1624 in Glenloch, Galloway in Scotland, and followed his father in becoming a Presbyterian minister. However, it was in Ulster that he was ordained, by the Army Presbytery in Cairncastle, County Antrim, on 7 May 1646. With his fellow Presbyters, he protested at the execution of Charles I in January 1649 and was one of only six or seven Presbyterian ministers who remained in Ulster during the persecution which followed. He exercised a valued ministry at this time, having to preach in remote places and some private homes.

He was one of sixty-four Presbyterian ministers ejected from their parishes in 1660, following the enforcement of Episcopal ordination. In 1663, he was arrested on suspicion of involvement in Blood's Plot and detained in Dublin for three months.

On 13 October 1674, Patrick Adair was installed as minister of Belfast's single Presbyterian congregation. He ministered there for the next twenty years until his death in 1694. It was during this period, and perhaps earlier, that Adair began to gather materials for writing the first history of the Presbyterian Church in Ireland.

Patrick Adair died in 1694, having graced the Presbyterian Church in Ireland for forty-eight years. His manuscript history of the Irish Presbyterian Church had unfortunately not been completed but provides a firsthand account of the earliest years of Presbyterianism in Ireland.

BELLFAST

440 Yards or ¼ of a Mile

Massacre at Drogheda
by Cromwell's troops

Contemporary mural testimony
to the legacy of Cromwell

subsequently refused to read the 'Representation' or concur with the advice of the Presbytery. These ministers, James Ker of Ballymoney and Jeremiah O'Quinn of Billy, were under sentence of silence for the following three years before finally agreeing to admit their errors and submit to the authority of the Presbytery. This same Presbytery meeting agreed to send two ministers to the Laggan district in the North West in order to strengthen the beginnings of Presbyterian organisation in that area and offer the Covenant to any congregation who would accept it.

The Presbytery 'Representation' drew a stinging rebuke from none other than John Milton, Latin Secretary in the Parliamentarian administration, who described Belfast as 'a barbarous nook in Ireland'. He was no more complimentary of the Presbytery, describing its members as, 'the blockish presbyters of Clandeboye', and their Representation as full of 'develish maile, impudence, and falsehood'. Certainly the Presbyterian support for the Royalist cause was winning them no friends in Parliamentary circles. In fact, some Scottish settlers combined with the Irish natives and besieged Sir Charles Coote in Londonderry. Curiously, this siege has been virtually erased from Protestant history, eclipsed by a later siege in 1689! In those confusing times, there were clearly divisions among the Ulster Scots – some being Royalists and others Covenanters.

The situation changed with the arrival of Oliver Cromwell in Ireland, at Ringsend near Dublin, on 15 August 1649. Briefly stated, he crushed all Irish resistance to the English Parliament. The controversial massacres that occurred at Drogheda in September – where Cromwell appears to have lost his self-control – and Wexford in October, in spite of his personal orders, have long sealed his obituary in Ireland. His stay on Irish soil was a mere nine months and fourteen days, yet 'the curse of Cromwell' changed the course of Irish history.

The Ulster Presbyterians were now subject to intense pressure under the Commonwealth regime. Yet another oath, 'the Engagement Oath', was requested of them. It was an oath of loyalty to the new regime. In June 1650, Colonel Venables ordered the Presbytery to appear before him in Dromore. They refused because one of their members, Rev John Drysdale of Portaferry, had been arrested. Venables then gave orders for all the ministers to be arrested. Some escaped but those who were caught were presented with the alternatives of taking the oath or leaving for Scotland within ten days. Only about six ministers remained at liberty and they operated 'undercover ministries' for some time, preaching to and encouraging their people in small groups and secret locations. The six remaining ministers were Ker (Ballymoney), O'Quinn (Billy), Gordon (Comber), Peebles (Dundonald), Ramsey (Bangor) and Kennedy (Donaghmore). On 23 May 1653, an order was given for the transportation of 260 leading Scots landowners from Ulster to Munster. The plan was eventually dropped.

Despite its active persecution of the Presbyterians, the Commonwealth administration

Oliver Cromwell by
Robert Walker
NATIONAL PORTRAIT GALLERY

O'Quinn's grave, Bushmills

favoured the establishment of sound preaching in Ireland. To that end, Independent and Baptist ministers were introduced. It was a strange contradiction that the very able Presbyterian preachers should be suffering persecution at this moment. In October 1651, Timothy Taylor was settled in Carrickfergus – to the loss of the Presbyterian John Greg who had been minister there since 1646. Gradually, the ministers who had fled to Scotland returned and resumed their ministries, though government suspicion was never far from the surface. Under the Protectorate, several Presbyterian ministers applied for and received annual payments of up to £100.

The growing number of Presbyterian ministers made it increasingly difficult for the entire Presbytery to meet in one place. Accordingly, in 1654, the Presbytery divided into three area meetings, each meeting dealing with ministerial settlements and other such business relevant to their locality. They were called the meetings of Antrim, Down and Route. Three years later, in 1657, the Route district was further divided and an additional meeting started for the Laggan area. Shortly afterwards, in 1659, another meeting was organized for the Tyrone area, making five in all. These local Presbyteries met in Synod or General Presbytery as deemed necessary. All this activity indicates the growing profusion of Presbyterian congregations. The actual number of Presbyterian congregations in the five Presbyteries was as follows: Antrim twelve, Down sixteen, Route ten, Laggan thirteen and Tyrone eight, making a total of fifty-nine congregations caring for the spiritual needs of about 100,000 people. The actual number of Presbyterian ministers operating in Ulster at this time exceeded the number of Presbyterian congregations, as some of them ministered in Church of Ireland parishes.

The Restoration

Cromwell died on 3 September 1658 and his son Richard succeeded him for a short time. Presbyterian congregations continued to thrive throughout Antrim, Down and Derry but now also in Tyrone, Armagh and further afield. Presbyterians in Ireland, as in England, worked with Royalists for a restoration of the monarchy and, eventually, Charles II returned to England from Scheveningen in Holland in May 1660 and his coronation took place in Westminster Abbey on 23 April the following year.

The Restoration was to usher in another period of persecution for Irish Presbyterians. Charles favoured an Episcopal Church as it supported his own belief in the Divine right of kings. The first sign of change was the abolition of the former Act, which had abolished Episcopacy in England, on the grounds that the Act had never been signed by a king. Charles saw to it that Episcopacy now became the established religion of England. An Act of Uniformity was passed in 1662. It required every minister to be ordained after an Episcopal fashion. Those already serving in the Church and who had not been so ordained had to submit to ordination by a bishop. No alternatives were contemplated. The General Synod met in Ballymena in 1661 and, due to the persecutions, was unable to meet openly again until 1690.

Irish Presbyterian Ministers in 1660

ANTRIM

Patrick Adair	Cairncastle
David Buttle	Ballymena
John Colthart	Drummaul (Randalstown)
Thomas Crawford	Donegore
James Cunningham	Antrim
Robert Cunningham	Broadisland
Robert Dewart	Connor
John Douglass	Broughshane
James Fleming	Glenarm
John Fleming	Ballee
Joseph Hamilton	Duneane & Grange
Robert Hamilton	Killead
Anthony Kennedy	Templepatrick
William Miln	Islandmagee
Alexander Osborne	Ballyclug
Andrew Rowan	Clough
James Shaw	Carnmoney
John Shaw	Ahoghill
Gilbert Simpson	Ballyclare

DOWN

Mungo Bennett	Drumaragh
James Blair	Dunboe
James Campbell	Loughbrickland
John Drysdale	Portaferry
James Gordon	Comber
John Greg	Newtownards
Archibald Hamilton	Benburb
Henru Hunter	Dromore
Alexander Hutcheson	Saintfield
George Keith	Drumglass
Henry Livingstone	Drumbo
Andrew MacCormick	Magherally
Thomas Peebles	Dundonald
Gilbert Ramsey	Bangor
William Reid	Ballywalter
William Richardson	Killyleagh
Donald Richmond	Holywood
Anthony Shaw	Belfast
Hope Sherid	Armagh
Andrew Stewart	Donaghadee
George Wallace	Holywood
James Watson	Magheralin (Tanderagee)
Hugh Wilson	Knock (Castlereagh)

ROUTE

Gabriel Cornwall	Ballywillan
William Crooks	Ballykelly
William Cuming	Kilraughts
Thomas Fulton	Drumachose (Limavady)
Thomas Gowan	Glennan
John Hamilton	Donagheady
Robert Hogsyard	Ballyrashane
James Ker	Ballymoney
John Law	Desertoghill (Garvagh)
Robert Stirling	Dervock
John Will	Glendermott

LAGGAN

Moses Chambers	Leckpatrick
John Adamson	
Robert Craghead	Donoughmore
John Crookshanks	Raphoe (Convoy)
Hugh Cunningham	Ray
Thomas Drummond	Ramelton
John Hart	Monreagh
William Semple	Letterkenny
Adam White	Clondevvadock (Fannett)

TYRONE

John Abernethy	Moneymore
Robert Auld	Magheracross
Thomas Boyd	Aghadowey
William Brown	Bellaghy
William Caldwell	Markethill
William Jacqu	Aghadowey
James Johnston	Lisnaskea
Thomas Kennedy	Donaghmore
William Keyes	Camus
William Moorcroft	Ardstraw
Robert Rowan	Maghera
James Wallace	Urney

Presbyterian Ministers ejected in 1661

NAME	CONGREGATION
John Abernethy	Desertlyn (Moneymore)
Patrick Adair	Cairncastle
John Adamson	Leckpatrick
Robert Auld	Magheracross, Co Fermanagh
James Blair	Dunboe
Thomas Boyd	Agahadowey
Michael Bruce	Killinchy
David Buttle	Ballymena
John Cathcart	Randalstown
James Campbell	Louhgbrickland
Gabriel Cornwall	Ballywillan
Thomas Crawford	Donegore
Robert Craghead	Donaghmore
William Crooks	Ballkelly
John Crookshanks	Convoy
William Cuming	Kilraughts
Hugh Cunningham	Ray
James Cunningham	Antrim
Robert Cunningham	Broadisland
Robert Dewart	Connor
John Douglass	Broughshane
Thomas Drummond	Ramelton
John Drysdale	Portaferry
James Fleming	Glenarm
John Fleming	Ballee
Thomas Fulton	Drumachose
James Gordon	Comber
Thomas Gowan	Glasslough
John Greg	Newtownards
Thomas Hall	Larne
Archibald Hamilton	Benburb
John Hamilton	Donagheady
Robert Hamilton	Killead
John Hart	Taughboyne (Monreagh)
Robert Hogsyard	Ballyrashane
Henry Hunter	Dromore
Alexander Hutcheson	Saintfield
William Jacque	Clongish, Co Longford
James Johnstone	Lisnaskea
George Keith	Dungannon
Anthony Kennedy	Templepatrick
Thomas Kennedy	Donaghmore
James Ker	Ballymoney
William Keyes	Belfast
John Law	Garvagh
Henry Livingstone	Drumbo
Andrew MacCormick	Magherally
William Moorcraft	Ardstraw & Badoney
Alexander Osborne	Ballyclog (Brigh)
Hugh Peebles	Aghalow
Thomas Peebles	Dundonald
Gilbert Ramsay	Bangor
William Reid	Ballywalter
William Richardson	Killyleagh
William Semple	Letterkenny
Gilbert Simpson	Ballyclare
James Shaw	Carnmoney
John Shaw	Ahoghill
Andrew Stewart	Donaghadee
James Wallace	Erney
Adam White	Fannet
Hugh Wilson	Castlereagh
Robert Wilson	Camus (Strabane)
John Wool	Glendermott

Other ministers were ejected from their parishes but it is uncertain if they were definitely Presbyterians.

Eight Church of Ireland bishops had survived the Interregnum, and twelve more were consecrated on 21 January 1661. The key appointments, as far as the fortunes of the Ulster Presbyterians were concerned, were John Bramhall as Primate and Jeremy Taylor as bishop of Down and Connor. These men were enthusiastic Episcopalians and determined to oust those Presbyterian ministers still within the Church of Ireland. The Irish Parliament passed a 'Declaration' in May 1661 requiring everyone to conform to the government and liturgy of the Church of Ireland. Taylor summoned all the ministers within his jurisdiction to a meeting in Hillsborough and ejected thirty-six Presbyterian ministers from their parishes because they refused to conform. This pattern was repeated throughout Ulster. Sixty-four ministers were 'ejected' and their parishes declared vacant. At that time, there were about eighty flourishing congregations and seventy Presbyterian ministers. A proclamation was issued which outlawed all unlawful assemblies, a measure which included the Presbyterian Synod and Presbyteries.

The ejected Presbyterian ministers largely continued to exercise their ministries in defiance of the authorities, in private houses and in small meetings. Only a few Presbyterian ministers (about eight) conformed to the new law. The rest refused to abandon their principles and suffered accordingly. The majority of Presbyterian gentry, rather than face the difficulties inherent in opposing government, conformed in face of this legislation. Perhaps the most notable case was that of Lord Montgomery of Ards who had twice before signed the Solemn League and Covenant yet now took the easier course. The suffering of the ordinary Presbyterian people was no less real. They were compelled to pay tithes to the Church of Ireland, and also try to support their own ministers and, if possible, look to the building of local Presbyterian meeting-houses (churches). Yet they 'voted with their feet', stayed loyal to their Presbyterian principles, and rejected the Episcopal system. Like many of his colleagues, the Rev William Cuming of Kilraughts was deposed for Non-conformity. His replacement, upon entering the church building on the following Sunday, was greeted by two sheep carcasses suspended from the ceiling beams!

After his defeat at Worcester, Charles II was on the run for six weeks. In this painting he is depicted hiding from the Roundheads in an oak tree. Despite a large reward being offered he was not betrayed. Many inns were subsequently named the Royal Oak.

Bishop Jeremy Taylor

Captain Thomas Blood
by Gerard Soest
NATIONAL PORTRAIT GALLERY

The vast majority of the deposed ministers continued their work in a quiet manner, without attracting undue attention. To remain anonymous was not always possible. Rev Thomas Kennedy, for example, was ejected in 1661 from the parish of Donaghmore (Carland in Co. Tyrone), where he had ministered for the previous fifteen years. Kennedy lived in a log house within the parish and he continued to minister from this dwelling. For doing so he was arrested and imprisoned in Dungannon for several years during which time he was denied visits, letters, food and clothing from his wife.

A few bolder spirits adopted a much more high profile approach to the situation and deliberately preached to large crowds, in which they openly criticised the bishops. The most notable firebrand preachers were Michael Bruce (Killinchy), John Crookshanks (Convoy) and Andrew MacCormick (Magherally) who had recently arrived from Scotland. Both Crookshanks and MacCormick died in Scotland in November 1666 with Covenanter forces at the battle of Rullion Green.

The most far-reaching change for Irish Presbyterians after the ejections of 1661 was that they never again ministered within the Episcopal Church buildings. They began to construct their own churches for worship. A new ecclesiastical situation emerged – and religious life in Ireland flowed from then on in one of three distinct streams: Roman Catholic, Anglican and Presbyterian.

Blood's Plot

As if circumstances were not difficult enough for Irish Presbyterians in the 1660s, the strange episode of 'Blood's Plot' brought further persecution upon a hard-pressed people. Several ministers were arrested and imprisoned. Only Blood's brother-in-law, Rev William Lecky, who had been deposed from a parish in County Westmeath in 1661, was implicated in the plot. Lecky was condemned to die but offered his life if he would conform. He refused, and was hanged in Dublin in December 1663.

Of the nineteen or so arrested ministers, ten were imprisoned in Carrickfergus, seven at Carlingford Castle and two others in Dublin. Most of them had never heard of the plot. They were offered a choice between leaving Ireland within two weeks or be sent to other prisons. Two chose to

Old Kilraughts

Blood's Plot
1663

COLONEL THOMAS BLOOD WAS BORN IN 1618 in Ireland and served in Cromwell's army, 1649–50. He received an Irish estate as payment for his services, but this arrangement was cancelled when the monarchy was restored in 1660. 'Blood's Plot' was to kidnap the Duke of Ormond, Lord Lieutenant of Ireland, in 1663, and hold him for ransom. The plot was foiled and Blood escaped. However, his brother-in-law and Presbyterian minister, Rev William Lecky, was tried and executed for his part in the plan. Nineteen other Presbyterian ministers were imprisoned upon suspicion of being implicated in this plot. All were eventually released.

In 1671, Blood almost managed to steal the crown jewels from the Tower of London. Incredibly, once again he evaded punishment. Charles II released him from the Tower and pardoned him, returned to him his grant of Irish lands and awarded him an annual pension of £500 per year.

Thomas Blood died in London of natural causes on 24 August 1680, but such was his reputation for trickery that the authorities later exhumed his body to verify that he was definitely dead!

The following ministers were arrested and imprisoned in 1663 under suspicion of involvement in Blood's Plot.

NAME	CONGREGATION
CARRICKFERGUS	
John Colthart	Drummaul (Randalstown)
James Cunningham	Antrim
John Douglas	Broughshane
Thomas Hall	Larne
Robert Hamilton	Killead
Robert Hogsyard	Ballyrashane
Willaim Keyes	Belfast
James Shaw	Carnmoney
John Shaw	Ahoghill
Hugh Wilson	Castlereagh
Timothy Taylor	Independent
Andrew Wike	Baptist
CARLINGFORD	
John Drysdale	Portaferry
James Gordon	Comber
John Greg	Newtownards
Alexander Hutcheson	Saintfield
Gilbert Ramsey	Bangor
William Richardson	Killyleagh
Andrew Stewart	Donaghadee
DUBLIN	
Patrick Adair	Cairncastle
Henry Livingstone	Drumbo
EXECUTED	
Willaim Lecky	Westmeath

(Hanged at Oxmanton Green, Dublin in December 1663)

Francis Makemie
Father of American Presbyterianism

Francis Makemie was born in County Donegal, near Ramelton, about 1657–58. His parents were both Scottish and had moved to this Laggan district some time earlier. The earliest certain date for his life is February 1676, when he was enrolled in the University of Glasgow as *Franciscus Makemius Scoto Hyburnus*.

On 26 January 1680, Rev Thomas Drummond, minister of Ramelton, introduced Francis Makemie to the members of the Laggan Presbytery as a student for the ministry. He was licensed sometime in the winter of 1681–82. He was subsequently ordained for service in Maryland, America, where he arrived in 1683. Makemie is credited with founding four or five congregations in Maryland and Virginia, and is most closely associated with the congregations of Rehoboth and Snow Hill.

He married into a wealthy family and soon became the largest land owner in Accomack County, with a farm of 5,109 acres. In the spring of 1706, Makemie drew together his fellow Presbyterian ministers to Philadelphia and they met as the first Presbytery on American soil. Francis Mackemie was elected Moderator at this first meeting.

On Wednesday 22 January 1707, Makemie was arrested in New York for preaching without a licence from the Governor, Lord Cornbury. Makemie was later acquitted but had to pay legal costs of £83.7.6. This trial marked a legal milestone in the history of religious toleration in America. A new law was passed forbidding the possibility of an innocent man being forced to pay for an unsuccessful prosecution.

Francis Makemie, the 'father of American Presbyterianism', died in the following year. He was fifty years old, and was buried on his farm in Virginia.

1706 FIRST PRESBYTERY

ARDENS SED VIRENS

Ramelton church

34

remain (Rev Keyes of Strabane and Rev Cathcart of Randalstown). Keyes was sent to Galway and Cathcart to Athlone. Many of the imprisoned ministers fled to Scotland but, upon their release, several were able to return to Ulster thanks to the influence and protection of individual 'persons of quality'. These were indeed dark days for the Ulster Presbyterians. However, they received some relief with the sudden death of Archbishop Bramhall in Dublin on 25 June 1663 and with that of Bishop Jeremy Taylor on 13 August 1667.

There were still examples of bitter and harsh persecution to be found. Bishop Robert Leslie of Raphoe – son of the former Bishop Henry Leslie of Down who had deposed the Presbyterian ministers in 1636 – had four ministers arrested and held under house arrest in Raphoe for six years. The ministers concerned – John Hart of Monreagh, Thomas Drummond of Ramelton, William Semple of Letterkenny and Adam White of Fannet – had refused to appear in answer to a summons from Bishop Leslie.

In 1671, Sir Arthur Forbes, commander of the Irish army and himself a Scot, successfully appealed for the liberation of all who were imprisoned in Ireland for the sole 'crime' of being Presbyterian. Among those released was a certain James Goodall, who had been imprisoned in Armagh for almost three years for drawing two loads of sand on Christmas Day – a holy day to Anglicans but an ordinary day for Presbyterians!

On 13 March 1672, Charles II had made a Declaration of Indulgence which was designed to ease the lot of all Non-comformists, including Roman Catholics. Parliament was incensed and he was later forced to withdraw it. In that same year, Charles arranged to make a payment to Sir Arthur Forbes, for distribution among Irish Presbyterian ministers who were suffering severe financial hardships. This *regium donum* (Royal Bounty) amounted to £600 and continued, with some breaks, until 1870. This payment demonstrates clearly the anomalous position of the Presbyterians in Ireland: recognised by the State but resented by the Church of Ireland – second class citizens. These small encouragements were important to the Presbyterian community. Their ministers felt confident enough to meet once more in Presbytery.

There are several examples of Episcopal persecution at this time in the Laggan district of the North West. In 1681, the Presbytery of Laggan declared a fast day in all their congregations. The local Church of Ireland clergy took exception to this and four ministers were arrested. The sentence passed was that they each pay a fine of £20 and sign a declaration that they would

Ramelton, County Donegal

James II by an
unknown artist

not offend the authorities in this manner again. None of the ministers would sign such a document and so they were each imprisoned, on 8 August 1681, in Lifford. Eventually they were released on 20 April 1682, after an imprisonment of 8 months. This act signalled an upsurge in persecution for the next two years and several Presbyterian churches were closed. The four imprisoned ministers were: William Trail (Lifford), James Alexander (Raphoe), Robert Campbell (Ray) and John Hart (Monreagh).

William Trail, who was Clerk of the Laggan Presbytery, resigned his charge in Lifford and emigrated to Potomac, Maryland, in America. Although he did return to Scotland after six years, his action in seeking liberty of conscience and freedom to minister planted a seed in the minds of others which quickly bore fruit. In 1684, a majority of the ministers in the Laggan district announced their intention of emigrating to America where there were new and exciting opportunities for ministers. They wanted to go 'because of persecutions and general poverty abounding in these parts'. Most famous in this regard was Francis Makemie of Ramelton, who emigrated to America and founded the first American Presbytery in 1706. He has thereafter been known as 'the father of American Presbyterianism'. Certainly Makemie's Ulster experience was significant in helping forge Presbyterian structures in the American colonies.

Charles II died on 6 February 1685 and was succeeded by his brother, James II. The new king, who openly supported Roman Catholicism, soon plunged all three kingdoms into turmoil. He was forced to abandon England and was replaced by his daughter Mary and her husband William of Orange. All of these events had far reaching consequences for the Presbyterians in Ireland.

LEFT: Detail of a page from the Laggan Minutes

Emigrant Ship leaving Belfast (1852)
by John Glen Wilson 1827–63

3 Irish Presbyterians 1685–1798

J AMES II SUCCEEDED HIS BROTHER CHARLES in February 1685. A new era had dawned. The new king's *Declaration of Indulgence* in 1687 suspended the operation of penal laws against Roman Catholics and Dissenters alike. Irish Presbyterian churches were reopened and public worship resumed. But James made himself unpopular with his open espousal of Roman Catholicism. He moved trusted Catholics into positions of influence and, on 20 June 1688, his wife Mary of Modena gave birth to a boy, James Francis Edward Stuart. It seemed that a Catholic royal succession was now secured.

Public opinion turned against James and Protestant noblemen invited William of Orange and his wife Mary to replace James. Mary was James' daughter so this was in fact an invitation for the king's eldest daughter and son-in-law to replace him. William arrived in England on 5 November 1688 and James, largely deserted by his army, fled to France in December. The ensuing conflict between James and William was one of European dimensions and was briefly to focus in Ireland with conflict in 1689, 90 and 91. James had the support of Louis XIV of France and William headed an alliance of European opponents which included Catholics and Protestants, determined to resist French dominance.

In Ireland, there was growing disquiet at James' policy of promoting Roman Catholics to positions of authority and influence. The preamble to the famous siege of Derry commenced on Friday 7 December 1688 and Presbyterians played a notable role. Ulster was rife with rumours that another massacre of Protestants and

William III and Mary, daughter of James II

Louis XIV receiving James II

St Columb's stained glass window depicting a scene from the Siege

THE RELIEF OF THE YEAR 1689   DERRY IN THE ...

Dissenters was about to occur. The approach of Lord Antrim's Catholic regiment, the *Redshanks*, at Derry in December precipitated a crisis. Rev James Gordon, Presbyterian minister of Glendermott, was in the city and advised shutting the gates to deny admittance to the troops. Others, including Ezekiel Hopkins, Bishop of Derry baulked at the thought of resisting King James' troops. Was it legitimate to defy a lawful monarch? A group of thirteen apprentice boys took matters into their own hands and raised the drawbridge at Ferryquay gate, thus closing the gates.

The Siege of Derry

The population of the city was about 2,000 at that time. On 21 December, the Redshanks were withdrawn and a Protestant garrison under command of Lieutenant Colonel Robert Lundy was admitted. Meanwhile James II landed at Kinsale on 12 March and made his way eventually, via Dublin, to the North West. Lundy gathered up a force consisting of all the Protestants in the locality of Derry, about 7,000 in all, and the city determined to resist James' forces. Several thousand Protestants flooded into the city, seeking refuge. The siege proper commenced on 18 April 1689 with about 30,000 people within the city walls. The vast majority of them, perhaps ninety percent, were Presbyterian, but most of the officers and leaders were Anglicans. On that day, James himself approached the city and offered terms, to be greeted

The Relief of Derry
by William Sadler (1782–1839)

Siege Price List

Rev George Walker recorded the following price list within the beleaguered city at the height of the siege

	s	d
Horse flesh: per pound	1	8
A dog's head	2	6
A cat	4	6
A pound of tallow	4	0
A pound of salted hides	1	0
A pound of horse flesh	1	0
A rat	1	0
A mouse	0	6
A horse pudding	0	6
A handful of sea wreck	0	2
A handful of chickweed	0	1
A quart of meal (when found)	1	0
A quarter of a dog	5	6
(fattened by eating the bodies of the slain Irish)		

Detail from Francis Nevill's 1649 map of the Siege of Derry. Ferryquay Gate which was shut by the Apprentice Boys is labelled 'New Gate'.

Reverend John Mackenzie
1649–94

A siege gun owned by William Conyngham of Springhill, County Londonderry. Willliam sent his wife Ann to Derry for her safety unaware of the impending siege.

NATIONAL TRUST NORTHERN IRELAND

with cries of 'No surrender', and a volley of shots. In the following weeks conditions deteriorated within the besieged city and food became scarce. One account details the 'market price' for basic materials. The Jacobite army was poorly equipped for such a siege. They lacked the heavy artillery necessary to breach the city wall. Eventually, the siege was lifted on Sunday 28 July, when supply ships broke through to relieve the city. This last great siege in British history had lasted 105 days.

There were eight Presbyterian and eighteen Episcopal ministers in Derry during the siege. St Columb's Cathedral was used by all for worship with an Anglican service in the morning and a Presbyterian service in the afternoon. Prior to this crisis the Anglicans had forced the Presbyterians to build their church outside the city walls and it had been destroyed. Denominational rivalry continued in the aftermath of the siege. Rev George Walker, rector of Donoughmore and military co-governor of Londonderry during the siege, afterwards published his *True Account of the Siege of Derry* but his account was challenged by Rev John Mackenzie, Presbyterian minister in Cookstown, who published his *Narrative of the Siege of Londonderry*.

William III landed at Carrickfergus on 14 June 1690. He travelled to Belfast where he stayed for five nights and was visited at the castle by a delegation of Presbyterians, led by their local minister, Patrick Adair, who presented him with a loyal address of welcome. The king proceeded to Hillsborough where he authorised an annual *regium donum* (Royal Bounty) payment of £1,200 to the Presbyterian ministers. (The previous payment of £600 authorised by Charles II in 1672 had been irregularly paid and then stopped altogether.)

The famous battle of the Boyne was fought on 1 July and although William was the victor, the battle was inconclusive. James II returned to France and the decisive battle was actually fought the next year at Aughrim, the bloodiest battle ever fought in Ireland. In 1691, the future for Presbyterianism in Ireland looked bright. Not for the first time, Presbyterian hopes were to be dashed.

Although William III was sympathetic to religious tolerance in Ireland, the Irish

AFTER THE SIEGE, a pamphlet war erupted with conflicting accounts from Anglican and Presbyterian perspectives. On the Anglican side was Rev George Walker, rector of Donoughmore in Tyrone, and elected governor during the siege. He wrote a *True Account* which emphasized the Anglican contribution and hardly mentioned the Presbyterians. Rev John Mackenzie redressed the balance by publishing his own *Narrative of the Siege of Londonderry*.

Mackenzie was born in 1649 in County Down. Following his education at the University of Edinburgh he was ordained in Derryloran (Cookstown) in 1673. He was one of eight Presbyterian ministers who took refuge in Derry during the siege and acted as chaplain to one of the defending regiments.

Walker's *True Account* was published in London in September 1689 and ran through several editions. The Irish Presbyterians were dismayed at this biased account. A plan was announced by which the Presbyteries of Antrim, Down and Laggan should fund Mackenzie and Captain James Gladstanes (a Presbyterian officer who had distinguished himself during the siege) to travel to London and give a true account of the part played by loyal Presbyterians in defending Derry. Not for the first time, the Church proved inefficient in collecting the necessary funds, and in exasperation, Mackenzie paid his own expenses and travelled to London with all haste.

He reached the capital in January 1690 and he published his own account within weeks, with the help of Thomas Lawrence, a Presbyterian bookseller in London. An anonymous pamphlet then appeared attacking Mackenzie's work. To this he replied and an unpleasant pamphlet war was halted by the death of George Walker at the battle of the Boyne on 1 July 1690.

John Mackenzie visited London again in 1694. He had an audience with King William during which he pressed for some protection for Irish Presbyterian ministers from the Episcopal courts. He died at Cookstown in 1694, aged 49 years.

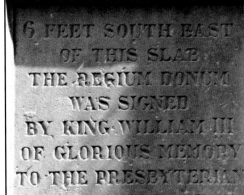

6 FEET SOUTH EAST OF THIS SLAB THE REGIUM DONUM WAS SIGNED BY KING WILLIAM III OF GLORIOUS MEMORY TO THE PRESBYTERIAN

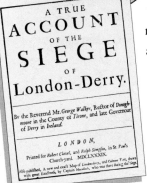

A TRUE ACCOUNT OF THE SIEGE OF London-Derry.

By the Reverend Mr. George Walker, Rector of Donough-moore in the County of Tirone, and late Governour of Derry in Ireland.

LONDON,

Printed for Robert Clavel, and Ralph Simpson, in St. Paul's Church-yard. MDCLXXXIX. and Calmer Fost, drawn

Also published, A new and exact Map of Londonderry, drawn with great Exactness, by Captain Mackelock, who was there during the Siege.

A NARRATIVE OF THE SIEGE OF London-Derry: Or, the late Memorable Transactions OF THAT CITY.

Faithfully Represented, To Rectifie the Mistakes, and supply the Omissions of Mr. Walker's Account.

By JOHN MACKENZIE, Chaplain to a Regiment there during the Siege.

The most Material Passages relating to other Parts of action and Siege are also inserted from the Memoirs of such as were chiefly concerned in them.

With Allowance.

LONDON,

Printed for the Author, and are to be Sold by Richard Baldwin, in the Old Baily. 1690.

ABOVE: St Columb's as it appeared in 1689, Reverend George Walker and the title page of Walker's Account of the Siege
RIGHT: Siege bomb with a detail from the Hillsborough Plaque

William III by an unknown artist

A piece of slate which represented an altar-stone in Penal times. Only seven inches by four, it could be easily carried by itinerant clergy.

NATIONAL TRUST NORTHERN IRELAND

Parliament was securely in the hands of the Anglican gentry and Bishops. The Dublin administration could frustrate and block London intentions and in the 18th century a three tier society emerged in Ireland. The first class citizens, an Anglican minority, clung to power and defended their position by a plethora of penal legislation. The second class citizens, the Dissenters of whom the vast majority were Presbyterian, at times felt the heavy hand of the Establishment against them. The third class citizens, the Irish Roman Catholic people, despite comprising the vast majority of the population were to be kept firmly in their place at all costs. Land was the indicator of wealth and power, and Irish land was slowly but surely accrued by the Establishment.

While the principal aim of the penal legislation was to make Irish Catholics harmless, it also impinged upon the Irish Presbyterians. From an Establishment perspective, the motives behind such legislation were mixed: the need for self-defence, out of vengeance, to make the whole nation Protestant. There was no co-ordinated government plan; individual Acts emerged over a period of time. Logically, if this legislation had been rigidly enforced, then the Irish Roman Church would have gradually withered. Initially enforcement was vigorous but later it became spasmodic as it became clear that a strict enforcement of the penal legislation was politically, socially and economically impossible. Perhaps most crucially of all, from an Anglican point of view, there was no serious or sustained missionary endeavour in the early 18th century.

The main complaint of Presbyterian ministers during William's reign, and afterwards, was that their marriages were not recognised in law. The root of this problem was that the Anglicans did not recognise Presbyterian ordinations and therefore couples married according to the Presbyterian form were regarded as mere fornicators and their children as illegitimate. Despite such discrimination, large numbers of Presbyterians from Scotland flooded into Ulster. They were fleeing successive poor harvests and famine in Scotland and were attracted by the idea of a new start across the North Channel. It has been estimated that as many as 50,000 or more Scots families arrived in Ulster between 1690 and 1715. Certainly, the number of Presbyterian congregations doubled in these years. In 1702, there were almost 120 Irish Presbyterian congregations, arranged in five Presbyteries.

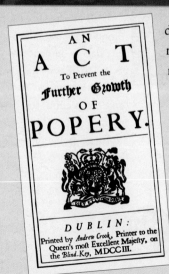

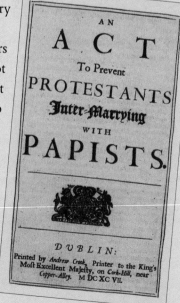

In that year, the Synod rearranged this territorial system into nine Presbyteries: Belfast, Down, Antrim, Coleraine, Armagh, Tyrone, Monaghan, Derry and Convoy. Structurally, these nine Presbyteries were arranged into three sub-synods: Belfast, Monaghan and Laggan, and, at the pinnacle of Irish Presbyterianism, was the General Synod which met annually.

The Sacramental Test Act

Queen Anne succeeded William in March 1702, and a new persecution was directed at the Irish Presbyterians. An Act was passed in the Irish Parliament in 1704 'to prevent the further growth of popery' but a clause was added, which obliged everyone who held any public office to take Communion according to the Church of Ireland rite. This *Sacramental Test Act* resulted in the expulsion of many Presbyterians from town corporations on which they had been serving, and in some cases, controlling. A plaque in the vestibule of First Derry Church records the names of ten Aldermen and fourteen Burgesses who were expelled from Derry Corporation under this Test Act. Half of the Burgesses in Belfast were Presbyterian; they were expelled in 1707. Presbyterians were also excluded from the magistracy, customs, excise, post office and all public offices. Throughout this time, Presbyterian people were compelled to pay tithes to the Church of Ireland, which they did not attend, and also support their own ministers.

There were several notable instances of harassment of Presbyterian people. In 1708, the Synod approved plans to install a Presbyterian minister in Drogheda where there had been a Presbyterian congregation before the Williamite wars. Commencing in September of that

IN COMMEMORATION OF THE UNDERNAMED MEMBERS
OF THIS CONGREGATION
WHO FROM LOYALTY TO THEIR CHURCH PRINCIPLES
RESIGNED THEIR SEATS ON THE CORPORATION
OF THIS CITY
AT THE PASSING OF THE IRISH TEST ACT IN 1704.

ALDERMEN:
ALEXANDER LECKY.
JAMES LENNOX, M.P.
HENRY LONG.
HORACE KENNEDY.
EDWARD BROOKS.
ROBERT SHANNON.
WILLIAM SMYTH.
WILLIAM MACKIE.
JOHN COWAN.
HUGH DAVEY.

BURGESSES.
ALEXANDER SKIPTON.
JOSEPH DAVEY,
SHERIFFS.
DAVID CAIRNS.
ROBERT HARVEY.
ROBERT GAMBLE.
JOHN DIXON.
FRANCIS NEVILLE.
JOHN RANKIN.
JOSEPH MORRISON.
JOHN CUNNINGHAM.
JAMES STRONG.
ARCHIBALD CUNNINGHAM.
JAMES ANDERSON.
JOHN HARVEY, CHAMBERLAIN.

First Derry plaque

Drogheda
DES CLINTON

A
SCRIPTURE-PLEA
Against a Fatal
RUPTURE,
And Breach of Christian
COMMUNION,
Amongst the Presbyterians in the North of IRELAND.

By JAMES KIRKPATRICK M. A.
Minister of the GOSPEL.

Rom. xv. 7. *Wherefore receive ye one another, as Christ
also received us, to the Glory of God.*
Gal. v. 15. *But if ye bite and devour one another,
take heed that ye be not consumed one of another.*

BELFAST:
Printed by JAMES BLOW, and
are to be Sold at his Shop, Anno
Dom. M. DCC. XXIV.

Regium donum seals

year, nine ministers were appointed to preach there successively. The local Church of Ireland representative, Dean Cox, had the first minister, Rev James Fleming of Lurgan, arrested on a charge of 'riot and unlawful assembly' and billed to appear before the Spring Assizes. The second minister to preach in Drogheda was Rev William Biggar of Bangor and he also was arrested and imprisoned for six weeks. This harassment eventually ceased in 1709, and Rev Hugh Henry was ordained as minister in Drogheda on 27 May 1711.

When the Monaghan Presbytery met in Belturbet in December 1712 for the purposes of building a new church in the locality, members were arrested and charged with 'holding an unlawful assembly and endeavouring to disturb the peace.' This case was eventually dropped on condition that the new building be located at least one mile outside Belturbet. Operating under such constraints, Presbyterian ordinations were rarely conducted openly but took place in private homes and usually in distant localities. Often, a newly ordained minister would only commence his ministry gradually and after a number of weeks or months, in order to avoid attracting the ire of the Establishment.

Pamphlet War

Throughout these unhappy times, a constant pamphlet war raged between Church of Ireland clergy and Presbyterian ministers. For example, Dr William King, who was born of Presbyterian parents, as Bishop of Derry published an attack upon the Presbyterian Church in a work entitled *A Discourse concerning the Inventions of Men in the Worship of God.* Presbyterian replies by Rev Joseph Boyse of Wood Street, Dublin and Rev Robert Craghead of Derry were soon in the public domain. One of the most famous Presbyterian works was by Rev James Kirkpatrick of Belfast's second Presbyterian congregation, entitled *Historical Essay Upon the Loyalty of Presbyterians.*

In 1714, the final year of Anne's reign, the *regium donum* was stopped, but only temporarily. It was resumed, and increased to £2,000 in 1718 under George I. Under the new arrangement, £1,600 was distributed among ministers in the General Synod and £400 among 'Protestant Dissenters' in the south of Ireland.

The Presbyterians in Dublin and in the south and west of Ireland differed from those in the Ulster counties. They tended to spring from English Presbyterian origins. Several southern congregations had started as Independent or Congregational and had evolved into Presbyterian. A number of these southern ministers met in Clonmel in 1697 to form a 'Munster Presbytery'. Relations between the General Synod and the southern Presbyterian ministers were cordial but unclear. It was common enough for ministers in northern Presbyteries to be installed in southern congregations and the Laggan Presbytery seems to have had specific responsibilities for supplying preachers for small groups of Presbyterians in the far south and west.

Anglican dominance and control continued to irk many Presbyterians. Probate of will required the sanction of Church Courts and so the question over the legality of Presbyterian marriages often caused additional anguish for grieving Presbyterian families. Many Church of Ireland clergy insisted upon 'reading over the dead' before burial could take place. A general economic recession in Ireland in the early 18th century increased Presbyterian discomfort and unsurprisingly, many individuals and families contemplated

A
DEFENCE
OF THE
SEASONABLE ADVICE,
IN
ANSWER
To the Reverend, Mr. CHARLES MASTERTOUN'S
APOLOGY for the Northern Presbyterians in IRELAND:
WHEREIN
The Differences between the Subscribers and Non-subscribers
are Stated, and the Reasonableness of their continuing
in Communion is Proved.

By JOHN ABERNETHY, M. A.
Minister of the GOSPEL. Author of
the *Seasonable Advice.*

To which is added
A
POSTSCRIPT
By the Reverend { N. WELD.
                 { J. BOYSE.
                 { R. CHOPPIN.

BELFAST:
Printed by JAMES BLOW, and are to

The Scots Confession, 1560

CHAPTER I
GOD

We confess and acknowledge one God alone, to whom alone we must cleave, whom alone we must serve, whom only we must worship, and in whom alone we put our trust. Who is eternal, infinite, immeasurable, incomprehensible, omnipotent, invisible; one in substance and yet distinct in three persons, the Father, the Son, and the Holy Ghost. By whom we confess and believe all things in heaven and earth, visible and invisible, to have been created, to be retained in their being, and to be ruled and guided by His inscrutable providence for such end as His eternal wisdom, goodness, and justice have appointed, and to the manifestation of His own glory.

CHAPTER II
THE CREATION OF MAN

We confess and acknowledge that our God has created man, i.e., our first father, Adam, after His own image and likeness, to whom He gave wisdom, lordship, justice, free will, and self-consciousness, so that in the whole nature of man no imperfection could be found. From this dignity and perfection man and woman both fell; the woman being deceived by the serpent and man obeying the voice of the woman, both conspiring against the sovereign majesty of God, who in clear words had previously threatened death if they presumed to eat of the forbidden tree.

LEFT: Shipping list 1771–3 of Scots-Irish migrating to America

ARDENS SED VIRENS

43

FOR NEWCASTLE AND PHILADELPHIA,

THE AMERICAN SHIP ACTIVE, 300 Tons Burthen, Robt. M'Kkown, Master, will be clear to sail for the above Ports on the first May next. For Freight or Passage apply to the Captain, or to Jones, Tomb, Joy, & Co. who engage to have sufficient Quantity of Provisions and Water on board.—Such Persons as intend going to America had best apply immediately, and engage their Passage.

Belfast, 30th March, 1797.

Those who are desirous to ship Linens by this favourable Opportunity, will apply to John Galt Smith and Son, or to Mr. John Boyd, Grocer, on the Hanover-Quay, Belfast, for Passengers, who will engage for them.

emigration to America as their best solution. Rev James McGregor, Presbyterian minister of Aghadowey since 1701, had been a twelve year old boy in Derry during the Jacobite siege. In 1718, he emigrated to Massachusetts, along with a significant portion of his congregation. The difficulty of the times may be judged by the fact that in that year the Aghadowey congregation had assets of 1 shilling yet owed their minister more than £80 in stipend! Interestingly, upon arrival in Massachusetts, these Ulster Presbyterians founded a town, which they called 'New Londonderry'.

The Irish Presbyterian Church was seriously weakened by an internal dispute over the issue of subscription – the principle of signing a doctrinal document as a means of proclaiming that you agree with the doctrines outlined in the document. The earliest Presbyterian ministers coming to Ireland had subscribed the Scots Confession of 1560 in this way at their ordination. This composition of John Knox and others had since been superseded in 1647 by the Westminster Confession of Faith.

The seeds of growing division were sown in 1705 by two events. Firstly, since 1698, the Synod emphasised that all men seeking to be licensed or ordained must subscribe to the Westminster Confession. Secondly, a group of Presbyterian ministers around Belfast formed a club under the leadership of Rev John Abernethy of Antrim. The club

Scots-Irish from Ulster became the pioneers and frontiersmen of early America

was known as *The Belfast Society*. They met regularly to read sermons to each other and discuss matters of faith. The members of this group professed themselves to be against the practice of subscription on principle, arguing that all creeds and confessions were of human origin and that the Bible was the only inspired summary of Christian doctrine. This stance, however, left others with a suspicion that members of this Belfast Society were using this argument about principle to mask their real beliefs which were, at best, a dilution of Christian truths.

THE Ship called the LORD RUSSELL of Belfast, lately from America, will Sail for Liverpoole in a few Days, to take in Loading there for Philadelphia, and will return to the Lough of Belfast, and Sail at farthest for said place, the 15th of February next; As the Ship will be Loaded, the Owners can only take on Board Fifty Passengers or Servants, and no more. If any Servants incline to indent, they may apply to any of the Owners, John Gordon, Samuel Mc. Tier, John Potts, and Hugh Barnet, of Belfast, and John Handcock of Lisburn, who will give good encouragement and usage: The said Owners have a quantity of very good Philadelphia Staves to Sell; also choice American Flour and Rum, which they will Sell at a reasonable Price.

Dated January 16, 1749.

The crisis broke in 1720 when Abernethy published a sermon on his views entitled *Religious Obedience Founded on Personal Obedience*. Other Presbyterian ministers were alarmed. Rev John Malcome of Dunmurry published a reply in a pamphlet entitled *Personal Persuasion no Foundation for Religious Obedience*. This issue struck a nerve within Synod and, incredibly, over fifty publications were eventually spawned by this growing controversy.

In an honest attempt to reconcile both views, the Synod, in June 1720, passed what became known as *The Pacific Act*. This Act was designed to enable ordinations and installations to proceed smoothly in Synod congregations. It reaffirmed the Synod attachment to the

Rev John Abernethy
1680–1740

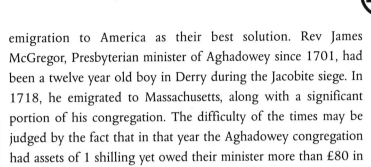

JOHN ABERNETHY was a son of the manse. His father, also called John, was minister in Brigh (1674–84), Moneymore (1684–91) and Coleraine (1691–1703). John junior was born on 19 October 1680 and ordained in Antrim on 18 August 1703. He was instrumental in the formation of the 'Belfast Society' in 1705, a group of ministers and some others who met regularly for discussion on all manner of subjects. Evidently, Abernethy was a capable and popular preacher because, in 1717, three congregations wanted him as their minister: Usher's Quay in Dublin, First congregation, Belfast, and Antrim. Contrary to the wishes of Synod, Abernethy opted for Antrim.

On 19 December 1719, Abernethy preached on Romans 14:5 before the Belfast Society and asserted that no Synod or church court had authority over the conscience of any individual. It was in the matter of the Synod's requirement for ministers to subscribe to the Westminster Confession of Faith that Abernethy's plea for the rights of conscience caused a furore.

Over fifty pamphlets on this controversy were published during the following seven years. Rev John Malcome of Dunmurry was Abernethy's earliest opponent; it was he who coined the adhesive nickname 'New Light' in describing the Non-subscribers. In June 1720, the Synod attempted to find a middle ground, a *Pacific Act*, by giving individual ministers the option of subscribing their own phrasing in place of Westminster wording.

This controversy threatened to disrupt regular church business in many localities and so in 1725 the Non-subscribing ministers were reassigned to one administrative grouping, a new Presbytery of Antrim. The suspicion of the majority of Synod ministers could not be relieved by such an administrative solution. The General Synod debated the situation from 18–28 June 1726 and, on a vote that was carried by a large majority of elders, but with ministers evenly divided (36–34), Synod separated from the Presbytery of Antrim without any formal excommunication.

In 1730, Abernethy was installed as minister of Wood Street in Dublin, in succession to the famous Joseph Boyse. In Dublin, he was soon embroiled in the struggle to secure repeal of the hated *Sacramental Test Act*. John Abernethy died on 1 December 1740.

Reverend Samuel Haliday
1685–1739

SAMUEL HALIDAY was born in 1685 in Omagh, where his father Samuel was a Presbyterian minister (1677–88). He was educated at the Universities of Glasgow (1701) and Leydon (1705), but was licensed in Rotterdam, where he subscribed to the Westminster Confession. In 1708, he was ordained in Geneva without subscribing to any confession, and thereafter professed himself a Non-subscriber. Haliday joined the General Synod in 1712 and was installed in First congregation, Belfast, on 28 July 1720, refusing to subscribe to the Westminster Confession. A disaffected minority in his congregation were formed into a Third congregation in Belfast. Feelings were running high and there was further controversy when Revs Samuel Haliday and James Kirkpatrick (Second congregation) were prevented from taking part in Communion Services in Third. In 1726, Haliday and his congregation withdrew from the Synod and joined the Non-subscribing Antrim Presbytery. He died on 5 March 1739, and was buried at midnight in the churchyard beside St. George's Church, High Street, Belfast.

1725
The Non-Subscribing Presbytery of Antrim

MINISTER	CONGREGATION
John Abernethy	Antrim
Michael Bruce	Holywood
Josias Clugston	Larne
Alexander Colville	Dromore
John Elder	Aghadowey
Samuel Haliday	First Belfast
Samuel Harper	Moira
John Henderson	Duneane
Robert Higinbotham	Coleraine
James Kirkpatrick	Second Belfast
John Mairs	Newtownards
Thomas Nevin	Downpatrick
Thomas Shaw	Ahoghill
Patrick Simpson	Dundalk
William Taylor	Cairncastle
Thomas Wilson	Ballyclare

NOTES
Colville was refused permission by the Presbytery of Armagh to join
Elder was a Subscriber
Higinbotham was a Subscriber. He later withdrew from Synod but returned in 1727.

Westminster Confession and Catechisms but permitted single ministers who were unhappy with individual phrases in the Confession, to offer their own expressions instead, and the local Presbytery was given authority to decide whether such alternative expressions were consistent with true doctrine.

This was an imaginative attempt to satisfy all parties but, as so often in Church History, it failed. Rev Samuel Haliday, a member of the Belfast Society, was installed in First Congregation, Belfast, on 28 July 1720. He refused to subscribe to the Westminster Confession and instead issued his own declaration. Despite the protest of four members of Presbytery who were present, the installation proceeded. The issue of subscription was the major topic of debate at the next meeting of Synod in 1721. An objection to Haliday's installation was sustained and those who had installed him were rebuked. The terms *Subscriber* and *Non-subscriber* now came into common usage.

One direct consequence of this controversy was that a proportion of Haliday's congregation refused to sit under his ministry and asked the Synod to sanction the formation of a Third Congregation, Belfast. (The minister of the Second Congregation, Belfast, was James Kirkpatrick, also a member of the Belfast Society). Their wish was granted, and in August 1721 Third Congregation, Belfast (later known as Rosemary Street), was erected in the face of opposition from Samuel Haliday.

In order to put an end to the constant confrontations between Subscribers and Non-subscribers, the Synod, in 1725, reorganised the congregations within the Presbyteries of Antrim, Down and Belfast in such a way that all the Non-subscribers, numbering sixteen congregations, comprised the Presbytery of Antrim. Individual families shifted allegiance. For example, Rev Abernethy lost about ninety families in Antrim and Rev Shaw lost about 100 families in Ahoghill. The Synod erected these people into new congregations. Although the Synod decided in 1726 to cease to hold communion with the Antrim Presbytery this proved to be a curious semi-separation because the Antrim Presbytery ministers retained their share of *regium donum* and pulpit exchanges still occurred. Their ministers continued to sit, deliberate and even vote in Synod.

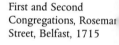

First and Second Congregations, Rosemary Street, Belfast, 1715

Scotland as seen from Murlough on the North Antrim coast

Arrival of the Seceders

Often in the history of Irish Presbyterianism there are echoes of shouts that originated in the Scottish mother church. Such was the case with the introduction to Ulster of that important branch of Presbyterianism: the people known as *Seceders*. They originated in Scotland due to the operation of an Act of Parliament in 1712 concerning Patronage, a system whereby a local lay patron had the right to choose a minister for a congregation. Initially, four ministers withdrew (seceded) from the Church of Scotland in 1733, and received the nickname *Seceders*. They formed themselves into *The Associate Presbytery*. Their protest was against this system but there were other factors. They were enthusiastic for sound and simple gospel preaching and were also missionary orientated, desiring to spread their doctrines.

In 1741, the Presbyterian people of Lylehill, about three miles from Templepatrick, applied to the Scottish Associate Presbytery for a supply of preaching. There were several reasons for this request. They cited the distance to the Templepatrick church as being too far. There was also a dispute concerning an expired lease on a farm in the locality. Some locals were aggrieved that Colonel Upton, an elder in the congregation, awarded a new lease to the minister, Mr Livingston (or his son), rather than a certain Samuel Henderson. Several temporary Seceder preachers supplied at Lylehill until, eventually, a licentiate, Mr Isaac Patton, arrived. He was ordained at Lylehill on 9 July 1746. Interestingly, this new brand of Irish Presbyterianism originated a mere sixteen miles from the place where Edward Brice had commenced his ministry in Ireland in 1613.

Initially, Isaac Patton was also responsible for a Seceder cause in Lisburn. Other Seceder preachers arrived and were warmly welcomed by ordinary Presbyterian people. They were perceived to preach with a warm devotion and often contrasted favourably with Synod of Ulster preachers, who appeared formal and cold. Among the earliest Seceder congregations in Ireland were: Markethill, Ballyrashane, Roseyards, Boardmills, Moira, Ray, Ballyroney, Newtown-Limavady, Ballybay, Bangor, Armagh, Aghadowey, Ballykelly, Balteagh, Dunboe, Kilraughts, Ballymoney and Derrykeighan (Dervock).

The Seceder advances in Ireland exposed weaknesses in the Irish Presbyterian Church. While Patronage had never been practised in Irish Presbyterianism, a Synod ruling in 1733

Reverend Isaac Patton
Seceders, Burghers and Anti-Burghers

REV ISAAC PATTON has the distinction of being the earliest Seceder minister to settle in Ireland. As a Probationer he was sent to Ireland by the Associate Presbytery in Scotland, and preached in Templepatrick, Belfast and Lisburn throughout May and June 1745. A call was made out and Isaac Patton was ordained on 9 July 1746 in Lylehill, with additional responsibilities for Lisburn and Belfast. His preaching was novel, using both homely and vulgar expressions, and he built up a sturdy Seceder cause. He ran a Classical School from his manse for many years. Other Seceder congregations were formed. In 1747 the Scottish Seceders split over the Burgess Oath which declared that only burgesses could engage in commerce or vote. Supporters of this Oath were known as 'Burghers' and opponents were known as 'Anti-Burghers'. This Scottish issue was transported to Ireland where the Seceders also split into Burghers and Anti-Burghers. When the Seceders themselves split into Burghers and Anti-Burghers, Rev Patton supported the latter. An Anti-Burgher Presbytery was formed in 1750 and an autonomous Synod in 1788, of which Rev Isaac Patton was the first Moderator. Rev Patton was an Ulsterman, born in 1720 and raised in the congregation of Myroe in County Londonderry. He ministered in Lylehill for over fifty years and, sadly, he finished his ministry under a cloud, being judged by many as unable to minister adequately due to age and infirmity. He retired in 1797, died on 31 May 1799, and was buried at Templepatrick.

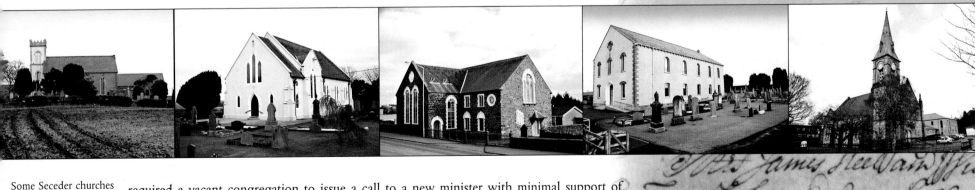

Some Seceder churches from left: Dervock, Roseyards, First Ballymoney, Aghadowey and Trinity Ballymoney

required a vacant congregation to issue a call to a new minister with minimal support of two-thirds of the votes. Two-thirds was calculated by both actual numbers and contributors to a minister's stipend. This 'two-thirds men and money' rule gave undue influence, or a

Upon his completion of three sessions in Glasgow, JAMES REID obtained his Master of Arts degree in 1816. He returned to Glasgow for the 1816–17 session during which he studied theology. He recorded informative details of his four return journeys to Glasgow, some of which are highlighted below.

I left Glasgow fair on the first of April, 1817, in company with Mr Crozier, to return by way of Portpatrick at 1 o'clock, on Tuesday. We got the length of Stewartstown that night at 6 o'clock, where we staid all night. We started in the morning, breakfasted in Irvine, and stayed two hours there. Thence we proceeded to Troone, Ayr, and ate something at Burns' Cottage, at 4 o'clock. Thence to Maybole and Kirkoswald, where we stopped all night. We started in the morning, breakfasted at Girvan, dined at Ballintrae, and slept in the Cairne. From the Cairne, we proceeded on Friday morning, breakfasted in Stranraer, and reached the port at 12 o'clock, just five minutes too late for the packet. We stayed here all day and set sail on Saturday and reached Donaghadee at 8 o'clock, after a passage of 10 hours. We reached Belfast and separated on Monday morning; when I got the length of Magherafelt that night, and the next morning to Dunneybragey, where I rested for seven days. I left this place on Monday morning, April 14th, at 7 o'clock, and reached Derry at 7 o'clock. And left Derry next day at 3 o'clock, and reached Ramelton on Tuesday evening, April 15: fifteen days after leaving Glasgow, having walked the distance of near 200 miles.

Francis Hutcheson

Sezerr's view of Glasgow University and Blackfriars in the late seventeenth-century

veto, to wealthier members of any vacant congregation – and caused considerable resentment. Other factors contributed to a general malaise within Synod congregations. The subscription controversy had left many ministers under suspicion regarding their orthodoxy. Also, there was a general reluctance to plant new congregations, and this left ministers open to the suspicion that they were simply protecting their share of the *regium donum* (more congregations would mean a greater division of the *regium donum* grant). In fairness though, it should be pointed out that the Synod was at that time trying to ensure that every Presbyterian minister received a minimum annual stipend of £40.

Influence of Glasgow University

Not surprisingly, the appearance of new and rival Presbyterian congregations was not well received by the Synod. In 1747, the Synod pronounced 'A Serious Warning' which was read from every pulpit and printed for circulation. It charged the Seceders with intruding into Ireland, making false charges against godly Synod ministers. The Seceder ministers portrayed the Synod ministers as slack in discipline and doctrine and as 'Government hirelings' because they received *regium donum*. In contrast, the 'purer' Seceder ministers were sustained solely by the contributions of God's people. In fact, both branches of Presbyterianism grew. By 1840, the Seceders had planted 140 congregations and in the same period the Synod of Ulster planted a further 130 congregations.

Part of the growing distrust of Synod ministers sprang from the fact that virtually all of them received their higher education in the University of Glasgow, where they came under the influence of such men as Francis Hutcheson. The son of Rev John Hutcheson, Presbyterian minister in Downpatrick and then Armagh, Francis Hutcheson had also been a licentiate of the Irish Presbyterian Church. He became Professor of Moral Philosophy at the University of Glasgow in 1729, and soon made a name for himself as an outstanding teacher. He was the first professor in Glasgow to abandon the normal practice of lecturing in Latin. His style was to walk about as he lectured, apparently without notes. In addition to courses on Natural Religion and Morals, he often lectured upon the evidences of Christianity.

In 1738, Hutcheson was on trial before the Glasgow Presbytery for teaching that the standard of moral goodness was the promotion of the happiness of others and that people could have a knowledge of good and evil without a prior knowledge of God. Such ideas were new, and often treated with suspicion, even hostility. Hutcheson was very influential in shaping the opinions of a generation of Irish Presbyterian ministry students and a source of ammunition for Seceders and others who believed that the Synod ministers were departing from the ancient truths.

The Seceders were not the only brand of Presbyterians to arrive in Ulster in the 18th century. The Reformed Presbyterians also established themselves. Their first minister in Ireland was William Martin, who was ordained at Vow, near Ballymoney, in 1757. The Reformed Presbyterians in Scotland grew out of the Covenanters who had not accepted the

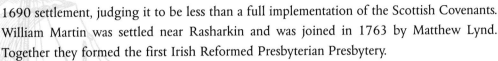

1690 settlement, judging it to be less than a full implementation of the Scottish Covenants. William Martin was settled near Rasharkin and was joined in 1763 by Matthew Lynd. Together they formed the first Irish Reformed Presbyterian Presbytery.

The Moravians also arrived. Rev John Cennick first preached in Ulster in 1746 and visited several locations. A small number of Moravian congregations were subsequently planted. In 1747, Rev John Wesley preached in Ireland and won some converts, mainly from the Anglican community. By 1760, there were about 250 members of the new 'Wesleyan Societies'.

Throughout the 18th century, the flow of emigration, mostly Presbyterian, from Ulster to America continued and increased. From 1730 onwards, the annual numbers were about 12,000. Exact figures are unknown, but estimates for the total in the fifty years before the American War of Independence (1770–79) vary from 100,000 to 250,000. Certainly, a significant number of Ulstermen fought in the American colonies for freedom from subjection to the British crown.

While Francis Makemie had set up the first American Presbytery in Philadelphia in 1706, the Moderator of the First American Synod in 1716 was also from Ulster (John Hampton, whose father had been minister in Burt, Donegal). Six ministers in this first Synod came from Ulster. Nor was the Ulster Presbyterian contribution in America confined to church

Signing of the Declaration of Independence 4 July 1776 Philadelphia by John Trumbull
YALE UNIVERSITY ART GALLERY

organisation. In relation to the famous Declaration of Independence, which was approved by the Continental Congress on 4 July 1745, it has been pointed out that there are truly amazing links with Ulster Presbyterianism. It was written by an Ulsterman (Charles Thompson of Maghera), first printed by an Ulsterman (John Dunlap of Strabane), first read in public by the son of an Ulsterman (Colonel John Nixon) and the first and only signature for a month was that of John Hancock, whose ancestors came from County Down.

The second half of the 18th century in Ireland is characterised by political unrest. Power continued to be exercised by an increasingly determined and paranoid minority in the Church of Ireland. The English Parliament had no desire to change the corruption in Ireland. In fact, English policy was to destroy the Irish wool and shipping industry, as

John Cennick
1718–55

JOHN CENNICK was born in Reading on 12 December 1718 and raised as a member of the Church of England. Converted as a young man, he was appointed by John Wesley as a teacher in a school for collier's children in 1740. He became a lay preacher and for a time assisted George Whitfield until 1745, when he joined the Moravians, the Church of the United Brethren, and was ordained a deacon in London. He travelled to Ireland and settled for a time near Ballymena. Here, he experienced success and is credited with founding the Moravian Church in Ireland. Although not the oldest of the Moravian congregations in Ireland, Gracehill is regarded as the 'mother church' because it was the only full-scale settlement built by the Moravians in Ireland. It consists of a centrally situated church, surrounded by homes for the congregation arranged in an orderly square. John Cennick published several collections of hymns and died in London on 4 July 1755, only thirty-six years old.

Gracehill
JAMES HAMILL ARPS

well as crippling the export of Irish cattle and sheep. All of these factors helped to ferment an atmosphere of general discontent, which permeated much of the Presbyterian community. Farmers could obtain only short-term leases, and faced unfair increases for tenancy renewals or fines for defaulting on agreements. Not surprisingly in such circumstances, Presbyterian emigration continued and was boosted by the Antrim evictions of the 1770s. Unable to pay, and their offer to pay interest on the fine in addition to their rent being refused, their rents were let to the highest bidder.

Lord Donegal's Antrim leases expired in 1770, and he demanded a payment of £100,000 for their renewal. Many tenants banded together and took direct action, for example 'houghing' (maiming) cattle in an attempt to discourage greedy or ambitious landlords from hiking rents. One such grouping was known as *The Hearts of Steel*. It was members of this group in County Armagh who killed a Presbyterian minister. On 6 March 1772, Rev Samuel Morrell of Tullylish was shot as he stood at a window in the house of a Gilford landlord, remonstrating with the rioters. These agrarian troubles continued for a number of years, and the resulting poverty and discontent was compounded by a massive slump in the linen trade in 1773. The normal fare for a passage to America at this time was £3.5.0 and could be paid for by an offer by the passenger to provide labour in America as payment. It was an option taken by thousands of Irish Presbyterians.

Morrell tablet in Tullylish church

Near this Place lie the Remains of the Reverend SAMUEL MORELLE, Diſſenting Clergyman of this Pariſh, who was killed on the ſixth of March 1772 (in the twenty eighth year of his Age) bravely defending the Houſe of SIR RICHARD IOHNSTON of Gilford BARONET, when attacked by thoſe lawleſs Inſurgents, called Hearts of Oak and Hearts of Steel, who under Pretence of redreſſing Grievances which never exiſted, diſturbed the Publick Peace in that year. He lived to the Welfare of his Country, to the Honour of his Prince, to the Glory of his God. He died fuller of Faith than of Fear, fuller of Reſolution than of Pain, fuller of Honour than of Days.

His particular Friend, SIR RICHARD IOHNSTON BARONET, who loved him living, and regrets him dead, hath cauſed this Monument to be erected to his Memory.

Manet poſt Funera Virtus.

Volunteer Camp and Manoeuvres at Belfast
c. 1782 after John Nixon

Formation of the Society of United Irishmen by Wolfe Tone, Samuel Nielson and Thomas Russell
NATIONAL LIBRARY OF IRELAND

The Volunteers

When the American colonists fought for independence from Britain, the sympathy of the Northern Presbyterians was solidly with the colonists. However, when France joined the conflict on the side of the colonists in early 1778, the same Presbyterians were prepared to side with England against this traditional continental enemy. Troops were withdrawn from Ireland for these American conflicts and so, companies of Volunteers were enlisted to maintain law and order in Ireland. The first Company was formed in Belfast in 1778. These Volunteers were given recognition by the Dublin administration but always maintained some measure of independence.

Many of the Volunteers were Presbyterians. They met regularly and, in addition to drill practice, discussed among themselves the new and growing ideas of political and economic reform. They passed resolutions at their meetings, calling for change. Amidst a new revolutionary climate in which there were many cries for freedom and equality, new legislation appeared, most notably a *Catholic Relief Act* in 1779. In 1780, the *Test Act* that had barred Presbyterians from all public office was repealed. In 1781, Presbyterian marriages where finally recognised in law. Over 100,000 Volunteers, mostly Presbyterians, met in the Presbyterian church in Dungannon in 1782 and pressed for further change.

The Government was in a weakened position, with low troop levels because of wars abroad, and confronted by articulate reformers backed by armed Volunteers. Several ministers played prominent roles in this Volunteer Movement. For example, Rev William Steel Dickson of Portaferry was a Captain in the local Volunteers. Reform became the burning issue. But, crucially, Presbyterians divided on how to measure progress. Many felt that the achievements of the 1770s were only a beginning, and other concessions and changes were to be grasped. Others felt that reform had progressed to a satisfactory conclusion.

America gained her independence in November 1782 and the Bastille fell in 1798. In Ireland, the radicals continued to press for further change, why not full Catholic emancipation? The conservatives urged caution. The French Revolution and the fall of the Bastille encouraged the radicals to believe that revolution could change Ireland as it had America and France.

The foundation of the United Irishmen in Belfast, in October 1791, marked a significant new development. This organisation was founded by Dr William Drennan, son of a Presbyterian minister, Rev Thomas Drennan of First Congregation, Belfast (1736–68). In addition to Drennan, the leading members of the United Irishmen were all Presbyterian:

Wolfe Tone
1763–98

THEOBALD WOLFE TONE was born on 20 June 1763 at 27 St Bride Street, Dublin. He was one of five surviving children out of sixteen and brought up as a member of the Church of Ireland. He entered Trinity College in 1781, but was suspended for a year for involvement in a duel. He graduated in 1786 and trained as a barrister in London. He eloped, and on 21 July 1785 married the sixteen-year-old Matilda Witherington. He commenced a career as a political writer and, in July 1791, he was invited to compile resolutions for the Society of United Irishmen formed in Belfast by Dr William Drennan. From 1794, Tone became more radical in his views, arguing for decisive action to secure reforms in Irish society. In pursuit of military assistance in fermenting revolution, he travelled to France, where he enlisted as an army staff officer. He was captured by British forces near Lough Swilly on 31 October 1798 on a French ship, and was transported to Provost's Prison, Dublin, where he was tried for treason. Although he requested death by firing squad, he was condemned to be hanged at 1pm on 12 November 1798. He cheated the hangman by cutting his own throat on the evening of 11 November and dying from this wound on 19 November.

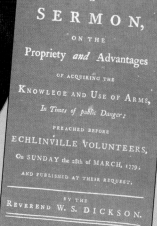

Reverend William Steel Dickson

Reverend William Bruce
1757–1841

WILLIAM BRUCE was born in Dublin on 30 July 1757, the second son of Rev Samuel Bruce, Presbyterian minister in Wood Street church, Dublin. He was a fourth generation of Irish Presbyterian ministers, supportive of Non-subscription from the 1720s. William graduated from Trinity College in 1775, and studied Theology at Glasgow and Warrington. He served as minister in Lisburn (1779–82) and Strand Street, Dublin (1782–90) before his installation in First congregation, Belfast, in March 1790. In addition to his installation in First, he was elected Principal of Belfast Academy. The First church was a member of the Non-subscribing Antrim Presbytery. Although Bruce had been a member of the Volunteers, he opposed the more radical ideas of the United Irishmen, for example, arguing for progressive Catholic emancipation. He became a strong advocate for the Act of Union. He resigned from the Belfast Academy in November 1822, and continued in First congregation with the aid of his son, also Rev William Bruce, who had been appointed co-pastor in 1812. Dr Bruce retired on 21 January 1834, due to deteriorating eyesight. He returned to Dublin, lost his sight completely, and died on 27 February 1841.

William Sampson, editor of the *Nortern Star*

Samuel Neilson, Robert and William Simms, and Sam McTier. The aim of the group was to unite Irishmen of all creeds and to achieve real parliamentary reform and break English dominance in Ireland. United Irishmen societies sprang up throughout the eastern portion of Ulster and became centres of radical fermentation.

In 1792, they produced their own newspaper, *The Northern Star*, which was an important means of spreading their propaganda. It was Roman Catholic emancipation which proved to be the decisive issue. While many Presbyterians were now radical in their politics and tactics, many more were conservative. For example, Drennan's friend, Rev William Bruce, minister of First Congregation, Belfast, declared himself to be in favour of a cautious advance. He also attacked the United Irishmen because they were 'an oath-bound society'. Even more outspoken in his attacks upon radical Presbyterians was Rev Robert Black of First Derry. He warned that radical politics would lead to government punishment. Yet, Black had earlier played a prominent role in the Volunteer Movement. Drennan retorted that Black, who was the agent for distributing the *regium donum* to Presbyterian ministers, had in effect been bought by government money.

In these turbulent times, sectarian conflict was never far from the surface. Some Protestants in mid-Ulster felt under increasing pressure from Roman Catholics with designs to participate in the linen industry. Paramilitary groupings formed: Protestant 'Peep o'Day Boys' raided Catholic homes and destroyed looms and Catholic 'Defenders' swore to retaliate. After a pitched battle at the Diamond in County Armagh in 1795, a new Protestant organisation was formed, the Orange Order. Could reform develop without bloodshed?

Irish Presbyterians were truly divided on these issues. Some ministers, such as Sinclair Kelburn of Second Congregation, Belfast, James Porter of Greyabbey and William Steel Dickson of Portaferry, were regular contributors to the *Northern Star* and some congregations regularly placed notices in its pages calling for parliamentary reform and additional civil rights. Increasingly, coercive government action, such as smashing the *Northern Star* printing press in 1797 and several public floggings, drove the United Irishmen into an underground structure. The case of the Presbyterian farmer William Orr, who was executed by the authorities on 14 October 1797,

Peep O'Day Boys searching for Defender arms in a Catholic household
LINEN HALL LIBRARY

William Orr
'I am no traitor'

WILLIAM ORR was a prosperous young farmer from Farranshane, about one mile from Antrim town. A Presbyterian of 'New Light' persuasion, he became a United Irishman and occasionally contributed to the *Northern Star* newspaper. On 15 September 1796, Orr was arrested and charged with administering a United Irishman oath to two soldiers, Hugh Wheatley and John Lindsay. He was imprisoned in Carrickfergus for one year without trial. When his case came to court, the jury could not agree on a verdict. The judge demanded a verdict and confined the jury from 7pm until 6am the following morning when they agreed upon a guilty verdict but added a recommendation that mercy should be shown. This recommendation was ignored and William Orr's execution was set for 7 October 1797.

Interest in Orr's plight was phenomenal. He was hanged at 2:45pm on 14 October 1797 at Gallow's Green, Carrickfergus. His final words stirred Presbyterian blood; 'I am no traitor. I die for a persecuted country. Great Jehovah, receive my soul. I die in the true faith of a Presbyterian'. The cry 'Remember Orr' was a rallying call as the United Irishmen in Antrim went into battle in the summer of 1798.

RIGHT: United Irishmen versus the Crown forces re-enact the Battle of Antrim in June 1998 commemorations

PETER COLLINS

did much to stir the feelings of frustration and injustice in County Antrim and beyond.

The pressure which had been mounting for some years had to find an outlet, and it did so in 1798. In the uprising and bloodshed of that year, Presbyterians fought on both sides. It proved to be a struggle of Irishmen against Irishmen. In the Presbyterian heartlands of Antrim and Down thousands of Presbyterians answered the call to arms and rebellion in the belief that this was their only means of gaining social justice in Ireland. The most notable battles were fought at Antrim on Thursday 7 June, at Saintfield the following day, and Ballynahinch on 12 June. However, the insurrection was soon put down and the ringleaders were hanged. Henry Munro, who led the rebels at Ballynahinch, was hanged in Lisburn on 16 June. Henry Joy McCracken, who had commanded the United Irishmen at Antrim, was hanged in Cornmarket, Belfast on 17 July 1798.

Undoubtedly the most famous Presbyterian fatality was Rev James Porter, minister of Greyabbey. He was hanged in

Reverend
Sinclair
Kelburn

SINCLAIR KELBURN was born in 1754, the only son of Rev Ebenezer Kelburn, minister of Plunkett Street and Usher's Quay, Dublin. He graduated from Trinity College in 1774 and undertook further study in the Universities of Edinburgh and Glasgow. He was ordained in Third congregation, Belfast on 8 February 1780. Although sympathetic with the aims of the Volunteers, Kelburn was opposed to their drill parade on Sundays, and clashed with Rev James Crombie of First congregation, who approved of such activities. Kelburn favoured Catholic emancipation and parliamentary reform and came under suspicion by the Government. He was arrested on 20 April 1797, taken to Kilmainham Jail in Dublin and held without trial. He was eventually released in October and returned to his congregation but his health was broken. Henry Joy McCracken, who was hanged in Belfast on 17 July 1798 for his part in leading the rebels at Antrim, was a member of Third congregation. Rev Kelburn, as his minister, attended him in his last moments on the gallows. Kelburn resigned from his church on 5 November 1799 and died on 31 March 1802, at forty-two years of age. He was buried at Castlereagh Presbyterian church graveyard.

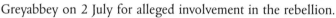

Henry Joy McCracken

Plaque to Henry Joy
McCracken in Rosemary
Street, Belfast

Greyabbey on 2 July for alleged involvement in the rebellion.

The Synod of Ulster did not meet in June 1798 because of the uprising, but did convene on 28 August at Lurgan. It was a time for assessing what had happened. The emerging consensus was that a series of local risings had occurred rather than a co-ordinated national uprising. The Synod reaffirmed its former position – that reform was a noble objective, but rebellion was wrong. It emerged that as many as

REV. JAMES PORTER
WAS BORN HERE 1753. HANGED AT
GREY ABBEY. CO. DOWN 1798.

HE SUFFERED BECAUSE OF HIS
SYMPATHY WITH THE UNITED
IRISHMEN AND SUPPORT OF
TENANT RIGHT.

Plaque to Rev James Porter
at Ballindrait

Report of the execution of
Rev James Porter in the
Minutes of the Synod of
Ulster – 29 August 1798

thirty ministers and eighteen licentiates had been actively involved in these risings. In addition to Rev Porter of Greyabbey, one licentiate had been executed, Archibald Warwick, at Kircubbin, on 15 October. Intriguingly, it is possible that another victim of public hanging, Rev Robert Gowdy of Dunover, who was hanged in July 1798, was a Presbyterian but no note of him survives in the Presbyterian records.

Several ministers fled the country in fear of arrest, for example Thomas Birch of Saintfield and John Glendy of Maghera. Other ministers were imprisoned and remained so for some time, for example William Steel Dickson of Portaferry, who was not freed until 1802.

The Synod recorded a loyal address to the king and distanced itself from 'the inexcusable crimes' of 'a few unworthy members of our body'. Attempts have been made to identify the

The site where Rev James Porter was hanged
at Greyabbey on 2 July 1798

Report of the arrest of
Rev William Steeel Dickson
in the Minutes of the Synod
of Ulster – 29 August 1798

53

3d.

WHO FEARS TO SPEAK?

Cover of 1948 pamphlet
for the Dublin 1798
Commemoration Committee

Presbyterian radicals as those with 'New Light' theology but this thesis does not bear investigation and is too simplistic. Irish Presbyterians could hardly avoid imbibing revolutionary ideas in the late 18th century, given their second-class status and little prospect of change. Within two generations they were to become the most vocal unionists in Ireland. The most obvious response of the Government to events in 1798 was structural, to pass the *Act of Union* in 1800 in the hope of tying Ireland to Britain and thereby gaining Irish loyalty by raising Irish standards.

The Synod recorded a loyal address
to the king – 29 August 1798

The Irish Parliament by
Francis Wheatley
LEEDS CITY ART GALLERY

I RONICALLY THE AIM of the United Irishmen had been to sever the link between Ireland and England, yet the Government response was to tie Ireland to Britain by an Act of Union which came into force on 1 January 1801. The most immediate consequence of this was the dissolution of the Irish Parliament by which the Anglican gentry and bishops had controlled affairs in Ireland.

The Union Jack – a combination of the flags of St George, England; St Andrew Scotland and St Patrick, Ireland

4
Irish
Presbyterians
1800–1900

The Government was obviously keen to win support from the Presbyterian community and attempted to do so by a substantial increase in the annual *regium donum* payment to Presbyterian ministers. The logic behind this was simple. If Presbyterian ministers owed the bulk of their income to a Government grant then they would be unlikely to preach rebellion. Not only was the royal bounty to increase (from £5,000 to c.£14,000) but the method of payment was controversially changed. Previously, the total grant was paid to the Synod and distributed to each minister equally. Thus in 1800 each minister received £32.

Now the Government proposed to make payments according to the size of a congregation; the largest to receive £100, the intermediate size £75, and the smallest £50. The largest grant would be paid to ministers with most influence. Only ministers who took an oath of loyalty to the Government could receive a grant. Also, the Government would pay the money to its own agent who would distribute the individual grants. They chose Rev Robert Black of Derry and paid him £400 annually for his trouble. The Synod was clearly not happy with these changes, interpreted as a blatant attempt to buy their loyalty, but eventually they crumbled under Government pressure and voted to accept the terms. Only Rev Henry Henry of Connor registered his dissent. Incidentally, Rev William Steel Dickson, now of Keady congregation, was barred from receiving any grant. The

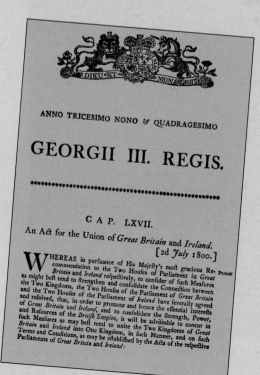

ANNO TRICESIMO NONO & QUADRAGESIMO

GEORGII III. REGIS.

CAP. LXVII.

An Act for the Union of *Great Britain* and *Ireland*.
[2d *July* 1800.]

WHEREAS in pursuance of His Majesty's most gracious Recommendation to the Two Houses of Parliament in *Great Britain* and *Ireland* respectively, to consider of such Measures as might best tend to strengthen and consolidate the Connection between the Two Kingdoms, the Two Houses of the Parliament of *Great Britain* and the Two Houses of the Parliament of *Ireland* have severally agreed and resolved, that, in order to promote and secure the essential Interests of *Great Britain* and *Ireland*, and to consolidate the Strength, Power, and Resources of the *British* Empire, it will be advisable to concur in such Measures as may best tend to unite the Two Kingdoms of *Great Britain* and *Ireland* into One Kingdom, in such Manner, and on such Terms and Conditions, as may be established by the Acts of the respective Parliaments of *Great Britain* and *Ireland*:

The Act of Union 1800

Belfast Academical Institution

Certificate in Arts awarded by Belfast Academical Institution

Rev Dr Henry Cooke by Daniel Macree, 1856

UNION THEOLOGICAL COLLEGE, BELFAST

PHOTOGRAPH BY BRYAN RUTLEDGE

56

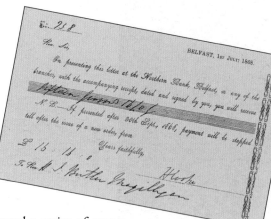

An 1868 *regium donum* voucher signed by Rev Henry Cooke

sixteen Southern Association ministers received similar treatment with grants of £100, £75 and £60 available. The Seceders were excluded at that time, but in 1809 their ninety-one congregations received grants of £70, £50 or £40 according to their size. The Reformed Presbyterians never received *regium donum* and, in 1811, they formed a Synod with twelve ministers.

The opening of the Belfast Academical Institution in 1815 triggered a series of events which dominated Irish Presbyterian affairs for thirty years. The Church of Ireland stranglehold on Trinity College, Dublin, meant that very few Presbyterians could obtain a university degree in Ireland. Candidates for the Presbyterian ministry usually travelled to Glasgow or another of the Scottish Universities to obtain degrees and theological training before their trials, licensing, and ordination in the Irish Presbyterian Church.

The new Belfast Academical Institution had a collegiate department and offered a Certificate in Arts on the model of the Scottish MA degree. Both the Synod of Ulster and the Seceder Synod agreed to accept this Belfast Certificate as equivalent to the Scottish degree. The Institute authorities also invited both Synods to appoint their own Divinity professors who could then teach within the Institution. This was a dramatic change in that Irish ministerial candidates could now receive all of their higher education in Belfast.

The Government was alarmed at this prospect of Presbyterian ministers receiving such an education, especially as former radicals such as William Drennan served on the governing body of the Institution. The Government tried to influence matters by hinting that its annual grant of £1,500 to the Institution might be withdrawn or that the *regium donum* might not be paid to ministers who had been educated in Belfast. The Synod ignored these threats and appointed Rev Samuel Hanna of Third congregation, Belfast as its Divinity professor.

Subscription Controversy

Within five years a new crisis engulfed the Belfast Institution. In October 1821, Rev William Bruce of First congregation, Belfast was appointed as professor of Latin, Hebrew and Greek in the Institute. At the 1822 meeting of Synod, held in Newry, Rev Henry Cooke unsuccessfully urged the Synod to withhold its

A stained glass window from First Congregation, Rosemary Street

Reverend Dr Henry Cooke

HENRY COOKE was born on 11 May 1788 at Grillagh, near Maghera. He studied Theology at Glasgow University and was ordained on 10 November 1808 in Duneane at age twenty years. He resigned in November 1810, tutored for a few months, and was installed in Donegore on 22 January 1811. He was minister in Killeleagh from 1818 until 1829 and in these years came to prominence as the staunch opponent of Arianism. He clashed in debate most notably with Rev Henry Montgomery of Dunmurray. As a champion of orthodoxy, Cooke's many supporters built May Street Church for him and he was installed as minister there on 24 November 1829. He served twice as Moderator, in 1841 and 1862, and was

President and Professor of Sacred Rhetoric in Assembly's College, Belfast from 1847–67. Technically, he resigned as minister of May Street but continued to 'supply the pulpit'. Rev Henry Cooke is, arguably, the most famous of all Irish Presbyterian ministers. He argued passionately for his theological and political views and gave his considerable and enthusiastic support to Church Extension and innumerable other worthy causes. Rev Henry Cooke died on 13 December 1968 and was interred in Balmoral Cemetery. His statue stands outside the Royal belfast Academical Institution, appropriately with his back to the building.

students from Bruce's classes on grounds that he was a professed Arian (that is, he denied the divinity of Jesus Christ). He was similarly unsuccessful at the 1823 Synod meeting in Armagh. In 1824, Cooke was Moderator of Synod and in January 1825 he was called upon to give evidence before a Select Committee of both houses of Parliament on the state of education in Ireland. Controversially, Cooke declared that in his opinion there were about thirty-five Arian ministers out of 200 in the Synod of Ulster and that the Belfast Institution could eventually become a 'Seminary of Arianism'.

Cooke's opinions were debated at the 1825 Synod meeting and another Subscription Controversy erupted. Henry Cooke made his reputation in these debates as the champion of orthodoxy and his chief opponent was Rev Henry Montgomery of Dunmurry congregation and also headmaster of the English School in the Belfast Institution. These two Presbyterian 'giants' clashed most famously in debate at the 1827 meeting of Synod in Strabane at which Cooke persuaded the Synod to vote on the question of whether members believed the traditional doctrine of the Trinity. In 1828, Synod approved a further proposal of Cooke's that all ministerial candidates should be examined by a Synod Committee as to their personal religion, knowledge of Scripture and doctrine before being licensed. The Non-subscribers recorded their protest and prepared to leave the Synod.

The 1829 Synod re-affirmed its intention to examine all ministerial students and the Non-subscribers gave notice of their withdrawal. The final act of separation occurred at a special meeting of Synod on 18 August 1829 in Cookstown. Their 'Remonstrance' was signed by eighteen ministers, fifteen students and licentiates, 197 elders and 314 seatholders. They eventually formed the Non-Subscribing Presbyterian Church in Ireland.

A number of factors were intertwined in this conflict. Subscription was again a thorny issue with all the former arguments replayed: the rights of conscience as opposed to the need to guard orthodoxy. Arianism was a major factor because undoubtedly some of the Non-subscribers were self-confessed Arians, for example, Rev William Porter of Newtown-Limavady. Politics was sprinkled through these stormy events. Cooke was a Tory and Government supporter and vehemently opposed to the Belfast Academical Institution while Montgomery was a Liberal and supporter of Catholic emancipation. Socio-economic factors may also be discerned in the controversy. Montgomery drew his main support from east Ulster (Porter being the only Non-subscriber west of the Bann) while Cooke played on the fears of mid-Ulster loyalists who feared Catholic advances. Finally, it is clear that there was also something of a personality clash between Cooke and Montgomery, each seeking to lead the Synod of Ulster.

It has been argued that the withdrawal of the Non-subscribers in 1829 led in turn to union between the Synod of Ulster and the Secession Synod in 1840. Other factors contributed to this union. Certainly the steady growth of the Seceders in Ulster was partially at the expense of Synod of Ulster weakness in doctrinal clarity. The suspicion that Synod ministers were less than

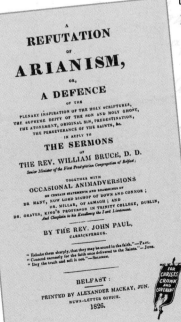

Rev Henry Montgomery and Rev Henry Cooke

The Arian Controversy

The climax of the 19th century conflict over Subscription within the Synod of Ulster took place on Friday 3 July 1829 in Lurgan. In an electric atmosphere, Rev Henry Montgomery spoke at considerable length in the morning, attacking and undermining the earlier pronouncement of Rev Henry Cooke. In the afternoon, Rev Henry Cooke rose and delivered his response. Both men received thunderous applause but it was Cooke who clearly carried the vote. At a Special Synod on 18 August the Clerk, Rev William Porter, presented a 'Remonstrance' signed by eighteen ministers, fifteen students and licentiates and 197 elders, in which they indicated their intention to withdraw. Seventeen ministers did so and on 25 May 1830 they formed the Remonstrant Synod of Ulster. The withdrawing ministers were:

MINISTER	CONGREGATION
Samuel Arnold	Narrow-Water
John Mitchel	Newry
Arthur Neilson	Kilmore
James Davis	Banbridge
James Lunn	Carlingford
Samuel Neilson	Dromore
John Watson	Greyabbey
John Mulligan	Moira
Henry Montgomery	Dunmurray
Fletcher Blakely	Moneyrea
David Whyte	Ballee
Thomas Alexander	Cairncastle
Robert Campbell	Templepatrick
Nathaniel Alexander	Crumlin
Alexander Montgomery	Glenarm
William Glendy	Ballycarry
William Porter	Newtown-limavady

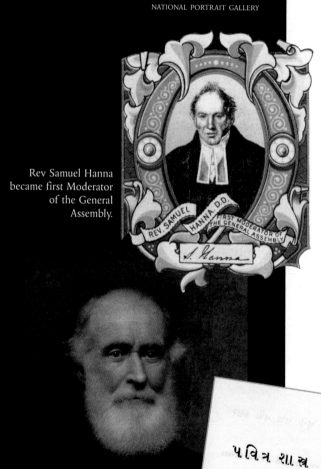

Robert Stewart, Lord Castlereagh, although born a Presbyterian, became an Anglican. He refused to intervene in the hanging of Rev James Porter of Greyabbey in 1798. Castlereagh also tried to bully the Synod of Ulster because he did not want Irish Presbyterian ministers educated in the Belfast Institution.

NATIONAL PORTRAIT GALLERY

Rev Samuel Hanna became first Moderator of the General Assembly.

Rev James Glasgow, first Irish Presbyterian Missionary to India

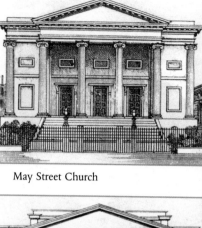

May Street Church

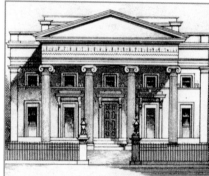

Linenhall Street Church

Rosemary Street Church

wholehearted in supporting the Westminster formularies encouraged Seceder causes. The victory of orthodoxy in the doctrinal controversies in the 1820s was followed by a reassertion of the practice of unqualified subscription to the Westminster Confession in 1835 and certainly helped to 'close the gap' between Synod and Seceder brands of Presbyterianism.

The Seceders themselves had suffered division into Burghers and Anti-Burghers but these factions had united in 1818. The Government also blurred the differences between the two Presbyterian Synods in 1838 by again changing the *regium donum* scheme. Those who had received £100 continued to do so, but all other Presbyterian ministers, whether Seceder or Synod of Ulster, now received £75. To qualify for the scheme, all new congregations had to consist of at least twelve families or fifty individuals and be able to contribute £35 annually to a minister's stipend.

Another important component in the 1840 union was the fact that the students of both Presbyterian bodies were receiving their training in the same Belfast Academical Institution and this situation fostered warm relations. The students started a united prayer meeting on 8 January 1839. They invited Rev John Coulter (Gilnahirk) to address them on the possible benefits of a union of the two bodies. This address, delivered on April 1839, was published and led to a wider debate on the possibility of union throughout Seceder and Synod of Ulster congregations. In 1839, memorials requesting union were presented to both Synods and committees were set up to explore the matter further.

Formation of General Assembly

On Tuesday 7 July 1840, the Synod of Ulster met in May Street Church and the Secession Synod met simultaneously in Linenhall Street Church. The union of these two bodies was proclaimed on Friday 10 July. At 11am both Synods ended their business and met in the city streets and processed together to Rosemary Street Church. Here, a new church court was constituted as the General Assembly of the Presbyterian Church in Ireland and Rev Samuel Dr Hanna was elected as its first Moderator. This significant event united 292 Synod of Ulster congregations with 141 Secession congregations, now forming a new united Church with a total membership of 650,000 Presbyterians.

The only black note was that the Seceder Moderator, Rev Alexander Rentoul of Ray, and about fourteen other Seceder ministers refused to join the new body. Happily most of them joined the following year on being given assurances about the use of Psalms in public worship.

One of the first acts of the new General Assembly was to commission two missionaries for work in India. Rev James Glasgow had only been installed in the Linenhall Street Secession Church less than three

પવિત્ર શાસ્ત્ર

THE HOLY BIBLE
IN GUJARATI
1952

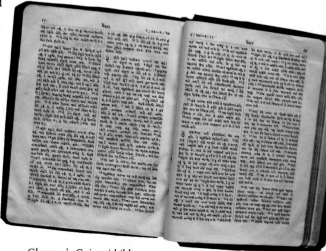

Glasgow's Gujarati bible

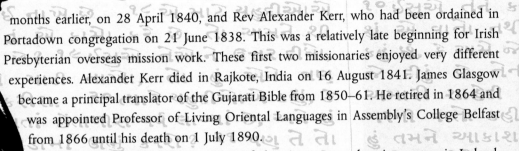

months earlier, on 28 April 1840, and Rev Alexander Kerr, who had been ordained in Portadown congregation on 21 June 1838. This was a relatively late beginning for Irish Presbyterian overseas mission work. These first two missionaries enjoyed very different experiences. Alexander Kerr died in Rajkote, India on 16 August 1841. James Glasgow became a principal translator of the Gujarati Bible from 1850–61. He retired in 1864 and was appointed Professor of Living Oriental Languages in Assembly's College Belfast from 1866 until his death on 1 July 1890.

Presbyterians played an active role in fashioning a new education system in Ireland. All of the main churches, Roman Catholic, Church of Ireland and Presbyterian founded and organised their own schools. For a time some of these Protestant schools were used as a

Alexander Kerr

FAR LEFT: Bellasis church school, Monaghan
The school, on the extreme left, was adjacent to the church with the boys room above the girls.

CENTRE: Spa church school, Ballynahinch

LEFT: The General Assembly's Committee Certificate on religious education to daily schools

means of evangelising the Roman Catholic people. In the early 19th century, Roman Catholics were increasingly indignant and hostile to this method of proselytism. This led to a suggestion that there should be a new National Education system based upon the principles of combined secular and segregated religious education. In other words, that all denominations should be taught together in National Schools but that religious education should be provided by the clergy of the respective denominations. The entire scheme was to be controlled by a Board of six commissioners: two Roman Catholic, two Church of Ireland and two Dissenters. Presbyterians were divided on these new proposals.

Rev James Carlile of Abbey congregation, Dublin, accepted an appointment as one of the Presbyterian commissioners but there was fierce opposition from many ministers. At the General Synod in 1834, a majority of ministers voted in favour of the new National Education scheme but the total vote, including elders, was opposed to it. Negotiations between the Synod and the Education Board broke down. The Synod continued to establish its own Presbyterian schools and pressed the Government to give grants to these schools. Eventually, in 1840, the Government conceded. Denominational education survived and flourished at the expense of this early experiment with integrated education.

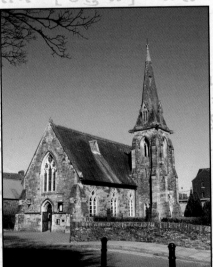

Clonakilty church, part of the Home Mission in the 19th century, is now a post office.

Evangelicalism was growing in influence throughout many churches in the mid-19th century and Irish Presbyterianism enjoyed its fair share. The Methodists had organised an Irish Mission as early as 1799 and discovered real success in sending Irish speaking

Stained glass window presented by the Former Pupils Association of First Derry School to First Derry Presbyterian Church in appreciation of the church's provision of education within the city from 1773–1995.

The Eviction by Erskine Nichol, 1853
NATIONAL GALLERY OF IRELAND

preachers throughout the south of Ireland. The London Hibernian Society was similarly active in Ireland as an offshoot of the London Missionary Society. Initially, Presbyterians were concerned to revive small Presbyterian causes in the south and west of Ireland. Notable in these endeavours were the efforts of Abbey congregation in Dublin. Rev Benjamin McDowell was appointed by the Synod in 1788 to tour west and south-west Ireland seeking small groups of Dissenters with the objective of organising further regular visits by Presbyterian preachers. Some Ulster ministers actively supported these efforts, most notably Henry Cooke and his close friend Robert Stewart of Broughshane. Co-operation between northern and southern Presbyterians led to the formation of the Home Mission in 1826.

The Workhouse where the unfortunate victims of the Famine often found themselves

The Irish famine of 1846 is infamous on a worldwide scale. The humble potato was the staple diet of thousands of Irish people and the blight which destroyed the crop spelt disaster in a situation where population growth had far outstripped the inefficient agricultural system. Government incompetence and ineffective emergency systems resulted in up to one million deaths and the emigration of about two million people. Private charity could never cope with a catastrophe on this scale.

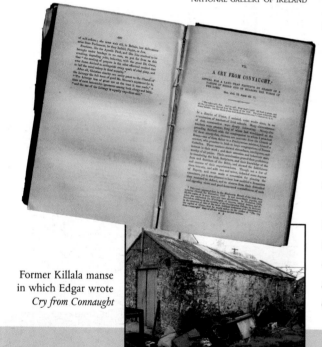

Former Killala manse in which Edgar wrote *Cry from Connaught*

Rev John Edgar was conducting evangelistic services in Connaught in September 1846 and was struck by the magnitude of the plight of the starving people. He wrote an appeal to his fellow Presbyterians, entitled, *Cry from Connaught*. About £16,000 was raised for relief work in response to Edgar's appeal. The full title of Edgar's work was, *Cry from Connaught: An appeal from a land which fainteth by reason of a famine of bread and of hearing the words of the Lord.* This linkage between famine relief and gospel preaching was resented by Roman Catholic authorities and led to charges of 'Souperism'. Edgar and others denied that they were trying to convert Roman Catholics into Presbyterians but were simply opening God's Word to them. Several new Presbyterian churches and schools originated at this time in Connaught but they were largely forced to close as the Roman

Rev John Edgar

Reverend Michael Brannigan

MICHAEL BRANNIGAN was born in Stewartstown in 1816 in a Roman Catholic family. Both Michael and his father were Irish School teachers with Rev Robert Allen in County Tyrone. Through conversation with Rev Allen of Stewartstown, and reading the Irish Bible for himself, Michael Brannigan was converted. In February 1845, the Belfast Theology students formed a Student Missionary Association and selected Michael Brannigan to be their missionary in Connaught. They undertook to support him in prayers and provide his salary. He arrived in Ballina in January 1846 and assumed responsibility for 112 Irish Schools scattered throughout Mayo and Sligo. In that harsh famine year alone, he founded a further thirty schools and twelve separate mission stations. It was in one of these stations, Ballinglen, that Rev Brannigan was installed as minister in 1848. He served here until his death on 15 November 1874. His church and manse were both destroyed by fire in 1864, but the resourceful Michael Brannigan had insured both! They were rebuilt and opened in the following year. That Church at Ballinglen was finally closed in 1959.

Ballinglen ruin today

61

Newtownstewart

Catholic Church became more proactive in establishing its own system.

While there was no large scale success in converting Irish Roman Catholics, the Presbyterian Church did experience a renewed evangelical self-confidence from the 1830s. New congregations were formed and missionary organisations and activities proliferated throughout the Presbyterian communities. During that decade, the Synod of Ulster grew by an incredible eighty-three new congregations, and the Seceders by a further thirty-seven new congregations. The new Presbyterian Church in Ireland added a further 137 congregations before the end of the 19th century.

One problem that was not tackled in 1840 was that of duplication. Many towns in Ulster today have two or more Presbyterian congregations, often originating in one from each of the uniting Synods. The wisdom of that day was to let both congregations continue but this is presenting fresh challenges in the 21st century when two or three Presbyterian congregations in a single locality could combine and be accommodated within any of the present buildings.

About half of all Presbyterian Church buildings were erected or enlarged during the 19th century. In addition, almost 400 manses were built in the fifty years after the 1840 union, aided by the creation of a Church and Manse Fund which originated in 1853. Building styles also changed with more ornate church buildings, including spires, becoming fashionable. Fitzroy Church in Belfast provides a typical example, being completed in 1874. Perhaps the new Church House complex in Fisherwick Place, Belfast which was completed in 1905, marks the high water mark of elaborate Presbyterian building.

The evangelical spirit within Irish Presbyterianism saw the formation of several missions in the mid-19th century. The Home Mission started in 1826, the Jewish Mission in 1841, the Colonial Mission in 1848, and the Continental Mission in 1856. Open-air preaching also grew in frequency as evangelical concern for the un-churched grew. One of the earliest ministers to engage in open air preaching

Abbey, Dublin

OPPOSITE:
Open-air preaching at the Custom House, Belfast
BELFAST CENTRAL MISSION

Belfast Town Mission

THE BELFAST TOWN MISSION began in 1827, when the Belfast population was about 40,000 but was rising rapidly and served by only five Presbyterian Churches: Rosemary Street, Donegall Street, Fisherwick Place, Berry Street and Alfred Place. The leading minister in the formation of the Town Mission was Rev Reuben John Bryce, son of Secession minister Rev James Bryce of Killaig, and principal of the Belfast Academy. His plan was to establish a number of stations throughout the poorer parts of Belfast from which mission agents would visit homes with tracts and in which they would conduct 'religious exercises'. The first mission agent was William Cochrane from Lisburn who had been converted under the ministry of Rev James Morgan in Fisherwick Place. Five stations were established during the first year: in Brown Street, Sandy Row, Cromac Street, Little Donegall Street and Mill Row. In 1843, the Town Mission was reconstituted under Presbyterian control, but

not formally connected to the General Assembly. The new congregations of Albert Street (1852), Argyle Place (1853), Great Victoria Street (1858), Duncairn (1861) and Donegall Pass (1869) were founded largely through the work of the Town Mission. The Annual Meeting on 17 January 1888 was given the following Mission statistics for the previous year. Visits paid to families totalled 43,973; to Institutions 302; to ships 657. Religious meetings had increased to 3,786 with an aggregate attendance of 170,418. Through the agents, 141 families were united to different churches. Young people at Sabbath Schools numbered 4,796 and at Bible Classes 669. When Belfast was designated a city in 1888, the 'Town Mission' became the 'City Mission.' By the year 1900, the population of Belfast had grown to 300,000 and the Mission had twenty-three agents.

Connor church. Scene of early Revival meetings

The railway and the well-developed Victorian transport system was essential in bringing crowds to meetings. Building also provided relief work. A discount was offered on rail tickets to attend the opening of the new College.

BELOW:
Open-air preaching off Commercial Court, Belfast
BELFAST CENTRAL MISSION

was William Johnston of Townsend Street congregation in Belfast. By the early 1850s the General Assembly was encouraging this activity.

1859 Revival

The year 1859 will forever be known as the year of the Revival in Irish Presbyterian history. This momentous series of events, in which 100,000 people were converted, did not happen overnight. Reports of a Revival on the eastern seaboard of America in 1857 prompted the General Assembly in 1858 to send Rev William McClure, minister of First Derry and Convenor of the Colonial Mission, and Rev William Gibson, Professor of Christian Ethics in the Presbyterian College, Belfast, to America to investigate the occurrence and to report back to the Assembly. The Revival began in the area of Kells in County Antrim and spread rapidly through surrounding areas.

This Revival challenged traditional congregational life. Numbers of worshippers multiplied as did meetings for prayer in homes and places of work. Special Church services and outdoor rallies gave focus to public enthusiasm. The largest such rally took place on 29 June 1859 in Botanic Gardens, Belfast when a crowd of about 40,000 attended. This event was chaired by the Moderator, Rev James Johnston of Tullylish. Because of the practical difficulty in hearing, this rally broke up into about twenty meetings throughout the Gardens and lasted four hours.

Not everyone was enthusiastic about events in 1859, as evidenced by the publications of two Presbyterian ministers. Professor Gibson warmly supported all that he saw and heard concerning the Revival and in 1860 he published his account in a book entitled 'The Year of Grace'. Gibson writes warmly of numerous incidents of good from all parts of Ulster. Also in 1860, the Rev.

Professor William Gibson

Isaac Nelson of Donegall Street congregation in Belfast published his 'The Year of Delusion'. Nelson saw the events of 1859 as a crude epidemic of mass hysteria and was offended by the rash of 'lay preaching' which sprang up everywhere. Modern research has indicated that the benefits of the 1859 Revival were certainly immediate in injecting new life into many congregations, but that such benefits were not sustained in the long term. In fact, although many Presbyterians were involved in the Revival, the greatest benefits were felt by the much smaller Brethren and Baptist groups.

University Education

Having been denied a university education in Ireland for so many years, the Presbyterian Church in Ireland built two Colleges in the mid 19th century. Presbyterian relations with the Belfast Academical Institution were never entirely harmonious, and, from the early 1840s, there was a growing desire for the Church to create its own College for higher education. The concept was almost killed at birth by a Government announcement in 1844 that it intended to create a new University in Ireland which would be open to students of all creeds or none. The result was the Queen's Colleges in Belfast, Cork and Galway. Why then should the Presbyterian Church create its own College?

A majority of the Assembly's College Committee felt the Church should concentrate upon providing a Theological College which ministerial students would attend after completion of their Arts course in a Queen's College. Consequently 'Assembly's College', as it became known, was built in Botanic Avenue and opened in December 1853. One serious complication in all of these developments was that in 1846 a bequest of £20,000 from Mrs Martha Maria Magee, widow of Rev William Magee (First Lurgan 1780–1800), was left to the Presbyterian Church for the purposes of creating a College of Arts and Theology. While a majority of Presbyterians believed this money could be used in the Belfast College project, an influential minority advocated a literal fulfilment of Mrs Magee's wishes in using her bequest to create a College offering a complete curriculum of Arts and Theology. A serious and costly legal debate ensued and eventually, in 1865, Magee College opened in Londonderry. Irish Presbyterians, who had for so long been discriminated against in higher

LEFT: Assembly's College, Belfast
ABOVE: Magee College, Londonderry

The Faculty of Presbyterian College c. 1863
From left: Prof WD Killen, Prof JL Porter, Prof H Cooke (president)., Prof J Edgar, Prof W Gibson, Prof JG Murphy

Emigration was the inevitable result
of both famine and eviction

Eviction scene by Willliam Lawrence
NATIONAL LIBRARY OF IRELAND

Rev Richard Smyth

education in their own country, now boasted the embarrassing riches of two Colleges. This situation continued until 1978, when Magee College and 'Assembly's College' amalgamated in the Belfast College building to form the Union Theological College.

The Tenant Rights

In the 19th century, the majority of Presbyterians were tenant farmers. Although northern tenant farmers were, generally speaking, better off than their southern counterparts, nevertheless an agitation for better tenant rights grew in the aftermath of the Irish famine in the 1840s. Many Presbyterian ministers were deeply and actively involved in this movement. There was an Ulster custom of allowing tenant farmers to be reimbursed for improvements made to their holdings, but this custom had no legal status and could be ignored by a landlord.

The Tenant Right Movement advocated a reform programme known as 'the 3 F's', fair rents, fixity of tenure (except for non-payment of rent) and free sale of a tenant's interest in a holding. This formula was the creation of a Presbyterian minister, Rev. Nathaniel McAuley Brown of Drumachose. In 1847, the General Assembly expressed its support for the 'Ulster custom' to be recognised in law. The rhetoric of the Tenant Right Movement increased in proportion to increasing evictions in the latter half of the 19th century, yet the Assembly continued to support the small farmers. Some conservative ministers, such as Henry Cooke, were offended by this stance and gave their support to the landlords.

When a National Right League was formed in 1850, the northern delegation was led by ten Presbyterian ministers and four Roman Catholic priests. There were, however, conflicting and sectarian understandings in this matter. Roman Catholic tenants tended to believe they were campaigning for the return of land which the British Crown had confiscated from their ancestors, and Presbyterian tenant farmers were campaigning for land which they believed had been legally given to their ancestors. It was Prime Minister William Ewart Gladstone who eventually began the process of solving the land problem with his Land Acts of 1870 and 1881. By these Acts the '3 F's' were conceded and later Acts enabled tenant farmers to buy their holdings and repay the State over a period of time.

1838 Sunday School notice from First Congregation, Belfast

Sunday Schools

While Sunday Schools first appeared in England in the 1780s, they were slow to become popular in Ireland. The origin of the first Irish Sunday School is not known but the first in Belfast was founded in 1784 by Henry Joy McCracken in connection with Third Belfast congregation in Rosemary Street. McCracken was later hanged as a leader in the United Irishmen rebellion in 1798. McCracken's Sunday School was primarily structured to teach literacy and numeracy to poorer children, and made use of religious literature for much of the former.

PREBYTERIAN HISTORICAL SOCIETY OF IRELAND

By 1809, there were only about eighty Sunday Schools among all denominations in Ireland. In that year, a non-denominational 'Sunday School Society for Ireland' was formed, though the Committee was dominated by Church of Ireland persons. By 1834, this Society had 2,746 schools in membership and 210,135 on the attendance rolls.

Controversy led to the creation of a separate Presbyterian 'Sabbath School Society' in 1862. Rev John Hall of Rutland Square congregation in Dublin was appointed as a Commissioner of National Education in 1861 and, as this system was opposed by the Anglicans, Hall was denied a seat on the Committee of the Sunday School Society unless he resigned as Commissioner. This he refused to do.

In 1862, a small group of leading Presbyterian ministers and elders established a new 'Sabbath School Society'. The leading personality was the Rev William Johnston of Townsend Street in Belfast. He was the Honorary Secretary of the new Society from its first meeting in 1862 until his death in 1894. Within ten years, there were 915 Sunday Schools in connection with the Society, teaching 62,102 students. The Society also distributed teaching materials, Bibles, New Testaments, Catechisms and appropriate books for congregational libraries.

Children's excursion
BELFAST CENTRAL MISSION

The Burning Bush

THE BURNING BUSH is probably the most commonly used and recognised symbol in Irish Presbyterian Churches. It is embroidered upon countless pulpit falls, and is carved into Church tables and chairs and hymn boards all over the country. Why did Irish Presbyterians adopt this symbol from Exodus chapter three? The earliest recorded use is by the French Protestant Church in the late 17th century with the Latin inscription *flagror non consumer*. The Church of Scotland has long used a burning bush with the inscription *nec tamen consumebatur 'not consumed'*. Irish Presbyterians have preferred yet another inscription; *ardens sed virens 'burning but flourishing'*. The earliest Irish use of a burning bush symbol was in the first edition of the twice weekly Presbyterian newspaper *The Banner of Ulster*, published on 10 June 1842. The editor, Rev William Gibson of Third Belfast, featured a burning bush with an open Bible beneath. On either side of the bush was an Irish wolfhound and an Irish harp. A shamrock and thistle were intertwined and an Irish round tower featured in the background. Within fifteen years the symbol was simplified to the now more familiar burning bush and Latin inscription.

First Home Rule Crisis

Gladstone believed passionately that he had to introduce legislation to solve the Irish problem which had dogged British politics for many years. The first step in his reform policy was to disestablish the Church of Ireland. That Church had failed to win popular support and, in 1869, Gladstone introduced his Irish Church Act by which disestablishment would become reality. Although some Presbyterians, most notably Henry Cooke, were opposed to this measure and attempted to rally Presbyterian support for the Church of Ireland, a majority of Presbyterians were more concerned with the implications for the Presbyterian Church in Ireland. The annual *regium donum* payment would also cease.

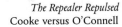

The Repealer Repulsed
Cooke versus O'Connell

This annual Government grant was worth almost £50,000 and guaranteed every minister about £70 per year. Ministers were given a choice: continue to take their payments for their lifetime or abandon their rights and the Government would pay a single lump sum to the Church for investment and to provide the basis of a Fund for future payment to ministers. This was no simple decision as many ministers depended

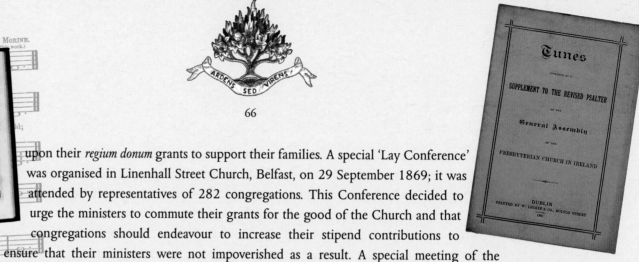

upon their *regium donum* grants to support their families. A special 'Lay Conference' was organised in Linenhall Street Church, Belfast, on 29 September 1869; it was attended by representatives of 282 congregations. This Conference decided to urge the ministers to commute their grants for the good of the Church and that congregations should endeavour to increase their stipend contributions to ensure that their ministers were not impoverished as a result. A special meeting of the General Assembly was subsequently held on Tuesday 25 January 1870 and was attended by 402 ministers and 274 elders. The vast majority of ministers agreed to gave up their rights. In response, the Government made a payment of £622,704. 6s. 5d to a new Commutation Fund. Only four ministers, from a total compliment of 562 ministers, maintained their personal payments.

In the latter half of the 19th century the Irish Presbyterian Church became entangled in three controversies: instrumental music, the use of hymns and communion wine. Today, the vast majority of Presbyterian congregations use instrumental music, sing hymns and use unfermented wine at Communion Services, but in the 19th century these issues created major debates within Presbyterian circles.

Church Music

The 1868 General Assembly was divided over the recent innovation of using instrumental music in public worship. The focus of the debate was the harmonium introduced in Sunday services in Enniskillen congregation on 8 March 1861. Other congregations had begun to follow this new trend. The Enniskillen minister, Rev Alexander Cooper McClatchy, was opposed in his action by Presbytery, Synod and General Assembly. Henry Cooke and others argued that there was a 'natural law' which prohibited such innovative practices in worship. Rev McClatchy and others argued that there was simply no Assembly law which prohibited the use of instrumental music in worship. The debate raged for several years, within the Assembly and outside it, by means of various pamphlets and newspaper articles. The younger ministers tended to side with the party arguing for liberty in this matter.

Organ behind the pulpit
Sinclair Seamans
SCENIC IRELAND

Window in High Kirk, Ballymena
GORDON GRAY

The storm clouds gathered. An Assembly resolution in 1873 requiring congregations with instrumental music to cease its use was ignored. A similar resolution in 1883, which threatened to discipline disobedient ministers, was only defeated by eleven votes. A 'Purity Party' was formed. It argued against instrumental music and other pollutants such as stained glass. In 1888, a threatened split of about 200 ministers was averted and a five year truce agreed. In 1891, the issue of instrumental music was raised again and the Assembly 'passed from the question'. This ended formal debate on this issue and gradually organs were introduced in virtually all congregations. Nowadays, of course, it is church organs that are under threat in several places, and

A poster advertising the 'Catch-my-Pal' movement

LIGHT V. DARKNESS

- WHITE SPOTS SHEW CHURCHES AND MISSION HALLS

"Light shineth in darkness"

MAP AREA

NEW CITY BOUNDARY

- PUBLIC HOUSES
- SPIRIT GROCERS
- DISTILLERS

"He maketh a shew of them openly"

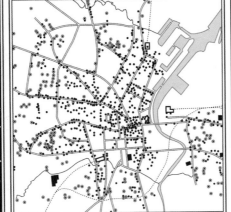

drawn by Maura Pringle based on an illustration from *A Brighter Belfast: the Story of the Shankill Road Mission*, 1898

there is a growing trend of introducing a much wider variety of musical instruments in worship.

The early Presbyterians had used the Scottish Psalter of 1564 in their worship. Indeed, the singing of the metrical psalms was a trademark of Presbyterian worship. A revised Psalter had come into use in 1650 and this was used in Ireland up to 1880. In the late 19th century, there was considerable controversy over the introduction of hymn singing in worship services. Some Seceder ministers had only joined the Union in 1841 after obtaining assurances that only the metrical psalms would be used in worship. Some Synod of Ulster congregations had been using paraphrases in their worship prior to 1840.

The introduction of hymns into Irish Presbyterianism caused much furore. There were many individuals who believed that the singing of Scripture was far superior to any 'man-made' composition and that the use of hymns opened the door to doctrinal error. Yet hymns were the newest aid in worship and Presbyterian congregations were susceptible to this new trend. In 1895, the General Assembly set up a Committee to select suitable hymns for a Presbyterian hymnbook. The same debate was taking place in the Scottish Church at that time and so a joint 'Church Hymnary' was produced in 1898.

Temperance

A storm blew up in Irish Presbyterianism concerning Communion wine. Despite the fact that John Calvin had expressed a desire to celebrate Communion on a weekly basis, he was denied this in Geneva and neither did the Scottish or Irish Presbyterian Church follow his ideal. The most common pattern in Irish congregations was to celebrate this sacrament twice each year, usually in Spring and Autumn. In 1875, the General Assembly was asked to give a definitive ruling as to whether Communion wine should be fermented or not. This request was inspired by the activities of the Total Abstinence Movement.

After debate, the Assembly ruled that 'a mild natural wine' should be used and that agitation on this subject should cease. But this debate would not die and the subject was discussed in 1878, 1888 and 1889. It was agreed in 1889 that each congregation should decide upon its own wine. The Presbyterian system is democratic if nothing else and no congregation illustrates this better than the response of St. Enoch's. Here it was decided that fermented wine would be served to those who desired it before the

The Temperance Movement

By the beginning of the 19th century, about 11.5 million gallons of spirits was being produced annually in Ireland with about 30% of this illicitly. Pubs and clubs proliferated in all the main towns. Dublin, for example, boasted 2,000 alehouses, 300 taverns and 1,200 brandy shops! Everyone drank, ministers and people alike. The Irish Temperance Movement was formed in 1829 by Rev Dr John Edgar of Alfred Place, Belfast. By example, he opened the parlour window of his Alfred Street home and poured the remaining contents of a gallon of old malt whiskey into the street!

In August 1829, John Edgar published letters in the Belfast News Letter advocating Temperance and soon local Temperance Societies were formed. The first was in New Ross on 20 August 1829 and The Ulster Temperance Society was founded in Belfast on 24 September. Incredibly, by March 1830 there were 3,000 such Societies in Ireland, England, Scotland and Wales. Edgar himself spoke at countless Temperance meetings all over the country and wrote some ninety tracts for the Movement. It has been estimated that as a result of his crusade, his own Secession church disciplined one in seven of its own ministers for drunkenness. From about 1832, a number of Temperance Societies took their cause further and advocated Total Abstinence. Edgar rejected this new position but nevertheless the new idea spread rapidly. His original pledge had been against whiskey but some thought this too narrow a basis as people could get drunk on wines and beer. On 4 July 1850, a 'Temperance Association in connection with the General Assembly' was formed by a group of fifteen ministers. This Association had a pledge of Total Abstinence and grew steadily in membership. In 1876, the General Assembly urged all Presbyterian people to adopt the practice of total abstinence from all intoxicating liquors as beverages.

While it is still the rule of the General Assembly that no alcoholic drink may be consumed on Church property, Irish Presbyterians are divided on the issue of private consumption. Some advocate teetotalism and some advocate temperance.

Pledge.

I hereby promise that with the aid of Divine Grace I will abstain from all intoxicating liquors as beverages.

Signed 28th January 1906.

William Bruce

A Sample of a Total Abstinence Pledge, 1906

68

Silver Communion serviceware – Ballycarry

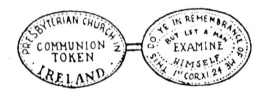

Stock token used in Drumbo up until about 1920

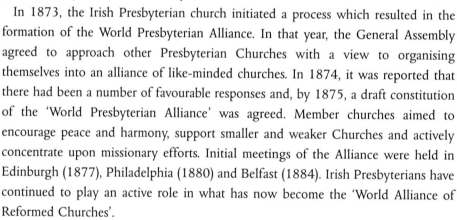

sermon and unfermented wine would be served to those who desired it after the sermon! Eventually, in 1905, the General Assembly recommended the use of non-alcoholic wine to Kirk Sessions. Today most congregations celebrate Communion on at least four occasions each year and only a very small number use fermented wine.

For years, Communion wine was consumed from large common cups, passed among the congregation. The use of small individual cups originated in the USA in the 1890s mostly for reasons of hygiene. Such reasons were legitimate. The congregation of Muckamore in County Antrim had two common cups from which an elder took a sip before passing them to the respective halves of the congregation. Some timid souls were put off if they sat behind the elder with the large walrus-like moustache and observed it dipping into the Communion cup before they were invited to partake of the contents! The use of individual cups at Communion has become the common practice today within Irish Presbyterianism.

Contemporary communion service in Lisburn using individual glasses

In 1873, the Irish Presbyterian church initiated a process which resulted in the formation of the World Presbyterian Alliance. In that year, the General Assembly agreed to approach other Presbyterian Churches with a view to organising themselves into an alliance of like-minded churches. In 1874, it was reported that there had been a number of favourable responses and, by 1875, a draft constitution of the 'World Presbyterian Alliance' was agreed. Member churches aimed to encourage peace and harmony, support smaller and weaker Churches and actively concentrate upon missionary efforts. Initial meetings of the Alliance were held in Edinburgh (1877), Philadelphia (1880) and Belfast (1884). Irish Presbyterians have continued to play an active role in what has now become the 'World Alliance of Reformed Churches'.

Second Home Rule Crisis

Even before he took office on 28 January 1886, Gladstone announced, on 17 December 1885, that he intended to introduce a Home Rule Bill for Ireland in the new Parliament. Most Presbyterians were shocked by the seventy-five year old's conversion to Home Rule; their natural political home was in the Liberal Party and they had supported his Irish Land Acts of 1870 and 1881. In response to calls from six Presbyteries, the Moderator, Rev James Weir Wigham of Ballinasloe in County Athlone, called a Special Assembly which met at noon on Tuesday 9 March 1886 in May Street Church, Belfast. The unanimous decision of this Assembly was to deplore Gladstone's move towards creating an Irish Parliament without safeguards for minority groups. The seventy-one year old Rev Matthew Macauley of McKelvey's Grove tried unsuccessfully to record a 'No' to the resolution but was not noticed by the Moderator.

The General Assembly reiterated its view on 16 June though on this occasion Matthew Macauley was the sole voice in opposition. The *Belfast Newsletter* summarised

Matthew Macauley

Presbyterian ministers 1882–3

Macauley's opinion:

He thought that the country and the Church were in the presence of a very serious crisis, and he thought the less said the soonest mended. In point of fact, they were like men standing upon the edge of a volcano, black with the smoke of recent eruptions and the trembling of the birth throes, of new ones; and therefore it was necessary upon their part to exercise self-restraint, to be very careful, even in the words they used, lest they did anything to provoke jealousy, bitterness, or strife in any part of the country (*Newsletter* Thur. 17 June 1886).

William Gladstone with his cabinet of 1868
NATIONAL PORTRAIT GALLERY

In fact, the Home Rule Bill was defeated in the House of Common in the previous week, on 8 June, by 341 votes to 311. Macauley was possibly alluding to the fact that there was serious rioting in Belfast even as the Assembly deliberated. Sectarian rioting had started in the Shipyard in June and continued until 25 October. At least thirty-two people were killed and over 270 injured. In some reports, the police were blamed for provoking much of the trouble while the *Belfast Telegraph* blamed 'roughs and corner loafers' (*B. Telegraph* Fri. 11 June 1886).

Gladstone introduced his Second Home Rule Bill in Parliament on 13 February 1893. Once again, a Special Assembly was called, and met in May Street Church at noon on Wednesday 15 March. 403 ministers and 254 elders attended, and the debate lasted five hours. This Assembly voted unanimously to defeat Home Rule despite attempts by Rev James Armour of First Ballymoney and Professor James Dougherty of Magee College to argue for a measure of self-government.

On Monday 7 June 1893, the General Assembly once again debated the issue and voted against Home Rule by 304 votes to eleven. The Home Rule Bill passed the Commons on 2 September by a majority of thirty-four votes but was then heavily defeated a week later in the Lords by a majority of 378.

The 1890, General Assembly established a central organising committee to link Guilds of young men and young women in congregations. Under the leadership of Rev Andrew Charles Murphy of Elmwood congregation, Belfast, a Young People's Guild was established and within five years there were 126 societies working in Presbyterian congregations.

As the century drew to a close, the Presbyterian Church in Ireland was in buoyant mood, consisting of 606 active ministers (including 103 missionaries) in 570 congregations. There were 165 students in training for the ministry, and 809 schools under Presbyterian management catering for 51,950 children. In addition, there were 1,099 Sunday Schools catering for 104,754 children. The 19th century had witnessed a consolidation of Irish Presbyterianism.

Rev JB Armour by William Conor
TRINITY CHURCH, BALLYMONEY

5
Irish
Presbyterians
1900–present

THE POPULATION OF IRELAND IN 1900 was 4,456,546 of whom 443,494 were Presbyterian. The main denominational breakdown in Ireland was: 74% Roman Catholic, 13% Church of Ireland and 10% Presbyterian. As had always been the case, the vast majority of the Presbyterians, 426,177 or 96%, were concentrated in Ulster. They were spread around the other provinces as follows: Leinster 11,735 (2.5%), Munster 3,312 (.7%) and Connaught 2,270 (.5%). The Church was led by 658 ministers, serving 565 congregations and spread throughout 36 Presbyteries.

In 1906, the new City Hall, Belfast, was opened the same year as the new Assembly Buildings, Fisherwick Place.

The Irish Presbyterian Church was a confident and influential church at the commencement of the 20th century and sure of its central place in society. The 1900 General Assembly which met in Dublin pronounced upon the sanctity of Sunday, urging people to protest against recently introduced Sunday postal services and newspapers. The imposing new £74,000 Church House and Assembly Hall in Fisherwick Place, Belfast, which opened on 5 June 1905, embodied the new confidence.

Dark clouds were gathering however, both religious and political. Deep suspicion of Roman Catholicism was confirmed in 1908 by the application of the *Ne Temere* decree. The Roman Catholic authorities declared that all marriages of Roman Catholics to Protestants were invalid unless they had been celebrated by a Roman Catholic priest. The children of mixed marriages in which a priest was not involved were declared illegitimate. In October 1910, a Roman Catholic husband, Alexander McCann, deserted his Presbyterian wife and took their

Church House, Fisherwick Place, 1906

The Battle of the Somme by JP Beadle
BELFAST CITY COUNCIL

72

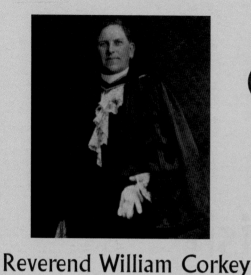

Reverend William Corkey

WILLIAM CORKEY was born on 15 June 1877 in Second Glendermott manse. His father, Joseph, was minister of that church (1860–1910). William and all seven of his brothers were ordained as Christian ministers and his three sisters all served as missionaries. William was ordained in Cullybackey on 6 December 1904 and he served as minister there for five years. On 28 June 1909, he was installed as minister of Townsend Street where he exercised an influential ministry for fifteen years. On 19 June 1924 he was installed as minister of Windsor where he served until his retirement on 1 September 1949. He was elected Moderator of the General Assembly in 1933. Rev Corkey was heavily involved in several church-wide ministries, for example: Orphan Society, Church Extension, Student Community Centre and Temperance. It was in Education that he came to prominence, leading a fight for the maintenance of Bible instruction to be given in schools under various Education Acts by which the State assumed responsibility for general education. William Corkey died on 20 February 1964 aged eighty-six years.

infant children, stating that on the basis of *Ne Temere*, they were not married. Rev William Corkey of Townsend Street congregation had married the couple and protest meetings were organised in Belfast, Dublin and other towns. The 1911 General Assembly protested loudly against the operation of the *Ne Temere* decree in the United Kingdom and instructed Irish Presbyterian ministers to warn their people against the dangers of mixed marriages.

Home Rule

The issue of Home Rule was again to dominate the religious and political scene in the early 20th century. On the eve of the 1910 election, eleven former Presbyterian Moderators took the unprecedented step of publishing a Manifesto in which they stated their preference for maintaining the union with Britain. Their chief complaint regarding a proposed independent Irish Parliament was that it would lead to 'clerical control' in all matters. An ominous opening shot in the forthcoming struggle was the passing of the Parliament Act on 30 August 1911, which limited the veto powers of the House of Lords over legislation passed in the Commons in three separate sessions.

The Presbyterian response to the gathering storm was to organise a Presbyterian Convention on the afternoon of 1 February 1912 in various locations in Belfast: Assembly Hall, Ulster Hall, May Street Church, Rosemary Street Church and Great Victoria Street Church. Interestingly, this Convention was organised without official Church sanction, and several speeches declared the folly of Home Rule, principally in terms of economic harm and domination by a Roman Catholic ascendancy. Rev William Patterson of May Street Church had a large union flag placed around his pulpit for the duration of this crisis!

Prime Minister Asquith's Home Rule Bill was introduced in the Commons on 11 April 1912, three days before the Titanic sank in the North Atlantic. On Easter Tuesday 1912, 100,000 men paraded at Balmoral against his proposals in a demonstration which commenced with a religious service led by the Church of Ireland Primate, Archbishop Crozier, and the Presbyterian Moderator, John Macmillan. On 7 June the General Assembly

The Presbyterian Convention.

If the electors of England and Scotland are not satisfied that the members of the Presbyterian Church as a whole are opposed to Home Rule then they must be first cousins to the ostrich. In size and enthusiasm the meetings which were held on February 1, 1912, have seldom been equalled and never surpassed. The demeanour of the delegates was most exemplary, all signs of bombast being absent. Instead there seemed to be a fixed determination to oppose in every way what they considered to be a menace to their religion and their well-being.

The Convention as reported in the March edition of the magazine the *Irish Presbyterian*

PRESBYTERIAN HISTORICAL SOCIETY OF IRELAND

Ulster day
PRONI

unanimously endorsed the sentiments expressed at the earlier unofficial Convention. Such harmony was only achieved though, after a midnight meeting which persuaded Rev James Armour of Ballymoney to withdraw his amendment on the subject.

Saturday 28 September 1912 was designated 'Ulster Day' and signatories were sought for 'Ulster's Solemn League and Covenant', the work of Thomas Sinclair, Clerk of Session in Duncairn congregation. Special services were held at 11am in many Presbyterian churches and copies of the Covenant signed in countless church halls. The unionist political leaders did not attend any church building on this occasion, but listened to Rev William McKean, minister of First Ballymacarrett, preach in the Ulster Hall.

Not everyone agreed with these developments. Rev John Waddell of First Bangor congregation encountered local opposition when he refused permission for the Covenant to be signed in his church hall. At the 1913 General Assembly, Rev James Armour referred to Ulster Day as 'Protestant Fools Day' but nevertheless, on Friday 6 June the Assembly debated Home Rule for over six hours and eventually voted by 921 to 43 against it.

On 24 April 1914, the Ulster Volunteers landed 35,000 rifles and five million rounds of ammunition at Larne and not one word was raised about this matter in Presbyterian circles. Asquith's Bill successfully passed in the House of Commons for the third time on 25 May 1914 and now only required Royal Assent to become law. Britain declared war on Germany on 4 August 1914 and, although the Home Rule Bill received Royal Assent on 18 September, the new Act was immediately suspended until hostilities with Germany should cease.

Women signing the Ulster Women's Unionist Council Declaration on Ulster Day.
PRONI

UVF gun-runners on the road from Larne, 24 April, 1914. Illustration by Carey and Thompson, *The Illustrated London News*
BELFAST CENTRAL LIBRARY

Reverend John Waddell

JOHN WADDELL was born on 8 January 1878, the third son of Rev John Waddell of Newington congregation. He had three brothers and three sisters. One brother, Henry, became minister of Trinity, Ballymoney (1926–55). Following his education at the Belfast Royal Academy, Queen's College and Assembly's College, John served a brief assistantship in First Derry before his ordination in First Bangor on 11 November 1902. John Waddell aroused the ire of his congregation in September 1912 when he refused to sign the Ulster Covenant or allow the Church Hall to be used for public signing. He resigned on 12 November 1914 and was installed in Egremont Presbyterian Church in Liverpool where he served for six years. He returned to Ireland and was installed in Fisherwick on 7 September 1920 and he ministered here for twenty-five years, retiring on 15 October 1945. He was the acknowledged leader of the General Assembly. John Waddell was Clerk of Belfast Presbytery from 1945 until 1949 and was elected Moderator of the General Assembly in 1937. His inauguration as Moderator was the first such ceremony to be broadcast. Rev Waddell's most important contribution to PCI was in his Convenerships of the Home Mission and Union Commission. John Waddell died on 26 February 1949.

First World War

In terms of deaths and injury, the First World War was the most costly conflict in the history of humanity. Fatalities and casualties soared to horrific proportions on all sides as the new technologies of 20th century warfare demonstrated an insatiable hunger for human lives. Irish Presbyterian churches house numerous war memorials which bear witness to those who 'made the ultimate sacrifice' and congregations still observe a respectful silence on Remembrance Sunday, recalling the names of congregational members who died in two World Wars.

In several Belfast congregations, considerable numbers of families suffered bereavement. For example, the Great Victoria Street congregation lost 122 members on active service. Four Victoria Crosses were awarded to Ulstermen for actions on 1 July 1916, the beginning of the Battle of the Somme, the first to Billy McFadzean of St John's, Newtownbreda. Not all Presbyterian casualties died on foreign fields. Mr Holden Stodart, a St. John Ambulance Brigader of St. Andrew's, Blackrock, was killed in crossfire during the Dublin Easter Rising in 1916. His

36th Ulster Division marching through Belfast on their way to France, 1915
PRONI

James Rentoul

Alexander Stuart
Assembly's College 1907–8

Reverend James Lawrence Rentoul

JAMES LAWRENCE RENTOUL was born in 1885 into a famous Presbyteriain ministerial dynasty. He was the eldest son of Rev Robert Rentoul (Clonmel 1892–1919). Both his grandfather and great grandfather were ministers: Rev James Rentoul (Garvagh 1827–85) and James Rentoul (Ray 1791–1822). His brother Alexander, and six of his uncles, where also Presbyterian ministers. James graduated from Queen's College, Galway, in 1906. He served assistantships in Adelaide Road, Dublin and Rosemary Street, Belfast, prior to his ordination on 20 May 1914 in Rostrevor. He married a daughter of Rev Moore of Killinchy. In May 1918, James enrolled in the Army Medical Corp and he left his wife and baby son to serve with his unit in France. In the early hours of Monday 30 September, Rev Rentoul, with two colleagues, was killed when a shell struck their dugout. The conflict ended forty-two days later, on 11 November. Rev James Lawrence Rentoul was thirty-three years old when he was killed. He was buried in La Baraque British Cemetery in the Aisne region of France, 8 kilometres north of St. Quentin.

name is recorded on the war memorial of that congregation along with those who died in action.

A total of fifty-three Irish Presbyterian ministers served as chaplains or medical attendants in the First World War, and two, who had been students together and both from the Newry Presbytery, died in action. Rev Alexander Stuart of Bessbrook congregation enrolled as a Chaplain and was killed on 24 October 1917 after only ten days at the front, the first Chaplain to die in the War. Rev James Lawrence Rentoul of Rostrevor congregation enrolled as a private in the Royal Army Medical Corps and was killed in action on 30 September 1918, within weeks of the war ending. Rev James Gilbert Paton of Terrace Row, Coleraine served with distinction as a Chaplain and was awarded the Military Cross. Another Presbyterian, Rev John Morrow Simms, served as Chaplain for thirty-three years, rising to the rank of Major-General and was Principal Chaplain to the British Expeditionary Force in France and Flanders during the war. He was elected Moderator in 1919. Yet another Irish Presbyterian, Rev Professor John Lawrence Rentoul, an uncle of the Rev JL Rentoul mentioned above, had emigrated to Australia and was Chaplain General of the Australian forces in this war.

When the conflict ended, thoughts in Ireland turned again to the matter of Home Rule. On 23 December 1920, a new Government of Ireland Act provided for two

Moderator of the General Assembly, the Rt Rev Major-General Simms unveils two memorials at York Street Church on 25 April, 1920.
PRESBYTERIAN HISTORICAL SOCIETY OF IRELAND

While Westminster worked out the details of the Province's political future there was sectarian rioting a the corner of York Street and Donegall Street, Belfast, 1920.
BELFAST TELEGRAPH

Parliaments in Ireland; one in Belfast for the six north-eastern counties and one in Dublin for the other twenty-six counties. There were serious implications for Irish Presbyterians. The Northern Ireland Parliament was opened in June 1921 and sat for eleven years in the Presbyterian College in Belfast while grand new Parliament buildings were erected at Stormont. In the South, guerrilla warfare against British forces led to the creation of an Irish Free State and southern Presbyterians were abandoned in the very position that northern Presbyterians had fought to resist; a religious minority under a Roman Catholic ascendancy. Yet the Presbyterian Church in Ireland always remained a Church for the whole island, albeit with over ninety per cent of its membership in Ulster.

Map of the proposed amendment to the border 1925 published in the *Morning Post*

Lloyd George's concept of a Council of Ireland which would bring both parts of Ireland closer together was never realised and in fact the Northern and Southern governments did not officially speak to each other until 1965! Partition came as a shock to minority communities of both sides of the new border. Presbyterian statistics indicate a sharp decline in their numbers throughout the southern Presbyteries. By 1922, Presbyterians had declined by 45% in Cork, 44% in Munster, 36% in Connaught and 30% in Athlone. The Dublin decline was smaller, at 16%, though still significant. Several landowners and business people withdrew in the chaotic period after the war; others were intimidated and some were murdered.

Several historians have noted that in the earliest years after Partition neither Irish Parliament succeeded in allaying the sectarian fears of their respective minority communities. The Presbyterian Church, although professing to be an all Ireland body, was, given its geographical distribution, in reality focused almost entirely upon the Northern perspective.

Lord Londonderry who proposed a new integrated primary education, by William Conor.

COLLECTION OF QUEEN'S UNIVERSITY, BELFAST

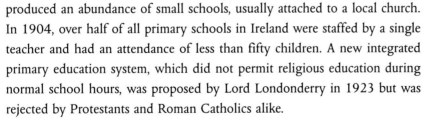

Drumkeen Presbyterian school which formed part of the church

Education

The education system in Ireland was largely denominational, following the rejection of the Government's original proposals in 1831. By the early 20th century, this denominational system had produced an abundance of small schools, usually attached to a local church. In 1904, over half of all primary schools in Ireland were staffed by a single teacher and had an attendance of less than fifty children. A new integrated primary education system, which did not permit religious education during normal school hours, was proposed by Lord Londonderry in 1923 but was rejected by Protestants and Roman Catholics alike.

The Roman Catholic Church refused to participate in any deliberations and the Presbyterian Church campaigned for six years to ensure that simple Bible instruction should be provided by teachers in primary schools. The Presbyterian campaign was led by Rev William Corkey, minister of Windsor congregation in Belfast. A new 1930 Education Act granted these demands and allowed State grants to such schools for running expenses and building projects. The Roman Catholic Church retained full control over their schools, and had to pay for this

Stranmillis College was set up as an integrated teacher-training college, however the Catholic Church refused to allow their students to attend preferring to establish their own institutions.

STRANMILLIS UNIVERSITY COLLEGE LIBRARY

Dr and Mrs O'Neill with their son Desmond

Reverend Frederick O'Neill

FREDERICK WILLIAM SCOTT O'NEILL was born in Belfast on 26 August 1870, a son of Edward O'Neill. He was educated at Royal Belfast Academical Institution and Queen's College, Belfast. In 1892, he graduated from the Royal University of Ireland with a first class honours degree in Mental and Moral Science and, after taking his masters in the following year, studied Theology at Assembly's College. He worked for one year as the first Theological Travelling Secretary for the Student Christian Movement. On 30 August 1897 he was ordained for missionary service in Manchuria where he served for forty-eight years. He worked through many difficulties including the Boxer Rebellion and the arrival of Communism. Rev O'Neill was awarded a DD by the Presbyterian Theological Faculty, Ireland in 1933 and was elected Moderator of the General Assembly in 1936. He retired on 7 June 1945 upon his release from a Japanese internment camp. Frederick O'Neill mastered foreign languages and became an expert in Chinese religions. He was an effective missionary and recognised the inherent difficulty of conveying Western metaphysical concepts to Chinese people. He published three books on mission work in Manchuria and died on 7 October 1952, aged eighty-three years.

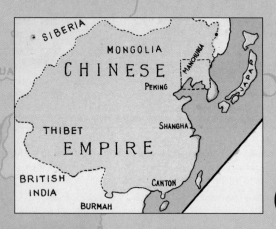

privilege. This differential in State support for primary schools was long a bone of contention among the main denominations in Northern Ireland.

During the 1920s the Presbyterian Church in Ireland experienced fresh revival and the drama of a heresy trial. There was a significant increase in missions and conversions within Presbyterian congregations in the immediate post-war years. New communicants reached a peak of 6,360 in 1923 (by comparison, the 2005 figure was 1,950). One of the most famous evangelists at this time was Rev William P Nicholson. Born near Bangor, County Down, in 1876, Nicholson had been ordained as an evangelist by the Carlisle Presbytery of the Presbyterian Church USA. He conducted many evangelistic missions in Ulster in the 1920s, often in Presbyterian churches and has been credited with helping avert civil war in the Province by the success of his campaigns.

Heresy Trial
The highest moment of Presbyterian drama in the 1920s was the heresy trial of Rev Ernest Davey, Professor of biblical criticism in the Belfast College. Davey was a brilliant scholar, graduating from the universities of Cambridge and Edinburgh, followed by his appointment in 1917 to the chair of Church History in the Presbyterian College, Belfast. In the 1920s, Davey appeared to some of his students and other Irish Presbyterians, especially Rev James Hunter of Knock congregation, to be misrepresenting the central Christian doctrines of the Incarnation and Atonement. Statements taken from Davey's publications, *Our Faith in God* and *The Changing Vesture of the Faith* were used to bring five charges against him in the Belfast Presbytery in March 1927. Davey was acquitted by the Presbytery but his accusers appealed against this decision to the General Assembly. The 1927 Assembly also acquitted Davey, by 707 votes to 82.

Rev J Ernest Davey

There is an interesting prequel to Hunter's pursuit of Davey. In 1914 Rev Frederick O'Neill, who served as an Irish Presbyterian missionary in Manchuria from 1897 until 1932, published an article in *The Witness* entitled, *The Miracle of the Kingdom*. Hunter took exception to some of O'Neill's views and notified the Belfast Presbytery that he intended to press O'Neill with specific questions. Nervous letters were exchanged between Presbytery leaders in Belfast and Mission leaders in Manchuria. O'Neill was informed of the gravity of this situation and urged to be cautious in his answers as a heresy trial would severely damage the standing of the Mission in Manchuria.

Although Hunter was not satisfied with the answers offered by O'Neill at the October 1915 meeting of the Belfast Presbytery, he abruptly withdrew his action against O'Neill. He did so as an act of compassion upon hearing of the death on 2 August 1915 of the O'Neill's sixteen month old son, Dermot. It seems that such a tragic loss on the mission field softened the heart of the minister of Knock congregation. There were no such mitigating circumstances twelve years later when he pursued Davey in the same Presbytery. Both Frederick O'Neill and Ernest Davey were elected Moderator of the General Assembly, in 1936 and 1953 respectively.

Following their rebuff by the General Assembly, James Hunter, who was by then retired from active ministry, and others who had mounted the campaign against Ernest Davey felt they had no option but to leave the Irish Presbyterian Church. As is usual in

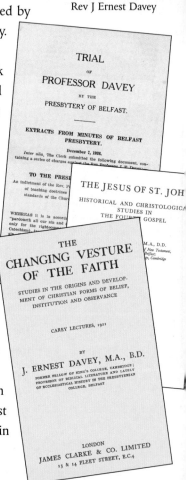

such circumstances, the schismatic group labelled the majority as 'apostates,' claiming that the false teaching in the Presbyterian College was permitted to continue unpunished. In October 1927, they set up the Irish Evangelical Church, from 1964 known as the Evangelical Presbyterian Church. Today the Evangelical Presbyterian Church consists of twelve congregations and, according to the 2001 census, less than 600 members.

Society was changing rapidly in the early 20th century. The Suffragette campaigns from 1910, and especially the efforts of women in the First World War, ensured that from 1918 women over thirty years of age could vote in parliamentary elections and this was extended to those over twenty-one years of age in 1928. The Church was also slowly responding to these changes. Women had made important contributions to the Irish Presbyterian Church for many years, they had played a key role in missionary work – both on the foreign field and with home support – but now they came more to the fore. An order of Deaconesses was founded in 1909. From 1926 women have been eligible for election as ruling elders, and the first woman minister was ordained in 1976. Mrs Edith Martin was the first female Theology student at Assembly's College (1927–30) and was ordained in Perth as a minister in the United Free Church of Scotland.

Women's Workers Union, 1913
NATIONAL LIBRARY OF IRELAND

The Presbyterian Church was still strong in the first half of the 20th century. A total of 45,500 new communicants were added to congregations in the 1920s and a further 43,996 were added in the 1930s. Numbers of students studying to become Presbyterian ministers also rose, reaching a peak of forty-seven in the year 1937. There was a surplus of ministers in later years and some men moved to England and Canada after the Second World War. In 1928, a centralised Church Extension scheme was launched to co-ordinate the formation of new congregations. Forty-five new churches were founded within fifty years, mostly located in the distinct V-shape formed by the Lagan valley in the west, incorporating Belfast and extending eastwards in two distinct arms; in South Antrim and North Down. Professional people were first to move out of central Belfast, and they were followed by skilled workers and many of the lower middle class. The 'Troubles' in the last three decades of the 20th century completed the exodus with several Church Extension causes developing in other towns such as Craigavon, Antrim, Ballymena, Lisburn, Carrickfergus and Bangor. As a result of these movements, by the close of the century the

Exodus of families from troubled areas, August 1971
EMPICS

Rev Cheryl Meban (née Reid)
STEPHEN LYNAS/PRESBYTERIAN HERALD

Female PCI Ministers

YEAR OF ORDINATION

	NAME	PLACE OF ORDINATION
1976	Ruth Patterson	Gardenmore
1979	Joan Barr	Newtownbreda
1983	Jean Mackarel	First Lisburn
1983	Patricia McKee	Belmont
1985	Helen Watson	Second Comber
1985	Marlene Taylor	Cooke Centenary
1986	Christina Bradley	Germany
1986	Elizabeth Stevenson	High Street, Antrim
1987	Katherine Meyer	Belmont
1987	Elinor Henning	Fisherwick
1988	Lesley Carroll	Rosemary
1988	Mary Hunter	Stormont
1988	Margaret Johnston	Newtownbreda
1990	Mairisine Stanfield	Regent St., Newtownards
1991	Barbara Kennedy	Cregagh
1991	Florence Taylor	Second Comber
1993	Nancy Cubitt	First Larne
1993	Gabrielle Ellis	Hillsborough
1994	Patricia McBride	First Lisburn
1999	Lorraine Kennedy-Ritchie	South Africa
2002	Cheryl Reid	Gilnahirk
2006	Amanda Best	Ramelton

ABOVE: Trainee Deaconesses at Union College Graduation
STEPHEN LYNAS/PRESBYTERIAN HERALD

Belfast Congregations 1962

In 1962, Belfast boasted seventy Presbyterian churches and in addition new causes at Garnerville, Saintfield Road and Taughmonagh.

These churches catered for 48,677 families (141,463 individuals).

The following congregations had over 1,000 families.

CONGREGATION	FAMILIES	INDIVIDUALS
McQuiston Memorial	1,550	5,150
Megain Memorial	1,500	5,000
Richview	1,370	4,760
Woodvale	1,224	3,743
Oldpark	1,100	3,300
Great Victoria Street	1,072	3,310
Bloomfield	1,036	2,662
Townsend Street	1,011	2,762
Sinclair Seamen's	1,000	3,000

Forty-three congregations had a membership in excess of 500 families.

30th Boys Brigade Company, Grosvenor Road,
c. 1910
BELFAST CENTRAL MISSION

powerbase of Irish Presbyterianism has shifted from the massive 19th century city churches to the wealthy provincial churches. In the mid 1940s Belfast boasted three congregations over 1,000 families (Agnes Street, McQuiston Memorial and Richview) and a further twenty-five over 500 families. In 1962 there were seventy-three Presbyterian churches in Belfast, nine with membership exceeding 1,000 families. Over seventy-five per cent of all Irish Presbyterians lived within forty miles of the centre of Belfast. The 'Troubles' saw the commencement of a very marked decline in Belfast Presbyterians.

McQuiston Memorial

Youth Work

The 20th century can be described with some justification as the century of 'youth work.' Certainly there was a significant increase in activities for young people. A plethora of youth organisations evolved: Sunday School, Boys' Brigade, Girls' Brigade, Scouts, Guides, Young People's Guild, Youth Fellowship, Youth Club and Children's Church.

From its inception in 1862, the Sabbath School Society had a Book Depôt for distribution of teaching material, Bibles and Catechisms. In 1905, this Depôt was developed as 'The Presbyterian Bookshop' and was based in the new Assembly Buildings in Fisherwick Place, Belfast and it was the financial success of this bookshop which continued to fund the Sabbath School Society. A 'League of Church Loyalty' scheme was launched in the early 20th century to encourage children attending Sunday Schools to also attend their local church services.

Today, Sunday School numbers in most denominations are in decline. The number of children in Presbyterian Sunday Schools and Bible Classes fell from 75,682 in 1950 to 34,291 in 2000; a drop of 55% in 50 years! This statistic, coupled with the fact that the vast majority of children in attendance today are already members of congregations, makes it clear that Sunday Schools are facing increasing difficulties in attempting to reach 'un-churched' young people. A further sign of difficulty is the growing trend of holding Sunday Schools at the same time as Sunday worship services thereby saving parents an extra journey to and from church. Today, an increasing number of churches are realising the necessity of employing a full-time youth worker in order to engage with young people.

Ecumenism

The Presbyterian Church in Ireland was in the forefront of all the major ecumenical developments in the 20th century. Discussions with the Irish Methodist Church aimed at a possible union commenced in 1905, and similar discussions with the Church of Ireland commenced in 1910. Both came to nothing: the former in 1926 because of Presbyterian refusal to accept ministerial itinerancy, and the latter in 1934, because of Church of Ireland refusal to accept the validity of Presbyterian ordination. Similar approaches were made to the Baptists, Reformed Presbyterians and

Scouts parade on St George's Day
DERMOTT DUNBAR

Congregationalists but all approaches were politely declined.

The Irish Presbyterian Church was a founder member of: The World Alliance of Reformed Churches, the 'United Council of Christian Churches and Religious Communities in Ireland' (from 1966 known as 'The Irish Council of Churches') founded in 1922, the British Council of Churches which was formed in 1942, and the World Council of Churches first Assembly which was held in Amsterdam in 1948. The new mood in the 20th century was clearly one of co-operation. The teaching of Jesus on unity and love seemed in sharp contradiction to the duplication among numerous Christian denominations.

The Presbyterian Church in Ireland noticeably changed tack in the 1970s, left the World Council of Churches (WCC) in 1980, and declined to join the new British Council of Churches in 1989. It is probably true to say that two issues led ultimately to PCI withdrawal from the WCC in 1980: racism and attitudes towards the Church of Rome. The apartheid regime in South Africa was universally condemned and the WCC established a Programme to Combat Racism in 1969. Voluntary contributions for relief purposes were placed in a Special Fund. The Presbyterian Church in Ireland did not give to this Fund. A grant of £43,000 was made from this Fund to the *Patriotic Front in Rhodesia* (now Zimbabwe); there were allegations that at least some of this money had been used to buy arms and that missionaries had died as a result of attacks by members of the Patriotic Front.

The other issue which flavoured all the debates within PCI on membership of the WCC was that of relations with the Roman Catholic Church. That Church had remained aloof from contacts with the Protestant Churches in Ireland but a thaw was signalled when Pope John XXIII opened the Second Vatican Council in 1962. While no doctrine was changed nor any claim withdrawn, the Roman Church did now regard other Christians as 'separated brethren' rather than heretics and schismatics. The 1965 General Assembly asked pardon 'for any attitudes and actions towards our Roman Catholic fellow countrymen which have been unworthy of our calling as followers of Jesus Christ.'

In September 1973, talks between representatives of the Irish Council of Churches and members of the Irish Roman Catholic hierarchy took place in the Ballymascanlon Hotel outside Dundalk. These meetings continued until 1988, exploring several theological and practical areas including, the Sacraments, the Creeds, Divine Revelation and Scripture, and the Church. However, agreement could not be reached on Ministry, and specifically that the structures of any future united Church should be based upon ordination by bishops.

Initial Presbyterian energy for such talks waned considerably. Many Presbyterians across Ulster were also annoyed at the constant sniping by Rev Ian Paisley against their Church. Paisley's populist political rhetoric and religious fundamentalism resonated with many Presbyterians. While they did not agree with his annual protests at the opening of each General Assembly, he did articulate their suspicions about ecumenism in general and closer links with Roman Catholicism in particular. The 'Free Presbyterian Church'

Interior of the new church at Carnmoney, County Antrim.
The occasion is that of the Board of Missions Overseas.

STEPHEN LYNAS/PRESBYTERIAN HERALD

Reverend Arnold Frank

ARNOLD FRANK was born in Suja, Hungary on 6 March 1859 to Jewish parents. When he was seventeen, Arnold travelled to Hamburg in Germany where he worked as a clerk. Through contact with the Irish Presbyterian Mission in Hamburg he was converted and baptised. He studied Theology at Assembly's College from 1877–83 and was ordained in Fisherwick Place on 17 June 1884. The following year he married Ella Kinghan, daughter of Rev John Kinghan. Rev Frank returned to Hamburg and served as a missionary to the Jews in the Jerusalem Church there for over fifty years. Over fifty missionaries and ministers came from this congregation during Rev Frank's ministry. A new church was built in 1912 and later a hospital too. In 1908, Arnold Frank was awarded a DD from the Presbyterian Theological Faculty, Ireland. From 1933, Dr Frank helped persecuted Jews and Jewish Christians. In 1936, his magazine *Friend of Zion* was proscribed by the Nazi regime; two years later he was imprisoned and the Jerusalem Church destroyed. In 1948, Dr Frank returned to Hamburg to witness the reopening of the Jewish Mission in a new church. Arnold Frank died on 20 March 1965, aged 106.

originated in 1951 in Crossgar, mainly comprising disaffected Irish Presbyterians, and currently has a membership of about 12,000 (2001 census).

In the 1970s, several Presbyterian ministers began to articulate the suspicions and distrust of many Presbyterians against the pervading ecumenical trends. A motion to suspend PCI membership of the WCC was debated on 21 November 1978 at a Special Assembly. This motion was carried by 561 votes to 393. Suspension was renewed in 1979, and the 1980 Assembly voted by 433 to 327 to withdraw completely from the World Council of Churches.

In 1989, the English Roman Catholic Church expressed a willingness to participate in a restructured British Council of Churches. The General Assembly of the Presbyterian Church in Ireland declined to join by 453 votes to 289. The Irish Roman Catholic Church also declined to join.

The most tangible expression of inter-church co-operation was the formation in November 1970 of a new 'Church of North India'. This involved a union of Anglicans, Baptists, Methodists, with the United Church of North India, which was itself a product of an earlier union in 1924 between Congregationalists and Presbyterians. Irish Presbyterian missionaries served in this latter Church in the area of Gujarat and Kathiawar. There was significant unrest in the Irish General Assembly about aspects of this new union since many ministers and elders believed that the proposed new church lacked a sound Reformed and evangelical basis. By 1970, the union took place and one Presbyterian missionary, Rev Donald Kennedy, became a bishop in the new Church.

Inter-church co-operation in Ireland is exemplified by the 'alternating ministry scheme' which the Presbyterian and Methodist churches have operated in some locations in the south of Ireland since the 1970s, the most successful cause being Limerick.

Overseas

Prior to 1950, the focus of Irish Presbyterian missionary activities was in India, China, and among Jews in Germany, Poland and Syria. These ministries had benefited from 180, 90 and 40 missionaries respectively. Since 1950, links with India continued and new relationships have been developed with churches in Jamaica (1952), Malawi (1956), Kenya (1966), Indonesia (1972), Nepal (1978) and Brazil (1987). In all a further 200 members of PCI have served in these countries as missionaries. In addition, links with Reformed churches in Europe have been re-established or strengthened.

The PCI links with partner churches run deep. Following the

In 1966 Rev Ian Paisley protested against ecumenical tendencies in the Presbyterian Church.
BELFAST TELEGRAPH

In October 2002 Rev David Irwin invited RC Bishop Tony Farquhar to preach in McCracken Memorial, Belfast.

The General Assembly 2005
STEPHEN LYNAS/PRESBYTERIAN HERALD

Rev Ken Newel in post-Tsunami Indonesia

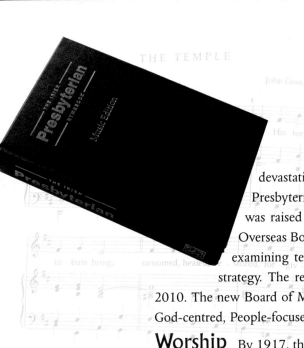

devastating earthquake in Gujarat in January 2000 the Moderator of the Presbyterian Church in Ireland appealed for financial aid and £453,000 was raised by Irish Presbyterians in response. Throughout 2003–05, the Overseas Board undertook a major Mission Review, *Mission in the Melting Pot*, examining ten key questions in relation to the Board's vision, purpose and strategy. The result has been the development of a mission plan for the year 2010. The new Board of Mission Overseas is seeking to develop a mission strategy that is God-centred, People-focused, Church-based and Forward-thinking.

Worship

By 1917, the majority of Irish Presbyterian congregations were using hymns in their worship services and, by 1940, there were only a handful of congregations which still resisted them. Several churches introduced organs as memorials to those who died in the First World War. A *Revised Church Hymnary* was produced in 1927. This book contained 707 hymns, arranged according to a doctrinal pattern, and won wide acceptance within a short space of time. The *Third Edition Hymnary* was produced in 1973, but struggled to displace the 1927 hymnbook. Many were upset by the fact that favourite hymns from the 1927 book were omitted in the 1973 publication.

Since 1973 there has been an explosion of growth in worship music and songs and many congregations have adopted their own songbooks for use in worship. As precentors were replaced by organists, so praise bands have become a common feature in many churches and the term 'musical director' is replacing that of organist. 'Powerpoint' is the latest addition to the worship technological repertoire. Announcements, praise words and sermon illustrations are increasingly projected upon screens, with varying degrees of competence. In a renewed attempt to develop a common denominational focus for worship, the most recent Irish Presbyterian hymnbook was published in September 2005. Psalms, paraphrases, established hymns and contemporary songs are included with modern and all-inclusive language. Time will tell if this publication will link Irish Presbyterian worship on an agreed template.

Decline

It is a curious fact that although there are more Irish Presbyterian congregations today than in 1840 when the General Assembly was formed, church membership has fallen by about 50% in the same period. The second half of the 20th century has witnessed an increasing rationalisation of resources, most noticeably in the creation of 110 joint and 12 triple charges. Many Ulster towns boast two Presbyterian churches when one building would suffice and the hard decision as to which building should close may have to be taken in the near future. All of the main churches in Ireland are experiencing similar decline.

Former Presbyterian church in Donegall Pass, now a thriving Chinese restaurant

The 1960s was the decade in which the Irish Presbyterian Church began to decline in strength and numbers. Various theories have been advanced for this decline: the advent of

Launch of the new hymnbook at the Waterfront Hall
STEPHEN LYNAS/PRESBYTERIAN HERALD

The Enniskillen bomb, 1987
PACEMAKER

EXPLOSIVES

If you know anything about terrorist
activities — explosives, threats, or murders —
please speak now to the
CONFIDENTIAL TELEPHONE

BELFAST 652155

Powerpoint in worship at Portrush

television, cheaper travel, secularism, the 'Troubles', but whatever the reason, the decline has continued and has been most pronounced at the beginning of the 21st century. All statistics indicate that the Presbyterian Church in Ireland is in serious decline; in the last half of the 20th century, total membership has dropped by 22% (from 363,112 to 284,704), baptisms have dropped by 68% (from 6,997 to 2,221), new communicants have dropped by 51% (from 3,921 to 1,929). In fact the problem is accelerating. Total PCI membership has dropped by 33% in the past thirty-five years, baptisms have dropped by 71%, new communicants have dropped by 49%, and numbers of children in Sunday Schools or Bible Classes have dropped by 58%. These are shocking statistics by any standard and it is clear that if these trends continue it is a mathematical certainty that some congregations will close.

There are obvious weaknesses in the Presbyterian Church in Ireland. In most congregations, a small number of overworked leaders carry the entire organisational workload. Many Irish Presbyterians rarely if ever attend church, and many merely attend Sunday worship services. Are too many Presbyterian congregations run like 'members only' clubs, providing comfortable suites of buildings for relatively small numbers of people to indulge in their favoured pastimes? This is a harsh question, but a vital question if PCI is to survive and grow in the 21st century.

Why do so many of our congregations have such little impact upon our immediate communities? Perhaps we are perceived to be largely irrelevant for modern life; reinforcements of peoples' caricatures of dead religion. In too many situations everything depends upon a single minister. It is surely a very unhealthy state of affairs when the minister must provide the energy to sustain all that a congregation does. However, it must also be acknowledged that some ministers tend to be personally insecure and seek to control all activities, taking the risk of stifling the gifts of other Christians.

Of course, the Irish Presbyterian Church, like any Church, requires the presence and power of the Holy Spirit in order to be effective. Given this spiritual dimension, it does also seem obvious that PCI must consider change if it is going to be effective. Indeed, the congregations that are currently coping with change and seeking to be relevant in modern life are thriving today and will continue to flourish in the 21st century.

Renewal
Life in Ireland has changed more in the past 100 years than at any time in the history of this island. Home design has advanced far beyond the dreams of our ancestors (with our double glazing, ensuite bathrooms and conservatories). New methods of food production and retailing have resulted in the demise of the corner shop and a pattern of daily shopping. We are all familiar with large hypermarkets, frozen foods, mass production and cooking with microwaves. Communications have moved on from letters which took weeks to reach their destination to telephones, faxes and e-mails. We can talk to and see relatives in Australia from the comfort

of our homes. Information is beamed into our homes on radio, television and computer, and school children grow up so quickly in our modern age.

Why should our neighbours be interested in the Gospel and our Presbyterian Church if we are perceived to be old fashioned? One of our greatest challenges is to change. Some of the elements of congregational life which are defended today as though they are sacrosanct were innovative in their day. Church organs only arrived in the late 1860s – and caused deep divisions within PCI – yet are defended today against modern instruments like guitars and drums. Choirs were only introduced in the 1870s, and most during the First World War, yet this form of singing is hardly appealing to the younger generation today. Clerical collars were introduced about 1900, yet are defended in some quarters as though the first disciples wore them!

No one can be sure of the future, but it seems that our general trend of decline will continue for some time. Experiences in other western countries provide clues as to what we might expect. There will be fewer congregations and more co-operation with other denominations, as local duplication may become a mere luxury in some places. Ministers will become 'team leaders' in congregations where more people can assume active responsibilities. There will be more investment in people

rather than buildings and informality will continue. Probably the smaller 'house group' structure will emerge as the most successful means of building for the future. Individuals will have to learn again how to 'gossip the Gospel' to their neighbours.

Beneath the grim statistics of a denomination that is rapidly shrinking lies a more positive hope for the future. There are genuine signs of renewal and spiritual life throughout the Presbyterian Church in Ireland. Both centrally, and in many churches, green shoots of spiritual renewal are emerging. The Coleraine Assembly in September 1990, and the 2020 Vision Assembly in 1997 were different from usual gatherings: the agenda was consciously designed to allow more time for worship, reflection and recognition of God's sovereignty.

Throughout its history, Irish Presbyterianism has been a Planter church, largely catering for people who already professed to be Presbyterian. As traditional church membership falls in Ireland and everywhere in Western Europe, the new challenge for the Presbyterian Church in Ireland is to win the un-churched. The congregations that are growing are those which provide a genuine caring community of faith, where members can exercise their gifts for the benefit of the whole body, and where teaching and lifestyle converge. It remains to be seen how Irish Presbyterianism will fair in the 21st century.

Youth Night, 2004
STEPHEN LYNAS/PRESBYTERIAN HERALD

Missions in India

THE FIRST PUBLIC ACT OF THE FIRST GENERAL ASSEMBLY was to send two missionaries to India: Revs James Glasgow and Alexander Kerr. These two ministers and their wives arrived in Bombay in February 1841, where they were encouraged by the famous Scottish missionary, John Wilson, to work in the Gujarati-speaking peninsula of Saurashtra, then known as Kathiawar. The harsh realities of overseas work were soon upon them. Within months, the Glasgow's infant daughter, Margaret, died, and, soon afterwards, Alexander Kerr also fell ill and died. In total, twenty-two Irish Presbyterian missionaries are buried in India; this figure does not include several wives and children.

The Gujarati hymnbook

Rev Tolleton Lutton Wells was buried in Surat Cemetry 1877, with Rev Samuel Gillespie beside him in 1928.

Children in church

FROM LEFT:
Evangelistic Camp, Kotarpur, March 1933: On the road and crossing the River Sabarmati

Scout camp at Vatva: Nathalal's patrol

ABOVE: Jama Masiid, Ahmedabad

Adam Glasgow

By January 1843, four new missionaries were working in this locality: Revs Adam Glasgow of College Square, Belfast, James McKee of Ballyreagh, Robert Montgomery and James Speers. Their first convert was a Muslim teacher, Abdur Rahman of Porbandar, who was baptised in 1843. On 30 January 1843, and on the direction of the General Assembly, the five ordained missionaries organised themselves as the Presbytery of Kathiawar. Life for early missionaries was difficult. Their children were sent home to Ireland at the age of five, and only saw their parents at seven-year intervals (this was later reduced to five years). Later, missionaries were able to send their children to boarding schools in India, though still over 1,500 miles away, and missionary families were united twice each year.

As the mission in Gujarat developed, several aspects of the work were initiated. Orphanages and hostels were opened in the 1860s. While the wives of the first missionaries were closely involved in missionary work, single female missionaries were also soon involved, often in educational or medical enterprises. A Ladies Zenana Association was formed in 1875, following the arrival of Miss Susan Brown in Surat. Miss M Forrest started the medical work in a small dispensary in Surat in 1876, which was soon seeing 10,000 women annually.

Susan Brown

The Irish missionaries set up schools as a useful means of engaging with local people. Common skills like literacy were believed to help combat local superstitions and prejudices and improve employment opportunities for pupils. The nurture of local Indian Christians into positions of church leadership was a relatively slow process. The first three Indian elders were ordained in Ranipur in 1875 and the first Indian minister, Rambhai Kalyan, was not ordained until 1888.

Undoubtedly, the Irish Presbyterian mission to India was successful. By the end of the 19th century, the Christian community associated with this mission counted as many as 4,321 people. Interestingly, the Irish Presbyterians working in Gujarat were known as the 'Presbytery of Kathiawar and Gujarat' and considered as a full Presbytery of the Presbyterian Church in Ireland a rather unique arrangement. In 1900, an autonomous 'Presbytery of Gujarat and Kathiawar' was finally formed.

IRISH PRESBYTERIAN STATIONS (UNDERLINED) ———

FROM LEFT:
Mr and Mrs Lyle,
Christmas, 1934
Mission House, Bhavnagar

Mission garden, Surat

Missions in China

Hugh Waddell

BEFORE THE EARLY 19TH CENTURY, China was closed to all missionary activity for over 150 years. The first Protestant missionary of this new era was Scotsman Rev Robert Morrison (1782–1834), who was sent by the London Missionary Society in 1807. In 1847, the English Presbyterian Church appointed Rev William Burns to missionary work in China. He founded the first Presbyterian Church in the city of Amoy (now Xiamen), one of the Treaty Ports. Burns died in April 1868, while trying to found a mission in the Treaty Port of Newchwang in Manchuria.

Manchuria, situated beyond the Great Wall in the extreme north east of China, became the focus of Irish Presbyterian missionary work in the following year. About five million people lived in Manchuria, where the climate produced short hot summers and long deep frozen winters. The first Irish Presbyterian missionaries to China were Rev Hugh Waddell, son of Rev Hugh Waddell of Glenarm congregation, and a medical doctor, James Hunter, of Belfast. They arrived in Newchwang on 29 April 1869.

Waddell and Hunter quickly established a Mission Station through a variety of activities: medical, evangelistic and educational. They became proficient in the local language and distributed large numbers of tracts in the locality. Hunter set up a small dispensary, which soon proved popular with local people. A school was started, and Waddell also began preaching regularly in the local language. The strains were enormous though: Mrs Hunter died and Waddell's health broke, forcing him to return to Ireland in 1872, with Hunter's infant son.

Waddell's replacement was Rev James Carson, James Hunter's brother-in-law. He served in China from 1874 until 1921. It was largely through the home support of Irish Presbyterian Sunday Schools that the mission survived and prospered during this early period. James Hunter pioneered missionary treks further inland. This pattern was repeated by subsequent missionaries, thus extending the influence of the Irish mission station. Five new missionaries arrived there between 1869 and 1889. Miss Sarah Nicholson was the first Zenanna missionary in China, starting her ministry in 1889. Before the end of the 19th century, twenty-two new missionaries were added to the mission team; nine of them were medical doctors. By the year 1900, Irish missionary work was well and truly planted in Manchuria, operating in a total of nine mission stations and ninety-three associated outstations. The mission employed over 210 Chinese converts and was responsible for thirty-

The grave of William C. Burns

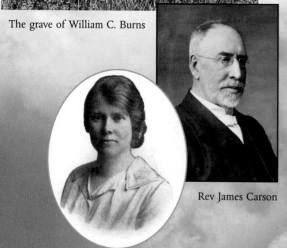

Margaret McCombe

Rev James Carson

Theological College, Moukden, 1910

James Hunter

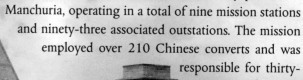

ARDENS SED VIRENS

87

The Great Wall of China

five day schools. The missionaries had gathered a community of 1,589 communicants and 375 children. The total number of Chinese believers in Manchuria at this time was reckoned to be about 19,000. Further developments saw the ordination of the first Chinese minister in 1896, and, three years later, a Theological College was established in West Moukden.

The 'Boxer Rising' in 1900 was a Chinese uprising against all things foreign; it was particularly vicious in the north of the country. Protestant missionaries suffered, with over 150 adults and 52 children killed. In Manchuria, however, all the Protestant missionaries managed to escape. The Chinese Christians took the brunt of the violence. In all, 332 members of the Manchurian church were martyred, and about one third of the total membership abandoned their faith.

During the post-persecution peace, the Mission Conference re-admitted lapsed Christians to membership of the Church, after a three-year exclusion from Communion. The Emperor died in 1908, and China underwent a period of political uncertainty that lasted for more than thirty years. The development of an indigenous church became the dominant issue for the missionaries in Manchuria. In 1922, a new executive Policy Committee was established, consisting of four Irish missionaries, four Scottish missionaries and fourteen Chinese Christians. A further step in this direction was taken in 1927, when the first regular meeting of a Chinese General Assembly took place, uniting sixteen regional churches, of which the Manchurian church was the largest.

Teachers and pupils of Manchuria Christian School, c. 1910

By 1931, there were twenty-three Irish missionaries in Manchuria and 181 Chinese agents. The Church, under Irish influence, counted 7,822 communicants, and 1,735 children attended thirty-nine Sunday Schools.

In September 1931, the Japanese army seized control of Manchuria, and, in 1935, the Church was accused of breeding Communism and other dangerous ideas. Pressure was brought to bear upon all schools to ensure that children conformed to rituals in which the Japanese Emperor was worshipped. The missionaries resisted and withdrew from their schools, but the situation became very grave when the Pacific war broke out in late 1941. Many missionaries were evacuated and went home, but those who stayed were quickly interned, mostly in Japan. Rev and Mrs Thomas Barker, Rev Harry Johnston and Miss Margaret McCombe were interned in Kobe, and later in Nagasaki, until the war ended. When the war started, the Irish missionaries were operating in an area which had 288 congregations, sixty-five Sunday Schools, twenty-two day schools, and employed 432 Chinese agents.

After the defeat of Japan, China was convulsed by a struggle between Chinese Nationalist and Communists, and the Manchuria region finally fell to the Communists in 1948. Initially, the church was largely ignored, but suspicion mounted against Christian activity in churches,

The first graduating class at Moukden with Dr J Ross and Dr TC Fulton

schools and medical centres. The majority of the remaining missionaries were eventually withdrawn during the autumn of 1949. Mission properties were handed over to local Christian control, and the last missionaries finally left Manchuria on 19 August 1950.

The Communist regime launched a persecution of the Chinese Church in 1966, with its so called Cultural Revolution. Church buildings were closed; the homes of Christian leaders were looted and destroyed. This Cultural Revolution ended in 1977 with the death of Chairman Mao: Christians reappeared and church buildings were progressively handed back to local groups. More than 4,000 churches reopened within a decade. The former Presbyterian tradition continues to influence the Chinese Church in the north-eastern territories.

While former Irish missionaries were invited back to preach, including for example, Dr Jack Weir, in the 1980s, there seems to be little prospect presently for active Irish missionary participation in the modern Chinese Church. Several Irish Presbyterian teachers have enjoyed spells in Chinese teaching institutions through the agency of the 'Amity Foundation', a non-governmental organisation established by Chinese Christians.

ARDENS SED VIRENS

The Chinese Bible

Mr and Mrs FSW O'Neill

An ornamental gate, Moukden

Mrs Stockman and children

Missions in Africa

Funded by PCI, Orphan children from the local township in Blantyre, Malawi, receive one meal a day from volunteers.
MAUREEN IRWIN

MANY IRISH PRESBYTERIANS SERVED AS MISSIONARIES in Africa from the latter part of the 19th century. However, they worked with independent missionary societies. The Presbyterian Church in Ireland first became involved in Africa in 1956, when a partnership was formed with the Church of Central Africa Presbyterian in Malawi. Rev William Jackson (1958–70) was the first Irish Presbyterian missionary. Before undertaking missionary service at Karonga for twelve years, Rev Jackson was the first minister in the joint Presbyterian/Methodist cause at Taughmonagh, South Belfast. He later became minister in Townsend Street church. Rev Terry McMullan made a significant contribution as Foreign Missions Convenor (1982–2002); he previously served in Malawi from 1969 until 1982.

About ninety Irish Presbyterians have served in Malawi since this partnership in mission commenced. Currently, sixteen Irish Presbyterians are working there in a number of ministries: secular and theological education, chaplaincy work, rural development, and nursing.

In 1975, a similar mission partnership was formed between the Presbyterian Church in Ireland and the Presbyterian Church of East Africa in Kenya. The first Irish Presbyterian missionary was Rev Dick Gordon (1975–80); he had previously worked in Kenya as chaplain in Thika High School. In October 1975, Rev Gordon commenced lecturing in St Paul's United Theological College, Limuru. Since 1975, about twenty Irish Presbyterian missionaries have served in Kenya. The current secretary of the overseas Board, Rev Uel Marrs, worked in Kenya from 1989 until 2002. The Presbyterian Church of East Africa is a growing church, which will require 300 new ministers over the next ten years. One exciting new development has been the arrival of African ministers at Union College, where they have successfully completed Master of Theology degrees. The most recent examples have been Revs Joseph Wakaba and Eric Njuru from Kenya, and Rev Binnie Mwakasungula from Malawi

At present, the Presbyterian Church in Ireland counts twenty-eight missionaries in Africa (twelve in Kenya and sixteen in Malawi).

Rev Uel Marrs

Rev Terry McMullan

Ekwendeni Mission Station, Malawi, which incorporates schools, a hospital and a church
DAVID IRWIN

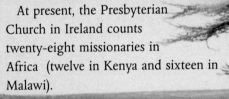

McCracken Memorial made possible the construction of a connecting road between the village of Tuum in north Kenya and a main road forty-five miles away. The area is war torn and trade was difficult. By employing five men from Tuum these families were able to send their sons for education and two have since returned to the village, one as motor mechanic and the other as a vet. Besides making trade of local agriculture safer the road has also opened up the area to tourists further expanding the local economy. The photograph shows guards protecting the men who were building the road.
DAVID IRWIN

Theological Education

Presbyterian College
Centenary Celebrations,
7 January, 1954

The original College emblem
set in the floor tiles at the
entrance to Union College

Irish Presbyterians did not possess their own theological College for over 200 years, and then built two within twelve years. The Presbyterian College, Belfast, opened in 1853, and Magee College, Londonderry, opened in 1865. Prior to this, the vast majority of ministers were educated in Scotland, mostly in Glasgow University. Trinity College in Dublin was the sole university in Ireland and, with very few exceptions, only Anglicans could matriculate. Presbyterians have always prized education and the Presbyterian Church in Ireland has a proud record in providing local education for the whole population. The Church has also consistently held to a belief in 'an educated ministry'. In other words, that perspective ministers should demonstrate appropriate gifts in mind and soul, principally in university level attainment with additional theological training. Travel to Scotland was arduous and expensive. The emergence of the Belfast Academical Institution in 1815 presented therefore new opportunities. The new Institution had a collegiate department and offered a Certificate in Arts on the model of the Scottish MA degree. Both the Synod of Ulster and the Seceder Synod agreed to accept this Belfast Certificate as equivalent to the Scottish degree, and both bodies appointed Divinity Professors. The Synod of Ulster appointed Rev Samuel Edgar of Rosemary Street church and the Seceder Synod appointed Rev Samuel Hanna of Ballynahinch church to teach their respective ministerial students. It was these Presbyterian ministry students who started a united prayer meeting. On 8 January 1839, they listened as Rev John Coulter of Gilnahirk addressed them on the possible benefits of a union of the two bodies. This address was published and led to a wider debate on the possibility of union throughout Seceder and Synod of Ulster congregations. The union took place on 10 July 1840 with the formation of the Presbyterian Church in Ireland.

Queen's College, Belfast, opened in 1849 as part of the University of Ireland, with sister Colleges in Galway and Cork. Theology was not on the curriculum. The Presbyterians opened 'Assembly's' College in 1853, in order to provide courses in Theology for

Magee University College Rugby
Club First XV, 1935-6

Union College, 2006

Advertisement to the Opening
of the College in 1853

Gamble Library showing the celebrated Lanyon ornamental ceiling

ministerial students. The main building was designed by Charles Lanyon and the opening ceremony, on 4 December 1953, was performed by Dr Merle d'Aubigne of Geneva, a celebrated Church historian. Magee College, in Londonderry, was opened in 1865. This College was named after its main benefactor, Mrs Martha Magee, whose will stipulated that £20,000 could be used for the provision of a College providing courses in both Arts and Theology. The executors of Mrs Magee's will insisted upon compliance with the precise terms of her will while many Presbyterians favoured using her money in the Belfast College and leaving the Arts courses to the new Queen's Colleges.

In 1881, the faculties of both Presbyterian Colleges were granted the right by Royal Charter to offer Theology degrees equivalent to any other institution in the United Kingdom. Thereby, the Presbyterian Theological Faculty, Ireland, came into existence and this body continues to award degrees under Royal Charter. The original Belfast College has added a chapel and accommodation wing. It was extensively refurbished in 2003 at a cost in excess of £2 million. The Northern Ireland Parliament met here from 1921–32 while Stormont was under construction. The building was occupied by the Department of Finance from 1941–48, following bomb damage to their premises.

In 1978, Magee College and Assembly's College were united by Act of Parliament, forming the Union Theological College, and occupying the Belfast buildings. Magee College became part of the University of Ulster. The study of Theology is more popular today than ever and there is a large and vibrant College community. Two-thirds of all Theology students in Queen's University take their course in Union College. While training for the ordained ministry of the Presbyterian Church in Ireland remains a primary role for Union College, the ministry students are by no means a majority of the student body. Today, there are over fifty ministry students out of a total of 186 undergraduate students. Flexible timetabling, and the introduction of evening classes in 1999, enables over forty part-time students to study for Bachelor of Theology and Bachelor of Divinity degrees. The current student body represents all the main denominations, and courses are taught in a healthy and enquiring environment in which souls are fed and minds are stretched. In addition, 'Union' currently caters for ninety postgraduate students, studying for Master of Divinity degrees or doctorates. The Magee Institute for Christian Training has been integrated with the College and, in 2006, some 590 individuals have participated in various courses, including Youth and Children's Ministry. Perhaps the greatest jewel in the Union crown is the *Gamble Library*. This is the largest theological library in Northern Ireland, and possibly all of Ireland, with over 65,000 books and about 12,000 pamphlets.

The College coat of arms consists of a shield with burning bush and inkpots. Two hands are depicted receiving the Word of God and the motto is taken from Proverbs 23:23, 'Buy the truth and do not sell it'. Based upon the revealed truth of Scripture, the Presbyterian College looks forward to training more and more students in view of preparing them efficiently for their various ministries in the Church.

Laurence Kirkpatrick, Professor of Church History, lecturing in the College Chapel.

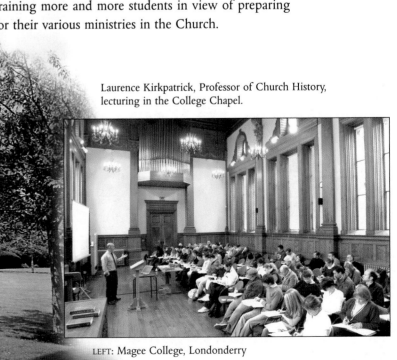

LEFT: Magee College, Londonderry

Other Irish Presbyterian Churches

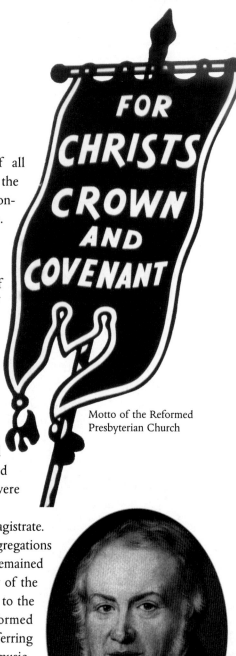

Motto of the Reformed Presbyterian Church

Tʜᴇ ᴘʀᴇsʙʏᴛᴇʀɪᴀɴ ᴄʜᴜʀᴄʜ ɪɴ ɪʀᴇʟᴀɴᴅ comprises over 95% of all Presbyterians in Ireland. Three smaller denominations also belong to the broader Presbyterian family: the Reformed Presbyterian Church, the Non-Subscribing Presbyterian Church, and the Evangelical Presbyterian Church.

The Reformed Presbyterian Church

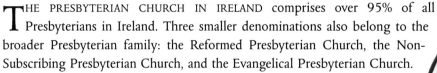

Dervock Reformed Presbyterian Church, Co Antrim

This Church originated in the aftermath of the Revolution Settlement of 1690, which was welcomed by most Irish Presbyterians as a vindication of their struggle for religious freedom. However, a minority of them were unhappy with the absence of any reference to the kingship of Jesus Christ: they harked back to the broader reformation aim of the 1643 Solemn League and Covenant. These Presbyterians formed themselves into Covenanting Societies and were in regular contact with similar Scottish Societies (they followed Richard Cameron and James Renwick). Notable early Covenanter preachers in Ireland included Alexander Peden and David Houston. A 'Reformed Presbytery' was formed in 1763. This was followed in 1811 by the creation of a Synod, consisting of twelve ministers and twenty-eight churches. The Reformed Presbyterian ministers were distinguished by the fact that they never accepted *regium donum* payments.

A schism occurred in 1840 over the issue of the powers of the civil magistrate. Under the leadership of Rev John Paul, five ministers and eleven congregations withdrew; they formed the Eastern Reformed Presbyterian Synod, which remained separate for sixty years. In 1902, this Synod joined the General Assembly of the Presbyterian Church in Ireland, though several churches decided to return to the Reformed Presbyterian Church. In their worship today, the Reformed Presbyterians continue to reject instrumental music and hymn-singing, preferring to maintain their tradition of metrical Psalm singing, unaccompanied by music.

In 2001, The Irish Reformed Presbyterian Church counted over 2,200 members (according to the Northern Ireland 2001 census), and contains thirty-nine congregations in four Presbyteries served by about thirty ministers.

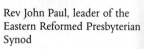

Rev John Paul, leader of the Eastern Reformed Presbyterian Synod

The Non-Subscribing Presbyterian Church in Ireland

This Church originated in 1830, following a dispute within the Synod of Ulster on the question of subscription to the Westminster Confession of Faith. The issue of whether a man-made confession of faith should be used as a basis of authority was central to the debate, as was the suspicion that the Non-subscribers adhered to Arian or Unitarian beliefs. Rev Henry Montgomery of Dunmurry led the Non-subscribers in forming a Remonstrant Synod on 25 May 1830. Seventeen Non-subscribing ministers withdrew and were organised into three Presbyteries: Armagh, Bangor and Templepatrick. Within a few years, Montgomery was forced to introduce a creed in order to control the lax theological views of some younger ministers. Heated arguments followed, and, by the time of his death in 1865, Henry Montgomery was out of step with many of his fellow Non-subscribers.

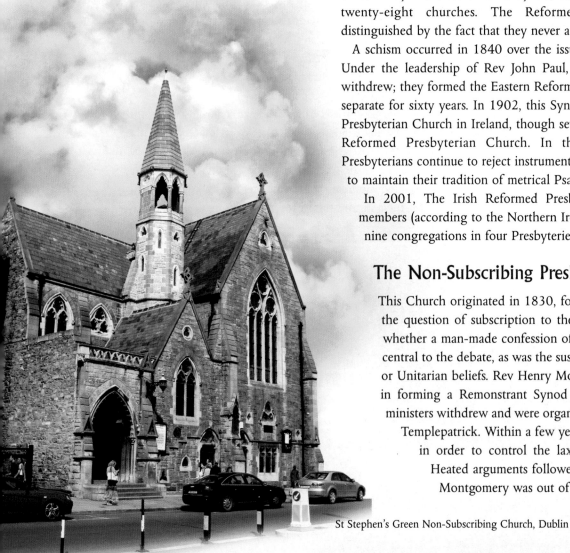

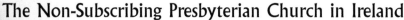

St Stephen's Green Non-Subscribing Church, Dublin

Henry Montgomery's
Church at Dunmurry

First Belfast Non-Subscribing Presbyterian Church

In 1910, the Remonstrant Synod and the Presbytery of Antrim amalgamated to form the General Synod of the Non-Subscribing Presbyterian Church in Ireland. The Synod of Munster, which had never practised subscription, joined with the larger body in 1935.

The ethos of the Non-subscribing Church today is 'faith guided by reason and conscience'. The Church advocates liberal tolerant Christianity. According to the Northern Ireland 2001 census, The Irish Non-Subscribing Presbyterian Church counted 1,233 members at the time. The Church consists of thirty-four congregations, served by less than twenty ministers.

The Evangelical Bookshop,
College Square East, Belfast

The Evangelical Presbyterian Church

In 1927, Professor Ernest Davey was accused by some of teaching heretical views in Assembly's College. However, the General Assembly did not find him guilty. The specific charges against Rev Davey were fuelled against a wider backdrop of concern about a general adoption of modernistic ideas within Irish Presbyterianism. The case against Prof Davey was

Knock Evangelical Presbyterian Church formed by Rev James Hunter in 1927

led by Rev James Hunter, a retired minister of Knock in Belfast.

When the heresy charges were rejected by both Belfast Presbytery and the General Assembly, Rev Hunter and a small minority of like-minded individuals left the Presbyterian Church and formed the Irish Evangelical Church. Later, the term 'Presbyterian' was added in brackets and, in 1964, the name was changed to The Evangelical Presbyterian Church. The views of this Church are well represented at the well-known Evangelical Bookshop in College Square East, Belfast. Interestingly, this bookshop was operating before the first congregation was formed.

According to the Northern Ireland 2001 census, The Irish Evangelical Presbyterian Church had 543 members at the time. The Church comprises ten congregations and ministers.

Stranmillis Evangelical Presbyterian Church

The Presbyterian Church in Ireland

Maps of Presbyteries and Congregations

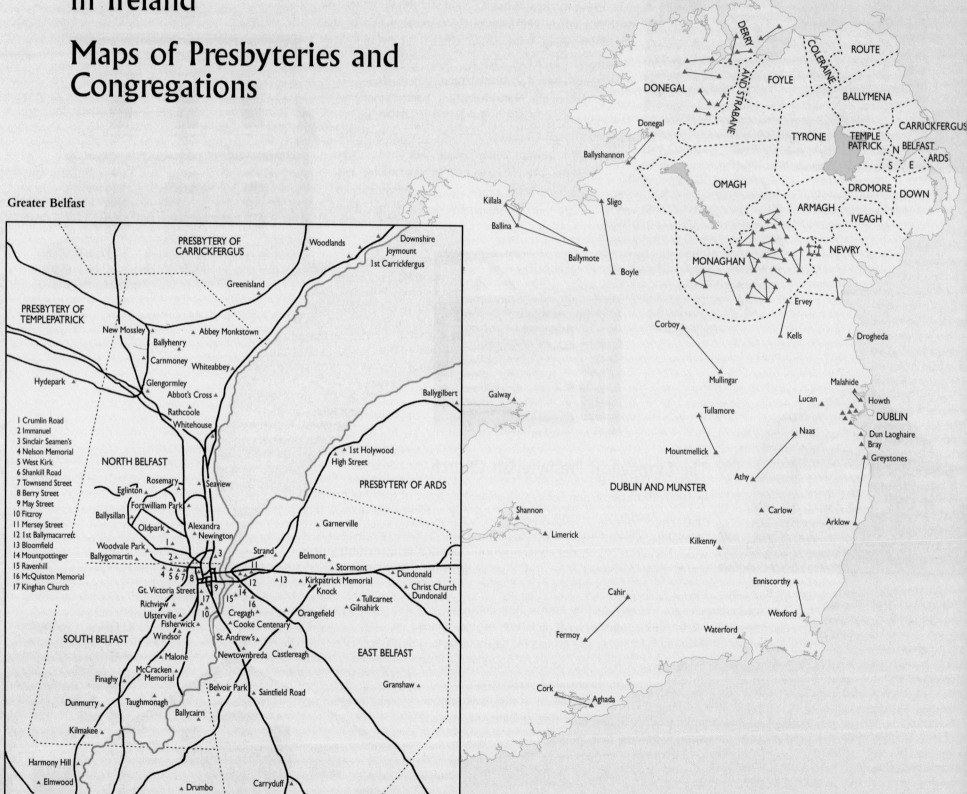

LEANNE HIGGINSON/GRAPHIC BASE

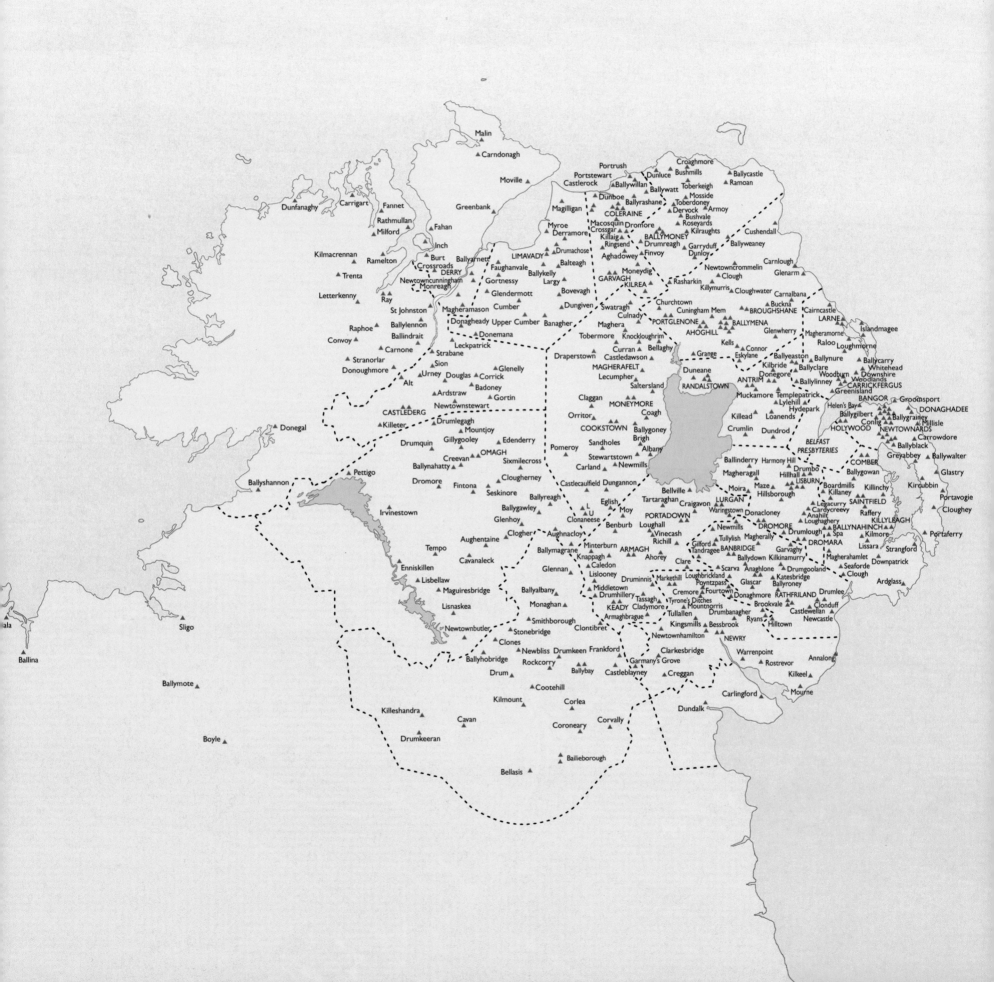

Strangford Lough
ESLER CRAWFORD

Ards Presbytery

Introduction

The Ards Presbytery includes more Presbyterians than any other Presbytery in Ireland. It contains thirty-five congregations and approximately 29,000 members. Geographically, the Ards Presbytery extends from Holywood in the north-west, cuts eastwards and southwards in a large arcing swathe across County Down, encompassing the towns of Bangor and Newtownards, and covering the entire Ards peninsula.

The 17th Century

In the earliest years of the 17th century, large tracts of this region came under the control of the Scottish Presbyterians, James Hamilton and Hugh Montgomery. The area had been devastated in the 'Nine Year War' (1594–1603) and these two men introduced Lowland Scots and English settlers. Montgomery gained the territory around Newtown Ards, Comber, Donaghadee and Greyabbey. Hamilton, later Lord Clandeboye, was the founder of the present Dufferin family, which acquired the Dufferin estate. The Church of Ireland at that time was in a shockingly poor condition with little money, dilapidated buildings and a dearth of ministers. Several Scottish Presbyterian ministers were invited to serve in Church of Ireland parishes in the Ards area: Robert Hamilton in Holywood from 1615, Robert Blair in Bangor from 1623, James Hamilton in Ballywalter from 1623 and John McClelland in Newtown Ards in the 1630s.

In the 1630s, these Presbyterian ministers were deposed by the bishops and a regular Presbyterian structure was not established in Ireland until 10 June 1642, when chaplains and elders from General Robert Munroe's Scottish army constituted themselves as a Presbytery at Carrickfergus. Almost immediately, requests came in from Presbyterian settlers in North and East Down seeking ministers to preach to them. Seven Presbyterian congregations were established throughout the Ards area in the 1640s and all survive to this day: Ballywalter, Portaferry, First Newtownards, First Holywood, First Bangor, First Donaghadee and Greyabbey.

Ballywalter

Rev John Goudy (1693–1733), one of the first ministers, here achieved some fame as a pastor who could predict future events. He earned the nickname: 'Goudy the Prophet.' The most famous of his 'prophecies' was to foretell the precise day, hour and circumstance of the death of Queen Anne on Sunday 1 August 1714. In 1818, the congregation split when a majority of the people formed a second congregation under Rev John Gibson. The two congregations reunited in 1925. Membership stands at 280 families today.

Portaferry

is situated at the southern end of the Ards Peninsula. The congregation's most famous minister was Rev William Steel Dickson (1780–1798). He was arrested on 5 June 1798, and imprisoned without trial, on suspicion of involvement with United Irishmen forces. Membership has declined steadily from 400 families in the early 19th century. In 1982, the congregation was linked with Kirkcubbin, but, in 2002, this was broken and a new link forged with Cloughey congregation. Membership stands today at sixty-five families.

First Newtownards

Rev John Mairs (1720–35) took the congregation into the Non-subscribing Presbytery of Antrim but, about 1723, a section of his congregation abandoned him and returned to the Synod of Ulster. Newtownards was a staunchly Presbyterian town in the 18th century. The ministry of Rev James Simpson (1790–98) came to an abrupt end during the chaos of the 1798 rebellion. Simpson was implicated and chose to flee from Ireland, travelling to America where he was out of reach of the authorities. Membership stands today at about 385 families.

First Holywood

was initially joined with Dundonald under the ministry of Rev Thomas Peebles, one of the Scottish army chaplains who had constituted the first Irish Presbytery at Carrickfergus. Rev Michael Bruce (1711–31) took the majority of the congregation into the Non-subscribing Antrim Presbytery. The smaller and poorer section of the church remained loyal to the Synod of Ulster and built a new church. Today, First Holywood is a very stable congregation, having a membership of just over 400 families.

Reverend Ruth Patterson

as born on 25 October 1944, the second
aughter and middle child of Rev Thomas and
uth Patterson. Her first eight years were spent
the congregation of Lylehill before the family
oved to Shore Street, Donaghadee in 1952.
ollowing studies at Queen's University and in
oronto, Ruth worked as assistant to the
resbyterian Chaplain at Queen's from
968–71. She obtained a Bachelor of Divinity
egree from Edinburgh University in 1974 and
ecame a student assistant in Gardenmore,
arne. It was in Gardenmore on 2 January 1976
at Ruth Patterson made history – being the
rst woman to be ordained in Ireland. On 16
ecember 1977, she was installed as minister of
ilmakee, Dunmurry, in the Presbytery of South
elfast. Out of her desire to bring people
gether and to foster a process of healing and
orgiveness, Ruth Patterson oversaw the birth in
988 of a new part-time work – 'Restoration
Ministries'. This was a non-denominational
entre for healing and reconciliation. The name
omes from the twenty-third psalm.
Restoration Ministries expanded to such an
xtent that Ruth resigned as minister of
ilmakee on 30 April 1991 in order to oversee
is special ministry in a full-time capacity. The
rganisation operates on a cross-community
asis as a non-denominational and charitable
ust. From the base at Restoration House Ruth
atterson provides a healing and caring
nvironment for those in our society who have
een victimised and hurt, or who are weary and
pent. Individuals are permitted to tell their
tory and be heard. Courses, seminars and
roup work help people to deal with areas of
oss. Relationships, friendships and trust are
uilt between people from all traditions. Today,
he support organisation, 'Friends of Restoration
Ministries', has a membership in excess of six
undred.

Michael Perrott

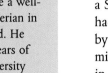

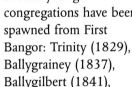

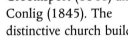

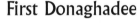

is one of the best-known Irish
Presbyterians of this generation. Although
born in London, much of his early life was
spent in Dublin, yet he has become a well-
known and well-respected Presbyterian in
Northern Ireland and further afield. He
became a Christian at seventeen years of
age and attended Cambridge University
where he read English and Theology.
Michael Perrott taught for a short time in
the Irish Bible Institute before working for
the Dublin YMCA. For ten years he
worked as an evangelist, travelling
considerable distances. He and his wife
Hilary joined First Holywood
congregation and Michael led the work in
the Belfast YMCA for fourteen years. He
developed a special interest in family issues
and became Director of Counselling and
Evangelism in the Belfast YMCA. Out of
this, grew 'Christian Guidelines', an
organisation that aims to provide several
streams of practical Christian education
and counselling. Marriage preparation
courses multiplied through Northern
Ireland under the auspices of Christian
Guidelines. Michael Perrott has now
retired from his active leadership role and
has explored a new outlet for his years of
experience by writing a bestselling book
entitled 'The Highway Code for Marriage'.
Based upon an acrostic on the word
'careful' it contains numerous personal and
life-related experiences of the author,
promoting Christian values in
Communication, Affection, Respect,
Encouragement, Forgiveness, Unselfishness
and Loyalty. Michael has since written a
practical book about procrastination
entitled 'Just Do It', and his 'Highway
Code for Parenting' is to be published
shortly.

First Bangor

was founded in 1642 by the Army Presbytery,
in that a Kirk Session was regularly
constituted. The first minister was
a Scotsman, Gilbert Ramsey. He
had been sent over to Bangor
by Rev Robert Blair, who had
ministered to the early settlers
in Bangor since 1623.
Several younger
congregations have been
spawned from First
Bangor: Trinity (1829),
Ballygrainey (1837),
Ballygilbert (1841),
Groomsport (1841) and
Conlig (1845). The
distinctive church building was
completed in 1831; it is a well known local landmark. This is one
of the largest congregations in the Ards Presbytery area.
Membership stands today at about 885 families.

First Donaghadee

was formed in 1646. The first minister, Rev Andrew Stewart, wrote
an interesting account of his early years in Ulster. The congregation
divided in 1821, when some members wished to remain loyal to
Rev William Skelly (1812–21) although he was deposed from
ministry (by one vote) by the Synod of Ulster. This minority group
formed a new congregation at Shore Street. Rev Skelly was restored
by the General Assembly in 1856. Today, First Donaghadee has a
membership of almost 300 families and has increased steadily as the
town has expanded since the
1960s.

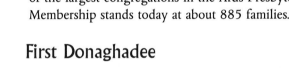

Greyabbey

was established around 1649. However, it struggled under the Commonwealth regime and was not re-opened until 1733. Clearly, the most notorious incident in the history of the congregation was the hanging of Rev James Porter (1787–98) within sight of his house on 2 July 1798, for complicity in the rebellion of that year. Porter's successor, Rev John Watson, joined the Remonstrant Synod in 1829. About one hundred seat holders remained loyal to the Synod of Ulster and built a new church which was given the significant name, Trinity. Membership today totals 170 families.

Reverend James Porter

was hanged at Greyabbey on 2 July 1798 following a guilty verdict passed on him by a military tribunal, which sat in the aftermath of the 1798 rebellion. He was the author of a series of satirical letters against the aristocracy of County Down, published under the title 'Billy Bluff and Squire Firebrand.' Porter was the only minister to be hanged, though two probationers suffered the same fate: Archibald Warwick of Kircubbin and Robert Goudy of Dunover. In all, sixty-three ministers and licentiates were suspected of involvement in the rebellion. Several fled to America.

The 18th Century

In the 18th century, five new congregations were added to the seven congregations established in the 1640s. They mainly served to 'fill the gaps' on the peninsula, reducing the distance people had to travel to worship. The most noteworthy development in the 18th century in this area was the formation of the first two Seceder congregations, at Newtownards and Ballycopeland.

Glastry

was formed in 1721 in order to ease pressure in Ballywalter, which served a wide area that included Greyabbey and Kircubbin. The most famous Glastry minister was Rev William Steele Dickson (1771–80), later an infamous supporter of the United Irishmen and minister in neighbouring Portaferry. Rev Alexander Porter Goudy was briefly minister in Glastry from 20 September 1831 until 1 May 1833 – a short ministry of just over a year and a half. He was a grandson of Rev James Porter of Greyabbey, who had been hanged in 1798 for complicity in the rebellion of that year. From December 2003, the congregation has been linked with Kircubbin and membership currently stands at almost 200 families.

Second Newtownards

was the earliest Seceder congregation in the Ards area. It was founded in 1753 in Conlig, halfway between the towns of Newtownards and Bangor. Earliest services were held in the open air. The Seceders had recently formed their first Irish congregation at Lylehill in County Antrim in 1743. The earliest ministers were all Scottish. The congregation moved to Newtownards in 1771. Three ministers covered a period of 129 years here: Rev David Maxwell (1812–59), Rev James Young (1860–1902) and Rev John Young (1901–40). The current building was opened in 1869. Membership today stands at just over 240 families.

101

linked with Portaferry, but has since been a Stated Supply served by the minister of Glastry. Membership stands at about ninety families today.

Millisle and Ballycopeland

Millisle was formed in 1773 under the care of the Synod of Ulster. Rev Andrew Greer (1777–1809) baptised 1,143 children during his ministry here! Millisle has the honour of producing the first Deaconess in Irish Presbyterianism, Miss Bessie Barclay. She was appointed a Deaconess in Woodvale Park, Belfast, before moving to Liverpool in 1915, where she worked in Brassey Street Institute for thirty years. She then returned to Belfast and lived to over 100 years of age.

Ballycopeland was the second Seceder cause in the Ards area and was also established in 1773. The first minister, Rev Alexander Grier (1773–77) married a daughter of Rev Isaac Patton of Lylehill, the first Irish Secession minister in Ireland. Rev Grier lived at Lylehill, outside Templepatrick, teaching in a school organised by his father-in-law; he travelled to Ballycopeland only for Sunday services. One of his pupils at Lylehill was the famous Henry Montgomery, future leader of the Non-subscribing Presbyterians. The most famous name associated with the congregation is that of Amy Carmichael who was baptised in this congregation on 19 January 1868. Amy Carmichael gained international fame for her work in Dohnavur, India, where she pioneered efforts to save young girls from lives of prostitution attached to Hindu Temples.

In 1906, Ballycopeland and Millisle were united. Membership today stands at around 400 families.

Kirkcubbin

was established in 1777, despite opposition from the Synod of Ulster and the congregation was not recognised by Synod until 1783. The first minister, Rev George Brydons (1778–1817), was chaplain at the execution of Archibald Warwick, a probationer for the Presbyterian ministry, hanged on 15 October 1798 for complicity in the 1798 rebellion of the United Irishmen. Warwick was a member of Kirkcubbin. From 1993–2003, Kirkcubbin was

Amy Carmichael

Amy Carmichael was born in Millisle on 16 December 1867 and baptised in the local Presbyterian church in the following month. She was one of seven children. Amy was converted about 1883 and founded a mission for Belfast linen girls in Cambrai Street in 1887. After brief spells as a missionary in Japan and Ceylon (Sri Lanka) and rejection for work in China, due to her frailty, she commenced missionary work in India in 1896. From 1900, Amy began working in the Dohnavur region of South India, rescuing children from temple prostitution. Amy Carmichael persevered in her work despite fierce local opposition, and built up a 'Dohnavur family' of over 100 children in a 10 year period. An orphanage, hospital, school and workshops were all built on the site. The children knew her as 'Amma' which means 'mother' in the Tamil language. Following a fall in 1931, Amy Carmichael was unable to walk and began to write. She was completely bedridden in 1935, by which time she had written thirteen books. Amy Carmichael served in Dohnavour for fifty-six years without a break. When Amy Carmichael died on 18 January 1951 she had written thirty-five books. She was buried at Dohnavur.

Background from a baptismal record relating to Amy Carmichael

The 19th Century

The 19th century saw the greatest expansion in the number of Presbyterian congregations in Ireland, including the Ards area. During this period, the number of Presbyterian churches more than doubled, from twelve to twenty-seven. Presbyterians were more numerous in the Ards peninsula in the 19th century than they are today. For example, a survey in 1838 indicated that in Portaferry there were 404 families (sixty-five in 2003), in Glastry 410 (190 in 2003) and in Kircubbin 302 (ninety-four in 2003).

Shore Street

in Donaghadee, was formed in 1821 as a result of a schism in what is now First Donaghadee at a time when Rev William Skelly was deposed from the ministry in the Synod of Ulster by a majority of only one. A minority of his congregation remained loyal to Rev Skelly. They formed a new congregation, originally known as 'Mr Skelly's meeting-house', and were received into the General Assembly in 1856. Rev Skelly received the sum of £200 in committing his building to the local Presbytery. Today, the membership counts 460 families and has grown steadily to become one of the largest congregations in the Ards peninsula.

Trinity

in Bangor was formed in 1829, in response to population growth. It was known as Second Bangor until 1894. The congregation moved to their current building on Main Street in 1888. In 1889, the second minister, Rev William Clarke (1879–92), was the first minister from the Ards Presbytery to become Moderator of the General Assembly (1889). In this same year, the church asked the Assembly to permit their name to be 'Christ Church, Bangor' but this request was refused. The new congregational name, 'Trinity Presbyterian Church' was finally agreed in 1894. Rev John Carson (1948–76) served as Moderator of the General Assembly in 1969. Membership today totals 470 families.

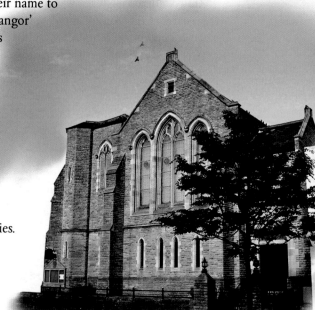

Ballyblack

was established in 1813 as the third Seceder cause in the Ards district. It started with a baptism in the cottage of Francis Boal, who had just moved to this area. He invited his home minister, Rev James McCullagh of Gransha, to baptise his child and invited many friends and neighbours. Regular house meetings continued, and the families who attended these gatherings finally decided to form a Seceder congregation. The original Church was replaced by the present building in 1872; the local farmers carried the stones to the site in their carts. Today, the congregation has a membership of 150 families.

Regent Street

in Newtownards grew out of a division within First Newtownards. In 1834, Rev James McCullough announced he would retire soon and requested that his son, Julius, should be appointed as his assistant and ultimate successor. A minority of the congregation did not agree and began holding services in the Court House. They were formed into a new congregation in 1834. Membership of the congregation declined in the later 19th century, from a peak of 300 families in 1870 to about 150 families in 1892 and 100 families in the late 1920s. In the past fifty years, the population of Newtownards has doubled and Regent Street has seen its membership increase from 190 families to 450 families.

Carrowdore and Ballyfrenis

Carrowdore was founded in 1830, when the Seceder minister of Ballyblack, Alexander McIlwaine, began conducting regular services in the village. The first minister of the new congregation, Rev David Parke, served for forty-two years (1830–72). This was followed by several short ministries. A number of ministers moved from Carrowdore to larger and more important congregations in Belfast and Carrickfergus.

Ballyfrenis, formed in 1843, was maintained through open-air and barn services for some years. The congregation was linked to the Scottish 'Associate Presbytery' and supplied by Scottish ministers. The first Irish minister here was Rev Hugh Fitzwalter Kirker (1886–1932).

On 1 July 1932, the congregations of Carrowdore and Ballyfrenis became a joint charge. Today the united congregation has a membership of just under 200 families.

Ballygrainey

was established in 1837. The first minister was John McAlister; he was ordained in Ballygrainey on 20 February 1838, but he resigned

three months later upon accepting a call to Third Armagh. The third minister, Mr Samuel McGaw, ordained on 19 August 1845, was subsequently degraded for immorality and deposed from the ministry on 2 April 1861. He emigrated to America. In the past fifty years congregational membership has increased by 100 families and today stands at almost 250 families.

Ballygilbert

was founded in 1841 due to increasing population in this area. Arguably, the most influential ministry has been that of Rev William

Regent Sreet

Park, one of three brothers, all Presbyterian ministers, whose father, also William Park, was minister of Glendermott. William Park junior was ordained in Ballygilbert on 1 January 1935 and ministered here for thirty-seven years, resigning on 31 December 1972. Rev Park was Moderator of the General Assembly in 1961 and Convenor of Union Commission for twenty-five years. Ballygilbert grew from 130 families to over 300 families under his ministry. Today the congregational membership is about 450 families.

Cloughey

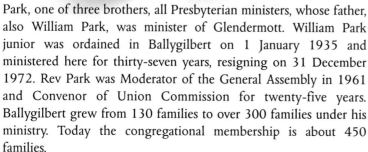

Cloughey was formed in 1841 following a Church Extension report to Bangor Presbytery in 1838 which declared that there were sufficient Presbyterians in 'the southern part of the back shore of the Ards' to merit the creation of a new congregation. The first minister was Rev James Gamble (1841–67), an uncle of Rev Henry Gamble (Ballywalter), and a name perpetuated in the Gamble Library in Union Theological College. Under the leadership of Rev David Palmer (1907–40), a hall was built in Portavogie and additional services commenced there. The congregation became known as 'Cloughey and Portavogie'. The link with Portavogie was broken in 2002 and a new link formed with Portaferry on 16 October 2002. Today about one hundred families belong to Cloughey.

Groomsport

In 1841, Presbyterians from First Bangor established a new congregation in Groomsport. Under the leadership of the first minister, Rev Isaac Mack (1841–77), a meeting-house (1843), a school (1844), a clock tower and a manse (1863) were constructed. The fifth minister, Rev John Nesbitt Moorhead Legate (1911–21), was a fourth generation minister with six uncles also Presbyterian ministers. He served as chaplain with the thirty-sixth (Ulster) Division in France from 1917–19. During the past fifty years, membership has more than doubled and stands today in excess of 400 families.

Portavogie

Presbyterians from this locality worshipped in Cloughey from 1841. In 1926 Rev Daniel Palmer (1907–40) commenced services in a new hall in Portavogie. These services were in addition to existing services in Cloughey. The congregation developed as 'Cloughey and Portavogie', utilising two buildings. From 1 July 1997 this arrangement became a joint charge; two congregations with their own structures, sharing one minister. In 2002 Portavogie became a separate congregation for the first time. The first minister of the single church was Rev Maurice Wade who was installed on 29 August 2003. The original hall had served the congregation well for eighty years and a new church opened in September 2006. Congregational membership stands today at 135 families.

Conlig

was founded in July 1845. Mr John Sinclair of Belfast, in whose memory the Sinclair Seamen's church is named, built the meeting-house largely at his own expense. By the 1940s, average attendance at Communion had fallen to only forty-five and concerns were expressed periodically by the Presbytery on a number of occasions that numbers were particularly low. But membership continued to decline and the Conlig minister was given the added responsibility of Kilcooley Church Extension services (1976–1979) and, later, Lisnabreen Church Extension services (1979–1981). In 1979, a pipe organ and stained-glass windows from Elmwood in Belfast were given to Conlig. Today, membership stands at just above 200 families.

Strean

in Newtownards was founded in 1866 by members of First Newtownards who were unhappy over the procedures in securing Matthew Macauley as successor to Rev Julius McCullough. Thomas Strean, from whom the church takes its name, had inherited his uncle's fortune and paid the entire cost of the new church building and most of the costs of building a hall and manse. Rev John Morrow Simms had been a member of Strean. He joined the army as a chaplain in 1887 and in 1915 was appointed Chaplain General. He was Moderator of the General Assembly in 1919. Membership has increased in the past fifty years from about 200 families to just over 300 families.

Greenwell Street

in Newtownards started as a result of the 1859 revival. Mr William McIlrath held meetings in a store room at the rear of his father-in-law's home at 27 High Street. He also commenced theological studies at the Presbyterian College in Belfast. Licensed by the General Assembly on 5 April 1867, he was called to 'the Greenwell Street Church', and ordained on 25 May 1869. Membership rose from 250 families in 1900 to 1,000 families by 1947. The present church building was opened on 19 February 1972 and current membership stands at 950 families; one of the largest congregations in Ards Presbytery.

High Street

in Holywood was formed in November 1855 by members of First Holywood. During the ministry of Rev Henry Osborne (1862–90), the Sunday School had 422 children on the roll and thirty-three teachers. Rev Osborne was also for a time editor of *The Evangelical Witness*. The eighth minister, Rev John Ross (1976–2000), was Moderator of the General Assembly in 1995. Membership now stands at just over 200 families.

Helen's Bay

was established as a result of services conducted in Helen's Bay Temperance Hall in 1892. Most of the earliest worshippers belonged to the nearby Ballygilbert congregation, but within two years they were convinced of a need to build their own church in Helen's Bay. Their first minister was Rev Thomas Johnston who retired from Second Bailieborough (July 1890) and lived in Helen's Bay. Fifty years ago, membership stood at 120 families, but it has recently risen to 220 families.

Hamilton Road

in Bangor was formed in 1897, the third Presbyterian Church in the town and the fifteenth Presbyterian Church to be formed in the Ards Presbytery during the 19th century. The first minister, Rev Robert Montgomery, installed on 17 February 1898, had to resign on 3 May 1898 due to poor health. The Faith Mission first held its Easter Convention in this church in 1924 and the Worldwide Missionary Convention has held its annual meeting here since 1936. The fifth minister,

Rev David Burke (1955–84), was elected Moderator of the General Assembly in 1978. Today, with 910 families, this congregation is one of the largest in the General Assembly and certainly has the largest number of contributing families in Ards Presbytery.

The 20th Century

In 1900, the Ards Presbytery counted twenty-seven congregations. Eight new churches have been established since, six in Bangor and two in Newtownards. From the 1960s the towns of Bangor and Newtownards have expanded rapidly and now dominate the Presbytery. There are nine Presbyterian congregations in Bangor and seven in Newtownards. However, while many congregations from the northern corner of the Presbytery are thriving, some of the smaller ones in the south are struggling as church attending Presbyterians dwindle, leading to various necessary links and unions.

Ballyholme

was founded on 5 November 1940. The first minister, William Erskine, was appointed on 23 January 1941 and served here for

thirty-seven years. The second minister, Rev Donald Watts (1980–2001), became Clerk of the General Assembly in 2003. Membership of this congregation has more than doubled over the past fifty years and today comprises just over 480 families.

West Church

is the sixth Presbyterian congregation to be formed in Bangor (and attained full congregational status in 1967). The first minister, Rev David Bailie (1961–98), engaged in a very distinctive ministry in Bangor West emphasising Christian renewal in the power of the Holy Spirit. Today, this thriving congregation has a membership of almost 1,000 families and holds three Sunday morning services.

Parkes have since served as ministers. Membership today stands at about 300 families.

St. Andrew's

started as a Church Extension cause on 25 July 1948, when a service was held in a nissen hut in the Clandeboye Road area of Bangor. Various ministers supported this work until the installation of Rev Ernest Logan, on 8 January 1953. A permanent church was opened on 13 April 1957 and the cause achieved full congregational status on 1 January 1962. Revs Kerr, McKee and

Reverend David Bailie

was born in 1929 and raised in the congregation of Duneane. He obtained a BA degree from Queen's University, a BD degree from Edinburgh University and served as student assistant in Trinity, Bangor. He was ordained in November 1954 for work as a missionary in Gujarat in India. There he initiated exciting developments, especially in Sunday School work which increased local involvement at leadership level. He returned to Ireland in 1959 and was installed on 11 October 1961 as the first minister of the new Church Extension charge of Bangor West. In Bangor, David implemented ideas that he had first employed in India – principally delegating responsibilities and encouraging everyone to get involved in congregational life. In 1968, David Bailie experienced a deepening of his faith through a fresh experience of the Holy Spirit in his life. It came about on the occasion of a series of meetings conducted by his former student associate in New College, Edinburgh, Rev Tom Smail. This spirit of renewal pervaded David's ministry and saw a tremendous growth in Bangor West. David Bailie retired in 1998. The congregation grew quickly and, today, Bangor West is one of the strongest congregations in the General Assembly.

and a new larger hall was provided for the work in 1978. The link with Strean was broken in 1984 and full congregational status was achieved in January 1994. Today, the congregational membership stands at just above 250 families.

Ballycrochan

grew out of a Church Extension cause that began when an option was taken on a site in the Donaghadee Road area of Bangor in 1973. The first services were held in October 1974 in a Play School hut with fifty-one people in attendance. Full congregational status was attained on 17 January 1982. In the late 1980s, there was immense pressure upon the facilities and two Sunday morning services had to be organised to accommodate worshippers. A new building opened in October 1990 and today the membership of Ballycrochan stands at 400 families.

Lisnabreen

grew from a Church Extension cause that began in 1967, when the Presbytery first discussed the possibility of starting work in the Bloomfield Road district of Bangor. A site was purchased in 1970 and a lightweight building erected for work. A new church building was opened in September 1990 and membership reached a peak of 300 families. Full congregational status was achieved on 21 January 1993 and membership today stands at just above 250 families.

Scrabo

New housing in the Comber Road district of Newtownards contributed to a considerable population growth, and the congregation of Strean decided to form a new church in that area. The Church Extension Committee purchased a site in 1969, and a new hall opened on 21 April 1972. Rev George Eagleson of Strean visited the locality and conducted services, assisted by Deaconess Pat Shirley. By 1976, over 250 families had joined the congregation

Kilcooley

was another Church Extension cause. This housing estate started to develop in 1966, and Church Extension identified it as a potential site for a new congregation. In November 1968, Rev Kennneth Weir of Conlig was asked to engage in the new work. He started Sunday services in the Primary School and visiting in the new houses as they were occupied. A Hall-church was opened on 15 October 1970. By 1980, membership reached 330 families and there was tremendous pressure upon the facilities. Full

congregational status was attained on 16 January 1983. Today, the membership of Kilcooley stands at 220 families.

Movilla

is the youngest congregation in Ards Presbytery. Church Extension first sought a site in this locality in the late 1970s and a suitable one was purchased in 1981. However, the decision to proceed was taken in 1994 only when planning permission for a new church was sought. The first minister, Rev David Porter, was installed in June 1995. He ministered here until 2 January 2001, just before full congregational status was achieved (16 January). Over 100 families joined in the first year and today, membership stands at 250 families.

Conclusion

The history of Ards Presbytery reflects that of the whole Presbyterian Church in Ireland. This region witnessed the arrival of Scottish Presbyterian settlers in Ireland and the subsequent establishment of Irish Presbyterian congregations. Seven of these have been founded over 350 years ago!

The recent and rapid growth of Bangor and Newtownards has brought much change in the Ards Presbytery. These towns dominate the area and have hosted a surge of Church Extension activity with the formation of eight new congregations in the past sixty years. In 1900, Bangor had a population of 6,000 rising to 15,000 by 1939. Today, the town counts over 71,000 inhabitants and boasts more Presbyterian congregations than any other Irish town. First Bangor, Hamilton Road and West Church constitute, with Greenwell Street in Newtownards, four of the largest congregations in Ireland. However, the overall picture in Presbyterian statistics shows a regular decline; even membership in most of the new congregations appears to have peaked in the 1970s–80s. Difficult decisions may have to be taken in the not too distant future in the lower Ards Peninsula district, where a number of smaller congregations may struggle to survive.

Armagh Presbytery

Introduction

Armagh Presbytery covers a region to the south and west of Lough Neagh. The historic ecclesiastical city of Armagh dominates the centre of this area. It is not a large city, with a population of less than 20,000, but boasts two Presbyterian congregations. The north-east of the Presbytery covers Craigavon (including Lurgan and Portadown), which was designated a 'new town' in the late 1960s. Like Armagh, Lurgan and Portadown are each served by two Presbyterian congregations.

The Armagh Presbytery contains thirty churches in all, served by seventeen ministers. Today, there are eight single charges, nine joint charges, one triple charge and one small cause served by a retired minister.

The 17th Century

Presbyterians first came to Armagh in the 17th century, as settlers moved south and westwards from Antrim and Down. These settlers travelled down the Lagan valley and into this fertile land. Six congregations were formed in the Armagh Presbytery in the 17th century: Armagh, Benburb, Minterburn, Clare, Lurgan and Vinecash. They cut a swathe across Armagh and its surroundings, and indicate a growing Presbyterian influence. Prior to the 1630s, Presbyterians and Anglicans co-operated as single congregations.

The earliest Presbyterian Church, Armagh, was organised sometime after 1641 by Rev Archibald Hamilton. He was a son of Rev James Hamilton of Ballywalter, nephew of the first Lord Clandeboye, and one of the earliest Presbyterian ministers to come to Ulster. In 1659, the population of Armagh was 409.

Francis Hutcheson

FRANCIS HUTCHESON was born on 8th August 1694, the second son of Rev John Hutcheson, minister of First Armagh (1697–1729). Francis studied for the Presbyterian ministry at the University of Glasgow from 1711; he was licensed in 1719. He declined a call from Magherally and opened an Academy in Dublin, on the invitation of several influential Presbyterian ministers in the capital. The reputation of his Academy was soon high. He married Miss Mary Wilson in 1725. Also in 1725, he published 'An Enquiry into the Origin of our Ideas of Beauty and Virtue'. This book went through several editions and was translated into French and German. He next published his 'Essay on Passions'.

In 1729, Hutcheson was appointed Professor of Moral Philosophy in Glasgow University, where his reputation reached a peak. He was regarded as one of the principal academics in his field. He was one of the first lecturers in Glasgow to abandon Latin and deliver his lectures in English. Hutcheson was a very popular lecturer in Glasgow, especially among the many Irish students. His guiding principle was benevolence and he is credited with the popular maxim, 'the greatest happiness of the greatest number'.

In 1746, Hutcheson was visiting his native Ireland when he became ill and died, on 8 August, his fifty-third birthday. His famous 'System of Moral Philosophy' was published after his death.

Reverend Ernest Best

was born in Belfast on 23 May 1917. He attended Methodist College, where he attained the nickname 'Paddy', which stayed with him throughout his life. He graduated from Queen's University, Belfast, with a first-class degree in Mathematics. He published several articles before studying for the Presbyterian ministry at Assembly's College (1939–41).

While assistant minister in First Bangor (1942–49), Best gained his PhD with a thesis on St Paul's doctrine. This was later published as 'One Body in Christ' (1955). From 1949–63, he was minister of Caledon and Minterburn. Such was his reputation that he was invited to be guest lecturer in New Testament at Austin Seminary, Texas from 1955–7. The local Presbytery approved and arranged for Rev Herbert Martin, retired minister of Mourne, to pastor Caledon and Minterburn for this period.

The call into academia could not be resisted and, in 1963, Ernest Best was appointed lecturer in New Testament in St. Andrews University. In 1973, he was appointed to the Chair of Divinity and Biblical Criticism in Glasgow University and he taught here until his retirement in 1982. 'Paddy' Best died on 1 October 2004, aged eighty-seven.

First Armagh

Precise details of the origins of First Armagh are lost, but it is known that Presbyterian worship was organised soon after the 1641 rebellion. One of the early ministers here, Rev Archibald Hamilton (1673–88), was a son of Rev James Hamilton of Ballywalter (1626–36). The third minister, Rev John Hutcheson (1697–1729) was father of Francis Hutcheson, the celebrated Professor of Moral Philosophy on Glasgow University (1729–46). Eighty people were killed in a train accident on a Sunday School excursion to Warrenpoint on 10 June 1889. Three ministers of this congregation have served as Moderators of the General Assembly: Rev Jackson Smyth (1880), Rev AW Neill (1948) and Rev Temple Lundie (1974). The current church was built in 1879. Membership today stands at almost 300 families.

The Armagh Disaster

At 10:15am on Wednesday 12 June packed Sunday School excursion tra carriages and 941 people left station, bound for the seaside t Warrenpoint. Before 11 o'clo passengers in the rear 10 carriage involved in Ireland's worst ever accident.

The engine was unable to carriages up the steep incline at E Bridge and stopped 200 metres sho summit. It was decided to secure the carriages on the slope and pull the carriages to the next station. How

Daniel Manderson (1884–1905) died in America where he was attempting to raise funds for renovation of the church. On 1st October 1928, Minterburn was united with Caledon. Rev Ernest Best (1949–63) became Professor of New Testament in St Andrews' University (1963–73), then in Glasgow University (1973–82). Today, this congregation has a stable membership of almost one hundred families.

Benburb

was formed sometime before 1660. The earliest known Presbyterian minister in Benburb was Mr Walkinshaw who ministered here shortly after the Restoration in 1660. The longest serving minister was Rev John Kennedy (1714–61). The congregation has never been large and suffered from a series of short ministries throughout most of the 19th century. The current church is the congregation's third and was opened in 1839. From 1977, Benburb has been united with Moy congregation. Today, there are fifty-eight families in membership.

Minterburn

was formed sometime before 1661. The first minister here was Rev John Abernethy who was ejected in 1661. His son, also Rev John Abernethy, was founder of the infamous 'Belfast Society'. Rev

Clare

is first mentioned in 1679, when the first minister was Rev John MacBride. Deep divisions among members in the early 19th century led to the establishment of a Seceder (later Reformed Presbyterian) congregation in the area. Rev Samuel Hutchinson (1967-85) became Deputy (1985–90) and Clerk of the General Assembly (1990–2003). The congregation has been linked with Ahorey since 1988, and currently has a membership of ninety families.

First Lurgan

was organised in 1686 with the ordination of Rev Hugh Kirkpatrick (1686–90). It was a poor and weak cause until well into the 18th century. The widow of the sixth minister, Rev William Magee (1780–1800), was Mrs Martha Magee, who inherited a fortune from her brother. She left over £60,000 to the Presbyterian Church in Ireland. Magee College in Londonderry was founded from part of this legacy. The present church was built in 1827. It was the scene of the great Synod of Ulster debate between Rev Henry Cooke and

Rev Henry Montgomery on Friday 3 July 1829, at the height of the subscription controversy. Membership today stands at just over 300 families.

Vinecash

is first mentioned in 1697, when Rev Alexander Bruce was ordained here. Several congregations grew out of it: Loughall, Richill, Portadown and Tartaraghan. The current church was built in 1879. Following the resignation of Rev Thomas Rowan (1910–23) in 1923, the church was vacant for sixteen years, until Rev William Wilberforce Pyper (1939–49) was installed on 3rd August 1939. From 1982, Vinecash has been linked with the congregation of Craigavon. Membership today stands at eighty-four families.

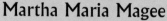

Martha Maria Magee

Mrs Martha Maria Magee was the widow of Rev William Magee, who was minister in First Lurgan from 1780–1800. Following the death of her husband on 9th July 1800, she moved to Dublin and became a member of Usher's Quay congregation. Mrs Magee outlived her husband by almost half a century and inherited considerable wealth from her unmarried brothers who were high ranking officers in the Indian Army. She died on 22 June 1846, and in her will left over £60,000 to various Presbyterian causes. £20,000 was left 'for the establishment of a Presbyterian College in Arts and Theology'.

Mrs Magee's Trustees, who included her minister, Rev Richard Dill, refused to allow this bequest to go towards the expense of establishing the Presbyterian College in Belfast, which opened in 1853, because it taught only Theology. The Belfast College only offered Theology courses because the new Queen's College in Belfast offered other subjects. Could Irish Presbyterians afford two Colleges? Neither side would give way and the argument over the Magee bequest was eventually settled in the Court of Chancery. The Trustees were entitled to use the bequest as they interpreted the will and, as a result, Magee College was eventually established in Londonderry, opening for classes in 1865.

Ulster Evangelical Society

The Ulster Evangelical Society was founded on 10 October 1798 in Armagh City. One of the principal aims of this organisation was to establish a system of itinerant preaching, employing laymen. The main leaders of the Society were Burgher Seceder ministers, most notably Rev William Henry (Tassagh), Rev David Holmes (Eglish), Rev Lewis Brown (Sixmilecross) and Rev John Lowry (Clonaneese). Such preaching was innovative in the late 18th century, but it was perceived by many ministers as a threat to their parish areas and an invasion of their ministry. It was the fear of many, and the sober judgement of a majority, that such enthusiasm could only lead to a form of Christianity that would be slave to emotional experiences.

The Society was condemned by both Burgher and Anti-Burgher Synods in 1799. As a result of these condemnations, Rev John Gibson (Richill) and Rev George Hamilton (Armagh) became ministers of Congregational churches. Hamilton later founded two of them, in Carrickfergus and in Straid.

Magee staff and students 1937–38

The 18th Century

The town of Armagh grew significantly during the 18th century. In 1750, there were 2,000 inhabitants, but only three dwellings with slate roofs. The city developed dramatically in the next forty years as a linen centre, boasting thirty-nine cloth mills within a six mile radius.

A further seven Presbyterian congregations were founded in the Armagh Presbytery in the 18th century. This brought the total number of Presbyterian congregations to thirteen. Of the seven new ones, three (Keady, Loughgall and Lislooney) were under the authority of the Synod of Ulster and four (Drumhillery, Tassagh, Ahorey and Redrock) belonged to the Seceders, who formed their first Irish congregation at Lylehill, County Antrim, in 1746.

The Orange Order was founded on 21 September 1795, in the home of James Sloan at Loughgall as a defensive Protestant organisation in opposition to the Roman Catholic 'Defenders' organisation. This was the outcome of sectarian conflict throughout this region in the 1780s and 1790s. The focus of the conflict was competition in the linen industry. Amidst such conflict and the Rebellion of 1798, the Ulster Evangelical Society was founded in Armagh on 10 October 1798. This organisation advocated itinerant gospel preaching.

First Keady

Prior to 1690, the Presbyterians in Keady worshipped in First Armagh. The first minister in the separate Keady congregation was Rev Thomas Milligan (1706–34). A minority formed a separate church in 1802 (Second Keady), because they objected to the ministry of Rev Henry McIlree (1797–1817). The current church (the fourth on this site) was opened in 1839. The congregation was linked with Armaghbrague in 1964. Membership now stands at just under seventy families.

Loughgall

grew out of Vinecash in 1711. Rev Robert Peebles (1758–61) opposed the Seceders in this locality and wrote a tract against their local leader, Dr Thomas Clark of Cahans. The fifth minister, Rev Robert Hogg (1803–30) was a distinguished scholar who also served as assistant astronomer to Very Rev James Hamilton in Armagh from 1799–1830. The congregation was linked with Tartaraghan in 1963. Membership has remained steady over the past fifty years at just under one hundred families.

Lislooney

grew out of Minterburn in 1714, as did Glennan, and was originally known as Kinnaird. The second minister, Rev William Ambrose (1732–65) was the son of Rev Willaim Ambrose, who had been minister of the undivided Minterburn congregation from 1693–1714. The church was linked with Knappagh on 1 April 1923. Membership has risen slightly of late and now stands at just over eighty families.

Drumhillery

was the earliest Seceder cause within the Armagh Presbytery. Formed in the early 1750s and originally known as Derrynoose, this congregation grew out of the labours of Rev Thomas Clark of Cahans. The present church was built in 1868. The Rev Vernon Corkey (1906–12) was the fifth of eight sons of Rev Joseph Corkey of Glendermott, all of whom became Presbyterian ministers. The congregation has been linked with Second Keady since 1971, and current membership stands at sixty-five families.

Tassagh

was formed in the 1760s, the second Seceder congregation in this area. The first minister, Rev William Henry (1771–1818), was a founding member of the Ulster Evangelical Society in 1798. The third minister, Rev Samuel Malcolmson (1824–42), was a grandson of the famous Seceder minister, Rev Thomas Reid of Drumgooland. On 18 February 2003, the congregation was linked with Cladymore and membership today stands at just over sixty families.

Reverend Thomas Campbell

THOMAS CAMPBELL was born at Sheepbridge, just outside Newry, on 1 February 1763. He graduated in Theology at Glasgow in 1786, and was ordained as the second minister of Ahorey Anti-Burgher congregation in 1797. He served as Moderator of the Anti-Burgher Synod in 1805–6 and supplemented his income by teaching in a Classical School, preparing young men for a university education. His attitude of openness and co-operation between all Christians was noted in that he was the only Anti-Burgher who subscribed to the Ulster Evangelical Society.

In 1807, aged forty-four, Thomas Campbell emigrated to America, where he continued to serve as a Seceder minister. However, he was deposed by the American Seceders on 10 April 1810 for the 'sin' of holding an open Communion. Undaunted, Thomas Campbell founded the 'Disciples', the first American indigenous church. He died at Bethany, West Virginia, on 4 January 1854, a month before his ninety-first birthday.

Today, the Disciples of Christ number over four million members. The 'Disciples' have not forgotten their Irish founder. In 1961, a Campbell memorial window was unveiled in Ahorey church and, in 1971, a church tower was added to the building in memory of Thomas Campbell.

Ahorey

Anti-Burgher Seceder congregation was formed in 1786 from the Seceder church at Markethill. The second minister, Rev Thomas Campbell (1799–1607), emigrated to America in 1810, and later founded the first US indigenous church, the 'Disciples of Christ'. In 1973, a new tower was added to the Ahorey church in memory of Thomas Campbell. Ahorey was linked with Clare in 1988, and membership today stands at 175 families.

Redrock

was a Seceder cause founded in 1799. The first minister, Rev James Harvey, served here for fifty-seven years (1799–1856). The congregation was united with Druminnis on 1 July 1924. Rev Joseph McKee has the distinction of having been minister here twice, from 1898–1905 in Redrock, and from 1926–42 in the united charge. Membership stands at 150 families.

The 19th Century

The Armagh region was opened up in the mid 19th century by the railway, arriving in Portadown in 1842, and Armagh in 1848. As in most Presbyteries, the 19th century saw the largest expansion in Presbyterian congregations. Sixteen new causes were formed, in addition to the thirteen already in existence. Five Synod of Ulster congregations (Second Keady, First Portadown, Middletown, Knappagh and The Mall, Armagh) and four Secession congregations (Caledon, Richill, Tartaraghan and Cladymore) were formed prior to the Union of 1840. A further seven (Druminnis, Waringstown, Armaghbrague, Moy, Hill St., Lurgan, Bellsville and Armagh Road, Portadown) were subsequently formed before 1900. The revival of 1859 certainly played some role in this expansion. The population in this Presbytery fell in the latter half of the 19th century. Armagh was overtaken in size by Lurgan in 1871, and by Portadown in the 1890s. The latter town in particular burgeoned, becoming the main market town for all of southern Ulster. First Portadown was founded in 1822, and Armagh Road, Portadown, in 1867.

Second Keady

was founded in 1802 as a result of disputes in First Keady. The first minister was Rev William Steel Dickson (1803–15). Due to suspicions that he was implicated in the Rebellion in 1798, the congregation did not receive *regium donum*. The original church was built in 1808; it was replaced by the current building in 1857. The congregation was united with Drumhillery from 1923–46. They were again united on 1 December 1971. Membership today stands at sixty-five families.

Caledon

was formed in 1807, the fifth Seceder congregation in this locality. The first minister, Rev John Allen (1814–23), left debts when he fled to America for which action he was suspended by the Synod. He returned to Ireland in 1826, and was restored to ministerial office. The congregation was united with Minterburn on 1 October 1928. Rev Barbara Ann McDonald was installed on 19 March 1993, the first woman minister to serve in the Armagh Presbytery. Today, the congregation has a stable membership of fifty families.

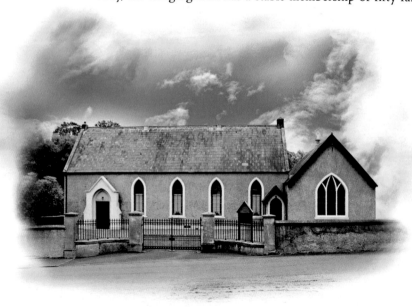

Reverend William Steel Dickson

WILLIAM STEEL DICKSON was born on Christmas Day 1744 at Carnmoney, near Belfast. He was taught classics and theology by Rev Robert White, minister of the neighbouring congregation of Templepatrick, and continued his studies at the University of Glasgow. Dickson was ordained and installed in Ballyhalbert (Glastry) on 6 March 1771.

Rev Dickson took an active interest in the Volunteer Movement and, on 14 March 1780, he became minister of Portaferry. In the years leading to the 1798 rebellion, William Dickson became an advocate for the reform ideas of the United Irishmen. On 5 June 1798, he was arrested on suspicion of complicity in sedition. Rev Dickson was confined to a prison ship in Belfast Lough from August 1798 until March 1799; he was then moved to Fort St. George in Scotland. He was finally liberated in January 1802, having been confined without trial for nearly four years.

Rev Dickson was installed in the new congregation of Second Keady on 4 March 1803, but, through Government interference, denied a share of the *regium donum*. His health deteriorated, and he resigned from his pastoral duties on 27 June 1815. He moved to Belfast, where he was supported by some friends. William Dickson died on 27 December 1824, two days past his eightieth birthday. Only a handful of friends were present when he was buried in a paupers' plot, in Clifton Street burying-ground.

Reverend Alexander Kerr

ALEXANDER KERR was born near Markethill in 1812. He graduated from the Old College Belfast (Belfast Academical Institution) in 1835 and was ordained as minister of First Portadown on 21 June 1838. It was to be a short ministry. The first General Assembly of the newly united Presbyterian Church in Ireland took the momentous decision to commission two of its own ministers, Rev Alexander Kerr and Rev James Glasgow (Castledawson 1835–40), as missionaries to India. They had been good friends as students in Belfast. These pioneer missionaries and their wives left Belfast on 29 August 1840, and arrived in Bombay on 26 February 1841. The famous Scottish missionary, John Wilson, encouraged them to base their work in the Gujarati speaking peninsula of Kathiawar.

Both families epitomised the high cost of missionary work in the 19th century. The Glasgows' daughter, Margaret Jane, was born on 16 March, but died on 11 June, less than four months after arriving in India. The Kerrs' son, Robert, was born on 15 April but Alexander Kerr contracted fever a few weeks later and died on 16 August. In a letter, James Glasgow wrote: 'Thus has the Lord begun to try us! Who shall be next, we cannot say.'

In all, twenty-two Irish Presbyterian missionaries are buried in India (not counting spouses and children). By January 1843, four new missionaries arrived, and mission stations were opened in Rajkot, Porbandar and Gogha.

First Portadown

was formed in 1822. The third minister, Rev Alexander Kerr (1838–40), was one of the first two Irish Presbyterian missionaries to India. He died on 16 August 1841, aged twenty-nine. The current church was opened in 1858. Two ministers have been elected Moderator of the General Assembly: Rev William John Macauley (1881–1916) in 1913, and Rev William Magee Craig (1948–83) in 1979. First Portadown is the largest congregation in Armagh Presbytery. Today, membership stands at 650 families.

Richill

congregation grew out of Vinecash. Meetings were first held in the locality in 1782 and a separate congregation was formed in 1824. The first minister, Rev James Sinclair (1824–36) left to join the Non-subscribers and the cause here struggled to survive. The congregation grew substantially at the time of the 1859 Revival. Today Richill congregation has a membership of just over 300 families, a very healthy increase in excess of 300% since the 1950s.

Tartaraghan

was a Seceder cause formed in 1823. The first minister, Rev James Shaw (1824–38), had been tutored by Rev Samuel Beattie of Ahorey. The church was built in 1825, and the congregation was poor for many years. Rev John Forsythe (1920–43) ended a series of short ministries. From 1 October 1962, this congregation was united with Loughgall. Membership has risen to a present total of eighty families.

Middletown

was formed in 1826 as a Seceder congregation. The first minister, Rev Samuel Hendrin (1827–67), was the last Irish Burgher student to study at the Secession College in Glasgow. The early years of this church were overshadowed by poverty; in 1840 the minister had only received £11 of his stipend (which should have totalled £24), and there was a building debt of £46. Middletown has been linked with a succession of neighbouring congregations throughout its existence and was most recently designated as 'Stated Supply' with Lislooney and Knappagh. Currently, membership stands at twenty families.

Cladymore

was a Seceder congregation. It grew out of a desire by locals to have their own minister rather than travel to neighbouring churches at Markethill, Mountnorris and Tullyallen. The first minister, Rev Robert Shields, was ordained on 4 October 1836. He died of fever during the famine of 1846, and, as a precaution against contagion, all his papers were burnt. Cladymore has been united with Tassagh congregation since 18 February 2003. Current membership stands at just over seventy families.

Knappagh

was formed in 1836 by the Synod of Ulster. The first minister, Rev Hugh Magill, resigned after only two years, 'under the influence of strong mental excitement caused by his arduous labours in organising a new congregation.' The congregation was briefly linked with Caledon (1920–23) before the present union with Lislooney, which came into effect on 1 April 1923. Membership has remained steady over the past fifty years at just over sixty families.

The Mall

was formed in 1837, when a section of First Armagh separated from their minister, Rev PS Henry, because of his Liberal political views and liberal theological views. The congregation was known as 'Third Armagh' from the time of the Union in 1840. It was united with Second Armagh (originally Seceder) on 1 April 1916. On 8 June 1953, the congregation's name was changed to 'The Mall'. Two ministers, Rev William Boyd (1939–50) and Rev John William Lockington (1981–89), later served as Moderator of the General Assembly, in 1967 and 1999 respectively. Membership today stands at 300 families.

Druminnis

was formed in 1841. It was originally known as Hamilton's Bawn. The first minister was Rev Henry Kydd (1842–62) and the church was built during his ministry. The congregation was united with Redrock on 1 July 1924, under the new ministry of Rev Thomas Bole. A new gallery was added to the church in 1974, with seating for an extra fifty people. Membership has risen from fifty to ninety families in the past fifty years.

Waringstown

was formed in 1846. Its first minister was Rev Michael McMurray (1848–84). The church is a creation of the famous architect Sir John Lanyon. Built in Florentine style with two ornate towers, the building was opened for worship on 5 June 1853. With a current membership of 350 families, Waringstown has more than trebled in size in the past fifty years. It is the second largest congregation in the Armagh Presbytery.

Armaghbrague

was formed in 1847, following a dispute in Tassagh. In July 1918, the congregation was united with Tassagh and this situation prevailed for forty-six years. The union was dissolved on 1 February 1964, and the present union with First Keady congregation came into effect under the leadership of Rev John Mark. There are forty-four families in Armaghbrague today.

Moy

was founded in 1849. The first minister was Rev James Shannon but he did not stay long, 21 August 1850–25 February 1851. Rev John Meharry (1871) was Moderator of the English Presbyterian Church in 1906. Rev Thomas Cairns (1872–77) is notable in that he later served as Moderator of the New Zealand General Assembly in 1886–7 and Moderator of the Presbyterian Church in Victoria, Australia in 1906–7. The congregation was united with Benburb on 1 January 1977. Currently, membership totals 140 families.

Hill Street

in Lurgan was formed in 1861 to cater for new converts after the 1859 revival. The third minister, Rev James Haire later became Professor of Systematic Theology in Belfast and Moderator of the General Assembly (1939). The eighth minister, Rev John Girvan, served here from 1972 until his retirement in 1984. He was Moderator of the General Assembly in 1981. Membership stands today at 324 families.

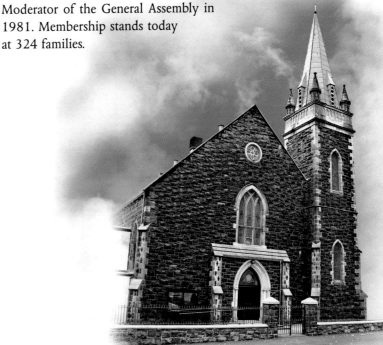

minister from 1887–93; he published a history of the Indian Mission of the Presbyterian Church in Ireland. The congregation name was changed from 'Second Portadown' to 'Armagh Road' in 1918. Rev George Wynne (1936–51) later served as Moderator of the General Assembly in 1975, though he died on 23 July 1975, only days after his election to the moderatorial office. Membership now stands at 330 families.

Bellville

was founded in 1862 as a result of enthusiasm from the 1859 revival. The church was built at private expense by two members of First Lurgan, the Bell brothers. Only Rev John Hutchinson (1863–1901) and Rev James Whiteside (1903–37) served in Bellville as a single charge. Between 1937–47 Samuel McCaughey, a student, cycled from Lurgan to conduct services here. Retired ministers served the church during the following twenty years. From 1967–98, the minister of Waringstown has cared for Bellville as stated supply. Around ten families are in membership at present.

Armagh Road

was formed in 1867 as the second Presbyterian congregation in the growing town of Portadown. Rev Robert Jeffrey served as

The 20th Century

There were high hopes in the late 1960s that the new town of Craigavon (incorporating the older towns of Lurgan and Portadown) would create a new centre in Northern Ireland, a modern environment with a fully integrated approach to planning. In step with this thinking, the new congregation of Craigavon was founded in 1967. It is the only new congregation in the Armagh Presbytery in the past 140 years. However, people did not relocate to Craigavon in the numbers anticipated, and the new congregation did not expand as expected.

Craigavon

Craigavon

developed as a Church Extension cause in the new city of Craigavon in 1967. Initial work was undertaken by Rev Andrew McComb and Rev James Campbell before Rev James Harrison (1971–90) was installed on 20 April 1971. The congregation was linked with Vinecash in 1982. Rev Andrew Thompson served as the second minister of the congregation from 1998–2004. The church has suffered three serious fires, on October 1987, February 1993 and May 2000. Membership today stands at just over one hundred families.

Conclusion

The Armagh Presbytery region constitutes a 'mixed' population with approximately 55% Protestant and 45% Roman Catholic. Presbyterians make up about 17% of this population. The largest congregation is First Portadown with over 700 families, compared to an average size of 155 families. Overall numbers for this Presbytery have remained stable over the past twenty years.

Bann Mouth, Lough Neagh
CENIC IRELAND

Slemish Mountain
SCENIC IRELAND
JILL JENNINGS

Ballymena Presbytery

Introduction

The name 'Ballymena' derives from the Irish *An Baile Meánach* meaning Middle Town, as it is literally the middle town of County Antrim. Ballymena Presbytery covers much of that central County area and is dominated by the town of Ballymena. There are thirty-one congregations within this Presbytery, served by twenty-nine ministers. Apart from three 'joint charges' (Kells/Eskylane, Glenarm/Cairnalbana and Newtowncrommelin/Carnlough/Cushendall), the other twenty-seven churches each have their own minister. This Presbytery is the third largest by total membership and financial contributions, after Ards and East Belfast. Membership stands at 9,440 families (2004 figure) and specified sources (income) at £2,556,108 (2004 figure).

The 17th Century

Presbyterians arrived in Antrim at the beginning of the 17th century as part of a general influx of Scottish settlers. The 'Ballymena estate' passed into the hands of William Adair, a Scottish laird from Kinhilt in south-western Scotland. During the 1641 Rebellion, the local garrison were forced to retreat to Carrickfergus. According to the 1669 hearth rolls, the population of 'Balymenoch' counted 106 households. This rose to 800 by 1707.

The earliest Presbyterian minister of whom there is any record was George Dunbar. He ministered in Larne from 1624–34, but also in Ballymena for part of this period. He was eventually deposed in 1634. Seven congregations were formed in the Ballymena area following the formation of the first Irish Presbytery in 1642: Ballymena, Broughshane, Glenarm, Ahoghill, Connor, Grange and Clough.

First Ballymena

traces its roots back to 1627 and the ministry of Scotsman Rev George Dunbar. Both Dunbar (1627–34) and the following Presbyterian minister, Rev David Buttle (1645–50), were deposed by government. A number of outstanding ministers served here. Rev Samuel Dill (1853–65) left to become Professor of Theology in Magee College, Londonderry. Rev Thomas Haslett (1892–1932) was convenor of Church Extension in the 1920s and Moderator of the General Assembly in 1925. Rev Eric Gardiner (1969–86) also served as Moderator of the General Assembly, in 1982. Membership of this congregation has remained steady over the past fifty years at about 550 families.

First Broughshane

was founded in the 1650s and was originally known as Braid. Arguably the most famous minister in this historic congregation was Rev Robert Stewart (1809–52), a close friend of the famous Rev Henry Cooke, and a fearless exponent of Trinitarian theology in the Arian controversy of the early 19th century. Stewart's successor, Rev Archibald Robinson (1853–86), left to become Professor of Sacred Rhetoric and Catechetics in 'Assembly's College', Belfast, from 1886–1902. During the 1859 revival, the church organised ten Sunday Schools with 100 teachers and 1,400 children. Membership now stands at just over 330 families.

Glenarm

was formed in the 1650s. The first known minister was a Scotsman, Rev Alexander Gilbert (1655–6). In the 1660s, the congregation was supplied for a time by the Covenanter, Rev David Houston, who eventually had his licence withdrawn by Route Presbytery. There was a six-year vacancy in the early 1700s because of a dispute over arrears owed to Rev John Lee (1693–1703). In 1829, Rev Alexander Montgomery (1801–29) and part of the congregation left the Synod of Ulster over the matter of Non-subscription and retained the church building. The current church was built after this schism. On 1 November 1919 the congregation was united with Cairnalbana congregation. Membership currently stands at just over seventy families.

Reverend Robert Stewart

ROBERT STEWART was born in April 1783 at Tullybane in the parish of Clough, County Antrim. He studied at the University of Glasgow from 1803–08 where he obtained an MA degree prior to his licensing by the Presbytery of Connor. He was ordained in Broughshane on 9 May 1809. The congregation voting which resulted in a call to Robert Stewart commenced after the close of morning worship and continued, with much rancour, until after 9pm. The Synod of Ulster thereafter discouraged such activities on Sundays. Rev Stewart was elected Moderator of Synod in 1816, a mere seven years after his ordination. It was largely due to the skilful negotiations of Robert Stewart – as Moderator – with Lord Castlereagh, that the Synod formed a relationship with the new Belfast Institution without Government opposition. When the Arian controversy arose in Synod, Stewart was the close ally of Henry Cooke, a colleague from student days at Glasgow, on the side of orthodoxy. In 1843, Robert Stewart was elected as the third Moderator of the General Assembly, succeeding his friend, Henry Cooke. He also took an interest in Presbyterian expansion in the south of Ireland and undertook several missionary tours. The congregation of Carlow was formed as a result of his efforts. He became ill in late 1851, and died on 26 September 1852. A memorial monument still stands in front of the church building.

First Ahoghill

was formed in the 1650s amidst trial and persecution. Financial hardship was severe in these early years. Annual stipend was £30, but, in 1690 the congregation was in arrears of £177 to their minister, Rev Matthew Haltridge (1676–1705), who nevertheless

Revival in Ahoghill

When Samuel Campbell of Ahoghill was converted on 9 December 1858, his first thought was to share his new faith with his family. On Christmas Day that year, he visited his brother, sister and mother, and shared his recent experience. Within a few days, all three had been converted. As in Connor, prayer meetings multiplied in the Ahoghill area, and the two Presbyterian ministers, Rev Frederick Buick (Trinity) and Rev David Adams (First), were both enthusiastic supporters of the revival movement.

The First Ahoghill church building had been opened in 1858; it could accommodate 1,200 people. The public manifestation of the revival occurred at the Communion Thanksgiving Service in First Ahoghill on Monday 14 March 1859. About 3,000 people attended. Rev Adams commenced the Service, but several members of the congregation were impatient to hear some of the converts speak. James Bankhead prayed in an excited manner and, in the ensuing commotion, Rev Adams believed the gallery might collapse. He ordered the building to be evacuated. The crowd spilled into the street and listened attentively in pouring rain to an appeal by James Bankhead, delivered from the steps of a house in the Diamond.

This event marked the public launch of the revival. By 26 March, there were thirty-five converts; by 7 April, 200; by 14 April, 400, and by 23 April the number had reached 1,000! It is no exaggeration to say that this event changed the face of Irish Presbyterianism, melting the formerly cold and religious nature of many congregations and giving impetus to a warm evangelical fervour.

Revival in Connor

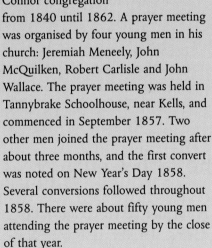

REV JOHN MOORE was a keen evangelical minister who led the *James McQuilkin* Connor congregation from 1840 until 1862. A prayer meeting was organised by four young men in his church: Jeremiah Meneely, John McQuilken, Robert Carlisle and John Wallace. The prayer meeting was held in Tannybrake Schoolhouse, near Kells, and commenced in September 1857. Two other men joined the prayer meeting after about three months, and the first convert was noted on New Year's Day 1858. Several conversions followed throughout 1858. There were about fifty young men attending the prayer meeting by the close of that year.

All of these developments had the support of Rev Moore. Other prayer meetings were started throughout the Connor congregation. As word of these events soon spread, Rev Moore was asked to address the General Assembly in 1858, and describe what was happening in his congregation. The 1858 Assembly set aside time to debate revival and also to pray for revival. This enthusiastic work throughout the Connor area continued that year, and, on 9 December, a young Ahoghill man, Samuel Campbell was converted, and this led to the revival spreading in Ahoghill.

continued his ministry until his death. The third minister, Rev Thomas Shaw (1710–31), joined the Non-subscribing Presbytery of Antrim in 1726, but the congregation rejoined the Synod of Ulster in 1732. The Revival occurred in this congregation during the ministry of Rev David Adams (1850–80). Membership has remained stable over the past fifty years at just above 400 families.

Connor

was formed in the 1650s and the first minister was Rev Robert Dewart (1658–61). Persecution and financial hardship were

common in the region for many decades, and the payment of stipend was often in arrears. The congregation is forever associated with the origins of the Revival in 1859, under the ministry of Rev John Moore (1840–62). About 1,000 people attended services and there were 100 prayer meetings throughout the district. Rev Samuel Lyle (1868–78) emigrated to Canada and was Moderator of the Canadian Presbyterian Church in 1911. Membership today totals 420 families.

Grange

was founded in the 1670s in conjunction with Duneane congregation. Services were held in each location on alternate Sundays. However, tensions arose between the two congregations and they parted in 1733. Grange congregation did not get its own minister until 1745 when Rev Francis O'Brien was ordained here. There was another link with Duneane from 1753–1813. This was during the ministry of Rev Robert Scott (1762–1808) who was accused of high treason in 1798, but subsequently acquitted. Membership stands today at 150 families.

Clough

was formed in the 1650s and the first minister, Rev Andrew Rowan (1650–61), was one of the few Presbyterians who conformed at the Restoration of Charles II in 1661. He became rector of Clough. Rev Joseph Douglass (1760–95) was a Captain in the Volunteers and often preached in his military uniform. The longest ministry in the history of this congregation was that of John Hall who was ordained in Clough on 17 June 1806 and retired on 14 March 1865. Rev James Glasgow, the earliest missionary of the Presbyterian Church in Ireland, was brought up in this congregation. Congregational membership currently stands at just less than 300 families.

Reverend James Glasgow

JAMES GLASGOW was born near Clough in County Antrim on 27 May 1805. The family were members of Clough. James Glasgow graduated with the General Certificate of the Old College, Belfast (Belfast Institution) in 1832, and was licensed to preach the Gospel by Belfast Presbytery in 1834. He accepted a call from Castledawson, and was ordained there on 6 October 1835.

At the first meeting of the General Assembly, on 10 July 1840, James Glasgow and Alexander Kerr were designated missionaries to India. James had married Mary Wightman earlier that year. The party left Belfast for India, but tragedy soon struck: the Glasgows' infant daughter died, and Alexander Kerr also died from the same fever. On 12 January 1842, James was joined in India by his younger brother, Rev Adam Glasgow.

Rev James Glasgow served the Presbyterian Church in Ireland well. From 1850 until 1861, he was the principal translator of the Gujarati Bible. He retired in 1864, and returned to Ireland, where he was appointed Professor of Oriental Languages in Assembly's College. He served in this post until his death at Portadown on 1 July 1890. Rev John Faris, of Cork congregation, is a great great grandson.

The 18th Century

A further seven congregations were formed during the 18th century. Four of them were planted by the Seceders. This period witnessed the development of the linen industry in this area. The linen business reached a peak in 1783, when Ballymena was one of nine leading brown linen markets in Ulster, with sales exceeding £100,000. The new Seceder congregation in Ballymena in 1769 reflects the growth of the town. The Moravian settlement at Gracehill was formed in 1765. In 1798, Ballymena was occupied 7–9 June by 10,000 United Irishmen who stormed the Market House (now the Town Hall) killing three defenders.

The Cuningham sisters

First Portglenone

was formed when Presbyterians, who had formally attended Rev Shaw in Ahoghill, disapproved of his attachment to the Non-subscribing Presbytery of Antrim in 1726. Six ministries used the original church building. The current church was built after the 1859 Revival, and was opened for worship on 12 February 1872.

Rev William McKay (1826–76) numbered twenty ministers among his ancestors and earned a reputation in his own lifetime as something of an oddity. His hair stood upright and he only possessed one shabby coat. He also specialised in prophecy, especially from the books of Daniel and Revelation. Congregational membership has risen by a healthy 30% in the past fifty years to 325 families.

Cuningham Memorial

was formed in the late 1720s. The first minister was Rev James McCreight (1730–57). The original name of the congregation was simply 'Cullybackey'. The name Cuningham Memorial was coined in 1881, on the occasion of the opening of the current church building which was paid for by Misses Catherine and Jane Cuningham, members of the congregation, in memory of their mother. Rev George Buick (1868–1904) was Convenor of the Presbyterian Jewish Mission and died in Damascus on 28 April 1904. Congregational membership has almost doubled in the past fifty years, standing now at 700 families. This is the third largest congregation in the Presbytery.

Trinity

in Ahoghill was formed in the 1750s as the first Seceder congregation in this area. Services were maintained for more than twenty years before the first minister, Rev Peter McMullan (1781–88), was ordained here. Rev Frederick Buick (1835–90) had an influential ministry here and was a keen supporter of the 1859 Revival. Two Trinity ministers became Moderator after leaving the congregation: Rev Victor Lynas (1943–47) in 1972, and Rev

William Fleming (1955–69) in 1987. Rev Harry Uprichard was installed on 16 April 1970, and served as Moderator of the General Assembly in 2005. Congregational membership has remained virtually unchanged in the past fifty years, at 250 families.

Buckna

was formed in 1756, in response to a petition from local people and despite a protest from some members of Broughshane. The new church was built in the shadow of Slemish mountain. Rev William Wray (1815–48) was noted in the locality for his strength and physique. Rev Thomas Jasper had the distinction of ministering successively in three congregations within the same Presbytery; Cairnalbana (1900–05), Portglenone (1905–17), and Buckna (1917–29). Membership currently stands at just over 250 families.

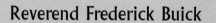

High Kirk

in Ballymena had its origin as a Seceder 'preaching station' in the Braid. The earliest name associated with this cause is the Scotsman Rev William Campbell in 1769. The Anti-Burgher Synod assumed responsibility for the congregation in 1798. It was during the ministry of another Rev William Campbell (1819–72) that the congregation moved into the town of Ballymena and, from 1840, it was known as 'Second Ballymena'. The name 'High Kirk' was used from the 1870s. In 1975, the congregation moved from High Street in the town centre, to Thomas Street on the outskirts. Rev Russell Birney (installed 1982) was elected Moderator of the General Assembly in 2002. Under his dynamic leadership, congregational membership has increased to around 750 families, making High Kirk the largest congregation in Ballymena Presbytery.

Reverend Frederick Buick

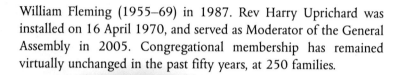

FREDERICK BUICK was the longest surviving minister from the first General Assembly in 1840. When he died on 17 January 1908, he was known as the 'Father of the General Assembly' at the age of ninety-six! Frederick Buick was born on St Patrick's Day 1811 in Navan, County Meath. He obtained the General Certificate from the Old College, Belfast (Belfast Institution) in 1832 and, as a Probationer, laboured in County Monaghan from November 1834 to lay the foundations for what became the Secession congregation of Ballyhobridge. He was licensed by Monaghan Presbytery in October 1834.

Rev Buick accepted a call to the Secession congregation in Ahoghill (later known as Trinity) and was ordained there on 3 November 1835. He spent his entire active ministry of sixty-five years in this congregation. Rev Buick oversaw major renovations to the church in 1840, and again in 1894. He played a prominent role in the 1859 revival, rejoicing in the many changed lives among his congregation and in the locality. He was buried beside his church and the inscription on his tablet reads: 'He was a good man, a true friend, a faithful pastor and an earnest preacher of the Gospel of Jesus Christ.'

Brookside

is the third Presbyterian congregation in Ahoghill, and was the first Burgher congregation of the Seceders in this locality. It started as part of a union with Randalstown around 1770. The first minister of the joint charge, Rev William Holmes, was installed on 11 January 1775. The first minister of a separate Ahoghill congregation was Rev John Marr (1800–44). After the union in 1840, this congregation was known as Third Ahoghill but later adopted the name Brookside. Rev Ivan McKay (1972–96) was elected Moderator of the General Assembly in 2003. Membership has virtually doubled in the past fifty years and currently stands at almost 350 families.

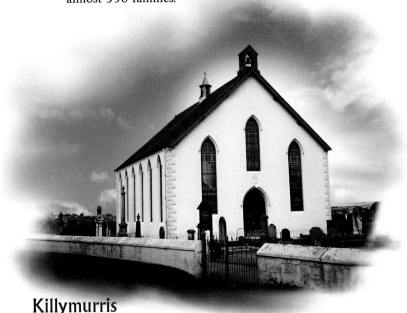

Killymurris

was formed in 1795, the second Burgher congregation within the Ballymena area. A split occurred within the congregation under the ministry of Rev John Wilson (1851–84) with a minority of people forming 'Second Killymurris'. The opposing factions were re-united upon the death of Rev Wilson. Since then the church has been

Reverend Russell Birney

REV RUSSELL BIRNEY was raised in Lisnaskea in County Fermanagh and worked in his father's grocery shop. The family belonged to Maguiresbridge congregation. In 1964, he commenced studies at Magee College, Londonderry, and this was followed by further study at New College, Edinburgh. Following an assistantship in First Carrickfergus, Rev Birney ministered in Downshire Road in Newry from 1973-1982. These were dark days in that locality with terrorist activity claiming Presbyterian and other lives.

From 1982–2005, Rev Birney ministered in High Kirk congregation in Ballymena. The congregation has grown to become one of the strongest in the General Assembly. Rev Birney has emphasised 'congregational body life' and the reality of the power of the Holy Spirit in peoples' lives. Under his leadership, High Kirk has managed change at a time when so many other congregations are struggling.

In 2002, Rev Birney was elected Moderator of the General Assembly and chose as his theme for the year: 'Living in God's Power'. He remains a firm believer in the maxim that it is not enough for the contemporary Church to have the right message, unless this is accompanied by visible and consistent Christian living. He retired in Autumn 2006.

Mary Steele

MARY STEELE is a remarkable lady! A native of Craigs and a member of Killymurris, Mary went to South Africa in 1959, to work as a nurse in a mission hospital. There, she met people who did not have a Bible in their own language. Mary returned to the United Kingdom, attended Bible College in Glasgow and later joined Wycliffe Bible Translators. She then moved to Ghana in West Africa to work on new Bible translations.

Today, Mary has completed two entire translations of the Bible; in the Konkomba and Bimoba languages. It took twenty years to achieve each translation. This huge endeavour involved analysing the sounds from local people, designing an alphabet and understanding how the grammar for each language operates. The Konkomba translation was completed in the 1970s by hand-written notes, and the Bimoba translation was completed with the aid of computers.

Throughout her years of hard work, Mary has been encouraged by the faithful prayer support of her congregation in Killymurris. Mary's enthusiasm has not abated. As she says herself: 'Quite simply, I can't think of any better way to spend one's life; if I had my time again, I would do exactly the same thing.'

STEPHEN LYNAS/PRESBYTERIAN HERALD

served by twelve ministers. Rev Francis Paul, Professor of Church History at Magee College (1911–22) and 'Assembly's College' (1922–41) was brought up in this congregation. Membership stands at 270 families.

The 19th Century

In 1800, the Ballymena Presbytery comprised fourteen congregations. By 1900, this figure had risen to twenty-nine, an average of one new congregation every seven years. The town of Ballymena developed rapidly during that period, with a population of 4,063 by 1843. Two new congregations in the town, founded in 1830 and 1863, testify to this growth. The Belfast-Ballymena railway was opened in 1848. The 1859 Revival dominated the religious landscape and many churches in this region recorded a marked increase in attendance and all activities. It was in the late 1800s that Sir Alexander Shafto Adair (later Lord Waveney) noted the 'seven towers' of Ballymena: Old Parish church, St Patrick's Church of Ireland, First Ballymena Presbyterian, All Saints Roman Catholic church, the Old Town Hall, Braidwater Spinning Mill and Ballymena Castle. The 'seven towers' symbol was soon associated with Ballymena. Only three remain today: Old Parish church, St Patrick's and All Saints.

Glenwherry

church was built in 1825, though Presbyterians in this area had before been attached to Ballyclare. The famous Covenanter fugitive Alexander Peden was sheltered in this region in 1682. There have been several notable and long ministries here, for example, Revs John Montgomery (1825–69), David Cummins (1889–1929) and David Connery (1929–64). Membership has remained steady at just under 200 families for the past fifty years.

Newtowncrommelin

was founded in 1826. It is situated nine miles from Ballymena in the foothills at the entrance to the Glens of Antrim. The first minister, Rev Joseph Anderson was ordained here in 1826; he resigned in 1834 to become a pioneer missionary with the Colonial Mission to Canada. Congregational numbers have declined in this rural area over the past fifty years and the church was united with Carnlough/Cushendall. Membership presently stands at seventy-five families.

West Church

in Ballymena, was the second Synod of Ulster congregation in the town and originated in 1830 on a site in Wellington Street. The first minister, Rev Alexander Patterson, was installed in 1830, but died of fever in 1847. The present church was built following the 1859 Revival, and the name 'West Church' was then adopted. In 1926, the building was destroyed by fire and re-opened after renovation on 14 November 1928. Membership has grown by 50% over the past fifty years and is currently recorded as 650 families, the fourth largest in the Ballymena Presbytery.

Rasharkin

was founded in the 1830s. The members of Finvoy had initiated the establishment of a 'preaching station' in the village and the new congregation grew from this venture. The first minister was Rev William Wallace. He was installed on 17 June 1834, and retired forty-eight years later, in 1882, after a ministry which encompassed early growth, famine and revival. The Free Presbyterians exploited tension within the congregation in the 1960s but, despite this, membership has remained virtually unaltered numbering around 200 families.

Churchtown

was founded in 1835 on a site given by Major Longford Hyland for a rent of 1 shilling every 25 years 'if demanded'. The first minister, Rev Andrew Mitchell, was ordained on 18 October 1836, but, due to illness, never commenced his ministry. Three ministers here served for a total of 141 years! They are Rev Robert Torrens (1839–75), Rev Henry Mulholland (1884–1930) and in recent memory the congregation was intricately linked with the Rev John Joe Rainey, who spent his entire ministry here, being ordained in Churchtown on 10 August 1933 and retiring on 8 August 1992. Rev Rainey later recounted that the suit he wore at his ordination cost £4 and his shoes 12/6 (62$\frac{1}{2}$p) and that his first car, a 1905 model, cost him £5! Membership currently stands at 140 families.

Third Portglenone

was formed in 1839 as the third Presbyterian, and second Synod of Ulster, congregation in the town. The second (Seceder) congregation had been founded in 1821. At the union of Synods in 1840, this second Synod of Ulster congregation was designated 'Third'. The Seceder congregation was dissolved in 1910, so that today Portglenone boasts two Presbyterian churches, First and Third. The first two ministers of 'Third' covered seventy-two years:

Rev Hutchinson Wood Perry (1839–69) and Rev Andrew Beattie (1869–1911). Membership has remained stable at around 150 families for the past fifty years.

Cloughwater

was formed in 1841; it was built up by a licentiate, Alexander Buchanan, later minister of Glendermott. The first minister was Rev William Davison (1843–66). Francis Petticrew, later to become

Professor Francis Petticrew

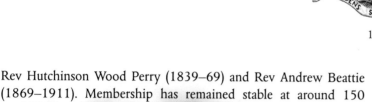

FRANCIS PETTICREW was born in 1832, into a farming family in the Broughshane district of County Antrim. He grew up in Cloughwater and studied at Queen's College Belfast, then at the Assembly's College, where he obtained a BA degree in 1855. He was licensed by Belfast Presbytery in May 1858 and ordained in Faughanvale, County Londonderry, on 17 February 1859. His ministry lasted twenty-seven years in this congregation and was invigorated by the 1859 revival. From 1886 until his death in 1909, Francis Petticrew was Professor of Theology in Magee College, Londonderry.

In 1868, the General Assembly debated the propriety or otherwise of employing instrumental music in congregational worship. Dr Petticrew was a staunch conservative and aligned himself with the 'Purity Party', which was strongly opposed to such innovations in worship. For several years, the Assembly passed resolutions ordering congregations to refrain from musical accompaniment to singing and, year after year, the 'guilty congregations' persisted in their innovations.

In 1883, about 200 ministers and elders of the Purity Party threatened to split from the Assembly over this issue. This group was also opposed to new architectural innovations in Presbyterian churches, for example stained-glass windows and spires. Under the influence of Dr Petticrew, a truce was eventually arranged and, in 1891, the matter was dropped. Prof Petticrew died on 3 August 1909.

Professor of Theology in Magee College, Londonderry, was brought up here. Rev Robert Herron (1927–55) was the Assembly Convenor of Students for the Ministry for many years. Congregational membership currently stands at 160 families.

Carnlough / Cushendall

was formed when these two churches were amalgamated on 1 July 1993. The Presbyterians of Cushendall had briefly helped support their own minister, Rev James Stewart (1708–19), but the cause did not flourish. They formed a congregation again in 1848. Carnlough was founded in 1892. Carnlough and Cushendall were made a joint charge on 1 November 1919, and the ministry of Rev William McCracken (1920–27) did much to establish the cause. 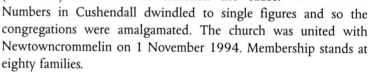 Numbers in Cushendall dwindled to single figures and so the congregations were amalgamated. The church was united with Newtowncrommelin on 1 November 1994. Membership stands at eighty families.

Eskylane

began in the early 1800s as a breakaway group from Kellswater Reformed Presbyterian Church. At the General Assembly in 1903, both Rev Samuel Moffett and his Eskylane congregation were admitted to the Presbyterian Church in Ireland. When Rev Moffett

retired in 1917, his church consisted of only twenty-six families and it was decided to unite it with Kells congregation. Membership today stands at just over fifty families.

Second Broughshane

was formed in the 1860s to cater for an increased number of worshippers in the locality as a result of the 1859 Revival. The first minister was Rev Robert Stewart (1864–67), a son of Rev John Stewart of Portstewart. It was during the ministry of the fifth minister, Rev John Gibson (1875–1911), that the congregation really flourished. Rev Gibson's son, Rev Joseph Gibson, was Clerk of the General Assembly and Moderator in 1950. Membership of this congregation has risen by over 50% in the past fifty years and now stands at just above 400 families.

Cairnalbana

was founded in 1862. The first minister was Rev Hamilton Martin (1863–99) and the church building was opened in 1867. The fourth minister was Rev William Ramsey (1905–31) and it was during his ministry that the congregation was united with Glenarm on 1 November 1919. The first minister of the united charge was Rev George Jackson (1931–70). Mr Jackson retired on 31 March 1970, and died six weeks later, on 16 May. Current congregational membership stands at just over 100 families.

Wellington

in Ballymena was formed in 1863 from a portion of the old 'Third' congregation in the town. The first minister of this new charge was Rev William Macloy (1863–81). He launched a monthly magazine, *The Christian Banner*, which he edited for five years from 1873. The Wellington Street site was developed and expanded further in the 1940s and again in the 1980s. In an imaginative move, the church is currently planning to relocate to a new site in the Galgorm Road area of the town and changed its name from Wellington Street to Wellington. Membership now stands at just below 750 families. Wellington is the second largest in the Ballymena Presbytery.

Kells

was founded in 1873, because the nearby Connor church could not accommodate the demand for seats. The first minister, Rev Thomas Eaton (1874–1900), was himself a convert of the 1859 Revival. He raised money for a church building by means of local donations and two fund raising trips to America. The church was opened in 1876. The congregation of Kells was united with that of Eskylane in 1917. Congregational membership stands at just over 250 families.

Harryville

in Ballymena was founded in 1899, and developed under the ministry of Rev William Currie (1900–07). The church was opened in 1902. Rev Currie was elected Moderator of the General Assembly in 1938. A

hall was added to the buildings in 1939, and membership doubled in the 1940s under the ministry of Rev Joseph Boyd (1940–54). Currently there are just over 350 families in membership.

The 20th Century

The congregation of Eskylane became a congregation within the Presbyterian Church in Ireland in 1903. The early part of the century saw the creation of three joint charges. In 1917, Kells and Eskylane were joined. This was followed on 1 November 1919 by the joining of Glenarm with Cairnalbana and Carnlough with Cushendall in 1993 and Newtowncrommelin added in 1994. In December 1937, Borough status was granted to Ballymena. In the second half of the twentieth century, the Church Extension Committee oversaw the creation of three new congregations within Ballymena: Ballyloughan (1981), Ballykeel (1983) and Ballee (1986) are the 'babies' in this Presbytery family. They brought the number of Presbyterian congregations in Ballymena to seven.

Glenariffe

Ballyloughan

gained full congregational status on 1 February 1981. The work started in June 1974, when 120 families joined the new cause. The church was opened in early 1978. Rev Joe Fell was installed by the Assembly's Church Extension Committee on 18 October 1973 and built up the work before resigning in 1988. Membership exceeded 300 families in 1977. The congregation is situated in an area of widespread social deprivation and, under the ministry of Rev David Brice (1989–2005), pioneered several pastoral care initiatives. Membership today totals 320 families.

Ballykeel

resulted from a Church Extension scheme which commenced in this area in the early 1970s. A new building on the site was opened in September 1974. Rev Brian Savage was installed on 3 March 1976 and, within three years, membership grew to over 300 families. A new extension was opened on 30 October 1982, and full congregation status was attained on 22 January 1983. There is a current membership of almost 150 families.

Ballee

arose out of pioneering work in this area which began in the early 1970s. Rev John McCullough was installed on 23 June 1977, and led the cause for nine years before resigning, when the congregation attained full congregational status, on 15 February 1986. The church building was opened on 3 April 1976, but suffered from serious structural damage following storm damage, when a wall collapsed shortly after the morning service on 14 December 1980. Membership today stands at almost 250 families.

Conclusion

The Ballymena Presbytery is rightly proud of its heritage. Presbyterianism has flourished here for over 350 years. However, as everywhere, the churches are facing challenges in the twenty-first century. There are enormous contrasts, from town to rural situations, from super church size to tiny communities. Perhaps the greatest challenge is for the Presbyterian congregations to demonstrate their relevance for this generation. Increasingly though, there are signs of rising sectarianism and social deprivation. Could too many congregations be perceived as middle-class comfort zones?

Belfast from Cavehill
SCENIC IRELAND

North Belfast Presbytery

Introduction

The Presbytery of North Belfast was created in 1963. Today, it consists of twenty-two congregations. Numerically, with just over 4,500 communicants, it sits between the larger East Belfast Presbytery (with almost 8,000 communicants) and the smaller South Belfast Presbytery (with 3,500 communicants). The Presbytery area extends from Ballygomartin to the north and west, incorporating the urban housing areas of Glengormley, Rathcoole and Monkstown. It is bounded by Carrickfergus Presbytery to the west and Templepatrick Presbytery to the north and east. The twenty-two congregations here range in size from eighty-eight families (New Mossley) to 1,147 families (Carnmoney) and there are no 'joint-charges', each congregation having its own minister.

The 17th Century

Two Presbyterian congregations were formed within the present bounds of North Belfast Presbytery in the 17th century. Of these, only Carnmoney congregation is a member of the General Assembly. This statement is misleading in that when it was founded in 1657, Carnmoney was separated by miles of green fields from the new town of Belfast. The oldest Presbyterian congregation in Belfast is 'First', founded in 1642, but is now a Non-subscribing congregation.

Shipyard from North Belfast
GORDON GRAY

Carnmoney

is the oldest congregation in this Presbytery, yet at the ordination of the first minister, Rev James Shaw, in May 1657, Carnmoney or Coole was a separate village on the lands that had been given to Sir Arthur Chichester. Four Presbyterian churches have occupied this site, and the current building was opened on 24 April 2004. The first two ministers were father and son: Rev James Shaw (1657–72) and Rev Patrick Shaw (1673–85). The cruciform church was replaced in 1714 by a simple square-shaped church. Today, Carnmoney with its impressive new building is one of the largest congregations in the General Assembly. Membership was around 300–350 families from the end of the 17th century, rising to 500 families in the early 20th century. Rapid growth took place in the twenty years between 1955 and 1975, when membership rose from 520 families to over 1,100 families.

The 18th Century

Although three Presbyterian congregations were formed within the modern Presbytery area in the 18th century, none of them are attached to the General Assembly today. The three were: 'Second' (in 1707), 'Third' in Rosemary Street (in 1722), and Donegall Street (in 1791). 'Second' became a Non-subscribing congregation and 'Third' united with Ekenhead in 1941 to form Rosemary congregation. Ballyhenry (formed in 1972) can trace roots through Cliftonville (founded 1885) to an earlier congregation formed in 1791, which used to meet in Donegall Street. It was in that century that the number of Presbyterians in Belfast increased significantly. The town was

prospering through import and export trade and professional and commercial classes grew. Not everyone prospered though, and the opening of the Poor House in 1774 is evidence that not all citizens made their fortune.

Rosemary Street meeting-house, 1783

The 19th Century

The population of Belfast expanded at a phenomenal rate during the 19th century. Over twenty congregations were formed in the North Belfast sector during these years of growth and eleven of them still operate although two, Alexandra and Immanuel, have adopted new names as a result of amalgamations with other churches. Several congregational names from this period are no more: Agnes Street, Bethany, Castleton, Clifton Street, Donegall Street, Duncairn, Ekenhead, Great Georges Street, James Street, Macrory, St. Enoch's and York Street. Many of the new congregations owed their origin to the pioneering urban mission work of the Belfast Town (later City) Mission (formed in 1827).

Whiteabbey

was founded in 1833, the name coming from a much older Dominican Abbey in the area, whose monks were distinguished by their white robes. The first minister was a Scotsman, Rev William Campbell; and he was ordained here on 12 November 1833. The current church was opened during the ministry of the third minister, Rev Robert Lynd (1860–75). His successor, Rev John Armstrong (1875), only preached on one Sunday in Whiteabbey. On the day after his first Sunday services, he became seriously ill and died within five months. This is the second largest congregation in North Belfast Presbytery with a current membership of 560 families.

Eglinton

has occupied its present site on the Ballysillan Road since November 1938. Previously, the congregation had worshipped in Eglinton

Reverend Robert Lynd

ROBERT JOHN LYND was born in 1833 at Greenfield, near Coleraine. He served with distinction in three congregations: Whiteabbey (1860–74), Academy Street (1875–82) and May Street (1882–1906). Within a year of Rev Lynd's arrival in Academy Street, the congregation outgrew their building and, in 1876, they relocated in the vacant Berry Street church building. (Rev Hugh Hanna and his congregation had moved from Berry Street to St Enoch's). In this same year, he married Sarah Rentoul – daughter of Rev John Rentoul (Ballycopeland, 1833–37, and Ballymoney, 1837–69) – and they had seven children. Rev Lynd played an active role in the anti-Home Rule movement and often spoke publicly at such rallies. He was elected Moderator of the General Assembly in 1888. He exercised an influence far beyond his May Street pulpit. Interestingly, his son Robert (1879–1949) held very different political views. Robert junior became a journalist and essayist in London, as well as a prominent member of the Gaelic League. He was also a fluent Gaelic speaker. In 1890, the degree of Doctor of Divinity was conferred upon Rev Lynd. Mrs Sarah Lynd died on 1 January 1898 and Dr Lynd died on 17 November 1906, aged seventy-three.

Reverend John Gailey

JOHN GAILEY was a native of Castlederg. He took his undergraduate course at Queen's College Galway and Belfast, graduating from the Royal University of Ireland in 1882. He studied Theology at 'Assembly's College' Belfast and was licensed by Donegal Presbytery on 3 June 1884. Gailey was ordained by Strabane Presbytery on 1 October 1884 in Second Ardstraw congregation. After fourteen years he left and was installed as minister of Ballysillan on 21 April 1898. He served here for almost twenty-three years. He resigned on 5 April 1921, and became Secretary of the Irish Temperance League (founded in September 1857). On 6 November he was installed as minister of Boyle congregation in Connaught Presbytery. He retired from active ministry on 30 April 1929 and died on 12 February 1932. His brother, Rev Andrew Gailey, was minister of Tullyallen (1893–1907) and Lucan (1907–39). His son, Rev Andrew John Gailey, was minister of Galway (1925–48), Deputy Clerk of Assembly (1948–62) and Clerk of Assembly (1962–3).

Street (from 1852), but had in fact originated as the third Secession cause in Belfast (in 1836) in Alfred Place. The second minister, Rev Edward Breakey (1845–49), died of typhus fever, which he contracted in the course of pastoral visitation. The congregation was briefly linked with Agnes Street (1926–38). Vibrant youth work continues with around 300 young people at various events each week. Membership currently stands at around 400 families.

benefactors of this congregation for many years. From the 1920s, many nautical furnishings and emblems were introduced to the church building, making it unique within the Presbyterian Church in Ireland. The ringing of a ship's bell still marks the commencement of Sunday evening worship. Family membership stands at just over 300 families today.

Whitehouse

was formed in 1866 to cater for new population expansion in this neighbourhood. On 29 July 1912, the Sunday School excursion train was attacked by a Roman Catholic mob in Castledawson. Rev Robert Barron (1875–1925), appealed for mercy when those responsible were tried in Londonderry – they were sentenced to

Ballysillan

was formed in 1838, following evangelistic work by Alexander Kerr, later appointed as missionary to India by the first General Assembly in 1840. The original church was opened on 27 October 1838, but the first three ministers served less than five years together. The longest serving minister was Rev William McCullagh (1850–87). The seventh minister, Rev John Gailey (1898–1921), resigned to become lecturer for the Irish Temperance League. Membership stands today at just over 500 families.

Sinclair Seamen's

was founded in 1857, but originated in the work of the Belfast Seamen's Friend Society which had operated from Pilot Street in the port district since 1832. The congregational name honours Mr John Sinclair, a generous supporter of the Seamen's Friend Society, who died in 1856. Members of the Sinclair family were the main

three months imprisonment with hard labour. The church building was destroyed in an arson attack on 2 August 2002 and a new church, retaining the frontage of the old, was opened on 19 February 2005. Membership is increasing and stands today at around 250 families. The congregation is planning to integrate with Duncairn and St Enoch's in the near future.

Crumlin Road

was formed in 1867 and initially met in the dining room of a local linen mill. A new church was opened in 1872 but this building was destroyed in an air raid on the evening of 15 April 1941. The congregation met in Edenderry School for thirteen years before the present building was opened. From the 1940s, the minister also acted as part-time Presbyterian Chaplain in the nearby Crumlin Road prison. Revs William Harrison, William Haslett, and William Vance served in this capacity until prison chaplaincy became a full-time post. Membership today stands at under 300 families.

Newington

was formed in 1875 as a result of initial mission work in this area by members of Rosemary Street. The second minister, Rev Thomas Johnstone (1910–43), was Moderator of the General Assembly in 1934. His criticism of the Northern Ireland Judiciary in respect of alcohol temperance led to him being charged with contempt of court and fined £100. Rev Johnstone refused to pay and was

Thomas Sinclair

THOMAS SINCLAIR senior was an elder in Duncairn. He served as one of two elders on the interim Kirk Session of the new 'Mariners' Church' under the leadership of Rev William Irvine (1854–61). Thomas' brother, John, died on 17 January 1856 at the comparatively young age of forty-seven. He had largely paid for the building of Conlig Presbyterian Church (opened in 1848). The brothers were prosperous business partners who founded their own trading company, J & T Sinclair, in 1834. The Sinclair family gave a large donation to build a seamen's church as a memorial to the late John Sinclair. The building was designed by the renowned architect Charles Lanyon and was opened on 7 October 1857. Thomas Sinclair acted as Treasurer of the new congregation until his death in 1867.

Thomas Sinclair junior was born in Belfast on 23 September 1838. He was educated at the Royal Belfast Academical Institution and Queen's College, Belfast. Sinclair graduated from the latter with a first class honours degree in Mathematics and a gold medal in 1856. He was awarded a Masters degree and another gold medal in 1859. He also was an elder in Duncairn and succeeded his father as Treasurer of Sinclair Seamen's congregation, a position he held for forty-seven years until his death in 1914. Interestingly, Sir Thomas Sinclair was a member of two congregations at the same time, Duncairn and Sinclair Seamen's, contrary to church law! Thomas Sinclair achieved fame in the campaign against Home Rule and is credited with composing the Ulster Covenant, which was signed by 237,368 Ulstermen on 28 September 1912. The organ in Sinclair Seamen's church was installed in 1924 by the Sinclair family as a memorial to Sir Thomas Sinclair, and a memorial tablet was also erected in the Assembly Hall in Belfast.

THE HIBERNIAN OUTRAGE.

ATTACK ON PROTESTANT CHILDREN.

Seizure of the Union Jack.

STATEMENT BY MR. BIRRELL.

In the House of Commons yesterday, Mr. J. GORDON asked the Chief Secretary whether he had any information with regard to the attack by Nationalists on Protestant school children attending the fête at Castledawson on 1st July; whether any children were injured,

Sectarian Strife

THE SUNDAY SCHOOL from Whitehouse Presbyterian Church set out on their annual excursion on Saturday 29 June 1912 to spend a day in Castledawson in County Londonderry. The party had its own band and the children carried flags and banners bearing Scripture texts. That evening, as they made their way to the train station, they met a parade of the Ancient Order of Hibernians. Provoked by the sight of Union Jack flags, the Hibernians attacked the Sunday School party. Some people were wounded and the children were terrified. Local Protestants intervened and more serious fighting ensued.

At the Sunday service in Whitehouse the following morning, Rev Barron urged his congregation not to talk about this incident in order to preserve community relations, but the newspapers published full details. Reprisals were taken against Roman Catholics, most notably in the Belfast shipyards. Roman Catholic workers were beaten and chased from the shipyards. Tension mounted throughout that summer and erupted on 14 September at a Celtic-Linfield football match (at Celtic Park), when serious fighting resulted in sixty casualties requiring treatment at the Royal Victoria Hospital.

Woodvale

was founded in 1895 with forty-three communicants. Its first minister, Rev John Milliken, was installed on 19 May 1896. The present church building, with seating for 1,000 people, was opened on 8 October 1899. The congregation grew quickly, as it was situated in a rapidly expanding housing area. A clock was added to the church steeple in 1949 as a memorial to those from this district who had died in the Second World War. Dorothy Shannon, who served as a Deaconess and later as a PCI missionary in India, was brought up in this congregation. Membership rose to a peak of 1,250 families in the 1950s and 1960s, and now totals 360 families.

prepared to serve a prison sentence but his fine was paid anonymously. The church was destroyed in an air raid in 1941, but was rebuilt upon the same site. Membership stands at about 300 families today.

Fortwilliam Park

was founded in 1885 to cater for the expanding Belfast population, with new housing following the development of the Antrim Road in 1830. The third minister, Rev James Breakey (1942–60), was elected Moderator of the General Assembly in 1955; he also served for many years as Convenor of the Foreign Mission in difficult post war circumstances. His successor, Rev John Thompson (1961–76), was later Professor of Systematic Theology in Union College, Belfast, and Moderator of the General Assembly in 1986. Macrory Memorial, which had been founded in 1895, was amalgamated with this congregation on 1 July 2005. Membership stands at 150 families today.

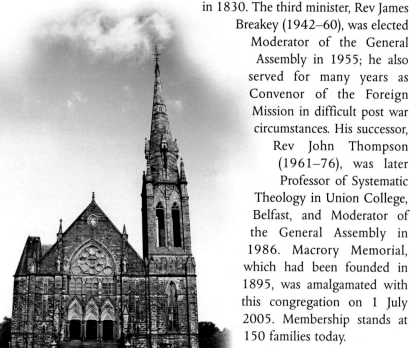

The 20th Century

Ten congregations within the North Belfast Presbytery were formed during the 20th century. Two of these, Ballyhenry and Rosemary, were 'ported' from older inner city congregations. Four church buildings in this district were completely destroyed in German air raids in 1941: Crumlin Road, Clifton Street, Newington and

York Street. Castleton was severely damaged, and the spire was never replaced. Unsurprisingly, most of these younger congregations represent further urban development as greater Belfast continued to expand.

Oldpark

was formed in December 1901. The first minister, Rev William McCoach, was installed in May 1902 and ministered here until his death in 1933 while attending the General Assembly. The current church, on the Cliftonville Road, was opened on 30 October 1904. It was during the ministry of Rev James Dunlop (1933–73) that this congregation reached its zenith. Over 1,100 families were in membership and the Sunday School catered for 680 children with ninety teachers. Rev Dunlop was elected Moderator of the General Assembly in 1964, an honour also bestowed upon his son, Rev Alistair Dunlop, in 2001. This locality has changed dramatically as

a result of sectarian strife and membership today stands at just over 100 families. The future of this congregation remains uncertain.

Contempt of Court

REV THOMAS JOHNSTONE was minister of Newington congregation (1910–43) and Convenor of the General Assembly's Temperance Committee for twelve years (1925–37). He was elected Moderator of the General Assembly in 1934. He will forever be remembered as the Presbyterian minister who was fined for contempt of court for comments he made in the General Assembly in 1934.

In presenting the Temperance Report to the Assembly on 9 June 1934, Rev Johnstone criticised the action of the Recorder in granting a Retail Spirit Licence for premises in Donegall Road, Belfast in contravention of a 1923 Act, which only allowed such a licence if the population of the town had increased by 25%. Rev Johnstone was examined by Lord Justice Best in the King's Bench Divisional Court and found 'guilty of gross Contempt of Court'. He was fined £100 and ordered to be detained and, if necessary lodged in Crumlin Road Jail until payment of the fine. Rev Johnstone was granted an extension of time to attend his son's ordination and marriage in the following week, but warned that he should then answer to the Court. Rev Johnstone declared that he would not pay the fine and that he was quite prepared to go to jail. Before his resolve could be tested, the authorities announced that the fine had been paid anonymously – the name of the benefactor has never been known. A special meeting of the General Assembly took place on 12 October and gave Rev Johnstone its full support. Johnstone was adamant that neither he nor any of his friends paid up. He hinted that perhaps the Authorities themselves paid the fine in order to restore public calm or perhaps the liquor people paid it to prevent any further publicity against their trade or his 'martyrdom'.

Communion Controversy

A CONTROVERSY STARTED in the General Assembly in 1875 when several ministers spoke in favour of using 'unfermented wine' at Communion services. The Assembly voted by 301 to twenty to maintain the custom of using fermented wine. The controversy grew and caused problems in several congregations including St Enoch's. In 1896, during the ministry of Rev Charles Davey (1892–1900), the Kirk Session were asked to provide a second table with unfermented wine for those who had scruples about taking fermented wine.

Rev Charles Davey

For many years thereafter it was the practice in St. Enoch's to provide two tables at a Communion service. There were not actually two physical tables in use; rather the same table was used on two occasions during Communion services. Those desiring fermented wine were served before the sermon and those who desired unfermented wine were served after the sermon. While such a compromise enabled the congregation to function with each communicant following the scruples of their own conscience, it should be noted that there is no historical or liturgical precedent for such a practice. This was a pragmatic decision taken in the interests of preserving congregational peace.

In 1905, as an indication of changing perceptions, the General Assembly rescinded its decision of 1875, and advocated the use of unfermented wine at Communion services.

Glengormley

originated from work undertaken in this neighbourhood during the 1880s by Rev Robert Barron of Whitehouse. A Sunday School and evening services were commenced but it was not until 5 June 1936 that a new congregation was established under the leadership of Rev Dr John Bain. The current church was opened on 17 November 1956. Dunlop Memorial was amalgamated with Glengormley on 1 September 1999. Membership in Glengormley reached a peak in the early 1970s with 1,000 families, current membership is about 550 families.

Seaview

was formed in 1936 amidst a new housing development in the Shore Road which had grown in the 1920s. Mr Kyle Alexander, a ministerial student, was appointed to this work and was ordained as first minister of the new congregation on 20 April 1939. The current church building was opened on 5 October 1940. Congregational strength reached a peak in the early 1970s with over 700 families in membership. The area has experienced some redevelopment and membership currently stands at about 300 families.

Alexandra

was formed on 1 January 1942 as a result of an amalgamation of York Street (founded in 1839) and Castleton (founded in 1896).

Reverend James Dunlop

JAMES DUNLOP was born on 6 August 1906. A native of Ballymena, he was raised within the Wellington Street congregation. He was educated at the Model School, Ballymena, Ballymena Academy and Trinity College, Dublin, where he graduated BA in 1929 with first class honours. His theological education was undertaken at Magee College, Londonderry (1929–30), Princeton Seminary (1930–31) and 'Assembly's College', Belfast (1931–32). He served as licentiate in the Church Extension charge in Greenisland and was ordained and installed in Oldpark congregation on 30 November 1933. He spent his entire ministry here and built the congregation up through his exceptional pulpit ministry.

Rev Dunlop was elected Moderator of the General Assembly in 1964. He was a joint-convenor of PCI Foreign Mission (1956–67), an occasional speaker at the Keswick Convention and Chairman of the Portstewart Convention (1957–77). Dr Dunlop retired on 31 August 1973 and died on 8 June 1980. His son, Rev Alistair Dunlop was minister in First Portglenone (1973–83) and Knock (from 1983). He followed his father as Moderator of the General Assembly in 2001. His grandson, also Alistair, has entered the ministry of the Presbyterian Church in Ireland as well, being licensed in 2006 by Templepatrick Presbytery in the congregation of First Antrim.

The York Street church was destroyed in an air raid on 15 April 1941 and the new amalgamated congregation met in the Castleton building. The first minister of the united church was Rev Rupert Gibson (1941–54) who was elected Moderator of the General Assembly in 1971. Mrs Charlotte Heathwood (née Kirkwood) served as organist for an incredible seventy-four years, from 1906–80. Congregational membership currently stands at 350 families.

Mrs Heathwood

Ballygomartin

was established under the labours of Rev Robert Elliott (retired from Duneane) who worked in the new housing area of Upper Ballygomartin in the late 1940s. A church was opened on 4 September 1954, being largely paid for from War Damage compensation from the old Clifton Street building, which had been destroyed by German bombs on 15 April 1941. The congregation was established under the ministry of Rev Robert Logue (1955–85). Membership totals almost 250 families today.

Rosemary

was formed on 1 October 1941 as a result of a union of Rosemary Street and Ekenhead. Rosemary Street had been founded in 1722, but the church building was destroyed by German bombs on the evening of 4 May 1941. The Ekenhead congregation had been founded in 1867, on a site at the corner of Frederick Street and North Queen Street. The church halls are known as the 'Ekenhead Halls' to mark the earlier link. Rev John Dunlop (1978–2004) had a significant ministry here and in the wider church. He was elected Moderator of the General Assembly in 1992. Membership totals just over 400 families today.

Rathcoole

was formed in the 1950s in a new housing development of 3,000 homes between Whitehouse and Glengormley. Rev William Davison was installed as the first minister of the new cause by the Church Extension Committee on 15 April 1955. Within a year there were two Sunday morning services, an evening service and thriving youth activities. Rev Robert Allen served as minister here for thirty-three years (1968–2001). Membership today totals 400 families.

Abbot's Cross

grew from services held in a temporary hall here in 1952. Harry Magill was ordained as the first minister on 22 January 1953 and served for sixteen years. The new church building opened on 9 March 1957 and a hall was added in 1964. Full congregational status was attained on 17 January 1960. The second minister, Rev William Fleming (1969–93), was elected Moderator of the General Assembly in 1987. Membership today stands at about 350 families.

Ballyhenry

was formed in 1972, when the inner urban congregation of Cliftonville 'ported' to the Ballyhenry area. Cliftonville had originally been formed in Donegall Street in 1792 and moved to Cliftonville in 1886. Services commenced on the Ballyhenry site on 5 March 1972, and full congregational status was attained in February 1975. Membership stands at just over 200 families today.

Immanuel

was formed on 14 October 1971 as a result of a union between Agnes Street (founded in 1871) and Bethany (founded in 1893). Rev John Girvan, minister of Bethany, was installed as first minister of the united congregation. Re-development has irreparably changed the locality, where Agnes Street and Bethany had a joint membership of 1,755 families in 1959. Today, membership of Immanuel amounts to 250 families. Plans are progressing to demolish the current church and open a new 350 seat church on this site.

TO THE GLORY OF GOD
AND IN GRATEFUL REMEMBRANCE OF
MARGARET MAGILL,
WHO FOUNDED IN THIS CHURCH IN THE YEAR 1889,
THE FIRST CHRISTIAN ENDEAVOUR SOCIETY
IN IRELAND.

ERECTED BY THE IRISH CHRISTIAN ENDEAVOUR UNION.
JUBILEE YEAR 1939.

Margaret Magill

MARGARET MAGILL was a young working class woman who was converted in Agnes Street in the late 1880s. She became a Sunday School teacher in that congregation, with responsibility for a class of girls who met under the gallery in the main church building. Margaret used innovative and successful methods of teaching, involving the girls themselves in the learning process.

In July 1889, a class of boys was amalgamated with the girls and a society was formed with an organising committee. Shortly afterwards, Margaret Magill investigated the aims and methods of the Christian Endeavour (CE) movement which had originated in Williston Congregational Church in Portland, Maine in February 1881. She was excited by the CE commitment to spiritual growth and mutual encouragement. As a result of her efforts, on 30 September 1889, the Agnes Street Young People's Society of Christian Endeavour was formally registered as No. 39 in Britain.

While the Christian Endeavour movement spread rapidly in Ireland, it is a fact that Margaret Magill remained resolutely in the background. She never held any position on a CE Council and was persuaded on only two occasions to appear in public in connection with the organisation.

Abbey Monkstown

attained full congregational status in February 1974. Work had commenced here with Rev Alexander Cromie in 1966. A temporary hall was opened for worship on 19 October 1968. An interesting plan to share this new initiative equally with the Methodist Church and the Church of Ireland did not progress and the present church building was opened on 28 November 1970. Rev Ernest Brown (1971–86) built up this cause. Membership stands today at just over 500 families.

New Mossley

is the youngest congregation in North Belfast Presbytery. The cause here started on 30 November 1980 in a temporary building under the leadership of a lay agent, Mr Willard Kelly. Rev William Harshaw developed the work for twelve years (1981–93), and the current church building opened in 1983. Full congregational status was gained in November 2005. The church is situated in one of the most deprived Housing Executive estates in the province and membership today stands at just over ninety families.

Conclusion

The Presbytery of North Belfast has been in decline since its formation in 1963. The table below indicates that the number of communicants has shrunk by 54% over a forty-year period. There are probably several reasons for this, including the 'greening' of much of this sector of the city, the population move to other locations and general secularisation.

YEAR	CONGREGATIONS	FAMILIES	COMMUNICANTS ON ROLL	ATTENDING COMMUNICANTS
1963	26	18,325	10,203	7,882
1973	25	16,217	8,416	6,432
1983	26	13,412	7,198	5,518
1993	25	11,191	5,731	4,488
2003	24	8,489	4,700	3,269

The old strength of the central congregations has passed as a result of extensive housing re-development in the latter half of the 20th century. Population density in these inner areas has been reduced and the traditional church is proving less attractive to new generations of people. Interestingly, the two strongest congregations within the Presbytery are Carnmoney and Whiteabbey where young professional families are attracted to fresh worship patterns. Many North Belfast congregations face an uncertain future and are struggling to cope with change.

Introduction

The Presbytery of South Belfast consists of nineteen congregations and was created in 1963. It is the smallest of the three Belfast Presbyteries, with 3,500 communicants (East Belfast has almost 8,000 communicants and North Belfast has just over 4,500 communicants). The majority of the congregations in this Presbytery originated in the 19th century, as Belfast expanded into previously green fields to the west and south of the early town centre.

South Belfast Presbytery

The 17th Century

Dunmurry is the only congregation in the entire South Belfast Presbytery which originated before the 19th century. Dunmurry was a separate village in the 17th century. The lack of congregations is not surprising when it is remembered that the town of Belfast boasted only five streets in the early 1600s – about 500 inhabitants in a thatched hamlet.

The Shankill Road

Dunmurry

was formed some time between 1676 and 1683. The most famous minister in the history of this congregation was Rev Henry Montgomery (1809–65). He was leader of the Non-subscribers and, in 1829, he and many members of the congregation seceded from the Synod of Ulster. A new congregation of Dunmurry was organised in 1860. Rev Robert Davey (1902–45) greatly strengthened the congregation. His two sons, John and Ray, became Presbyterian ministers and his daughter Beth was a missionary in Gujarat. Congregational membership currently stands at just over 250 families.

152

The 18th Century

There was no congregation formed in the South Belfast Presbytery area during the 18th century. Shortly before 1761, the first Seceder (Anti-Burgher) congregation in Belfast was formed. Initially, the people met in a house in the vicinity of the Old Lodge Road, then, from 1782, they moved into new premises in Berry Street. In 1839, the congregation moved into a new church in Linenhall Street and again, in 1887, to the Crescent in the University area of the city. The congregation was formally joined with Fitzroy on 1st January 1976.

The 19th Century

This century witnessed the phenomenal growth of Belfast and an accompanying growth in Presbyterian congregations. A total of eighteen Presbyterian churches were formed within South Belfast Presbytery. Of these, twelve are still operating. The congregations of College Square, Albert Street, Elmwood, Donegall Pass, Fountainville and Broadway were all formed during the

Reverend Ray Davey

ROBERT RAYMOND DAVEY was born into an Irish Presbyterian ministerial family. His father Robert was minister in Dunmurry from 1902–45. His brother John was a missionary in India (1932–63), minister of Aghadowey (1963–72) and Moderator of the General Assembly in 1962. In 1940, Ray Davey resigned as assistant in First Bangor to become a field worker with the YMCA. He helped establish a centre in Tobruk to help cater for the physical and spiritual needs of those involved in the desert warfare. In 1942, he was captured by German forces and held as a prisoner of war near Dresden. After the War, in 1946, he was appointed Presbyterian Dean of Residence in Queen's University, Belfast. Through his experiences in working among students, Ray Davey caught a vision of a new society in Ireland characterised by love and brotherhood. He gave expression to his vision by acting as part-time leader in the new Corrymeela Centre, opened in Ballycastle in 1965. A 'Corrymeela Community' developed and Ray Davey pioneered cross-community activities at the Centre. From 1974 until his retirement in 1980, Ray Davey was the full-time leader and public face of Corrymeela. The Centre has attracted world-wide fame with a ministry of cross-community contact and reconciliation. In recognition of his achievements, Rev Ray Davey has received honorary degrees from the University of Ulster, Queen's University, Belfast, the National University of Ireland, Maynooth, and the Presbyterian Theological Faculty, Ireland.

19th century but were closed in the 20th century.

When Queen Victoria visited Belfast in 1849, she was taken to the new Queen's College (now Queen's University), which was built at what was then the outer limits of the town. It was in the later years of the 19th century that the city extended into the areas between the radiating roads of Stranmillis, Malone and Lisburn. Fisherwick moved from its original location in Fisherwick Place to its current location on the Malone Road in 1901.

Fitzroy

originated in 1813 as the second Seceder cause in Belfast. The people worshipped for seven years without a settled minister and in several locations. In 1820, they called Rev John Edgar (1820–48) and built their first church in Alfred Place. In 1837, the congregation moved to a larger building in Alfred Street. They moved again, in 1874, to the present buildings in University Street. Remarkably, only six ministers have led this congregation over the past 190 years. Donegall Pass (founded in 1869) was joined with Fitzroy in 1973, and Crescent congregation (founded in 1769) was similarly joined in 1976. Rev Ken Newell was installed here on 15 January 1976. His ministry has been marked by the distinctive role he has played in our divided society. Family membership stands at 230 today.

Fisherwick

originated in Fisherwick Place, on the site of Church House. The original church was opened on 23 September 1827. The first minister, Rev James Morgan (1828–73), did much to establish the cause of Foreign Mission within Irish Presbyterianism. The congregation moved to its present location on 29 April 1901. Four Fisherwick ministers have served as Moderator of the General Assembly: Morgan in 1846, Williamson in 1896, Waddell in 1937 and Withers in 1968. Today, the congregation actively engages with a large and migrant student population in the area. Membership stands at about 450 families.

Reverend John Edgar

JOHN EDGAR's birth date is uncertain – he was not sure himself! It is known that he was held as a child in the arms of an uncle who watched the battle of Ballynahinch in 1798. His father, Rev Samuel Edgar, was Secession minister in Ballynahinch (1793–1826) and the Seceder Professor of Divinity in the Belfast Institution (1815–26). Samuel was followed by his son David in Ballynahinch, and by his son John in the Belfast Institution. Both boys were taught in their father's Academy in Ballynahinch. On 14 November 1820, John Edgar was ordained in the recently formed second Secession congregation in Belfast. His congregation moved to a new building in Alfred Place in 1821, then to larger premises in Alfred Street. In addition to his growing congregation, John Edgar concentrated his efforts to establishing the Temperance Movement (from 1829) and famine relief in Connaught (from 1846). He was elected Moderator of the General Assembly in 1842. After resigning from congregational duties in 1848, John Edgar devoted his free time to mission work in the South and West of Ireland, as well as Church Extension work in Belfast. He died on 26 August 1866 and his congregation moved into their current church in University Street in 1874.

Reverend Wylie Blue

REV WYLIE BLUE was a preacher of unusual power and originality. He exercised a long and distinguished ministry in May Street from 1916-46. Alexander Wylie Blue was born on 11 May 1869 in Campletown, Argyllshire. He graduated from Glasgow University in 1894 and studied Theology at the United Presbyterian Theological College in Edinburgh. He served as minister in John Street, Glasgow (1900–05) and St. George's Sunderland (1905–16). During his thirty years as minister in Belfast, Wylie Blue gained a reputation for dramatic pulpit eloquence. He toured the United States and Canada in 1919–20 as part of the Ulster Delegation in opposition to Home Rule and also ministered in Australia for several months in 1932, 1946 and 1947. In appearance, his long hair was distinctive and seemed to add a certain prophetic quality to his preaching. Throughout his ministry, his power to re-create biblical scenes in the minds of his congregation was renowned. In preaching, he used his whole body, not just his voice. In 1939, he was awarded a Doctor of Divinity degree by the Presbyterian Theological Faculty, Ireland. Rev Wylie Blue retired on 6 May 1946 and died peacefully on 15 July 1956, at the age of eighty-seven.

154

May Street

was formed in 1829. The first minister, Rev Henry Cooke, preached here until his retirement in 1867. The second minister, Rev John

MacIntosh (1868–81), was American, a native of Philadelphia. The sixth minister, Scotsman Rev Wylie Blue (1916–46), was renowned for his pulpit eloquence. As a city centre congregation, May Street has suffered from population movement and the 'Troubles'. New efforts are underway in the early 21st century to revitalise it as an urban mission base in the heart of Belfast. Membership today stands at less than one hundred families.

Ballycairn

was founded in 1830 near Drumbo village. The first minister, Rev Adam Montgomery, ministered here for fifty-eight years. The current church was opened in 1926, during the ministry of Rev Samuel Clarke (1908–31). Rev William Latimer (1931–49) was a son of the Irish Presbyterian historian Rev WT Latimer. He was followed in 1949 by Rev Marshall McCreery who had been a missionary in Manchuria for twelve years. He retired on 31 August 1974. Membership has remained stable over the past fifty years at about 175 families.

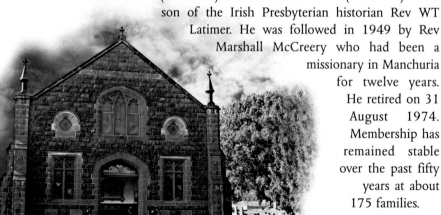

Malone

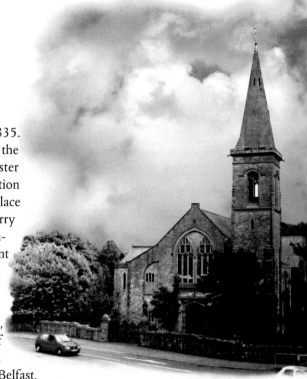

was established in 1835. At that time, it was the only Synod of Ulster Presbyterian congregation between Fisherwick Place and Lisburn (Dunmurry had joined the Non-subscribers). The current church was opened on 18 June 1899. The third minister, Rev James Haire (1912–19), became Professor of Systematic Theology in 'Assembly's College', Belfast, and remained a member of the congregation. He was elected Moderator of the General Assembly in 1939. Rev Haire was succeeded by Rev James Gilbert Paton (1920–36), who served as Moderator of the General Assembly in 1931. New church halls – known as the 'Paton Memorial Halls' – were opened in September 1946. Membership currently stands at about 350 families.

Townsend Street

was founded in 1833 on a site at what was then the periphery of Belfast (as its name suggests). The original church was officially opened on 26 April 1835. The congregation was an offshoot from Fisherwick Place (which had opened in 1828). The current building, with a seating capacity of 1,400, was opened on 18 October 1878 during the ministry of Rev William Johnston. He had the distinction of being elected Moderator of the General Assembly for two successive years, 1872 and 1873. The Townsend Street area has undergone radical development over the past thirty years and the West Link carriageway cuts through the parish area. Membership currently totals about 160 families.

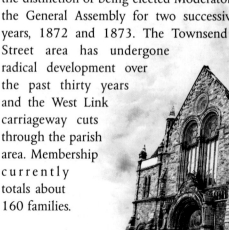

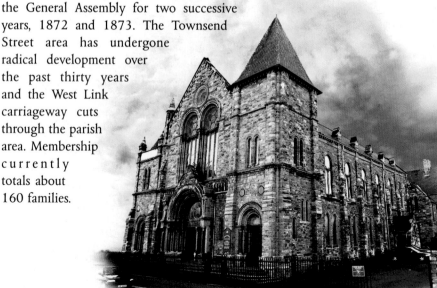

Reverend William Johnston

WILLIAM JOHNSTON was born on 2 January 1818, the eldest of five children of Rev John Johnston of Tullylish (1811–62). He served as minister in Berry Street from 17 May 1842 until his installation as the third minister of Townsend Street on 21 September 1847. William Johnston served his congregation for forty-five years. He exhibited enormous energy in various ministries. For example, he worked for twenty-seven years as the first Honorary Secretary of the Presbyterian Orphan Society, which was founded in 1866. He also managed sixteen National Schools.

William Johnston was elected Moderator of the General Assembly in 1872, and again in 1873, following his father who had been Moderator in 1858. In 1873, he was instrumental in forming a Society for the Orphans of Presbyterian Ministers and Missionaries. William Johnston was the acknowledged leader of the General Assembly in the 1870s, and the congregation of Townsend Street grew very significantly under his ministry; so much so that the church was rebuilt and opened on 13 October 1878. He devoted the later years of his ministry to the task of establishing new congregations in Belfast, retired from active duty on 6 September 1892, and died on 10 January 1894.

Great Victoria Street

originated in 1858 out of work by the Town Mission in the Sandy Row district. The current building was opened on 13 January 1861. An amazing 769 members of this congregation served in the Forces during World War I. Of these, 122 died on active service. Membership reached a peak of more than 1,400 families in the 1920s. The interior of the church was re-designed following serious fire damage on 18 March 1957. An even more radical restructuring

took place in 1997–8 to produce a dual-purpose building. Membership stands today at about 180 families.

Berry Street

originated in 1869 with the work of the Town Mission in Academy Street. During the ministry of Rev Robert Lynd (1875–82) the congregation expanded beyond the limits of their building in Academy Street. The current church building in Berry Street was occupied in 1876 when Rev Hugh Hanna's congregation moved to St Enoch's. The fourth minister, Rev James Crawford (1882–1902), played a leading role in the 'Instrumental Music' controversy, arguing against new innovations. Rev Glyn Owen exercised a notable ministry here, especially among students before moving to Westminster Chapel in London. This inner city congregation has dwindled to less than twenty families in recent years and has been cared for by Richview's minister.

Windsor

was founded in 1887. A certain Mr Robert McQuiston of Colinview Terrace (now Tates Avenue), who died in 1882, left £7,000 for the construction of a new church in his neighbourhood. Belfast was expanding rapidly at that time and the new congregation was much needed. The second minister, Rev John Irwin (1899–1924), was Moderator of the General Assembly in 1918. His successor, Rev William Corkey (1924–49), also served as Moderator of the General Assembly (in 1933). Dr Corkey was deeply involved in Church Extension, Youth Work and the

Presbyterian Orphan Society. Membership of Windsor congregation currently stands at about 200 families.

Richview

was originally known as 'Donegall Road'. It was formed in 1895 as a result of mission work undertaken by members of Elmwood. Under the energetic ministry of Rev John McIlrath (1895–1920), membership reached 500 families by 1912. The neighbouring Fountainville church building was destroyed by a fire on 1 February 1920 and thereafter the two congregations united under the name 'Richview'. Membership exceeded 1,400 families in the late 1950s but has since fallen to around 300 families.

Nelson Memorial

was founded in 1896 as an extension church in the upper Shankill area. The church building was provided by Miss Mary Nelson in memory of her brother, Rev Isaac Nelson, who had died in 1888. The church was built upon her own land and was officially opened on 12 May 1896. During the ministry of Rev Robert Milford (1929–74), an elder of the congregation was honoured by the opening of The Henry Taggart Memorial Hall in New Barnsley. Unfortunately, this outreach venture did not survive the 'Troubles' and subsequent population shift. Membership currently stands at about 120 families.

The 20th century

Eight new congregations were formed in the South Belfast Presbytery during the 20th century and six of them are still operating. The relatively brief existence of Springfield Road (1957–70) and Suffolk (1961–94) bear testimony to the demographic changes in some localities as a direct result of serious civil strife. It is a salutary lesson to note that every congregation within this Presbytery, with the exception of Ballycain, has experienced a drop in family membership over the latter half of the 20th century.

Musical Controversy

REV JOHN CRAWFORD was minister in Berry Street for twenty years (1882–1902). He played a leading role in the 19th century 'music controversy' in Irish Presbyterianism. The controversy started in the General Assembly in 1868, when it was reported disapprovingly that the congregation of Enniskillen had recently introduced a harmonium in Sunday Services. A debate and pamphlet war raged within the Presbyterian Church for the next twenty-four years. Two groups emerged: the 'Purity Party', which resisted all musical instruments and innovation, and a 'Liberty Party', which welcomed musical accompaniment and experimentation in worship.

Rev Crawford supported the Purity Party. Although neither side could deliver a 'knockout blow' to the other, change proved irresistible. Most congregations used the *Scottish Psalter* of 1650 in their worship and, in 1880, an Irish *Revised Psalter* was published. An indication of Presbyterian resistance to change is that as late as 1917 at least sixty congregations were still using the 1650 *Psalter*! Fractious debates on musical instruments in the General Assembly came to a head in 1885, when the anti-instrumentalists withdrew to the accompaniment of hisses and laughter to hold their own protest meeting.

In 1892, the General Assembly voted to 'pass from the question' and, officially, there the matter ended. Thereafter, congregations have decided what was right for their situation and many installed organs as memorials to members who had died in the First World War.

Reverend Isaac Nelson

ISAAC NELSON was born in 1809 in Belfast. His father was a grocer in Barrack Street. Isaac served as assistant classical master in the Belfast Academical Institution for nine years before entering the Presbyterian ministry. He was ordained on 27 August 1837 in First Comber. On 31 March 1842, he was installed as minister in Donegall Street (Cliftonville). Rev Nelson had a flair for languages with expertise in French, German, Greek and Hebrew. He was particularly hostile to the 'enthusiasm' displayed in the 1859 Revival. When Professor Gibson published his supportive 'The Year of Grace', Nelson responded with a series of twelve tracts collected under the title 'The Year of Delusion'. He was regarded by some of his contemporaries as a man suffering personal bitterness against the Presbyterian Church in Ireland because he had been overlooked in the appointment of a Professor of Greek in the Belfast College. Whatever the truth of that suspicion, Nelson resigned from his congregation in 1880 to become a Home Rule Member of Parliament for County Mayo. He held his seat for five years. Isaac Nelson returned to Belfast where he died on 8th March 1888. He was buried in Shankill graveyard and his sister contributed to the founding of Nelson Memorial congregation in his memory.

Ulsterville

was a product of planning by the Belfast Church Extension Committee, which secured a site at the foot of Tate's Avenue and Donnybrook Street in 1894. The earliest meetings were conducted in a hall under the name of 'Lower Windsor' but the congregation was known as 'Ulsterville' from 1902. The first minister was Rev Thomas Rodgers (1902–29). The present church on the Lisburn Road was opened on 5 January 1924. Membership currently stands at about 130 families.

Shankill Road Mission

was started in 1898, when Albert Street congregation built the 'Albert Hall' for mission work on the Shankill Road area. The minister, Rev Henry Montgomery, resigned from his congregation in 1902 to work in this mission. On 10 July 1910, the mission was designated a Presbyterian congregation. Its minister was empowered to operate irrespective of a parish boundary, and the successive ministers were selected by the Belfast Presbytery. Rev

Montgomery was elected Moderator of the General Assembly in 1912. His ministry flourished until his retirement in 1924. The fourth minister was Rev William Patterson Hall (1939–48), who had earlier been a singing evangelist with the Irish Mission. Membership of the Shankill Mission today numbers about one hundred families.

Reverend Henry Montgomery

DR HENRY MONTGOMERY was a native of Bangor, County Down. He was ordained on 15 August 1882 in Albert Street, Belfast. The congregation opened mission buildings, called the Albert Hall, on the Shankill Road, in 1898. Rev Montgomery resigned on 2 September 1902, in order to devote all of his time to work in the Albert Hall under the care of the Church Extension Committee of the Belfast Presbytery. This new mission was given the status of a congregation on 10 July 1910 with the name, 'Shankill Road Mission'.

Henry Montgomery was elected Moderator of the General Assembly in 1912. He retired from his preaching and pastoral responsibilities on 1 April 1924, but continued to organise the social activities of the Mission until 1 January 1936. His funeral was one of the largest seen in the locality with the entire Shankill Road coming to a standstill to bid farewell to its own 'Dr Barnardo'.

McCracken Memorial

arose out of a meeting held in the old hall of St. John's Parish Church in 1930. A new Presbyterian congregation was recognised in 1932. The current church building was opened on 1 December 1934 and paid for out of the estate of Miss Mary McCracken of Omeath, Newry. A Church Hall was added in 1956 and named the Dowling Hall after the first minister Rev David Dowling (1932–57). Membership of McCracken stands at about 300 families today.

Lowe Memorial

originated on 14 March 1930, when services were first held in a wooden hall on this site. Full congregational status was gained on 13 October 1932. The church was named after Rev William Lowe, former Clerk of the General Assembly, who had died in March 1931. The first minister was Rev Alfred Martin (1935–72). He built up the congregation and was elected Moderator of the General Assembly in 1966. The congregation further developed under the outstanding teaching ministry of Rev Alan Flavelle (1972–86). The congregation came through an interesting but painful dispute over infant baptism in the early 1990s. Membership today stands at about 450 families.

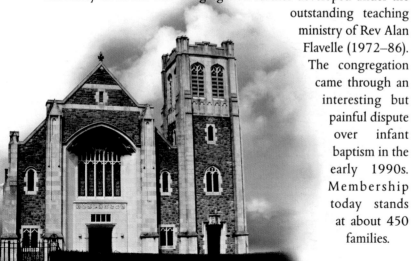

Where there's a Will?

On 23 November 1907, Miss Mary McCracken gave instructions for the preparation of her will and the disposal of her estate. She was suffering from cancer and subsequently died on 1 March 1908 at the age of sixty. The bulk of her estate was to be invested until such time as there were sufficient funds to build a church in memory of her parents. She gave instructions for the new church to be cited 'a decent distance from Fisherwick'. Her executors were to 'choose a lovely bright spot with the sun shining on it'. The will stipulated that the name of the new church was to be 'McCracken Memorial Church' and that this name should be carved in granite above the door. In order to ensure that this stipulation should be complied with, she gave instructions that if the name should ever be changed then the entire property would revert to ownership by the Methodist denomination.

Further unsavoury stipulations were made in Miss McCracken's will. She had an obvious umbrage against a family named Wylie for she stated: 'There are not any of the Wylie family or their relatives or connections to interfere or meddle in this church' otherwise again, the property would revert to the Methodists. Similarly she stipulated that the Wylie family were to be denied any memorial window or tablet in the new church. One wonders at the nature of the offence that produced such odium on the part of Mary McCracken.

A further clause in her will was to cause problems. She named the man she wished to be the first minister of the new church. By the time the church opened in 1932, this minister was sixty-five years old. He was offered £100 to renounce his 'claim' to be minister of McCracken, but refused unless he was paid £500. Having received this increased amount he later increased his demands but eventually settled for £500. One can say that this is certainly not the most edifying episode in Irish Presbyterian history.

Taughmonagh

started as a joint Presbyterian/Methodist cause in 1954. The overseeing congregations were McCracken Memorial Presbyterian and Osborne Park Methodist. A succession of six short ministries saw the cause slowly develop. Taughmonagh was briefly a Stated Supply with Suffolk congregation in the mid 1970s. Under the innovative and enthusiastic leadership of Rev Bill Moore (1981–2002) membership continued to rise and currently stands at around 150 families.

Kilmakee

originated from services held in a wooden hall in Seymour Hill, which commenced in June 1958. The current church building was opened on 19 September 1959. The cause was originally under the care of Dromore Presbytery and was added to South Belfast Presbytery on 1 January 1963. The new church gained full congregational status in February 1976 and continues to minister to the Seymour Hill and Conway estates on the outskirts of Dunmurry. The first female minister in Ireland, Rev Ruth Patterson, ministered here from 1977 until 1991. Congregational membership currently stands at 250 families.

West Kirk

was formed in 1971 by an amalgamation of the former congregations of Albert Street (originally formed as 'Falls Road' in 1852 and re-located in Albert Street in 1854) and Argyle Place (originally formed in 1853 in Alfred Place and re-located in Argyle Place in 1864) in the Argyle Place church. Rev Brian Moore

exercised a notable teaching ministry here from 1971 until 2001. Today, membership stands at around 400 families.

Conclusion

Recent statistics indicate that Presbyterianism in South Belfast is under severe pressure. As the table below illustrates, the total number of families has fallen by **67%** in the past forty years and the number of communicants by **62%**.

YEAR	CONGREGATIONS	FAMILIES	COMMUNICANTS ON ROLL	ATTENDING COMMUNICANTS
1963	25	14,122	9,670	7,298
1973	24	11,030	7,971	6,067
1983	21	7,760	5,518	4,268
1993	20	6,306	4,872	3,603
2003	19	4,662	3,678	2,498

Population movement within the Presbytery sector has changed the nature of South Belfast. Urban redevelopment has reduced the number people living nearer the city centre. As a direct consequence some city centre churches are struggling to survive. Several urban mission initiatives have been tried by some congregations in an attempt to provide a relevant ministry in the heart of the city. Other areas have become 'green' and this also has encroached on some congregations, for example Suffolk and Lowe Memorial. The Night Light ministry, around Shaftesbury Square, is an exciting initiative.

Introduction

The Presbytery of East Belfast is the largest of the three Belfast Presbyteries which were created in January 1963. The Presbytery area encompasses an extensive swathe of the city from the centre, extending outwards and east of the River Lagan, collared by Carryduff in the south, Granshaw and Dundonald to the east. It consists of twenty-seven congregations ranging in size from 140 families (Mersey Street) to over 900 (Knock). This Presbytery represents the most Presbyterian section of Belfast.

The 17th Century

It is not surprising to discover that only two congregations in this Presbytery, Dundonald and Castlereagh, trace their origins to the 17th century and that both were located at some distance from the infant settlement. Indeed, the town of Belfast did not expand eastwards across the River Lagan until the 19th century. Formerly, this land was part of the vast Castlereagh estates though the modern name Connswater harks back to the earlier owner, Conn O'Neil. Dundonald was originally linked with Holywood and, what is nowadays known as Castlereagh, was located at Knock and Breda.

Belfast from the
Castlereagh Hills
SCENIC IRELAND

Parliament Buildings, Stormont
GORDON GRAY

East Belfast Presbytery

Dundonald

is one of the oldest Presbyterian congregations in Ireland. Its first minister, Rev Thomas Peebles, had arrived in Ulster in 1642 as a Chaplain in Major-General Munro's army. He served as Clerk of the Army Presbytery. He was installed at Dundonald in 1645, and ministered also in Holywood. The second minister, Rev Gilbert Kennedy (1670–88), was a father-in-law of Rev William Tennant, founder of the Log College (forerunner of Princeton Seminary) in America. The current church was opened on 4 July 1839. Rev Ivan McKay (minister from 1996) was Moderator of the General Assembly in 2003. Congregational membership totals about 470 families today.

Castlereagh

was originally a joint charge with one congregation gathered at Knock and the other at Breda. Its first minister was Rev Hugh Wilson (1652–61 & 1663–91). His eventful ministry was marked by ejection by Bishop Taylor in 1661, arrest and imprisonment in relation to Blood's Plot in 1663. The two churches came together under the name 'Castlereagh' and built their distinctive church on the present site in the 1720s. The eighth minister, Rev John Given (1854–70),

Reverend William Tennent

WILLIAM TENNENT was born in Ireland in 1673. He graduated from Edinburgh University in 1695 and married Catherine Kennedy, daughter of Rev Gilbert Kennedy (Dundonald) on 15 May 1702. The first of their four sons, Gilbert, was born on 5 April 1703. William Tennent was ordained into ministry in the Church of Ireland in 1706. About 1718, the family emigrated from County Armagh to America and settled in Pennsylvania. William changed to the Presbyterian denomination and in 1726 he was settled as minister of a congregation at Neshaminy, about twenty miles north of Philadelphia.

It was here that he built a primitive academy for training young men for the ministry. This enterprise became known as 'The Log College'. Tennent's teaching was unashamedly evangelical and was instrumental in establishing Presbyterian ministries as far west as Ohio and southwards into Virginia and North Carolina.

The famous evangelist George Whitfield worked with William Tennent in 1739. He described the College as a rough room measuring about twenty feet in length. It was the first Presbyterian educational establishment above basic school level in America and led to the establishment of sixty-three similar institutions, the most famous descendent being Princeton Seminary. William Tennent retired from pastoral ministry in 1742, but continued to teach in his beloved College. He died on 6 May 1746.

Reverend James Little

JAMES LITTLE was born in Rathfriland and brought up in Glascar. After serving as Assistant in the Shankill Road Mission, he was ordained on 20 September 1900 in Dundrod, where he ministered for ten years. From 1910–15 he served as minister of Knoxland Church in Dunbarton before returning to Ireland. He was installed in Castlereagh on 4 November 1915 and served as minister there until his death on 31 March 1946.

Rev Little published several devotional books. In addition to his duties as minister in Castlereagh, he was elected Member of Parliament for County Down at Westminster in 1939, and served in this capacity until his death in 1946. Three other Irish Presbyterian ministers have been elected to Westminster: Rev Professor Richard Smyth (1874–78), Rev John Kinnear (1880–85), Rev Martin Smyth (1982–2005). In addition, during the Stormont regime, Rev Robert Moore served as Minister of Agriculture (1948–60) and Rev Professor Robert Corkey served as minister of Education (1943–44).

In 1944, the General Assembly decreed that no minister may hold any publicly paid job in addition to being an Irish Presbyterian minister. Rev James Little was succeeded as minister of Castlereagh by his son, Hastings, who had been Assistant to his father for some time. Rev Hastings Little was ordained in Castlereagh on 5 September 1946.

had previously served as a missionary to the Jews in Hamburg for seven years. He was subsequently appointed Professor of Oriental Languages and Hermeneutics in Magee College, Londonderry. The eleventh minister, Rev James Little (1915–46), also represented County Down as a Member of Parliament at Westminster from 1939–46. Congregational membership currently stands at just above 300 families.

The 18th Century

The population of Belfast rose from 8,500 in 1757 to 20,000 by 1800, but little of this was in East Belfast. The only congregation formed in the area was a Seceder cause at Gilnahirk. The location was probably chosen as a compromise for families 'poached' from the nearest Synod of Ulster congregations at Castlereagh and Dundonald.

Gilnahirk

was a Seceder cause that originated before 1759. In the course of that year, the people secured the site on which the current church was built, although the original building was not complete until 1787. At the time of the 1798 Rebellion, a majority of the congregation supported the cause of the United Irishmen. The minority separated to form Granshaw congregation. The current church was opened in 1840, during the ministry of Rev John Coulter (1820–60), Moderator of the General Assembly in 1851. Following the Second World War, housing development transformed this district. Membership currently stands at 400 families.

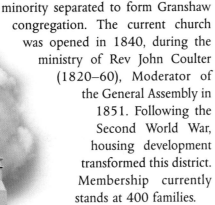

The 19th Century

In 1780, there were ninety-six dwellings in what is now 'East Belfast'. Industrial development of the Ballymacarrett sector commenced in 1786, with the establishment of a glass making factory and, by 1830, there were almost 800 dwellings. In 1843, the Long Bridge with its twenty-three spans was replaced by the new Queen's Bridge, and East Belfast grew rapidly. Corn mills, weaving, rope making and shipbuilding all added to the development and thirteen new Presbyterian congregations were formed to cater for the bludgeoning population. Of these, only one has since closed, Megain Memorial. This congregation originated in 1890 and was amalgamated with Mersey Street in 1991.

Granshaw

was a Burgher Seceder congregation that grew out of a dispute in Gilnahirk at the time of the 1798 Rebellion. A loyalist minority left and were seeking their own minister from 1800. The first minister, Rev James McCulloch, was called on 7 September 1802, but not installed until 9 August 1803. The current church building was

opened in May 1879, although an original plan for a west wing was never added. Membership was never large in Granshaw and at successive vacancies in the 20th century the suggestion of amalgamation with neighbouring congregations was floated – but consistently rejected. Membership now exceeds 300 families and has grown by over 60% in the last fifty years.

Ballymacarrett

was the first congregation to be formed in the County Down area of Belfast. The people came together under the leadership of Drs Henry Cooke (May Street) and James Morgan (Fisherwick); the building was opened in 1837. The first two ministers each served as Moderator of the General Assembly: Rev John Meneely (1838–81) in 1876, and Rev William McKean (1881–1917) in 1906. The church was renovated and partially reconstructed in 1898. The fifth minister, Rev William Thompson (1939–63), left to become Director of the Samaritans. From 1969, civil disturbances adversely affected this locality and the Army occupied the congregation's former school property from September 1969 for three years. Membership stands at just under 300 families today.

Carryduff

was formed in 1840 and the church was opened in 1841. The fourth minister, Rev Samuel Wilson (1903–26), presented new oil lamps to the

congregation and these lamps still form part of the church furnishings. Rev Thomas Stuart ministered here between 1926 and 1935. The church hall bears his name. His father, four brothers and his son were all Presbyterian ministers! The population of the Carryduff area has risen from 200 to 4,000 in the past fifty years and congregational membership has also risen by 33% in the same period to stand at about 450 families today.

Newtownbreda

arose out of evangelistic work begun by students for the Presbyterian ministry in this locality in 1840. The first minister was Rev Andrew Crawford (1844–61). He had been involved in the preliminary work. This congregation was one of the first to introduce music to Sunday Services and so figured prominently in the controversy of 1868–74. The present church building, with its distinctive spire, was opened on 13 March 1892. Membership increased dramatically in the 1950s as a result of new housing and a second Sunday morning service was introduced in 1957. There are currently about 550 families in membership.

Belmont

arose out of meetings organised in this area by Ballymacarrett. The church was designed by WJ Barre (who also designed the Albert Clock) on a site donated by Liberal MP, Sir Thomas McClure. It was opened on 26 January 1862. The first minister, Rev John Moran (1862–80), was responsible for the Irish revision of the metrical Psalms in 1880. Rev John MacDermott (1880–1920) was elected Moderator of the General Assembly in 1903. The Right Honourable Viscount Craigavon, first Prime Minister of Northern Ireland, was a member of Belmont. Membership stands at just over 700 families today.

Mountpottinger

grew out of concerns expressed by Rev Meneely, minister of Ballymacarrett. This new congregation, originally known as

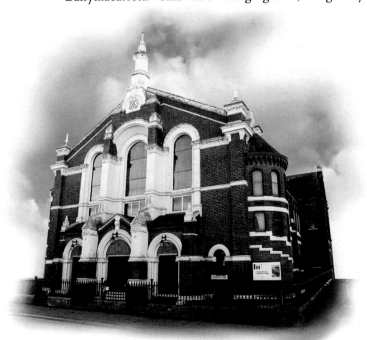

William McFadzean VC

BILLY McFADZEAN was a member of Newtownbreda. He was one of 116 young men and women from this congregation who served in the armed forces in World War I, and the first of nine members of the Ulster Division to be awarded the Victoria Cross. On the first day of the battle of the Somme, on 1 July 1916, the 14th Battalion of the Royal Irish Rifles left their front line trench in Theipval Wood to attack the German lines. As the troops advanced towards their own front trench a box of Mills bombs (hand grenades) fell to the ground and some of the pins dislodged. Realising that they would explode within seconds, Private McFadzean shouted a warning to his colleagues and threw himself on top of the grenades. He was killed instantly but his sacrificial action undoubtedly saved the lives of those around him.

Private McFadzean's father, also William McFadzean, received his son's VC from King George V on 28 February 1917. A memorial plaque was placed in the church on the first anniversary of the battle. Mr McFadzean senior was Clerk of Session in the congregation from 1924 until 1930.

Reverend John Moran

JOHN MORAN was born in Donegal on 20 February 1820. He was ordained in First Ballybay in County Monaghan on 24 March 1846 but only stayed there for six months, resigning on 27 October in the same year. He was installed in the congregation of Sandys Street, Newry on 16 November 1846, where he served for fourteen years. His third and final congregation was Belmont, where he was the first minister from 28 March 1862 until his death on 9 June 1880. Rev Moran's chief contribution to Irish Presbyterianism was his leading role in the production of a *Revised Psalter* in 1880 in replacement of the earlier *Scottish Psalter* of 1650.

Prior to 1880, Presbyterian praise was in a generally low state with many congregations attempting only a few tunes. The *Revised Psalter* offered about 120 tunes and also a recasting of words and removal of obsolete words. The 1880 Psalter grew out of a wider controversy within Irish Presbyterianism concerning music and hymns and was a link towards the production of the Church Hymnary in 1898. Rev John Moran supported change and printed a collection of one hundred hymns, which were used in Belmont during his ministry. He died on 9 June 1880 at Bellagio, on the shores of Lake Como in Italy.

'Second Ballymacarrett', was sanctioned by the General Assembly in 1865. A church building was completed in 1869, with its name changed to 'Mountpottinger' in 1873. Membership increased greatly in the 20th century, but this area has been subject to extensive redevelopment in later years as a result of the 'Troubles'. Families in connection with this congregation now total about 185.

from almost 900 families in the 1960s to just over 200 families today. In 2001, the congregation was linked in a new mission partnership with Bloomfield in order to sustain a ministry in this area.

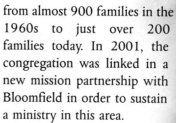

McQuiston Memorial

was originally known as 'Willowfield' and grew out of work by the Church Extension Committee on the Castlereagh Road in 1889. The congregation was formed on 20 December 1892. Its name was changed to McQuiston Memorial in honour of Mr WJ McQuiston, who left his entire estate for the creation of a Presbyterian church. A new church was opened on 28 February 1897. This congregation was the largest in the General Assembly in the 1960s with a membership of over 1,500 families. Recent redevelopment has changed the area and current membership stands at just over 500 families.

Knock

was formed in 1872 to provide a focus for the increasing number of Presbyterians in the locality. The name was changed to 'Dundela' in 1875 but reverted to 'Knock' during the ministry of Rev James Hunter (1889–1924). Rev Hunter was instrumental in forming what is now the Evangelical Presbyterian Church. The original church has been enlarged twice, most recently in 1907, when it was lengthened and had galleries added. Knock is one of the strongest congregations in the General Assembly with annual specified sources in excess of £370,000. Membership has risen sharply in the past fifty years and now stands at just over 900 families.

Westbourne

originated from work commenced in 1874 among the numerous Presbyterians living in the east end of Ballymacarrett. The church building opened on 10 October 1880. This locality was greatly affected by the 'Troubles' from 1969, and membership dropped

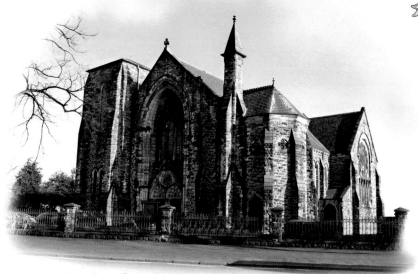

Cooke Centenary

was organised in 1890, following a plan by Belfast Presbytery to mark the centenary of Dr Henry Cooke in 1888. The church was opened on 1 May 1892. The first minister, Rev John Macmillan (1892–1930), was elected Moderator of the General Assembly in 1911. The third minister of the congregation was Rev John Barclay (1949–54), who later served as Professor of Church History and Principal of 'Assembly's College' in Belfast. Membership now totals just over 450 families.

Bloomfield

was formed in 1898 from meetings which had earlier originated in the National School in Bread Street East. The church opened on

4 December 1897, halls were added in March 1926, and the church porch was completed in 1956. The second minister, Rev John Orr (1946–76), was elected Moderator of the General Assembly in 1973. In 2001, the congregation was linked in a new mission partnership with Westbourne. Membership peaked in the early 1970s at just over 1,000 families but now stands at just under 500 families.

Reverend James Hunter

BORN IN 1863 in Newtownstewart, James Hunter was ordained on 10 April 1888 in Sandys Street, Newry, but resigned on 12 November in the following year. On 5 December 1889, he was installed as minister in Dundela congregation (now Knock) where he ministered for thirty-five years until his retirement on 9 July 1924. During his long ministry, the church building was enlarged twice. Rev Hunter pioneered the use of instrumental music in church services and a small American organ was used in Knock from 1892. The annual performance of Handel's 'Messiah' commenced in Knock in 1916.

James Hunter is forever associated with the 'heresy trial' of Prof Ernest Davey in 1927. It was James Hunter who brought formal charges against Prof Davey based upon statements made by the latter in two books that he had published. Davey was acquitted by the General Assembly by 707 votes to eighty-two and, in protest, James Hunter resigned his membership of the Presbyterian Church in Ireland in July 1927 to become the leader of The Irish Evangelical Church (now The Evangelical Presbyterian Church). Rev James Hunter died on 20 September 1942.

Reverend John Barkley

JOHN MONTIETH BARKLEY was born on 16 October 1910, son of Rev Robert Barkley (Malin, Aughnacloy, Loanends and Claremont). He was ordained on 26 September 1935 in Drumreagh congregation. He was installed in Second Ballybay on 4 May 1939, and, in a later union, Rockcorry on 26 March 1947. He accepted a call to Cooke Centenary congregation where he was installed on 1 February 1949. From 1954 until his retirement in 1981 John Barclay was Professor of Church History in 'Assembly's College' (now Union Theological College) in Belfast and was Principal from 1976. His publications were numerous and his lectures were famous for their personal anecdotes. John Barkley was well known for his deep interest in history, liturgy, inter-church relations and doctrine. His Doctor of Divinity degree was awarded by Trinity College, Dublin in November 1949, and was only the eighth such degree ever awarded by Trinity and the first awarded to a Presbyterian minister. John Barkley died on 20 December 1997 in his eightieth year.

Ravenhill

met for the first time on 29 May 1898. Initially, an 'Iron Church' was erected on the current site and the present church was opened on 4 June 1905, one day before the new Assembly Buildings in Fisherwick Place. Rev William Nicholson conducted a memorable mission in Ravenhill in 1923. The church was extensively damaged by fire on 4 March 1979, but re-opened on 10 October 1981. Membership stands today at about 235 families.

The 20th century

During the 20th century, industry and population continued to expand in East Belfast. The shipyard of Harland and Wolff grew to become the world's greatest shipyard epitomised by the ill-fated launch of the Titanic on 31 May 1911. Other important industries such as linen reached a peak in the 1950s and the second half of the century witnessed the decline of many once formidable industries. The last three decades of the century were dominated by serious civil disturbances. Twelve new congregations were formed in East Belfast during that period.

Cregagh

arose out of services held in Brown Memorial School, Redcar Street, by a small group of people who had belonged to the Secession congregation in Botanic Avenue. Services moved to an 'Iron Church' on the Cregagh Road in 1902, and full congregational status was

Reverend William Nicholson

WILLIAM PATTESON NICHOLSON (later to be known affectionately in Christian circles as 'WP') was born on 3 April 1876 at Cottown, near Bangor, County Down. He was one of seven children; his father, John, was a captain in the merchant Navy. Brought up in Albert Street Presbyterian Church in Belfast, he followed his father in going to sea at sixteen years of age. William Nicholson returned to Bangor in 1899, and was converted on 22 May. He undertook study in the Bible Training Institute in Glasgow and travelled to America where he was ordained on 15 April 1914 as an evangelist by Carlisle Presbytery of the Presbyterian Church USA.

Rev Nicholson returned to Northern Ireland in 1920 to conduct a series of missions over the following years; thousands of people flocked to hear his unique, vivid, straight-talking style of preaching. His sermons often lasted longer than one hour.

One such mission was held in Ravenhill Presbyterian Church in 1923. During this mission, hundreds of men from the shipyard marched together to Ravenhill and, on one particular evening, the crush at the door moved a pillar supporting the gates. Thereafter, this was known as 'the night of the big push'. Over one hundred new communicants joined Ravenhill within three months of Nicholson's mission. The march of the shipyard men is commemorated in a memorial window in the church building in memory of Mr Harry Magill.

William Nicholson died on 29 October 1959 and was buried in Clandeboye Cemetery on the outskirts of Bangor.

Reverend David Stewart

DAVID STEWART was born in Saintfield on 10 July 1868. He graduated from the Royal University of Ireland in 1894 and was ordained in Tralee, in Munster Presbytery, on 31 March 1897. He then accepted an invitation to undertake pioneer work in the Cregagh district of Belfast, commencing his new work on 1 January 1903. The new congregation of Cregagh was organised on 24 July of that year, and Rev Stewart was installed as the first minister there on 22 October. He gave forty years of unbroken service to this new cause.

Rev Stewart had a passionate interest in church history. Founding member and later Convenor or Co-Convenor of The Presbyterian Historical Society for thirty-seven years, he composed several congregational histories and historical pamphlets. His best known books are: *The History and Principles of the Presbyterian Church* (published in 1907) and *The Seceders in Ireland* (published in 1940).

David Stewart retired on 30 April 1943 and received an honorary Doctor of Divinity degree from the Presbyterian Theological Faculty Ireland in 1944. He died on 25 May 1961.

Magill memorial window

attained in 1903 under the name 'Cregagh'. The current church was opened on 20 September 1928. The first minister, Rev David Stewart (1903–43), contributed significantly to Irish Presbyterian history with several publications. Congregational membership totals just over 400 families.

Strand

was formed on 1 November 1903, under the name 'Strand, Sydenham'. Services were held in a hall for several years until the present church was opened on St. Patrick's Day 1924. The site for the Lecture Hall was donated to the congregation by a Miss Duffin at an annual rent of one shilling. The fifth minister, Rev William Chestnutt (1927–65), served as Convenor of the Colonial Mission for thirteen years. He was awarded a Doctor of Divinity degree in 1950 by McGill College, Montreal. Membership stands today at about 250 families.

Kirkpatrick Memorial

arose out of work commenced in Ballyhackamore by James Tolland of the City Mission in 1893. Services were held in the Jubilee School. Mr Tolland left to train for the Presbyterian ministry and returned in 1910, being ordained on 27 August 1912 as designated Missionary in Ballyhackamore. The congregation was organised under the name 'Ormiston' in 1914. Money from the will of Rev James Kirkpatrick of Dunluce for a new congregation in Belfast was given to Ormiston, and the current church, named 'Kirkpatrick Memorial Church', was opened on 27 June 1924. Membership currently stands at about 200 families.

Stormont

grew out of a 1921 plan by Belfast Presbytery to plant a new congregation in this area of the city. Rev William McConnell was appointed as Stated Supply in 1932 and continued this initial work until his retirement in November 1936. A hall was opened in 1931. Its first minister, Rev John Park, served this new church for thirty-nine years (1937–76). The current church was opened on 18 September 1955. Congregational membership has risen by 30% in the past fifty years and currently stands at over 500 families.

Mersey Street

was a Mission Hall in Severn Street under the auspices of Megain Kirk Session. The initial hall was built in 1930. A succession of Superintendents worked here until 1958, when licentiates and Assistant Ministers were appointed. The church was remodelled in 1973, with additional furniture from Argyle and Agnes Street. In 1991, this cause attained full congregational status. This is the smallest congregation within the presbytery with a membership of 140 families.

Orangefield

grew from Belfast City Mission activities here in 1935, in the new housing development on the Castlereagh Road. The original wooden hall was replaced by a brick hall in 1939. Full congregation status was attained in 1941, with 230 families. Its first minister was Rev Malcolm Parke (1941–75). A new church was opened on 6 September 1957, and a halls complex on 3 September 1971. Plans are currently in hand to develop a new suite of buildings on the site at a cost of about £3M. Membership of this congregation has risen by over 40% since the halls opened and stands today at about 600 families.

St. Andrew's

was formed as an offshoot of Cregagh on 3 September 1949 and gained full congregation status in June 1950. War compensation from the former York Street church helped to finance the scheme and a new hall-church was opened on 5 January 1952. The congregation shared a church building with the local Methodist

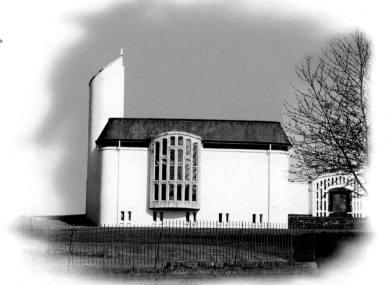

church, with each congregation retaining separate halls. This sharing arrangement has not lasted and there are current plans for each community to worship in separate buildings. Membership today stands at about 275 families.

Garnerville

was a Church Extension cause that started in November 1950 in a converted stable in the grounds of Garnerville House. In September 1952, the work moved to a wooden hall at the foot of the Circular Road. The work returned to the Old Holywood Road after thirteen years, and the present church building was opened on 4 September 1965. Full congregational status was granted on 1 January 1975. The third minister of the congregation was Rev Joan Barr (1980–2000), the first female minister to serve in the Presbytery of East Belfast. Congregational membership currently stands at just over 350 families.

Saintfield Road

originated in services conducted in Knockbracken Orange Hall under the auspices of the Church Extension Committee. The first minister, Rev James McAdam, was installed on 5 January 1960 and established the congregation, working here until his retirement in

1987. Sixty-seven families joined the congregation on Rev Adam's first Sunday. The current church was opened on 13 January 1962, and full congregational status was granted on 10 January 1965. Membership today stands at around 325 families.

Belvoir Church

originated from services which commenced in a hall in this new housing development on 24 February 1963. There were about 1,500 new dwellings in the Belvoir Park development. The church was opened on 1 May 1965 and full congregational status was granted on 18 February 1973. The church building had to be completely rebuilt following damage sustained when the nearby Police Forensic Laboratories were destroyed by a terrorist bomb in 1992. Membership today stands at about 185 families.

Christ Church, Dundonald

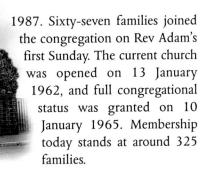

grew out of services in this area which commenced in a wooden hall on the Millar's Lane site in June 1965. Sunday School numbers exceeded 300 in 1968. Miss Janet Wood, the Senior Deaconess of the Presbyterian Women's Association, worked in the new congregation for six years from 1968. The current church building was opened on 19 September 1970 and the hall complex was completed in January 1973. Full congregational status was granted in February 1974. Congregational membership today stands at about 325 families.

Tullycarnet

was formed following services commenced here on 2 September 1968 in temporary accommodation. Housing development did not proceed as originally anticipated and this reduced the potential of the congregation for further development. There were 300 families claiming membership in 1974. Rev George Moffett (1984–2003) did much to establish this cause and also acted as Presbyterian Chaplain in the nearby Ulster Hospital, Dundonald. A hall was added to facilities in April 1989, and full congregational status was granted in 1990. Membership currently stands at just over 200 families.

Conclusion

Although East Belfast Presbytery is the largest and strongest of the Belfast Presbyteries, it is suffering similar decline to the others. As the table below indicates, overall communicant membership has fallen by 43% in the past 40 years.

YEAR	CONGREGATIONS	FAMILIES	COMMUNICANTS ON ROLL	ATTENDING COMMUNICANTS
1963	24	17,607	12,096	9,752
1973	27	18,039	12,047	8,746
1983	28	14,849	10,380	7,967
1993	27	13,421	9,425	6,750
2003	27	10,719	7,983	5,602

There are bright spots amidst the general shrinking trend. Knock congregation remains one of the strongest Irish Presbyterian congregations. Orangefield congregation has witnessed significant new growth. The Westbourne-Bloomfield link is an interesting experiment in which a stronger outer area congregation helps a weaker inner one.

Carrickfergus Presbytery

Introduction

The Presbytery of Carrickfergus covers the southern and eastern areas of County Antrim and contains twenty congregations. The main urban centres are: the ancient castle town of Carrickfergus, the seaport of Larne and the market town of Ballyclare. Each of these centres has experienced recent population growth and they have become significant dormer towns to Belfast. Presbyterians have always been numerous in this part of Antrim and this continues in the present century.

The 17th Century

The Carrickfergus district was the cradle of Irish Presbyterianism. Following the formation of the first Presbytery on 10 June 1642, seven congregations were formed in this locality in the 17th century. The town of Carrickfergus was the principle centre of English occupation in Ulster and therefore the natural base for the expansion of the new church. In this turbulent century there were frequent interchanges with Scotland and the 'mother Church' with ministers and people moving in both directions according to the severity of persecution on either side of the Irish Sea.

Carrickfergus

First Carrickfergus

can possibly claim the distinction of being the first Irish Presbyterian congregation. It was in this garrison town that the first Presbytery was formed on 10 June 1642. The first resident minister was Rev John Greg (1646–49) who later served in Newtownards (1649–70). The original thatched church was replaced by a T-shaped church building in 1724. The current church building was opened, on the same site, on Sunday 8 February 1829. The minister at that time, Rev Seaton Reid (1823–38), was arguably the most distinguished minister in the history of this congregation. Congregational membership currently stands at about 800 families.

Ballycarry

was founded in 1642 from the people to whom Rev Edward Brice, the earliest known Presbyterian minister in Ireland, ministered

Reverend Seaton Reid

JAMES SEATON REID was born in Lurgan on 19 December 1798, the eleventh son and sixteenth child of Forrest and Mary Reid. His older brother Edward was the Presbyterian minister in Ramelton from 1806 until 1838. Seaton Reid has left a memorable account of his regular journeys between Ramelton and Glasgow. He graduated from Glasgow University in 1816, and was minister in Donegore (1819–23) and Carrickfergus (1823–28). He was Clerk of the Synod of Ulster (1830–41) and Professor of Church History in the Belfast Institution (1838–41). It was Seaton Reid who read the Act of Union at the formation of the General Assembly on 10 July 1840. In 1841, he was appointed Professor of Church History in Glasgow University, fulfilling this task until his early death on 26 March 1851, aged 52. Seaton Reid will forever be honoured as the author of the comprehensive *History of the Presbyterian Church in Ireland*. Volume One appeared in 1834 and Volume Two followed in 1837. Reid was still working on the final volume when he died but his work was completed by Professor Killen and published in 1853.

Andrew Jackson

ANDREW JACKSON was the seventh President of the United States of America. The family home was at Boneybefore, to the east of Carrickfergus. His parents, Andrew and Elizabeth, worshipped in Ballycarry congregation before emigrating to America in 1765. Andrew was born there on 15 March 1767 and orphaned at age fourteen. Andrew Jackson was elected a U.S. senator and, after several successful military exploits, was appointed a major general in the U.S. army. In 1791, he married Rachel Robards, but discovered then that Rachel was not in fact legally divorced. They 'married' again in 1794. Jackson's political opponents used these unusual circumstances to blacken his character. Andrew Jackson played a decisive role in the 1812 Battle of New Orleans against the British. As a popular American hero, he was twice elected President of the United States (1828 and 1832). First US President who did not come from the aristocracy, Jackson showed strong leadership and vetoed twelve pieces of legislation (more than the first six presidents together). He retired in 1837 to his farm, The Hermitage, where he died on 8 June 1845.

(1613–36). Andrew and Elizabeth Jackson, parents of seventh American President, Andrew Jackson, were members of this congregation before emigrating to America in 1765. In 1829, Rev William Glendy (1812–29), with a portion of the congregation, broke from the Synod of Ulster to join with the Non-subscribers. Eight of the nine elders and the majority of the congregation built the present church and remained under the authority of the Synod. Rev Gabrielle Farquhar (née Ellis) was installed here on 16 September 1994, the first female minister of a congregation in this Presbytery. Membership stands at 280 families today.

Cairncastle

was formed in 1646, in the immediate aftermath of the establishment of the Army Presbytery in Carrickfergus in June 1642. The first minister, Rev Patrick Adair (1646–74), was ordained here on 7 May 1646 and preached in the parish church for fifteen years. He wrote the earliest history of Presbyterianism in Ireland. Rev William Taylor (1715–34) took the congregation into the Non-subscribing Antrim Presbytery in 1725, but the people rejoined the Synod of Ulster in 1734. Rev Thomas Alexander (1793–1829) and a minority of the congregation joined the Non-subscribers in 1829 and retained the church building. The current church was opened on 24 May 1831. Membership stands at just over 200 families today.

First Larne

was one of the early congregations formed in South Antrim in the wake of the first meeting of the Army Presbytery in June 1642. Following a controversy over subscription, a number of the families resolved to remain loyal to the Synod of Ulster and built their own church in 1716. The building was replaced in 1835. Rev Henry Molyneaux (1831–71) was elected Moderator of the General Assembly in 1853. The seaport of Larne was shocked and distressed by the sinking of the ferry *Princess Victoria* on 31 January 1953 with a loss of 128 lives, and the congregation still remembers that tragedy by standing for a silent tribute on the nearest Sunday to the anniversary. On 5 March 1978, due to the construction of a new approach road to the port of Larne, fourteen feet above ground level and only twenty feet from the church building, the congregation moved to a nearby site and constructed their present church. Membership stands today at just under 900 families, the largest membership in this Presbytery.

Reverend James Cochrane

JAMES COCHRANE was the first son of Moses Cochrane, a farmer in the Saintfield area. The date of his birth is unknown, but he graduated from Glasgow University in 1813. He was ordained in First Larne on 22 December 1815 having previously served as a tutor to a family called Craig in nearby Carrickfergus. He 'married' a daughter of that family but the matter was investigated by the Presbytery. On his own admission, Mr Cochrane performed the marriage himself in May 1815, with no witnesses present and without any public announcement – all highly irregular! The Synod suspended Rev Cochrane from office for one year though the congregation refused to pay any of the supply preachers. Rev Cochrane was reinstated in August 1817. In 1822, he was suspected of stealing £10 which had been entrusted to him to pass to Rev James Horner in Dublin for poverty relief work. The postmaster in Saintfield recalled handling a letter addressed to Rev Horner, but the same minister never received it. In the wake of this mystery, the Presbytery declared Rev Cochrane to be guilty of 'folly and imprudence'. Two years later, on 11 May 1824, the Presbytery found Rev Cochrane guilty of stealing £5, which had been donated for the work of the London Missionary Society. On this occasion he was permanently suspended from ministry. His congregation paid £45 for their minister, wife and family to travel to America. They sailed from Belfast on the *Louisa* on 12 September 1824.

First Islandmagee

was formed in the aftermath of the Army Presbytery meeting in Carrickfergus in 1642, although Rev Edward Brice of Ballycarry ministered to Presbyterians here as early as 1613. Rev Henry Main was ordained in 1647, but his ministry was brief. A succession of Scottish ministers laboured in the congregation until the longer ministry of Rev John Murphy (1789–1828). The first church was built in 1674. The longest ministry in the history of this congregation was that of Rev David Steen, who was ordained here on 14 August 1877 and he retired after 51 years, on 3 November 1928. The present church was built in 1901. Membership currently totals 270 families.

Ballyclare

was founded in the mid 1650s. The first minister, Rev Gilbert Simpson, was ordained here on 9 August 1655. Although deposed for Non-conformity in 1661, he continued to minister to his people until his death in 1675. Rev Thomas

Reverend Harold Allen

HAROLD ALLEN was born in Belfast on 31 December 1921. He graduated BA in 1951 from Trinity College Dublin, then studied Theology, and was ordained in Ballyclare on 17 February 1955. Rev Allen remained there until his retirement on 13 September 1987. While a student at Trinity and Boys' Auxiliary leader, Harold was one of a number of young people who visited the Ruhr area of Germany in an early post-war cultural enterprise. He stayed in the town of Dorsten where he made lifelong friendships. Several subsequent exchange visits took place and links were established between the Dorsten and Ballyclare churches. The Borough of Newtownabbey is now officially linked to the town of Dorsten. In recognition of his important contribution to mutual understanding, Harold Allen was created a Member of the Order of Merit of the Federal Republic of Germany in 1987, the year of his retirement. Harold Allen died on 24 January 1994. In August 2000 the Town Council of Dorsten named a road in their town *Harold Allen Straße*, in honour of Rev Harold Allen.

Archibald McIlroy

ARCHIBALD McILROY was born in 1859 in a farmhouse on the outskirts of Ballyclare. He was brought up in the local Presbyterian congregation and said later of his relatives, 'most of the male sex were ruling elders in the Presbyterian Church, while their womenfolks ruled them.' Following education at James Pyper's Mercantile Academy and Belfast Academical Institution, Archibald McIlroy worked in the Ulster Bank. He married a daughter of Rev Adam Montgomery of Ballycairn. About 1895, he began to write, and his first book, *When Lint was in the Bell*, was published in Belfast in 1897. It was followed by several other very popular books entitled *The Auld Meetin'-House Green*, *A Banker's Love Story* and *The Humour of Druid's Island*. He also published several articles in the Presbyterian newspaper, *The Witness*. A strong supporter of Tenant Rights, Archibald McIlroy developed popular lantern slide shows, which he distributed throughout Ireland and England. His writings were very popular with Ulster people in America. Archibald McIlroy died on 7 May 1915 as he was returning from a successful trip to the United States. He was a passenger on board the liner Lusitania when it was torpedoed by a German submarine off the Kinsale headland. Fifteen hundred passengers and crew also perished.

Wilson was ordained on 27 February 1711, but joined the Non-subscribing Presbytery of Antrim in 1726. In 1856, a section of the congregation separated from the Non-subscribing Presbyterian Church and formed a new congregation within the General Assembly. Rev Harold Allen (1955–87) pioneered links with the town of Dorsten in Germany. Congregational membership has risen by an incredible 82% in the past fifty years and stands today at about 620 families.

Raloo

was formed in the 1650s, but did not have its own minister until Rev Robert Kelso was ordained in Larne on 7 May 1673. This minister was released from this charge after only three years through lack of support. The congregation was formed again in 1838. Rev James Whiteford was ordained here on 10 March 1840. He served for forty-eight years before retiring on 13 April 1888. Membership today totals just over 200 families.

The 18th Century

There were only three new congregations formed in the Carrickfergus region in the 18th century. Ballynure was attached to the Synod of Ulster, and the Seceders established two congregations, in Larne and Islandmagee, from the labours of one busy minister. The Subscription Controversy caused significant upset with divisions erupting in several congregations, most notably in Ballycarry, Cairncastle, Larne and Ballyclare.

Ballynure

was formed in 1723 for Presbyterians wishing to disassociate themselves from nearby Non-subscribing gatherings. Rev Clotworthy Brown ministered here for a time but was never installed by the Synod and in 1748 he joined the Non-subscribing Presbytery of Antrim. Rev James Whiteside McCay was minister for over twenty years (1826–47) and his son, Rev Andrew McCay, was

minister for six years (1859–65) before moving to Castlemaine, in Australia. Later, he gained a Professorship in Church History. Andrew's oldest son, born in Ballynure in 1864, became Lieutenant General Hon. Sir James McCay. Membership currently numbers about 285 families.

Gardenmore

was the first Seceder cause in this Presbytery area. Precise details of its origins are unknown, but the church was opened in 1769. Seceders in this locality were served by Revs Isaac Patton of Lylehill (from 1746) and William Holmes of Ballyeaston (from 1768). The second church building was opened in 1870. In 1885, the church name was changed from *Second Larne* to *Gardenmore*. Rev David Hanson (1892–1939) was Deputy Assistant Chaplain General and supervised the building of the current church in 1915. Rev Victor Lynas (1947–87) was elected Moderator of the General Assembly in 1972. Membership currently stands at about 680 families.

Second Islandmagee

was a Seceder congregation formed as a result of the labours of Rev William Holmes of Ballyeaston (1768–1813). Together with the Larne congregation (now Gardenmore), the people called Rev John Nicholson as their first minister (1785–99). Rev Nicolson also taught Classics in the Belfast Academy. The first church was built in 1796. The Seceder minister preached on alternate Sundays in Larne and Islandmagee. However, this arrangement ended with the creation of two separate congregations in 1827. Although fewer local people are employed in agriculture, new families have moved to this quiet corner of East Antrim. Membership currently totals about 180 families.

The 19th Century

Whereas most Presbyteries indicate a significant numerical growth in new congregations in the 19th century, this is not the case in the Carrickfergus area. This is probably because there were already substantial congregations at the time, following the colonisation of the South and East Antrim from the early 17th century by the Scottish Presbyterian settlers who constituted the majority of the population. Five new congregations were formed within this Presbytery district in the 19th century. The largest of these was Joymount, which was a much needed second congregation in Carrickfergus.

Loughmorne

was formed in 1804 as a Covenanting cause within the Reformed Presbyterian Synod of Ireland. The first minister was Rev John Paul (1805–48), who withdrew from the jurisdiction of the Reformed

Synod in 1840 and formed the Eastern Reformed Synod in 1842. When negotiations in 1893 for union between the Reformed Presbyterians and the General Assembly broke down, the Loughmourne people asked to be received into the Presbyterian Church in Ireland. Rev William Close (1848–1903) oversaw the new link in 1893. In 1903, the Belfast Water Commissioners acquired twenty farms within this parish and thereby weakened the congregation, which was subsequently united with Woodburn on 1 July 1957. Membership stands at eighty-five families today.

Ballylinney

was founded in 1834; the church building was opened on 11 September 1836. Interestingly, seating was only installed in the following year! The first minister, Rev Isaac Adams, was ordained here on 20 June 1837; he gave a lifetime's work, retiring in 1880. A gallery was added to the church in 1858. The second longest

ministry in Ballylinney was that of Rev Ernest McConnell, who was ordained here on 8 December 1921 and retired on 30 September 1958. Membership currently stands at about 310 families.

Joymount

congregation was formed in 1852 as the second Presbyterian cause in the town of Carrickfergus. It is built near the site of Sir Arthur Chichester's 17th century palace, Mountjoy. The church building was opened on 21 September 1856; its first minister was Rev James Warwick (1852–82). In 1977, the congregation initiated a new cause in the eastern suburbs of the town by opening the Carlisle Hall (in memory of Rev Tom Carlisle who was minister from 1936 until 1969). This initiative eventually became the congregation of Downshire. Membership of Joymount totals about 750 families today.

Woodburn

developed from work by Mr Hans McCoubrey, an agent of the Belfast Town Mission, who started services here in 1873. He was ordained on 2 January 1866 as the first minister and served until his retirement in 1900. There were 200 families in membership at that time; however, this number was halved after 1903, when the Belfast Water Commissioners acquired several farms within this parish. Rev John McFall, who was ordained here on 11 May 1948, oversaw the union with Loughmorne on 1 July 1957, and retired in January 1989. Membership today stands at about 120 families.

Magheramourne

This church was built in 1876 by Mr Quinton Hogg of London as a mission hall for his workers from the nearby limeworks. Quinton Hogg was the grandfather of Baron Hailsham, Lord Chancellor (1970–74 and 1979–87). Local Presbyterians desired to be formed into a new congregation. In 1880, they gained possession of this building and were recognised as a Presbyterian Church. The first minister was Rev David Graham (1881–92). The longest ministry here was that of Rev Thomas Docherty who was minister from 1896 until 1955! Membership peaked at 225 families in the 1950s and stands today at about 145 families.

The 20th Century

In the 1960s and 1970s, the population of Carrickfergus rose from 4,000 to 17,000. The man-made fibre industry in the town made it an attractive location. Larne also developed with industry and as a busy ferry-port and gateway to Scotland. Five new congregations were formed, in Whitehead, Greenisland, Larne and two in Carrickfergus.

Greenisland

arose out of Church Extension work, which started here in a wooden hall in 1932 under Mr James Dunlop (Moderator of the General Assembly in 1964). A site for a church building was leased from Greenisland Golf Club in 1935, and the church was opened on 6 September 1941. The first minister was Rev William Hall (1935–39). A new hall and other accommodation were added to the main church building in 2004. Membership stands today at about 400 families.

Whitehead

was formally established in June 1900. The origin of this cause was in hall meetings, commenced in Whitehead in 1898, and the opening of a school. The first minister was Rev David Knox (1900–25) who was also editor of the monthly magazine, *The Irish Presbyterian*. Several attempts were made to heal an ongoing breach with the congregation in Chester Avenue, Whitehead. These efforts were unsuccessful and the latter cause became a Congregational Church. Membership today totals about 375 families.

Craigy Hill

originated as a Church Extension initiative in 1956, in the new housing development of Larne's Craigy Hill area. Rev Bill Boyd was installed as the first minister on 27 September 1956 in a temporary wooden hall. A new church building was opened in March 1961. This cause attained full congregational status in January 1965, and a church hall was added to the suite of buildings in 1967. Rev Jackson Buick (1970–82) had a vigorous and influential ministry here. Membership today stands at about 350 families.

Reverend Jackson Buick

JACKSON BUICK was born on 8 October 1921 near Randalstown in County Antrim, and was brought up as a member of First Antrim congregation. Leaving school at fourteen, Jackson worked for a time in the linen trade before serving for twelve years in the Belfast City Mission, attached to Ballysillan congregation. He then studied Theology at Magee and 'Assembly's' Colleges. After an assistantship in Richview, he became minister in Second Newtownards (1963–70) and Craigy Hill (1970–82). It was in the new congregation of Craigy Hill that Jackson Buick displayed boundless enthusiasm and evangelical vigour. His ministry there was an outstanding success and the church grew rapidly. On 2 June 1982, Rev Buick commenced a new full-time ministry as Presbyterian Chaplain to Crumlin Road Prison. Once again, his efforts were very much appreciated and he served in this capacity until his retirement in 1988. In recognition of his work in the prison, Jackson Buick received the MBE. He then undertook pastoral responsibilities in Bloomfield and Glengormley. In May 2004 Rev Jackson Buick was awarded an honorary Doctor of Divinity degree by the Presbyterian Theological Faculty Ireland in recognition of his services to the Presbyterian Church in Ireland.

Downshire

is the fourth congregation in the town of Carrickfergus and the youngest within this Presbytery. This new cause grew out of work initiated by Joymount, when they opened the Carlisle Hall on 30 April 1977 in the Victoria Road area of Carrickfergus. This work came under Church Extension control in 1985, adopting the name *Downshire*. Rev Morris Gault was installed on 29 May 1985, and a new church building was opened in February 1988. Full congregational status was attained on 13 January 1993. Membership currently amounts to just over 250 families.

Woodlands

was spawned from outreach activities by First Carrickfergus congregation in the Sunnylands district of the town. Rev Norman Brown was installed as the first minister on 24 February 1977, and the new premises were opened in October 1978. A Deaconess, Miss Elsie Colgan, assisted in early development work. After only four years, full congregational status was attained on 7 January 1981. Membership peaked in the early 1980s at almost 500 families. There are currently about 250 families in membership.

Conclusion

At face value, the congregations of Carrickfergus Presbytery are flourishing. Attendances are healthy and there are encouraging signs of life throughout the whole Presbytery. The challenge for these congregations, as for every congregation, is to present a relevant gospel message for an increasingly secular society. Several churches are investing in additional staff in order to meet demands and such trends are likely to continue in the 21st century.

Coleraine Presbytery

Introduction

The Presbytery of Coleraine is dominated by the plantation town of Coleraine with its five Presbyterian congregations. Prior to the establishment of Londonderry in the first decade of the 17th century and its later dominance of the North West area, County Coleraine was the name of this region, west of the River Bann.

The 17th Century

The town of Coleraine was developed by the Irish Society as a plantation town. The pre-Reformation church of St. Patrick's was re-roofed and all the new settlers, Scots and English, worshipped in this church. Of the eight Presbyterian congregations which were formed in this area during the 17th century, First Coleraine is the earliest. In 1641, Rev Thomas Vesey of Camus took refuge in Coleraine. He later subscribed to the Solemn League and Covenant, ministering to the Presbyterian people until his appointment as Rector at the Restoration. Presbyterianism was therefore organised in Coleraine during the early 1640s. Initial manpower shortages are illustrated by the fact that a blank call – bearing thirty-four local signatures and dated 25 July 1673 – was sent to Scotland in the hope of securing the services of any Presbyterian minister.

Mussenden Temple and
Benown Strand

SCENIC IRELAND

First Coleraine

was organised in the early 1640s under Rev Thomas Vesey who ministered successively as an Anglican, Presbyterian, Independent and Anglican minister. During the ministry of the Irish speaking Rev Robert Higinbotham (1710–70), the congregation temporarily withdrew from the Synod of Ulster due to the Subscription controversy. The original church, built at the corner of Abbey Street and Cross Lane, was replaced in 1827 at a new site in Upper Abbey Street. Membership stands today at about 450 families.

Ballywillan

was formed after the dismissal of Rev Gabriel Cornwall from the parish church in 1661. A Presbyterian cause was formed and Rev Cornwall continued his ministry until his death in 1691. The original church building was replaced by a second church in 1828 and this in turn was replaced by the current building in 1889. Rev Matthew Woodburn (1862–77) died aged thirty-six and was the father of Professor George Woodburn of Magee College, Londonderry. Another son, James, was minister of Fitzroy Avenue congregation (1922–42) and Moderator of

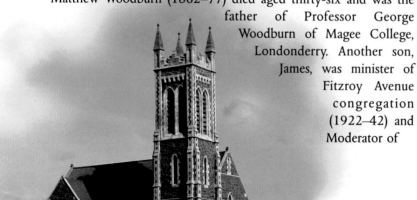

Reverend Robert Higinbotham

ROBERT HIGINBOTHAM was born in County Antrim in the late 17th century. He graduated from Glasgow University in 1710 and was ordained in First Coleraine on 26 December 1710. In 1714, he was found guilty by the Synod of Ulster for failing to keep a promise he made to marry Mrs Martha Woods of Four Loanends, Belfast. His defence before Synod was that his father would not approve of the marriage. Synod summoned Mr Higinbotham senior and tried, unsuccessfully, to secure approval for the marriage. Rev Higinbotham was given three months in which to marry Mrs Woods or face deposition from the ministry. He complied.

Robert Higinbotham had sympathy with the cause of the Non-subscribers and was determined enough to publish his sympathy in 1725. Several families left First Coleraine and formed Second Coleraine in protest. The Synod reprimanded him for his publication and in a fit of pique he withdrew his congregation from the Synod and joined the Non-subscribing Antrim Presbytery. Two years later, he and his congregation were re-admitted to the Synod and he was admonished to live at peace with his former members who were now constituted as a second congregation in Coleraine. Clearly, no score of his wrongs was kept as Robert Higinbotham was elected as Moderator of Synod in 1746. He played a leading role in opposing the Seceders at every opportunity. He died on 6 October 1770, having served as minister in Coleraine for sixty years.

Reverend James Frazer

JAMES FRAZER retired on 18 February 2001, after thirty-nine years ministry in Ballywillan. This was an outstandingly successful ministry, which saw membership rise from 168 to 450 families. Two Sunday morning services are held throughout the year and a gallery had to be added to the church to accommodate the expanding numbers attending. In the summer months one of the morning services requires a video link to overflow facilities. Jim Frazer is a man who has quietly gone about his ministry. In 1979, he took a six month sabbatical at Princeton Seminary in America and returned with fresh ideas for Ballywillan. Sunday evening musical events in the summer conveyed the concept of an open church and people were attracted. Nine minute Sunday morning sermons in a seeker friendly context proved a winning formula. These services were supplemented and balanced by a longer and deeper teaching format in the evening and everything was underpinned by various sharing and learning programmes delivered through an extensive house group network. In recognition of his ministry, Rev Frazer was awarded a Doctor of Divinity degree by the Presbyterian Theological Faculty Ireland in May 2001.

Reverend James McGregor

JAMES MCGREGOR was born near Magilligan in 1677 and ordained as minister of Aghadowey on 25 June 1701. Unhappy with religious persecution and economic hardship, Rev McGregor and a number of families from his congregation emigrated to New England in the summer of 1718, their convoy of five ships arriving in Boston on 4 August 1718. Perhaps the reason for this voyage is to be found in the fact that, in his absence, the Presbytery were concerned to discover that he was owed more than £80 in stipend. James McGregor and his friends settled at Nutfield and founded a new town which they called Londonderry. On their first day at Nutfield, James McGregor preached to the settlers in the shade of an oak tree, from Isaiah 32:2. Each settler was allocated 120 acres. They introduced the potato and the small flax spinning wheel to this locality. Their new church, which measured fifty feet in length and forty-five feet in width, with one gallery, was opened in 1722. It was the first Presbyterian Church in New England. James McGregor contracted a sudden fever in 1729 and lasted only a few days. He died, at the age of fifty-two, on Wednesday 5 March 1729. His son, David, became minister of a second Presbyterian church in the west of the district.

TBF Thompson

THOMAS BACON FRENCH THOMPSON was born in 1915 in Garvagh. He worked for his father, a general merchant. By a combination of entrepreneurial skill and hard work in the transport and haulage business, he rose to become a very significant businessman in Northern Ireland. He was converted in July 1947 and his business interests and success grew to such an extent that his diverse commercial outlets have a combined turnover of around £150 million. TBF is an elder in Garvagh Presbyterian Church. In 1978 TBF and his late first wife Kathleen established the TBF and KL Thompson Trusts in order to support numerous charitable works. Countless individuals and Christian ministries have benefited from generous financial assistance from TBF Thompson Ministries. In 1990, TBF received an honorary Doctor of Science in Economics degree from the Queen's University, Belfast and an OBE at Buckingham Palace. He celebrated his ninetieth birthday in 2005.

the General Assembly in 1940. Rev James Frazer was ordained here on 21 September 1961 and exercised an outstanding ministry during which the congregation grew substantially. He retired on 18 February 2001 and was awarded a Doctor of Divinity degree by the Presbyterian Theological Faculty Ireland. Ballywillan has more than tripled in size in the past fifty years and membership today stands at about 475 families.

Aghadowey

was formed in 1655. Its first minister was Rev William Jacque (1655–60). The third minister, Rev James McGregor (1701–18), is reputed to have fired the canon in Londonderry in 1689 to announce the approach of the relief ships. In 1719, he emigrated to America with a number of families and founded Londonderry in New England. The current church was built in 1830, during the lengthy ministry of Rev John Brown (1813–71). The congregation was linked with Crossgar in 1976. Membership stands at about 165 families today.

First Dunboe

was formed in 1656 under the ministry of Rev Thomas Fulton (1656–58). In 1718, Rev James Woodside (1698–1718) emigrated to America with about a third of the congregation. He ministered at Brunswick and Boston. A new church was built in 1785. It was enlarged in 1830, by raising the walls and incorporating a gallery on three sides. Rev John Mark (1867–1906) was a vigorous

First Garvagh

was founded in 1658. Its first minister was Rev John Law (1658–73). Rev James Browne (1795–1839), the tenth minister, baptised the famous Henry Cooke. His daughter married a minister, and five of his grandsons were ministers. Three of his granddaughters married ministers. He baptised 710 children in the first eleven years of his ministry. In 1908, the congregation of Third Garvagh was dissolved and their building became the hall for both First and Main Street, Garvagh. The current church building at Kilrea Road was opened on 17 November 1971. Membership stands today at 175 families.

supporter of the tenant right movement and the church hall, which was opened in 1908, was built in his memory. The current church was built in 1936 and the cost was cleared by two former members of the congregation, John and David Crawford, of Parkersburg, USA. Membership has risen by a healthy 80% over the past half century and stands today at about 360 families.

Ballyrashane

was formed in 1657 and the first minister was a Scotsman, Rev Robert Hogsyard (1657–73). A 'sod church' was built after 1661 at Knockinkerragh and replaced in the early 18th century when a new church was built behind Brookhall. A third church was built at Ballyrashane crossroads in 1824 but this was replaced by the current building in 1846. A memorial tower was added after the First World War. Rev Thomas Mullin (1948–78) was the author of many books on local history. Membership stands today at about 170 families.

Macosquin

originated sometime before 1680 but the first church was not built until 1705. Rev John Thompson (1727–71) was a son of Lieutenant

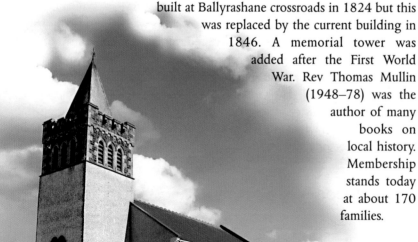

Colonel Thompson, who played an active role in the Siege of Derry. A new church was opened on 3 July 1786. Rev Clarke Houston (1823–66) was Clerk of Coleraine Presbytery for thirty-two years and author of several Presbyterian articles. The congregation was linked with that of Crossgar from 1922 until 1964. Membership stands today at 200 families.

1756. In the 1770s, the Boveedy people desired separation from the larger Kilrea faction and became a Seceder cause after 1780. The first Seceder minister was Rev Adam Boyle (1781–1841). A section of the congregation separated to form a Seceder church in the Associate Presbytery in the 1840s, but dissolved in the 1890s. The current church was built about 1845. Boveedy was united with Second Kilrea in 1923. Membership stands at sixty families today.

The 18th Century

In many ways the 18th century was a continuation of Presbyterian plantation in this locality. Agriculture and an infant linen industry provided an economic base for local families. Seven new congregations were formed within the boundaries of Coleraine Presbytery in the 18th century. The earliest, New Row and Killaig, originated because of Subscription controversies in First Coleraine and Aghadowey respectively. The other five were Seceder congregations. In addition, Boveedy became a Seceder church after 1780. Many Presbyterians emigrated to America in this century and contributed significantly to settlement expansion in New England.

First Kilrea

grew out of a Presbyterian church at Boveedy, which served the surrounding districts. Rev William Gilchrist ministered here from about 1680 until his death in Derry during the siege. The second minister, Rev Matthew Clark (1697–1729), had been wounded in the Siege before studying for the ministry. A church was built in Kilrea about 1770. The minister, Rev John Smyth (1749–88), preached on alternate Sundays in Kilrea and Boveedy. The Boveedy people broke the link soon afterwards. The current church was opened in 1849. Rev Ivan Wilson had the distinction of twice serving as minister here; from 1963 until 1967 and again from 1976 until 1985. Membership of this congregation stands at just above 150 families.

Boveedy

grew out of early Presbyterian worship in a wider area under the ministry of Rev William Gilchrist. The first church was built in

Reverend James Bryce

REV JAMES BRYCE came from Scotland where he had been minister in Wick and settled in Killaig on 16 August, 1805. An Anti-Burgher Seceder of strong principles, he was the only minister who refused to countenance acceptance of the *regium donum,* the annual Government grant to supplement minister's stipend. His principles cost him financially. He survived upon an annual stipend of £26 while his neighbouring Church of Ireland minister received £730 per annum and the Presbyterian minister of Aghadowey received £185 (£100 *regium donum* and £85 stipend). To help make ends meet he conducted Classical Schools in Coleraine and at his home. His stance on *regium donum* was admired by some, and he nurtured seven other small congregations in the Associate Presbytery. James Bryce died on 24 April 1857 in his ninetieth year, having preached twice on the Sunday prior to his passing. Three sons had distinguished careers in education: Reuben was Principal of Belfast Academy, Archibald was Principal of the High School, Edinburgh, and James was Principal of the High School, Glasgow.

New Row

was formed in Coleraine in 1727, when about ninety families left the 'First' congregation in protest at the slackness of Rev Higinbotham in relation to subscription to the Westminster Confession of Faith. The original name was 'Second' and the first minister, Rev Charles Lynd (1728–51) was Moderator of the General Synod in 1733. A new church was built in 1832 and enlarged in 1875. Rev William Wilson (1896–1918) tragically died in a car accident while working with the YMCA in Le Havre on 20 March 1918. In 1959, the official name of the church was changed from Second to New Row. Rev 'Harry' Allen (1979–98) was elected Moderator of the General Assembly in 1996. Membership totals just over 500 families.

Killaig

was formed by members of Aghadowey, who disapproved of the Non-subscribing stance of Rev John Elder in the 1720s. However, they did not secure their own minister until 1765, when the Seceder Rev Samuel Moore was ordained. A new church was opened in 1803, and the name Killaig was adopted during the ministry of Scotsman Rev James Bryce (1805–57). In 1816, Killaig and six other churches formed the Associate Presbytery of Ireland and became a United Free Church of Scotland congregation. The congregation joined the Irish Presbyterian Church in June 1922 and was united with Crossgar from 1967 until 1977. It has been united with Main Street, Garvagh since 1977. Membership stands today at about fifty-five families.

Ballywatt

was the second Seceder cause in this locality and was formed in 1748 when some members of Ballyrashane congregation, in co-operation with families from Roseyards and Derrykeighan, applied

to join the Anti-Burgher Synod. The first minister was Rev John Tennent (1751–80) and a church was built at Carnabuoy. A new church was opened at Ballywatt in 1832 and the congregation then adopted the name Ballywatt. The church was rebuilt in 1895 during the ministry of Rev William Currie (1891–1904). Membership stands today at about 166 families.

Killaig. From 1976, Crossgar and Aghadowey have been united. Membership stands at seventy-five families today.

Second Dunboe

was formed as a Burgher cause in 1788, although an application had been made to the Anti-Burgher Synod forty years earlier. Until 1800, the new cause was joined to that of Crossgar. The original thatched church was replaced by a slated church in 1822. The longest serving minister was Rev Joseph Keers who served here from his ordination on 28 May 1874 until his death on 13 October 1923. A major refurbishment was undertaken in the church in 1980. The congregation was united with Ringsend on 1 January 1995. Membership stands at almost one hundred families.

Main Street, Garvagh

was formed about 1771, when Rev James Harpur was ordained in the Secession charge at Knockloughrim and given the additional responsibility of caring for Seceders in Garvagh. The first minister was Rev Thomas Mayne (1773–1825), son of Rev Thomas Mayne of Drumgooland. The current church building dates from the early 19th century. The congregation did not join the General Assembly until 1841 upon receiving assurances concerning the ongoing value of psalm singing. In 1977, the congregation was united with that of Killaig. Membership stands today at just over 200 families.

Crossgar

was formed about 1787 to serve the Macosquin parish. Initially, the people shared the services of Rev Charles Campbell (1788–1800) with Seceders in Dunboe but separated in 1800. The church was rebuilt in 1835. Crossgar and Macosquin were united from 1922 until 1964. Unable to support its own minister, the church became a Stated Supply. Briefly, from 1967–76, Crossgar was united with

Terrace Row

was the first Seceder cause in the town of Coleraine. It was formed in 1796, and the original building was at Waterside. The current church at Terrace Row was opened on 6 July 1834. It was extended during the ministry of Rev Robert Wylie (1871–1913). The fifth minister, Rev Gilbert Paton (1913–20), had a distinguished war record. Rev Edwin Torrie (1920–54) had a memorable ministry in Terrace Row and enjoyed a long retirement. When he died in 1975, aged eighty-nine, he was the 'Father of the General Assembly'; the longest ordained minister at that time. It was during his ministry

that the congregation adopted the name Terrace Row, in preference to Third Coleraine. Rev David Clarke, installed here on 17 September 1980, was elected Moderator of the General Assembly in 2006. Membership totals 450 families today.

The 19th Century

Six new congregations were formed in this area during the 19th century. Three of them – Portstewart, Portrush and Castlerock – originated out of preaching activities undertaken in the busy summer months when people were travelling to the North Coast for leisure. The 1859 Revival swept the region, bringing newness of life to many congregations.

Portstewart

was formed in 1829, though summer preaching had been organised here for several years beforehand. The church building was completed in 1827. The first minister, Rev John Stewart, was ordained on 1 September 1829 and served here until his death on 28 January 1874. The church was rebuilt and opened in August 1904. It was enlarged, with added halls, during the ministry of Rev Samuel Fitzsimmons (1946–67). A further renovation and extension was completed in 2004. Membership stands today at just over 400 families.

Reverend Gilbert Paton

JAMES GILBERT PATON was born on 20 April 1882 in Chapleton, Lanarkshire, son of Rev Walter Paton, a minister in the Free Church. In 1892, the family retired to Londonderry and became members of Great James' Street. Gilbert was educated at Foyle College; he later became a minister in the Irish Presbyterian Church, serving in Ballykelly (1907–10), Downshire Road, Newry (1910-13), Terrace Row Coleraine (1913–20) and Malone (1920–36). His two brothers, James and John, were both ministers in the Scottish Church. The First World War commenced within ten months of Gilbert Paton's arrival in Terrace Row. He was the first Presbyterian minister to volunteer for service with the YMCA and was commissioned as a Chaplain with the rank of Captain. He served for three-and-a-half years with the 10th Battalion of the Royal Inniskilling Fusilers. He was awarded the Military Cross in 1917 and a Bar in 1918. The award was made for bravery under fire. Captain Paton helped evacuate wounded soldiers under heavy shell and machine-gun fire. Most notably, he assisted in carrying a wounded man four miles to an aid station. Gilbert Paton did not stay long in Terrace Row when he returned to Coleraine. He accepted a call to Malone in 1920. He was elected Moderator of the General Assembly in 1931 and died on 22 February 1936.

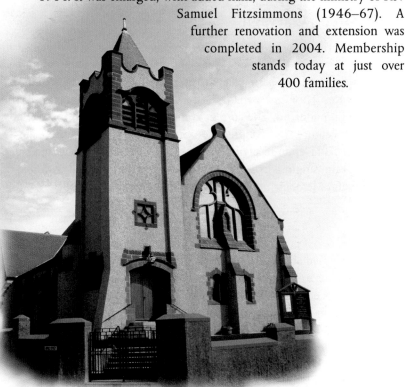

Second Kilrea

was formed as a Seceder cause in 1833. The earliest meetings were held in a linen cloth sealing room in Bridge Street in the town. The first minister, Rev James McCammon (1833–39) was ordained on 18 June 1833 at an open-air service attended by 2,000 people. He was injured while helping in the building of the church, which opened in 1838, and died on 16 March 1839. Rev Joseph Dickey (1840–83) was the great grandfather of Dr Maureen Gordon, wife of the eleventh minister, Rev Richard Gordon (1980–95). In 1923, the congregation was united with Boveedy. Membership now stands at ninety families.

There is an amusing entry in the Kirk Session Minute Book in 1900: 'The meeting having been constituted with prayer, it was reported that the Minute Book of Session had disappeared. It was unanimously resolved to use unfermented wine for communion in future.'

Ringsend

was formed in 1835 but the origins go back to the 1820s. An

Orange parade at Ringsend in 1826 resulted in fighting and bloodshed. Peace was restored when Rev John Brown of Aghadowey came to the locality and preached several times in the open air. In consequence, some local people desired to have their own church. The original church building was enlarged in 1897; a side wall was extended and the roof was raised. The most famous minister of this congregation was Rev Robert Moore (1912–60). He was also a Member of Parliament and cabinet Minister for twelve years. On 1 January 1995, the congregation was united with Second Dunboe. Membership currently stands at about eighty-five families.

Reverend Robert Moore

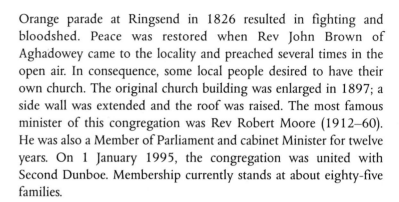

ROBERT MOORE was born at Ringsend in 1886. Educated at Coleraine Academical Institution and Queen's College, Galway, he graduated in the Royal University of Ireland in 1908 and pursued theological studies at Magee College, Londonderry. He was ordained in Ringsend on 5 March 1912 in succession to his uncle, also Rev Robert Moore. Initially, Robert Moore lived in his own home but upon his engagement he declared his intention of living in the manse. However, the manse was in poor repair so Rev Moore resigned his charge on 2 September 1931 and accepted a call to Mosside. The people of Ringsend then renovated their manse and Rev Moore was not installed in Mosside but returned to Ringsend on 19 November 1931. Rev Moore was President of the Ulster Farmers' Union from 1937 to 1940 and again from 1941 to 1942. He was a member of the Ulster Unionist Party and sat as Member of the Northern Ireland Parliament for North Londonderry from 1938 until 1960. He served as Minister of Agriculture from 6 May 1943 until his death on 1 September 1960.

Moneydig

was formed in 1835 although preaching activity in this locality had started some years previously. A site was secured from the Marquis of Waterford, rent free, and the church was completed in 1837. Slates were provided free of charge from the Waterford estate. The first minister, Rev Patrick Killough, was ordained on 12 December 1837; he served here until his death on 21 August 1856. A manse was bought during the ministry of Rev William Latimer (1923–31) and a church hall was built in 1971 during the ministry of Rev

Ernest Ferguson (1964–76). Membership stands today at about 155 families.

Portrush

grew out of a request from local Presbyterians in 1836 to have preaching in the town, at least during the popular summer months. The cause gained full congregational status in 1841. The first minister, Rev Jonathan Simpson (1842–90), had considerable difficulty in building a church and travelled 14,000 miles throughout America and also in Scotland in search of funds. The church was completed in 1844 and significantly extended following the 1859 Revival. Further extensions were required in 1924, as summer attendances were large due to the popularity of the town as a holiday destination. Today, the congregation maintains a ministry to many summer visitors and students attending the nearby university. Membership stands today at 300 families.

Castlerock

was formed in 1874 though summer services were held here from 1862. A church building was opened on 17 July 1870 on a site given by the Clothworkers Company and the first minister, Rev William Irwin, was installed on 2 March 1875 and served until his death on 7 May 1908. The fourth minister, Rev William Forbes Marshall (1928–54), was an accomplished poet and historian. An expert on the Ulster dialect, he published several books including *Ulster Sails West* and *Ballads from Tyrone*. Membership has more than doubled over the past fifty years and stands today at just over 200 families.

The 20th Century

While Sunday church attendance in many congregations peaked in the late 1960s, several congregations in this Presbytery have experienced new and substantial growth. Three new congregations were formed under the auspices of Church Extension: Hazelbank and Ballysally in Coleraine, and Burnside in Portstewart. Overall, Presbyterian families claiming a connection to the congregations within Coleraine Presbytery has increased significantly over the past fifty years.

Hazelbank

was formed in 1973 with services commencing in February of that year. Rev Bill Addley, Chaplain at the University of Ulster, acted as

Stated Supply. Rev Sam Millar was installed as the first minister on 5 September 1974. Full congregational status was attained on 7 January 1982. Rev Millar retired on 30 April 2003. The second minister, Rev Alan Johnston, was installed on 10 January 2004. Membership today stands at about 280 families.

Ballysally

was founded in 1977 in response to the growing population of Coleraine. A dual-purpose hall was opened on 24 September 1977. Rev Brian Kingsmore, minister of Ballywatt and, from 1978, Chaplain in the University of Ulster, was appointed as Stated Supply. Rev Kingsmore was installed as minister here on 30 September 1982 and resigned on 31 December 1983. Rev William McKeown was minister from 1984–1991 and was followed by Rev George Moore (1991–96). Rev John Coulter was inducted as minister in December 1996 and as yet this cause has not attained full congregational status.

Burnside

was formed in 1974 with services commencing on 3 November of that year. Rev Sam Millar of Hazlebank carried the early responsibility. Rev Eric Boreland was installed on 6 April 1978 and a church hall was opened on 31 March 1979. Rev George Cunningham ministered here on 20 January 1983 and served until 1995. A new church building, costing half-a-million pounds, was opened in November 1990 and full congregational status was gained on 1 January 1995. Rev Dr Charles Cameron was installed on 9 February 1996 but he returned to minister in Scotland in September 1998. Rev Richard Gregg was ordained on 1 June 1999 and membership today stands at about 175 families.

Conclusion

It is encouraging to note that more than two thirds of the churches in this Presbytery are growing numerically. Some, most notably Ballywillan and Castlerock, have experienced extraordinary growth. Coleraine Presbytery occupies an attractive area and the desire for people to reside here seems certain to continue in the 21st century. The total number of Presbyterian families has risen by one third over the past five decades and totals over 5,600 today. As in other localities, many congregations are experimenting with new styles of music and broader concepts of ministry.

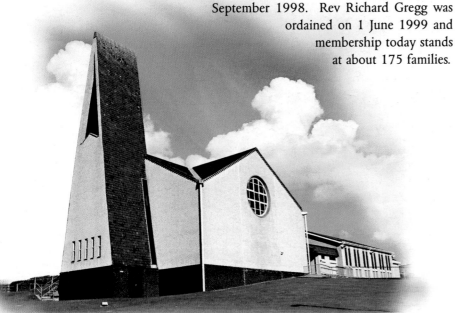

Derry and Strabane Presbytery

Introduction

The Presbytery of Derry and Strabane is dominated by the plantation city of Londonderry. There are thirty-three Presbyterian congregations within this area, served by eighteen ministers. Eighteen congregations have less than 100 families in membership and ten of these are situated in the Republic of Ireland. The largest church, Ebrington, has over 450 families, and the smallest congregation, Inch, counts only fourteen families. Londonderry in the second city of Northern Ireland and has a population of around 100,000.

The 17th Century

Traditionally, the city of Derry was founded by St Columba in AD 546. The name Derry comes from the Irish word Doire or Daire, meaning oak grove. The original oak grove was on an island in the Foyle and the water around it gradually dried out to become the 'Bogside'. Derry was fortified in 1613, and renamed Londonderry in honour of the London Companies, which were given responsibility for Plantation in this area. The name of the city is still contentious in the 21st century. Eight Presbyterian congregations within the Derry and Strabane Presbytery can trace their origins to the 17th century.

The Grianan of Aileach overlooking Lough Foyle

Monreagh

is the oldest congregation in the Laggan district. The first minister, Rev Robert Cunningham (1645–55), successfully appealed to the Scottish Assembly to send ministers to this area. A new church was built during the ministry of Rev William Boyd (1725–72). A number of families left Monreagh during the ministry of Rev Patrick Davison (1776–86) being opposed to his Unitarian views. They formed the congregation of Crossroads. The longest ministry here was that of Rev William Robinson who was ordained on 12 January 1900 and retired on 30 September 1944. The congregation was united with First Derry on 18 November 1987. Membership today totals about sixty-five families.

First Derry and Claremont

First Derry was formed in the 1640s though the name of the first minister is unknown. Rev Robert Craighead (1690–1711) clashed publicly with Rev William King, Bishop of Derry. Unusually, from

Reverend Robert Black

ROBERT BLACK was born in 1752 at Clare, County Armagh. He graduated from the University of Glasgow in 1772 and was licensed by Armagh Presbytery in 1776. Robert Black married his cousin Margaret. He declined a call to Keady and was ordained on 28 June 1777 in Dromore, County Down. This congregation now rejoined the Synod of Ulster, having withdrawn at the height of the Non-subscription controversy in the previous ministry of Dr Colville. Rev Black was an enthusiastic officer in the Volunteers and often preached in his Volunteer uniform. He was installed in First Derry on 7 January 1784, elected Synod Agent for the *regium donum* in 1788, and rose to become the recognised leader of the Synod. He shrank from the excesses of the United Irishmen and warned against civil uprising. In 1803, Rev Black (he was awarded an American DD degree in 1800) negotiated the much appreciated increase in *regium donum* but at the much despised price of congregational classification. In fact Black himself benefited in the new scheme in that his agency of the *regium donum* was now a Government appointment as opposed to a Synod appointment. Black lost his power when the Synod stood up to the machinations of Lord Castlereagh over the Belfast Institution and last attended Synod in 1817. He died on the evening of 4 December 1817 when he committed suicide by jumping from the bridge in Derry and drowning in the River Foyle.

Reverend Richard Smyth

RICHARD SMYTH was born the second of four surviving sons to Hugh and Mary Smyth, at Carnculagh near Dervock on 4 October 1826. All four boys entered the ministry of the Presbyterian Church and two became Moderators, Richard in 1869 and 70, and Jackson (First Armagh) in 1880. Richard was converted as a youth and graduated from Glasgow University in 1850. He was ordained on 20 June 1855 in Westport, County Mayo, but did not stay long, being installed in First Derry on 21 May 1857. When Magee College opened in 1865 Richard Smyth resigned from First Derry and was appointed Professor of Oriental Languages in the College. In 1869, aged forty-three, he was elected Moderator and led negotiations with Government on compensation in relation to ending *regium donum* payments. In the following year, Smyth was re-elected Moderator and also moved to the Chair of Theology in Magee College. Smyth supported the cause of tenant farmers, his own parent having suffered eviction when he was a child, and in 1874 he was elected as a Liberal MP for County Derry. The burden of public life, in addition to his teaching and preaching duties, led to a breakdown in his health. He died on 4 December 1878, aged fifty-two.

1736 until 1865 the congregation had two ministers who worked together as colleagues. The present church building was opened in 1780 just prior to the ministry of Rev Robert Black (1784–1817) who was the acknowledged leader of the Synod of Ulster for many years. Rev Richard Smyth (1857–65) was later Professor of Oriental Literature at Magee College and MP for the city of Derry. Membership fell dramatically with the arrival of the 'Troubles'. The congregation was linked with Monreagh on 18 November 1987. Claremont congregation was formed in 1901 following initial work in the locality by students of Magee College. The Rev John Barkley (1929–45) was father of Professor Barkley of Assembly's College, Belfast. Membership reached 400 families in the early 1960s but diminished rapidly during the 'Troubles', especially following the murder of an off-duty policeman member returning to his car after a service in the church.

First Derry and Claremont were united on 1 January 1997 under the name 'First Derry and Claremont' and total membership stands today at 280 families.

marriage charge'. The longest ministry here was that of Rev Andrew Alexander who was ordained on 31 August 1749 and died on 30 April 1809.

Sion Mills congregation was formed in 1866. Its first minister, Rev David Gordon (1866–78), left to become a missionary in New Zealand. The second Minister, Rev John McMillan was ordained on 26 June 1879 but resigned on 30 April 1880.

Urney and Sion were united on 11 August 1881. Membership stands today at 170 families.

Urney and Sion

The first minister in Urney was Rev James Wallace (1654–74) who continued his ministry even though he was deposed for Non-conformity in 1661. The second minister, Rev David Brown (1677–89), died in Derry during the siege. Rev William Holmes (1696–1734) was temporarily suspended in 1697 on a 'scandalous

Ardstraw

The first minister, Rev William Moorcroft, was here in 1655; he was also responsible for work in Badoney in 1657. Rev Samuel Haliday (1692–1718) ministered in Ardstraw on an annual stipend of £27 and 27 barrels of corn. His son was the famous Rev Samuel Haliday of First Congregation, Belfast. The current church was built in the 1870s. In 1741, a new congregation of Clady was formed out of Ardstraw though it was re-united with the mother congregation in 1884. In 1946, the congregation was united with that of Douglas, which was founded in 1831 as an offshoot of Clady congregation. Membership now totals 170 families.

(1766–98), was a great-great-grandson of Rev Andrew Stewart of Donegal, one of the Fathers of Irish Presbyterianism. Rev Crawford established an Academy at Strabane and several Synod of Ulster ministers received their theological training here. Rev Alexander Porter Goudy (1833–53) became a leading minister in the General Assembly and its Moderator in 1857. A Seceder congregation was formed in Strabane in 1816 and was united with First in 1911. On Christmas Day 1938, the church building was destroyed by fire. A new church was built within the bounds of the manse and incorporated the bell from the old church. The building was opened on 2 May 1957. Membership stands at about 230 families today.

Badoney

Rev William Moorcroft ministered here in 1657. Rev Alexander McCracken (1710–43) was followed by his son Rev Hugh McCracken (1751–66). A new church was built upon the site of the original during the ministry of Rev Thomas Johnston (1843–75); the famous Irish politician, Mr Daniel O'Connell, was a generous contributor. In 1884, the congregation was united with that of Corrick. Local co-operation was extended further in 1970, when Glenelly joined what is now a triple charge. Upon discovering dry rot in their church recently, the people took the courageous decision to demolish it and build a new church, which was opened in 2002. The cost of £265,000 was raised within one year. Membership stands at sixty-five families today.

Strabane

The first minister here, Rev Robert Wilson (1659–89), died in Derry during the siege. The fourth minister, Rev William Crawford

Burt

This cause is situated in County Donegal and was originally linked to First Derry. The earliest minister with sole responsibility for ministry in Burt was Rev William Hempton (1673–89). The Session Minute book, dating from 1677 is in the archive collection of Union Theological College, Belfast. The second minister, Rev Andrew Ferguson (1690–1725) established Burt as a strong cause. His son, Rev John Ferguson, was a founding member of the first American Presbytery of Philadelphia. On 1 October 1951, Burt was united with Buncrana. In January 1973, Burt became part of a wider union which included Buncrana, Fahan and Inch. This union was broken in 1987 and Burt became a Stated Supply of Claremont. On 1 July 1996, Burt was united with Second Derry (Strand and Buncrana). Membership stands at 40 families today.

Reverend Alexander Goudy

ALEXANDER PORTER GOUDY was born in February 1809 in Ballywalter, County Down. His middle name, Porter, honours his grandfather, Rev James Porter of Greyabbey who was hanged in 1798. He was educated at the Belfast Institute and graduated with the General Certificate of the Old College Belfast in 1826. His first pastorate in Glastry was a brief eighteen months, September 1831 until March 1833, and he was installed in the larger and wealthier congregation of Strabane on 20 March 1833. He was still only twenty-four years old. In 1839, he was one of four Presbyterian ministers who responded to a literary attack upon the validity of the Irish Presbyterian Church by Dr William King, Anglican Bishop of Derry, with a publication entitled 'Presbyterianism Defended'. The same four ministers published again in 1840 with 'Plea of Presbytery'. This publication marked a new confidence within Irish Presbyterians, daring to confront the hierarchy of the Church of Ireland. Rev Goudy vigorously supported the cause of using the Magee Bequest to build a College in Derry. He also supported the cause of liberals in politics, much to the annoyance of Dr Henry Cooke. In 1857, Alexander Goudy was elected Moderator of the General Assembly but he did not fulfil his year of office. After travelling to Dublin in December 1858 to deliver the funeral sermon of Rev Richard Dill, he took suddenly ill in the Verdon Hotel and died at 10am on Tuesday 14 December. His wife arrived at the hotel from Strabane only a few minutes after the demise of her husband.

The 18th Century

Nine congregations within the Derry and Strabane Presbytery trace their origins to the 18th century. The five churches formed in the first half of the century were members of the Synod of Ulster and the four formed in the second half of the century belonged to the Seceders. The Strabane Academy, which was formed in 1785 by Rev William Crawford, is noteworthy as Presbyterians sought university level education without recourse to expensive travel to Scotland.

First Castlederg

was formed about 1700 at the instigation of Rev William Holmes of Urney. Some of his congregation, along with members of Ardstraw, comprised the nucleus of the new congregation. The first minister was the Irish-speaking Rev John Dunlop (1710–13). In 1793, a section of the congregation formed a new church at Drumquin. The current church was built in the early 1800s during the ministry of Rev James Henderson (1791–1818) and the architect was Mr Vincent Craig, a brother of Sir James Craig, the first Prime Minister of Northern Ireland. Rev Henderson drowned on 20 December 1818. In November 1827, a section of the

Carndonagh

The first minister, Rev Robert Neilson (1690–98), struggled to survive among a poor people but the cause became established in the 18th century. Rev Reuben Rogers (1808–46) was assisted and then succeeded by his son, Rev Robert Rogers (1844–47). A new church was built during the ministry of Rev Robert Morrison (1884–1925) and opened in 1886. From 1 December 1965 the Carndonagh minister became Stated Supply for Malin. This relationship was further developed when the congregations were united in 1969. Membership stands at 45 families.

200

congregation formed a church at Killeter and in September 1837 Rev John Crockett of Killeter was installed as minister of Castlederg. The congregation was linked with Killeter on 1 April 1977. Membership stands today at about 175 families.

Moville

was formed in 1715. the first minister was Rev Thomas Harvey (1715–18). He returned to Moville for a second period from 1727

until 1747. The original church was situated at Clare, some three miles closer to Londonderry. The current church was built in Moville town during the ministry of Rev John Bell (1861–92). Rev Robert Porter was ordained on 24 May 1892 but died aged twenty-six on 28 September 1894. Moville was united with Greenbank on 1 May 1959. Membership today stands at about thirty families.

Malin

church was built on the seashore in 1717 because this land was deemed to belong to no-one, and Presbyterians were discriminated against by the land owning Episcopalians. Until a new road was constructed, the sea swept around the building twice each day. The local Roman Catholic chapel was built on the seashore for the same reason. The congregation enjoyed a total of sixteen ministers as a separate charge. The two longest ministries here were Rev James Canning (1798–1838) and his son, Rev John Canning (1832–77). The shortest ministry was that of Rev Joseph Thompson (13 June

1878–3 September 1878). On 1 December 1965, Malin became a Stated Supply of the minister of Carndonagh and was united with this congregation in 1969. Membership stands at thirty-one families.

Fahan

was formed in 1719 and initially linked with Buncrana, for over 100 years, until 1834. The second minister, Rev Joseph Reagh (1748–70) emigrated to America. Rev John Macky (1842–54) resigned to undertake missionary work in New Zealand. The congregation was united with Inch in 1896. This union became a three-pointed charge with the addition of Knowhead in 1959. Rev Robert Stewart served as minister on two occasions, 1959–61 and 1964–68. On 31 December 1972, the union with Knowhead was dissolved and the congregation became a Stated Supply to the minister of Burt and Buncrana. The congregation was linked with Great James Street in 1974 and then with Waterside on 1 July 1995. Membership stands today at just under fifty families.

Knowhead

is also known as 'Muff' and originated about 1749. The second minister, Rev Stephen Brizzle (1776–80) was deposed by Presbytery for celebrating marriages illegally. The congregation was united with Greenbank from 1952–58 and then with Fahan and Inch from1959–72. The present union with Ballyarnett was effective from 1 January 1973. The first minister of the new union was Rev Robert Simpson (1973–80) who left to become Director

of Northern Ireland Marriage Guidance. Membership stands at sixty-five families.

Second Derry (Strand and Buncrana)

The second Presbyterian congregation in Derry was formed in 1780 by a section of the original Derry congregation. They were linked with Crossroads. The first minister, Rev Walter Galbraith (1782–1810), was presented with four calls but was directed by Synod to accept the call from Derry. He resigned the Crossroads ministry in 1793. The original church was situated in Fountain Street but a new and larger church on Strand Road was opened on 12 March 1848. A gallery was added in 1885. Rev John Henry (1882–90) became Professor of Church History at Magee College (1890–1911) and was elected Moderator of the General Assembly in 1902. He was succeeded by Rev William Lowe (1891–1909) who served as a distinguished General Secretary of the Assembly (1909–1931) and its Moderator in 1921. Rev William Montgomery (1941–67) was elected Moderator of the General

Assembly in 1963. The congregation of Strand (Second Derry) was united with that of Buncrana on 30 September 1988, becoming one congregation on 1 July 1996, with the name, 'Second Derry' (Strand and Buncrana) and in union with Burt. Membership now stands at about 160 families.

Reverend William Lowe

WILLIAM JAMES LOWE was raised as a member of First Ballynahinch. His early career was as a teacher, after which he entered Queen's College, Galway, in 1877, and was the leading scholar in science for his three years there. He graduated BA from Queen's University in Ireland in 1883 and then undertook theological studies in the Presbyterian College, Belfast. William Lowe was ordained on 2 April 1884 in Mountnorris congregation in County Armagh where he served for five years. He then undertook a brief ministry in Islington congregation, Liverpool (1889–91) before his installation in Strand congregation, Londonderry, on 27 February 1891. While there he clashed with Baptist propagandists. A series of his sermons on the issues of conflict emerged later as a book entitled, 'Baptism, its Mode and Subjects'. On 4 June 1895, he was appointed Clerk of the General Assembly and in 1900 he was awarded a Doctor of Divinity degree by the Presbyterian Theological Faculty Ireland. On 1 July 1909, he resigned as minister of Strand, having been appointed General Secretary of the Presbyterian Church in Ireland on 11 June 1909. Dr Lowe was elected Moderator of the General Assembly in 1921 and received an honorary LL.D degree from Dublin University in 1925. He had a distinguished career in Church House, wisely guiding many Moderators and directing affairs of the Presbyterian Church. William Lowe died suddenly on 18 March 1931 at seventy-seven years of age. The new church at Finaghy in South Belfast was named 'Lowe Memorial' in his memory.

Crossroads

This Anti-Burgher Seceder cause was formed by a number of Monreagh families who were dissatisfied with the New-Light ideas of Rev Patrick Davidson. For a time this new cause was known as 'Taughboyne'. A church was built in 1783 and Rev Walter Galbraith preached here and in Derry until 1793 when he left Crossroads. Rev Samuel Craig spent a lifetime here (1805–54). Rev Hugh Irwin (1874–85) left to become a missionary in New Zealand. In 1956 Crossroads was united with Newtowncunningham and, from 1 November 1974, Crossroads became Stated Supply to the minister of Carlisle Road, Londonderry. The congregation was united with Carlisle Road on 1 Sept 1989. Membership totals about thirty families.

Second Castlederg

originated as a Seceder preaching station organised by the Ardstraw Seceder congregation. The congregation was known for a time as Dergbridge. A new church was built in 1859 and a gallery was added in 1870. Rev John Stirling (1880–91) visited America in 1888 where he collected £460 with which to build a manse. Rev Gustavus Henderson (1892–1909) was succeeded by his brother Rev William Henderson (1910–35). From 1 October 1966, the minister of Second Castlederg became Stated Supply to Alt. On 1 Feb 1991, the congregations were united. Membership now totals about 190 families.

Corrick

This was a Burgher Seceder cause formed in 1798 by members of Badoney who were dissatisfied with Rev Charles Hempill. The new congregation was also known as 'Badoney' and 'Second Donemana'. The name 'Corrick' came into use in the mid 19th century. In 1884 the congregation was united with Badoney during the ministry of Rev Jackson McFadden who continued as minister of the united charge for a further fifty-one years until his death on 31 May 1938. A three-point charge was created on 1 July 1970 when Glenelly was added. Membership today stands at about thirty families.

The 19th Century

Fourteen of the current congregations within the Derry and Strabane Presbytery originated in the 19th century. Of these, only Leckpatrick and Magheramason remain as single charges. Numbers in the countryside area declined in the latter half of the 20th century and from 1881 several congregations were united in order to provide a viable ministry for a single minister.

Newtownstewart

was formed in 1802 and the first minister was Rev John McFarland (1804–26). He was suspended in 1824 for irregular celebration of marriages and in 1830 deposed from ministry. The second minister, Rev Charles Adams (1827–42), was suspended for the same

reasons. A Seceder congregation was established in Newtownstewart in 1826 and, following unsuccessful attempts at union in 1877 and again in 1900, they eventually united in 1903 during the long and successful ministry of Rev David Morton (1890–1950). The current church was built in 1910 on the site of the original church. On 1 July 1970 the congregation was united with Gortin. Family membership today stands at forty.

Killeter

originated as part of Castlederg but separated in 1827. Rev William Hamilton was ordained here on 20 February 1838 despite more than one third of the people requesting a postponement. The Synod later declared the ordination irregular and removed Rev Hamilton from the congregation. During the ministry of Rev James Lyons (1937–75) Killeter acquired a glebe of 140 acres, possibly the largest of any Irish Presbyterian Church. The congregation was united with First Castlederg on 1 April 1977. Membership today stands seventy-five families.

Inch

is a small island off the coast of Donegal and the Presbyterians here originally worshipped at Burt. They formed a separate congregation in 1831 and their first minister was Rev Samuel Armour (1833–53). In 1850, the congregation consisted of twenty-two families. In 1896, they were united with Fahan and this union in turn became a three-pointed charge with the addition of Knowhead from 1959 until 1972. From 1 January 1973, Inch became a Stated Supply for the minister of Strand with services held twice each month. It has been a Stated Supply for the minister of Ebrington since 1996. Inch is the smallest church in this Presbytery with a membership of fourteen families.

Douglas

was formed in 1831 as a separation from Clady. The first two ministers covered a period of 105 years. Rev James Alexander (1831–67) was followed by Rev Robert Dick (1868–1936) who was one of the last Presbyterian ministers to own his own house and farm. The congregation was united with Ardstraw in 1946 and a new church was opened in April 1958, replacing the original T-shaped building. Membership stands today at about 175 families.

Alt

was formed out of the Seceder cause at Drumlegagh (Second Ardstraw). The first minister, Rev Samuel Stewart (1834–81), had grown up in Drumlegagh congregation. The church was built in 1835, enlarged in 1899 and almost completely rebuilt in 1911. The congregation grew at a time when the local Presbyterian population fell by half. The shortest ministry here was that of Rev Herman Brown, who was ordained in Alt on 29 May 1942 and resigned on 31 July 1942. From 1952, the congregation became a Stated Supply under Donaghmore for ten years and then Second Castlederg before union with the latter church on 1 February 1991. Family membership today stands at twenty families.

Glenelly

was formed in 1835 following services conducted by Rev Charles Hempill of Badoney. Rev John Moore was ordained on 12 May 1836; he used to preach in a thatched cabin on the site of the present church until his retirement on 14 June 1869. Many Presbyterians in this locality emigrated, and the congregation was united with Gortin on 1 June 1946. On 18 October 1946, Crockatanty was added to the union. From 1 July 1970, Glenelly has been united with Badoney and Corrick congregations. Family membership today stands at thirty-seven families.

Leckpatrick

was formed in 1836; the church building was opened in this same year. The first minister, Rev Moses Chambers (1838–63), was a native of County Donegal. In 1898, the interior of the church was entirely altered and refurbished. A church hall was built in 1955, and a new manse in 1963 replaced the original, built in 1878. Family membership has almost doubled over the past half century and now stands at 190 families.

Carlisle Road

was a Seceder cause that started in the Fountain Street area of the city in 1837. The first minister, Rev John McFarland (1838–42), was ordained in the later accommodation in London Street, a former theatre. The new church in Carlisle Road was opened on 23 March 1879 during the ministry of Rev Robert Ross (1850–94) who was Moderator of the General Assembly in 1888. His son was a local MP, High Court Judge and Lord Chancellor of Ireland. Crossroads became a Stated Supply in 1977 and the two congregations were united on 1 September 1989. Membership stands now at a little under 200 families.

Gortin

was formed in 1842 following work in the locality by Matthew Logan who was then ordained as minister on 13 August 1842. He was a strong advocate of Temperance and ministered here until his death on 19 August 1884. His daughter, Fanny, was a missionary in Damascus for thirty years. Rev Adam Whyte (1885–1936) followed and built two schools in the area. The congregation was united with Glenelly on 1 June 1946 with Crockatanty was added on 18 October 1946. A new union with Newtownstewart was formed on 1 July 1970. Membership stands at about forty families today.

Ballyarnett

was formed in 1843 by a minority of Knowhead congregation who disapproved of the appointment of Rev John Bleckley. The first two ministries here were long and distinguished: Rev Robert McCreery (1848–92) and Rev John Gregg (1892–1944). Uniquely, the church was built in the centre of an old racecourse and local Roman Catholic people assisted in its construction. The congregation was united with Knowhead on 1 January 1973. Membership currently totals about 150 families.

Greenbank

was formed by a section of the 'Old Moville' congregation who built a church here in the 1860s. The longest ministry here was that of Rev Samuel Irvine who was ordained on 21 March 1861 and retired in 1893. The congregation was united with Knowhead from 1952–58 and then with Moville from 1 May 1959. Family membership stands today at almost forty families.

Magheramason

was formed in August 1878 by a section of Second Donagheady congregation. They had shown determination for two years in pressing the need for a new church in the locality. The first minister, Rev Thomas Boyd (1879–84), established a regular congregation of eighty families. Both Rev James Hamill (1893–96) and Rev Joseph Caskey (1896–1908) left Magheramason to become ministers in the Free Church in Scotland. Perhaps the most influential evangelical ministry here was that of Rev Frederick Wallace (1925–61). Family membership has virtually doubled over the past fifty years and now stands at about 300 families.

Waterside

was formed in 1866 as a new Derry congregation on the east side of the river. The original name of 'Clooney Terrace' was dropped in favour of 'Waterside'. The first minister, Rev Thomas Croskery (1863–75) was appointed Professor of Logic in Magee College and was a prolific author. A gallery was added to the church in 1877 and there were 350 families in membership in 1923. Rev Robert Wilson (1923–28) was later Principal of Assembly's College,

206

Belfast, and Moderator of the General Assembly in 1957. The congregation was united with Fahan on 1 July 1995. Membership today totals about 265 families.

Ebrington

was formed in 1896 following services in a small Temperance Hall in Spencer Road which commenced two years earlier. The first minister was Rev Leslie Rankin (1896–1944) of Garvagh. Two Ebrington ministers have become Moderator after leaving: Rev William Craig (1945–48) in 1979, and Rev Robert Dickinson (1960–73) in 1985. Rev Bill Addley (1974–87) left to undertake missionary service in Brazil and was later Professor of Practical Theology in Union Theological College, Belfast. The congregation of Inch became a Stated Supply in 1996. Family membership stands today at about 450 families, the largest in this Presbytery.

Reverend Thomas Croskery

THOMAS CROSKERY was a native of Carrowdore in County Down. Born on 26 May 1830, he was brought up in the congregation of Rev Samuel Nelson in Dromore, in membership of the Remonstrant Synod. As a student Thomas Croskery came to accept the doctrine of the Trinity and joined the General Assembly. He worked for a time as a journalist before studying for ministry in the Presbyterian Church. He was licensed in 1851 and, after preaching in twenty-six vacancies, became minister successively in Creggan (1860–63), Clonakilty (1863–66) and Waterside, Londonderry (1866–75). In 1875, he was appointed Professor of Logic, Belles Lettres and Rhetoric at Magee College, a position he fulfilled for four years. From 1879 until 1886, he served as Professor of Theology in the same College. Thomas Croskery published several books and contributed numerous articles to various journals and periodicals. Perhaps his most famous publication was his 'Refutation' of the principles of the Plymouth Brethren. Professor Croskery died on 3 October 1886. Two sons, James and William, were also Presbyterian ministers in the congregations of Mountjoy and Tully respectively.

The Strabane Academy

WILLIAM CRAWFORD was born in 1739, first son of Rev Thomas Crawford (Crumlin), grandson of Rev Rev Andrew Crawford (Carnmoney), great-grandson of Rev Thomas Crawford (Donegore) and great-great-grandson of Rev Rev Andrew Stewart (Donegore). William was ordained in Strabane on 6 February 1766. In 1784, he was awarded a Doctor of Divinity degree from Glasgow University and in the following year, he opened an Academy at Strabane for training candidates for the Presbyterian ministry. The Academy was recognised by the Synod of Ulster and offered home education as a much cheaper option than the custom of sending ministerial students to the University of Glasgow. A similar Academy was founded by Rev Moses Neilson at Rademon. Considering the financial saving in undertaking local education, it is not surprising that a considerable number of ministers received their training in Dr Crawford's Strabane Academy. The enterprise does not appear to have survived Dr Crawford's move to Holywood and the opening of the Belfast Institution in 1815 gave new opportunities for home education for ministerial students. Rev William Crawford ministered in Holywood from October 1798 and died on 4 January 1800.

The 20th Century

From 1905, there were six Presbyterian churches within Londonderry, five on the west bank of the Foyle and a sixth on the east bank. This Presbytery has witnessed a flurry of congregational unions from the 1940s. This has been specially marked since the 1970s, pairing small congregations within close proximity but also linking a city church with a smaller church on Fahan peninsula. The civil disturbances which erupted in Londonderry in 1969 resulted in a major population move from the Cityside to the Waterside of Londonderry. Some 12,000 Protestants have abandoned the Cityside, leaving less than 1,000 in that area. Unsurprisingly, this has impacted upon the Presbyterian congregations in the city which have all experienced a major haemorrhaging of members. Prior to 1969 there were 10,000 Presbyterians living within the city. Kilfennan is an obvious success story in this move but there have also been casualties, with strong congregations declining markedly. Claremont closed its doors in 1996 and Strathfoyle is a notable example of an abortive attempt at church extension.

Kilfennan

was opened on Saturday 11 September 1982 and was the first Presbyterian church to be built in Londonderry for seventy-five years. The origin of this new congregation was the imaginative decision of the people in Great James Street in 1978 to 'port' from the Cityside to the Waterside. The project was undertaken in partnership with Church Extension. The new building was multifunctional in design, combining beauty and practical durability. The first minister, Rev Edgar McKinney (1982–92), enjoyed tremendous success in establishing this new cause. Membership today stands at 375 families.

Conclusion

This Presbytery is dominated by the city of Londonderry. The future challenges facing the city churches will multiply as their loyal congregations age. New challenges may emerge on the Waterside also. As this area becomes more mixed, it will be interesting to see if Presbyterians will stay or move again. This Presbytery has many successful joint charges and such arrangements look set to continue.

TS Mooney

THOMAS SMYTH MOONEY, or 'TS' as he was universally known, was born on 6 February 1907 and raised in Dromore Original Secession Church; he was converted in his teens. He worked for forty-five years in the Derry branch of the Belfast Savings Bank and was an elder in Great James Street congregation. He contributed significantly to student life in Magee College, Crusaders camps, Christian Workers' Union, the Portstewart Convention and several other Christian organisations. TS was ordained as an elder in Great James Street in 1945, and became Clerk of Session in 1971. He retired from his beloved bank in 1970. TS was the best known elder in Irish Presbyterianism and seemed to always have something relevant to say at every General Assembly. Reputed for his pithy sayings, he was once asked why he had never married. He replied, 'The attractive were not available and the available were not attractive'. Despite the decline within the congregation due to the exodus of Presbyterians from the city side, TS was always the loyal and cheerful elder. He enthusiastically embraced the new opportunity for the congregation to relocate and was instrumental in ensuring that Kilfennan opened in September 1982 as a happy and united congregation. Membership rose from 110 families to 350 families within six months. TS died on Friday 25 January 1986.

Errigal mountain

Donegal Presbytery

Introduction

The Presbytery of Donegal consists of twenty-one congregations, all of which are situated in the Republic of Ireland and none of which are single charges. Congregational distribution is clustered in the north-west of the County, the exception being Donegal and Ballyshannon in the south-west. Congregational size varies from 13 to 215 families with an average of sixty-seven families. Presbyterianism has a long and distinguished history in this area but recent experience has been one of gradual shrinkage and increasing congregational unions.

The 17th Century

Scottish settlers began to arrive in this area in 1611 and it is known that some Presbyterian ministers worked among these early Planters. The Royal School at Raphoe was founded by a charter granted by Charles I and dated 15 December 1637. The 1641 Rebellion resulted in many settlers returning to Scotland and the record of the early ministries has been lost. As the bulk of the new settlers arriving from Scotland were Presbyterian, it is no surprise to discover that nine congregations in Donegal Presbytery today can trace their origins to this early period. The 17th century was marked by bitter rivalry from the established church. With a bishop in Derry, and another in Raphoe, only twelve miles distant, the Episcopal authorities regularly flexed their muscle against the Presbyterian ministers. Several ministers and many people emigrated, most notably Francis Mackemie, the 'father of American Presbyterianism'.

Ray

congregation was the second Presbyterian cause in the Laggan, after Monreagh. The first minister of Ray, Rev Hugh Cunningham (1646–61), had been a Chaplain to the Earl of Glencairn's regiment in 1642 and present at the formation of the Army Presbytery in Carrickfergus on 10 June 1642. In 1752, the majority of the congregation declared support for the Seceders and gained control of this church building, but the minority loyal to the Synod of Ulster expelled them by resorting to legal action. The Seceders formed their own congregation, later known as *Second Ray*. This early Seceder cause had three generations of Rentouls, father James, son Alexander and grandson James, as ministers from 1791–1881. Both congregations united in 1927 and the first minister of the united charge was Rev James Lorimer (1927–37). This united charge was in turn united with Newtowncunningham on 1 July 1974. Membership stands at about 130 families today.

Trinity, Letterkenny

was built up under Scotsman Rev William Semple (1647–74) who initially preached in the Church of Ireland. He suffered many

hardships under bishops and the Commonwealth, most notably being imprisoned in Lifford for six years, 1664–70, by Bishop Robert Leslie of Raphoe for Non-conformity. A Second congregation was formed in 1821 by a minority of the congregation but re-united with First in 1858. The seventh minister, Rev John Kinnear (1848–99) supported tenant rights and was elected MP in 1880. The original church was rebuilt in 1907 but burnt out in an act of vandalism on 31 August 1921 as part of the 'Troubles'. This event brought Presbyterians in Letterkenny closer together and resulted, in 1925, in a united single Presbyterian congregation in the town. The new congregation adopted the name Trinity. In addition to First congregation, this union included two other churches, Third (formed in 1840) and Gortlee Reformed Presbyterian church (formed about 1785). Letterkenny was united with Trenta on 1 February 1975. Today, Letterkenny is the largest church in Donegal Presbytery with 215 families in membership.

Reverend John Kinnear

JOHN KINNEAR was born in 1823, the son of Rev John Kinnear, minister of Lower Clonaneese. He was ordained in First Letterkenny on 27 December 1848 and took a keen interest in the rights of tenant farmers. Local landlords did not approve of his sympathies with the Tenant Right Movement and blocked his appointment as Chaplain to the new Letterkenny Hospital. During 1868 he travelled in the United States for five months. He stood as a Liberal candidate in the 1880 general election and sensationally won the seat from the Marquis of Hamilton who represented the landlord interests. He did defend his seat in the 1885 general election, judging that politics in the locality had become too nationalistic. Dr Kinnear, awarded an honorary DD from Washington University in 1874, was a staunch opponent of the use of instrumental music in Sunday services. His practice was to preach for fifty minutes without manuscript and his services invariably lasted two hours. He retired on 6 August 1899, outliving his wife and three children, and died on 8 July 1909.

Reverend Samuel Dill

SAMUEL DILL was born on 22 August 1772 into a notable Presbyterian dynasty. Son of John Dill, a Fannet farmer, both Samuel and his older brother Richard became Presbyterian ministers – as did their cousins Francis and Richard. Samuel was ordained on 16 July 1799 in Donoughmore and spent his entire ministry of forty-five years here. He was extremely zealous for Christian truth and clashed with Arians and Moderates. He suspended a Mr Wauchop from communion because the Castlefin hotel owned by this gentleman was a venue for cock-fighting, card playing and horse-racing. In 1805, Mr Wauchop took Rev Dill to court on a charge of 'defamation of character' and claimed £500 damages. A Lifford court awarded Mr Wauchop 6d damages. An indignant plaintiff pursued the case in Dublin and Rev Dill was £300 out of pocket on legal costs before the case was settled. Samuel Dill could afford this sum as he married 'into money' and inherited a large house and farm. He died on 10 December 1845.

Ramelton

was formed in 1654 and the first minister, Rev Thomas Drummond was deposed by Bishop Robert Leslie in the year of his installation and later imprisoned in Lifford Castle from 1664 until 1670. In 1681, Rev Drummond introduced Francis Mackemie to Laggan Presbytery as a student for the ministry. A Seceder congregation was also formed in Ramelton sometime before 1761, and was later known as *Second Ramelton* or the *Scots church*. The first regular minister here was Rev Samuel Gamble (1808–57). A Third Ramelton congregation was formed, for reasons long forgotten, on 22 December 1837. The first minister of Third was Rev Matthew Wilson (1839–49), father of Professor Wilson of Assembly's College, Belfast. Rev Thomas Killen was minister of Third (1850–57) and later a highly influential minister who was elected Moderator of the General Assembly in 1882. Second and Third united in 1903, and First united with Second and Third on 1 May 1967. Ramelton was united with Kilmacrennan on 1 January 1991. Membership totals 135 families today.

Fannet

was formed in 1654. Originally linked to Rathmullan, it was known as Clondevadock. The first minister, Rev Adam White (1654–72), was deposed by Bishop Robert Leslie in 1661, and imprisoned in Lifford Castle from 1664 until 1670. Several of the earliest ministers were local men. The longest ministry was that of Rev James Keating (1859–1903). The church was united with Rathmullan from 1931 until 1951. Fannet was united with Milford from 1 May 1951 and, on 1 January 1982, a three-point charge was

created when Rathmullan was added. Membership today stands at thirty families.

Donoughmore

was formed in 1658, when Rev Robert Craighead became minister. Although deposed by Bishop Leslie in 1661, he avoided imprisonment and stayed here until 1690. The original church building was replaced in 1875. During extensive renovation work, an electrical fault resulted in the accidental destruction of the church on 19 February 1975, after which a new church was built. Rev John Sproule (1934–70) was appointed Stated Supply of Stranorlar from 1 October 1966 and the two congregations were united on 1 July 1972. Rev Elinor Henning became the second woman minister in Donegal Presbytery, when she was installed on 19 March 1988. Membership today stands at eighty families.

Convoy

was the location where Revs Weir and Adair from Scotland administered the Covenant in 1644. The earliest known Presbyterian minister was Rev John Crookshanks 1660–63. Mr Samuel Halliday followed in 1664 and, uniquely, officiated here for twelve years before being ordained in December 1676. He was father of Rev Samuel Haliday of First Belfast congregation. For a short time, 1700–1717, Convoy was the centre of the Presbytery of Convoy. Rev David Fairly ministered here for sixty-five years (1711–76), and Rev James Taylor followed for sixty-one years (1766–1827). Convoy united with Carnone on 1 August 1957. Rev Patricia McKee, the first woman minister in Donegal, was installed in the joint charge on 14 June 1985 and served here for five years. Membership today stands at 100 families.

Ballyshannon

was originally linked with Donegal. The first minister, Rev William Henry, was ordained on St Patrick's Day 1674. Rev Henry was

arrested by Bishop Otway of Killala in 1677 while preaching in Connaught, and imprisoned in Dublin. Details of his death are unknown due to lost records. A church was built in College Street in 1672. It was used by the congregation until May 1834, when Ballyshannon separated from Donegal. The church was also known as *Mountcharles*. A new church was then built on the Mall. With thirteen families, this is the smallest congregation in Donegal Presbytery.

Ballindrait

was originally known as Lifford and was formed about 1671. The first minister, Rev Wiliam Trail (1672–82), was imprisoned for eight months for observing a Laggan Presbytery fast in 1681 before successfully appealing before the Privy Council in Dublin. Rev James Porter, who was executed at the time of the 1798 Rebellion, was raised in this congregation. In 1882, Miss Houston, granddaughter of Rev Cunningham of St. Johnston, left her father's house and farm as a manse and glebe to the congregation. A union with Ballylennon was in place from 1 July 1923 until 1 July 1965. On 1 January 1972, the congregation was united with Raphoe and membership currently totals thirty-two families.

Donegal

was formed in the 1670s and was originally known as *Raneeny*. The first minister, Rev William Henry, was ordained in 1674 and also ministered in Belleek and Greystown. A Second congregation was formed by the Seceders in the early 1820s employing Licentiates to

213

build up the work. A church was built in 1827 and Rev William Niblock (1825–68) conducted a Classical Academy here. First and Second united as a single charge in 1884. The current church was built in 1886 upon the site of the Seceder church. In 1952, Rev Dr Thomas Barker was appointed Stated Supply and was elected Moderator of the General Assembly in 1956. Donegal and Ballyshannon have shared the services of a minister since 1959. The Second church is used for Sunday services and the First church is used once a quarter. In addition, summer services are conducted in Rosnowlagh, one of the few wooden churches in Ireland. Ancillary rooms were added in an extension in 2006. Membership today stands at forty-five families.

The 18th Century

Six congregations today trace their origins to the 18th century. The Seceders brought an injection of enthusiasm and building activity to this locality and generally made inroads among the poorest people. Their first church was formed at Ray in 1747 and this was followed by further causes at Carnone in 1755, then further north at Crossroads in 1781. The spectre of emigration haunted the Presbyterian community throughout this century with people leaving for America with hopes of attaining freedom of worship and economic prosperity.

Dunfanaghy

was formed in 1702. Originally linked with Kilmacrennan, its first known minister was Rev Robert Drummond (1702–12). The link

USA Connections

DONEGAL PRESBYTERIANS have long associations with America. Some of them emigrated as early as the 17th century due primarily to persecution from local bishops or poor economic conditions. Rev Thomas Wilson of Kilybegs was the earliest example, leaving in 1681, after which his congregation became extinct. During penal times in the early 18th century, a majority of ministers in this locality declared their intention to seek religious freedom by emigrating to America. Rev William Trail of Ballindrait went to Maryland and prepared the way for Francis Mackemie. Rev Thomas Craighead of Donegal sailed from Derry in 1714. Most Donegal emigrants passed through Philadelphia into Pennsylvania and founded congregations in Lancaster County. They formed a Donegal Presbytery in 1732. Recent links have been developed between the congregations of Donegal Springs (America) and Donegal (Ireland) with the former founded by members of the latter in 1714. As a mark of the links between these congregations, the minister and elders from Donegal Springs were present when a mature Irish Oak was planted in the grounds of Donegal Church in June 1975 on the occasion of the tercentenary celebrations. An American White Oak tree stands in the grounds of Donegal Springs and is between 300 and 400 years old.

was broken in 1829. The present church was built in 1878. By the mid-20th century this locality was a popular summer holiday destination and congregational attendance rose notably in these months. The church was linked with Carrigart on 1 May 1951. Membership currently stands at twenty-six families.

Kilmacrennon

was formed in 1702 and was linked with Dunfanaghy until 1829. Rev Robert Watts was ordained on 4 March 1885 but died on 4 December 1889. He was a son of Professor Robert Watts of Assembly's College, Belfast. The congregation was linked with Trentra from 1929 until 1963 and then became a Stated Supply to the Ramelton minister. Union with Ramelton took effect on 1 January 1991. Membership today stands at thirty-seven families.

Stranorlar

originated in impoverished circumstances in 1709. When the first minister, Rev Robert Wilson (1709–27), resigned the Synod thought seriously about dissolving the cause. The longest ministry here was that of Rev James Curry (1881–1940) and in 1906 the current church was built. Rev Jim McClure (1955–65) had been raised in this congregation. The congregation was united with Donoughmore on 1 July 1972 and Rev Elinor Henning was installed in the joint charge on 19 March 1988. Membership totals seventy families today.

St. Johnston

originated in some controversy when Rev William Gray, formerly of Monreagh (1699–1721), returned after a short time in Dublin and conducted regular worship in the town of St. Johnston. Several families from his former congregation joined him and eventually, in 1731, the new congregation was formally recognised. The original church was replaced by the present building in 1829. Unusually, this Presbyterian Church has a tower and the neighbouring Church of Ireland and Roman Catholic churches do not. The church was united with Ballylennon on 1 July 1965. Membership stands at about seventy families today.

Raphoe

was formed in 1751, the local Presbyterians having worshipped at Convoy previously. Rev William Ramsey (1786–1827) is reputed to

have only ever produced thirteen sermons, and these he preached on a rota basis for many years. Rev William Killen (1829–41) left to become Professor of Church History in Assembly's College, Belfast. An additional congregation, Second Raphoe, was formed in 1855 and was served by four successive ministers before First and Second united on 8 August 1923. The Second building was no longer used for worship in 1950. On 1 January 1972, the congregation was united with Ballindrait. Membership stands today at just over 150 families.

Carnone

was originally known as Donaghmore and was formed in 1757 as the second Seceder congregation in the locality. The first minister, Rev Robert Law (1757–93), was a native of Ballindrait and had been licensed by the Synod of Ulster in 1746. His license was withdrawn in 1752 and he joined the Anti-Burghers. Membership peaked in 1846 with 280 families. In 1923, the church was united with Alt. Rev Thomas McCandless was minister on two occasions, 1894–1908 and 1928–41. Rev Herman Brown served as minister for only two months, 27 May 1942 – 31 July 1942. The union with Alt was dissolved in 1948 and, on 1 August 1957, a new union was formed with Convoy. Rev Patricia McKee, the first woman minister in Donegal, was installed in the joint charge on 14 June 1985 and served here for five years. Membership currently stands at fifty-four families.

The 19th Century

Six congregations today trace their origins to the 19th century. In only one location, Ballylennon, did a Seceder cause prosper and that soon united with the Synod of Ulster congregation in the same town. Neither Methodist nor Baptist causes had any success in this area with Presbyterian people remaining loyal to their own Church. The once all-powerful Church of Ireland was disestablished in 1870 and relations with Presbyterians much improved. Many of the Presbyterian ministers supported the Land League Movement, seeking to improve the security and prospects of poor tenant farmers.

Rathmullan

was formed in 1828 to ease travel for local Presbyterians who had previously worshipped in Fannet. The longest ministry was that of Rev John McFarland (1860–1907). Rev James Edgar (1931–44) had been a licentiate of the Reformed Presbyterian Eastern Presbytery before joining the General Assembly. The church was

united with Fannet from 1931 until 1950 and was then a Stated Supply to Rev Samuel Thompson, minister of Ramelton, until 1971. From 1 May 1971, the minister of Milford and Fannet was appointed as Stated Supply and the present three-point charge was created on 1 January 1982. Membership currently stands at just less than twenty families.

1974 and with First and Second Ray since 1 July 1974. Membership currently stands at sixty-two families.

Ballylennon

was the locality for new Seceder and Synod of Ulster churches within six years of each other. The Seceders ordained Rev John Lecky on 29 September 1829 and built a church shortly afterwards. The Synod of Ulster built a church and then ordained Rev George Hanson on 10 February 1835. These two ministers became firm friends and both resigned in 1878, enabling the congregations to unite on 5 December 1878. Rev Alexander Lecky, son of Rev John Lecky, had a long ministry here (1878–1929). The church was united with Ballindrait from 1 July 1923 until 1 July 1965 and then united with St. Johnston from 1 July 1965. Membership stands at sixty families today.

Newtowncunningham

was formed on 10 February 1830 though Presbyterians in the district had sought to form a congregation as early as 1792. The first minister was Rev William Scott (1830–80). Two ministers later served as Moderator of the General assembly; Rev George Thompson (1880–98) in 1923 and Rev John Knowles (1912–22) in 1954. The church was united with Crossroads from 1957 until

Trenta

was formed in 1836 and the first minister, Rev Sampson Jack, was ordained on 20 April 1837. He died on the ferryboat at Derry while travelling to Belfast to attend an Assembly Committee on 20 October 1879. The church was united with Kilmacrennan from 1929 until 1963, when the minister of Ray acted as Stated Supply here. This arrangement continued for twelve years. From 1 February 1975, the congregation has been united with Letterkenny. Membership currently stands at thirty-three families.

Milford

was established on 15 May 1837. The first minister, Rev Robert White (1837–73), spent his entire ministry here and was a pioneer

in the Tenant Right Movement. His son John became Lord Mayor of Belfast in 1919. The third minister, Rev William Young, also served here for his entire ministry from 1881 until 1931. The church was united with Carrigart from 1937 until 1951, and then with Fannet from 1 May 1951. On 1 January 1982, a three-point charge was created, when Rathmullan was added. Membership today stands at thirty-eight families.

Carrigart

was formed in 1844 for Presbyterians in this locality who had previously worshipped in Ramelton. The first minister was Rev Francis McClure who was ordained on 13 March 1844 and died on 15 September 1882. The church was united with Milford from 1937 until 1951 and then with Dunfanaghy from 1 May 1951. The first minister of the new joint charge was Rev Peace

Montgomery (1951–53) who had been a missionary with the English Presbyterian Church in China. Membership today stands at twenty-seven families.

The 20th Century

The present Presbytery of Donegal was formed on 1 January 1962 from the former Presbyteries of Donegal, Letterkenny and Raphoe. The Presbyterian population in Donegal continued to decline throughout this century and every congregation within the Presbytery is in union with another, with Fannet, Milford and Rathmullan forming a triple charge. With some notable exceptions, modern ministries tend to be of a short duration, interspersed by lengthy vacancies. A similar problem is faced by Monaghan Presbytery. Over the past fifty years the number of Presbyterian families in membership with Donegal congregations has fallen dramatically from 2,500 to just under 1,500. This fact alone has dictated the number of congregational unions.

Conclusion

The loyalty of Donegal Presbyterians is well testified and twenty-one congregations today are witnessing to the Reformed faith throughout the County area. The small numbers in congregations present problems in maintaining or increasing facilities. Good relations between Presbyterian and Roman Catholic neighbours is a hallmark of this area. The Donegal Presbytery is vulnerable in times of ministerial shortage, tending to absorb several lengthy vacancies, which in turn drains the already limited resources.

Downpatrick
SCENIC IRELAND

Down Presbytery

Introduction

Down Presbytery contains twenty congregations and extends over the area on the western side of Strangford Lough, stretching from Comber in the north to Ardglass in the south, from Killyleagh in the east to Ballynahinch in the west. The Presbytery was formed on 1 January 1963 and many of the current congregations previously belonged to the old Comber Presbytery, now defunct. Currently, there are three joint charges within the Presbytery and fourteen single charges.

The 17th Century

Eight congregations within Down Presbytery trace their origins to the 17th century. All of the early ministers knew hardship and persecution yet Presbyterianism put down strong roots in this locality. Collectively these congregations are widespread, indicating the extent of Presbyterian settlement in this part of County Down.

220

First Comber

was formed about 1645. The first minister, Rev James Gordon was ordained here in that year and deposed for Non-conformity in 1661 but he later joined the Episcopal church. Rev John Orr was ordained on 6 January 1724. He joined the Non-subscribing Presbytery of Antrim and was consequently deserted by most of the congregation which remained loyal to the Synod of Ulster. Rev Isaac Nelson (1838–42) started his ministerial career here before moving to Belfast and notoriety in the wake of the 1859 Revival of which he strongly disapproved. Rev John McKean exercised a lengthy ministry in Comber (1916–64) and was elected Moderator of the General Assembly in 1952. Membership stands at just over 550 families today.

First Killyleagh

was originally linked with Killinchy. It was formed from Presbyterian families who worshipped here as early as 1622 under

Rev John Bole who was imprisoned in 1639 for refusing to take the 'Black Oath'. His successor, Rev Thomas Murray, was crucified by Irish rebels during the 1641 rebellion. The third minister, Rev William Richardson (1649–70), was also imprisoned, on suspicion of complicity in Blood's Plot. The most famous minister here was Rev Henry Cooke (1818–29) unquestionably the leading Presbyterian minister in his lifetime and leader of the cause to oust Arianism from the Synod of Ulster. The present church was built during Rev Cooke's ministry, with Cooke acting as architect, and was one of the largest rural congregations in Ulster at that time. When Rev William Witherow was installed on 5 April 1882 he was one of twenty-eight individuals who had preached for the position and he left after only ten months. The church building has been internally refurbished in 2004 with comfortable chairs replacing solid pews. Membership stands at 190 families today.

Downpatrick

originated about 1655 under the ministry of Rev John Fleming and nothing is known of him after 1661 when he was deposed by Bishop Jeremy Taylor. Father, Rev Thomas Nevin, son, Rev William Nevin, and grandson, also Rev William Nevin served here from 1711 until 1789. In 1825, during the ministry of Rev James Neilson (1792–1838), a section of the congregation formed a new church and sought more evangelical preaching. The new church was known as *Infirmary Street*. Within ten years a gallery was added to the building. The current church was opened on 31 March 1955. In 2005 the church was united with Ardglass. Membership totals 128 families today.

Killinchy

was originally linked with Killyleagh under Rev John Bole in the early 1600s. The first church was built in 1670 in the ministry of Rev Michael Bruce (1657–61 & 1670–89). A new church was built in 1714 and replaced by the current cruciform building in 1739. Rev Samuel Watson was ordained in September 1797 but suspended in 1835 for his Arian views. At that time, with a section of the congregation, he joined the Remonstrant Synod and tried unsuccessfully to retain possession of the church building. A distinctive three-faced clock was installed in the church in 1811, replacing the former hour glass used to judge the length of sermons. Membership stands at about 570 families today.

First Saintfield

was originally known as Tonaghneave and was formed in 1658 and the first minister, Rev Alexander Hutcheson served from that date until his death in 1711, apart from two years in Dublin (1690–92). His grandson, Francis, was Professor of Ethics and Moral Philosophy in the University of Glasgow (1729–46). The present church was built in 1777, during the ministry of Rev Thomas Birch (1776–98) who was implicated in the Rebellion of the United Irishmen in 1798. Rev Stewart Dickson served as minister for fifty-six years (1887–1943). In 1890 the interior of the church was renovated, including the replacement of the old pulpit and pews. Major renovations to the ancillary buildings were carried out in 1998–9. Membership currently stands at just over 400 families.

Reverend Thomas Ledlie Birch

THOMAS LEDLIE BIRCH was born in 1754, the sixth son of John Birch, a prosperous farmer from Gilford. He graduated from Glasgow University in 1772 and was ordained in Saintfield on 21 May 1776. His first task was to supervise the building of a new and larger church which was opened in 1777 though seating was only added in November 1778. Thomas Birch was attracted to the ideals of the United Irishmen and in Saintfield, in January 1792, he formed the first company of United Irishmen in County Down. In 1795 a section of his congregation left and formed a Seceder cause in the town. During the 1798 Rebellion the Down United Irishmen assembled in Saintfield on 9 June and about 100 people were killed in clashes with the Yorkshire Fensibles. Rev Birch was arrested and tried in Lisburn for treason on 18 June. His defence was that he was burying the dead and attending to the wounded, not engaging in rebellion. Although convicted, he was permitted to emigrate to Pennsylvania. He published an exaggerated account of the battle of Ballynahinch in 1798 and died on 12 April 1828.

Clough

was originally called Drumca and the first minister, Rev Thomas Maxwell, served here from 1680 until 1705. In 1829 a Non-

subscribing section of the congregation seized the building and joined the Presbytery of Antrim. In 1836 a successful legal suit regained the building for the Subscribers under the ministry of Rev Francis Dill (1829–42). The church was united with Seaforde on 5 March 1923. The congregation has a notable reputation in the 20th century for providing PCI missionaries. Membership currently stands at 130 families.

Ardglass

was an extremely important trading port in the 17th century and had a Presbyterian congregation at nearby Ballee in the late 1690s. The fourth minister, Rev Josiah Ker was ordained here on 18 March 1799 but suspended on 26 August 1809 upon declaring himself an Arian. He was succeeded by Rev David White who, with a majority of the congregation, joined the Non-subscribing Remonstrant Synod in 1829. A new church was formed in Ardglass on 1 October 1839. On 1 May 1923 the church was united with Strangford. The congregation operated without a Kirk Session of its own from 1877 until 1973 when two elders were ordained. Strangford amalgamated with Ardglass on 30 September 2003 and the congregation was united with Downpatrick in 2005. Membership currently stands at thirty families.

First Ballynahinch

was formed about 1696 under the ministry of Rev William Reid (1696–1704). In 1735, and again in 1831, there were serious disputes over electing a minister but schism was avoided. The present church was built in 1751 during the ministry of Rev John Strong (1744–80). Rev Marisine Stanfield was installed on 8 January 1993, the first woman minister in Down Presbytery. Membership totals 280 families today.

Margaret McCombe

MARGARET McCOMBE was brought up in Clough congregation. She served as a missionary in Manchuria from 1923–1947. On 24 May 1942 Margaret and other missionaries in the city of Hulan were transported by the occupying Japanese to Nagasaki. They were under house arrest there, on 9 August 1945, when the Americans dropped an atomic bomb on the city. She recalled the ear splitting explosions and the flash of bright light. One and a half square miles in a densely populated section of the city was destroyed and the windows on the exposed side of their building were shattered. Margaret has written of her vivid memories of that time; death and injury and the whimpering of children. In the early hours of 18 August the local police chief came to tell the missionaries that Japan had surrendered and hostilities had ended. Margaret McCombe's niece, also Margaret, was a PCI missionary in Nepal and her sister, Violet, was a missionary in Lebanon.

Margaret McCombe, 1923

The 18th Century

Five new congregations were formed within the current Down Presbytery area in the 18th century. With the exception of Kilmore (formed 1713) this century belonged to the Seceders and their four congregations form a solid square in the heart of this Presbytery. The area was also noted for the numerous educational establishments which were organised by Presbyterian ministers. Such establishments were valued by Presbyterian people and a useful means for ministers to supplement what was too often a meagre stipend.

Kilmore

Trinity Boardmills

was formed as a Burgher Secession cause, and originally known as Killaney, in 1749 under Rev Andrew Black (1749–77) who helped establish other Seceder congregations at Ballynahinch, Loughaghery and Lissara. A schism developed in 1811 when Rev John Sturgeon decided to accept the *regium donum* and the disaffected section formed Second Boardmills. Rev George Shanks (1840–89) was one of the earliest ministers to use unfermented wine at Communion. The average length of service of the first six

Kilmore

was formed in 1713 though the first minister, Rev Thomas Elder, was not installed until 14 June 1716. Rev Moses Neilson was ordained here on 8 April 1767 and conducted a famous Classical School at Rademon until his retirement, due to blindness, in 1810. He was succeeded on 13 June 1810 by his son, Rev Arthur Neilson, who led the congregation into membership of the Non-subscribing Remonstrant Synod in 1829. Upon his death in 1831 the majority of the congregation reverted to the Synod of Ulster. The current church was opened on 1 September 1833. Membership stands at 120 families today.

James Thompson

Presbyterian Classical Schools

In the 18th century a remarkable number of Presbyterian ministers operated Classical Schools in the Down Presbytery area. University education was only available in Scotland for Presbyterians and this was expensive and inconvenient. Additionally, such teaching was an obvious opportunity for a minister to supplement his stipend. Rev James McAlpine (First Ballynahinch 1714–32) operated such a school in Killyleagh from 1697–1714 and had about 160 students. Several ministers were educated here but probably the most famous pupil was Francis Hutcheson, later to become Professor of Ethics and Moral Philosophy in the University of Glasgow (1729–46). Rev Moses Neilson (Kilmore 1767–1810) also ran an impressive Academy at Rademon from 1767 until 1810 and this work was carried on by his son, Rev Arthur Neilson (Kilmore 1829–31). Rev Samuel Edgar (Second Ballynahinch 1793–1815) operated a Classical School in his home at Ballykine. His most famous pupil was James Thompson, later to become Mathematics Professor in Glasgow University and father of Lord Kelvin. Such educational endeavours represented attempts to alleviate the genuine economic hardship experienced by many young men at that time in preparing for ministry.

ministers was thirty-seven years. The first minister of Second Boardmills was Rev John Shaw (1816–25) who had been a member of the congregation before his ordination. When First Boardmills joined the General Assembly in 1840 a section of the congregation objected and seized the building. Upon receipt of £350 as compensation they withdrew and formed another congregation, Killaney, in 1846, a few yards from First Boardmills. There were now three Presbyterian churches within half a mile of each other. On 6 June 1925 Killaney joined the General Assembly and was united with Second Boardmills on 30 July 1925. First Boardmills was united with Second Boardmills and Killaney on 1 May 1974. For several years all three buildings were used for services on a regular rota. On 1 July 2002 both congregations amalgamated under the name Trinity, Boardmills and agreed to use only the First church building for services. Membership currently stands at about 190 families.

Lissara

was formed as a Seceder congregation in 1770 and early meetings were held in a mill at Ballydugan. The cause was initially weak and therefore linked with a Seceder church in Ballynahinch (now Edengrove). The first minister, Rev Thomas Fryar was ordained on 2 May 1774 but died on 12 January 1775. Lissara gained independence in 1793. The present church was opened on 14 April 1866. An argument during a vacancy in 1950 led to some members leaving and the formation of the Free Presbyterian Church. Membership currently stands at 190 families.

Rev Ian Paisley at Crossgar in 1951

Birth of Free Presbyterianism

Rev William McClure retired as minister in Lissara on 1 July 1950. A number of events led to heated exchanges, wild allegations and a schism. Voting for a new minister in October 1950 was challenged, as was voting for new elders in November and threats to form a separate congregation were issued. An added complication was the fact that Rev Ian Paisley was due to conduct an *Old Time Gospel Campaign* in Crossgar in 1951 and a dispute arose over whether the Lissara Hall could be used for such an event. In January the Presbytery deferred a decision on use of the hall but advertisements appeared in the local press in February announcing that the mission would be held in the hall. When permission was not granted, five former Lissara elders issued a 'manifesto' on 11 March announcing that on Saturday 17 March the Free Presbyterian Church of Ulster would be officially constituted in Killyleagh Street Hall in Crossgar. The new separatist grouping was born amid claims that the Presbyterian Church in Ireland was like Sodom and Gomorrah and should be left to the flames of God's wrath and judgement.

Reverend Walter Moffatt

WALTER MOFFATT was born on 13 August 1810, son of Rev William Moffatt, Seceder minister of Moira. When he was thirteen years old he attended the Belfast Institution and three years later, at age sixteen, he was appointed assistant to Dr James Thompson, head of the Mathematics Department and father of Lord Kelvin. Walter was converted at this time and he became an enthusiastic Secretary of the Belfast Town Mission. He was licensed on 5 May 1830 and declined an offer to assist Rev Dr John Edgar in Linenhall Street. Instead, he accepted a call to the young Seceder church in Saintfield. He was ordained on 9 March 1831 and although his ministry was short, only six years, the congregation doubled in that time. Walter Moffatt preached as often as fifteen times in a week in frequent travels far from Saintfield. He was instrumental in establishing a Seceder church in Derry (Carlisle Road) and also in Dublin (eventually to become Clontarf). He resisted invitations to be minister in Usher's Quay and also to succeed James Thompson in the Belfast Institution. His health was never robust and he was laid low by tuberculosis in late 1835. After several bouts of illness, Walter Moffatt died on 30 March 1838 at the young age of twenty-seven years.

Edengrove

church was formed by the amalgamation of Second and Third Ballynahinch on 19 June 1949. Second was a Burgher Seceder cause which originated in 1774 and was initially linked with Lissara. It became independent in 1792. Rev Samuel Edgar (1793–1825) was later the Seceder Professor of Divinity in the Belfast Institution. A majority of the people wanted his son, David, to succeed as minister and were prepared to wait two years until he completed his theological studies. Rev David Edgar was minister from 1829 until 1889. A minority disagreed with the delay and formed a Third congregation. Rev John Davis paid for the Third church by preaching in America for two years (1849–51). Second and Third united in 1927 and then adopted the name Edengrove upon their amalgamation in 1949. The present building was completely renovated in 1971. Membership now totals 265 families.

Second Saintfield

was formed as a Burgher Seceder congregation in 1795 due to dissatisfaction in the old Saintfield congregation with Rev Birch's sympathies with the United Irishmen. The second minister, Rev Walter Moffat was a gifted evangelist and known as the 'McCheyne of the Irish Seceders'. His reputation was enhanced by the fact that he died after

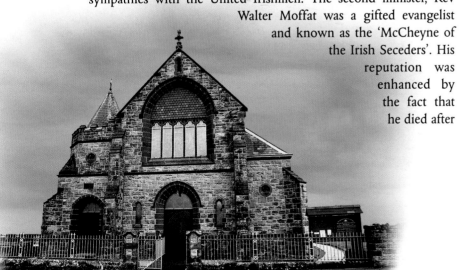

only seven years service. The present church was built upon the site of the original in 1892. Extensive renovations were carried out in 1966–7. Membership now totals over 250 families.

The 19th Century

This century began as the previous century had ended, with the Seceders forming new congregations: Magherahamlet in 1825, Seaforde in 1826 and Second Comber in 1838. Four more churches were founded after the union in 1840. Another trait in this century was the Presbyterian fondness for schism. Two extra churches emerged in Boardmills and another in Ballynahinch. By 1900 there were twenty-three churches spread over this sector of County Down.

Magherahamlet

was formed in 1725 as a result of open-air services conducted by Rev Samuel Edgar of Ballynahinch and was originally known as Drumgavlin. Local elder Robert McIlwaine built a small school for the early services and then replaced this with the first church on the same site. The cause prospered in the aftermath of the trouble in Second Ballynahinch in the 1820s. The church was united with Spa on 1 June 1925. Membership stands today at ninety families.

Seaforde

was formed in 1825 as a Seceder church; the first minister, Rev Robert McCormick, was called on 1 November 1825 and installed on 18 April 1826. The church is situated about a quarter of a mile outside the village of Seaforde and the congregation was united with Clough on 5 March 1923. Numbers have always been small and membership stands at forty families today.

Second Comber

was formed in 1838. The first minister was Rev John Rogers (1839–69), who later became Professor of Sacred Rhetoric in Assembly's College, Belfast. The church building opened on 3 October 1840. Rev David Taylor (1877–96) was later Secretary of the Presbyterian Orphan Society (1896–1941) and Moderator of the General Assembly in 1899. A new refurbishment and extension is currently being undertaken to the already extensive ancillary buildings. This is the largest congregation in Down Presbytery with over 750 families.

Ballygowan

was formed in 1838 and the first minister was Rev John Gamble (1838–54). The church is a large barn style and had no form of heating until the early 1900s! A distinctive and imposing three storey school built with blue cut stone was purchased by the congregation in 1918 for use as a Sunday school. Several 20th century renovations and extensions culminated in the opening of a large new hall in 1981. The longest ministry here was that of Rev William McLernon (1900–46). Seven members have become Presbyterian ministers, including two Moderators: Rev William Craig in 1979 and Rev John Girvan in 1981. Ballygowan is the second largest congregation in Down Presbytery with 600 families,.

Second Killyleagh

was formed in 1840 but was mooted ten years earlier by members of First Killyleagh who were unhappy with the selection of Rev Andrew Breaky to succeed Rev Henry Cooke. Rev Alexander McCreery served here for fifty-eight years, from 1852 until 1910. An attempt by Union Commission to amalgamate First and Second

in 1919 was stoutly and successfully resisted. Rev Samuel McVicker (1920–28) was the first ex-service student to be ordained in the Irish Presbyterian Church and was both an Irish hockey and rugby international. Rev Clifford Boggs served here for fifty-two years, from 1928 until 1980. Two brothers were also ministers: Rev Ernest Boggs (Faughanvale 1931–74) and Rev Robin Boggs (Clough and Seaforde 1938–51). Membership totals almost 250 families.

Raffrey

was formed in 1843 following services in the village conducted by several neighbouring ministers. The first minister was Rev Ringland Fisher (1843–88). The third minister, Rev William Watson (1895–1902), was later Clerk of the General Assembly from 1928 until 1953 and Moderator in 1941. Rev Martin Smyth (1957–63) was later Member of Parliament for South Belfast from 1982 until 2005. Membership stands today at about 225 families.

Spa

is the youngest church within Down Presbytery, having been formed in 1872. The town was a popular health resort in the 19th century and one wealthy visitor, Robert McQuiston after whom McQuiston Memorial church is named, paid for a church in the town. The church opened on 16 July 1872 and services were conducted by neighbouring ministers for two years. The first minister was Rev William Wilson (1874–79). The church was united with Magherahamlet on 1 June 1925. Membership stands at 115 families today.

The 20th Century

While it is true that no new congregations have been formed in this area in the 20th century, this is not to say that there has been no activity. The first half of the century witnessed reunion and harmony. In 1925 Killaney joined the General Assembly and united with Second Boardmills. Two years later Second and Third Ballynahinch united and then amalgamated in 1947 under the new name of Edengrove. In 1974 the two Boardmills congregations united and in 2002 amalgamated under the name Trinity. The Free Presbyterian Church was formed in 1950 from a schism in Lissara.

Conclusion

County Down has long been a Presbyterian heartland. There are currently almost 5,500 Presbyterian families in membership of the twenty churches in this Presbytery. This number has risen over the past fifty years by almost 10%. Masonic and Orange influences are also discernable. On the surface this is a healthy Presbytery but the challenges, as ever, are to remain relevant by presenting the Gospel in a relevant manner to an increasingly secular society.

Spa church

Introduction

The Presbytery of Dromore covers the north eastern portion of County Down and contains twenty-two congregations. It is bordered by Belfast on the east and Lough Neagh on the west. The main urban centre is the city of Lisburn which boasts five Presbyterian churches. The whole area has experienced recent population growth and several towns, most notably Hillsborough, Dromore and Dromara have attracted thousands of new dwellings.

The 17th Century

Six congregations within this Presbytery can trace their origins to the 17th century. These were fairly well spread throughout the area: Drumbo and Lisburn to the north-east, Ballinderry to the north-west, Dromore to the south-west, and Anahilt to the south-east. The development of Presbyterianism is discerned within these congregations in that the first four ministers were all Scotsmen, but, towards the close of the century, Revs Alexander McCracken of Lisburn and Samuel Ferguson of Moira were Ulstermen.

Dromore Presbytery

Flax field

Drumbo

is the oldest Church in Dromore Presbytery. It was formed about 1655, when Rev Henry Livingstone, a nephew of Rev John Livinstone of Killinchy, was minister. He remained here until his death on 7 April 1697, and several stones bearing his initials survive from his church. Rev Thomas Gowan (1706–16) was author of several books. He was a son of Rev Thomas Gowan, who founded a Philosophy School at Antrim. The current church was built in 1750. Rev Samuel Hanna (1795–99) achieved later fame as the first Moderator of the General Assembly. In 1830, a section of the congregation separated to form another church in the neighbouring parish at Ballycairn. Rev Barkley Wallace (1926–63) exercised a lengthy ministry here and published a history of the congregation. Membership stands at just over 350 families today.

First Dromore

was formed about 1660 and the first minister was Scotsman Rev Henry Hunter. The congregation was split during the 18th century

over the Subscription controversy. Alexander Colville, son of Rev Alexander Colville (1700–19), was denied Synod ordination for refusing to subscribe to the Westminster Confession. In December 1724, he was ordained in London and, on 25 October 1725, irregularly installed here by the Synod of Munster. In 1730, he joined the Non-subscribing Antrim Presbytery and a section of the congregation formed a second church in Dromore. The present church can accommodate 800 people and was opened in November 1915. Membership stands today at about 250 families.

Anahilt

was sometimes called Hillsborough and was formed about 1662, when Rev John McBroom was installed here. His tombstone is still visible in Anahilt graveyard. The fifth minister, Rev John Semple (1749–58), clashed with local Seceders and published a pamphlet against their influence. The current church was built during the ministry of Rev Josias Mitchell (1887–1925) as was a manse and school. On 1 September 1974, the congregation was united with that of Drumlough. Membership totals just over 100 families today.

Ballinderry

was originally formed in the early 1670s though the people could not maintain the stipend promised to their first minister, Rev Matthew Haltridge (1673–74). A new congregation was formed in 1713 from Glenavy and Moira. The short ministry of Rev Clotworthy Brown (1746–47), who was a Non-subscriber, prompted the formation of a Seceder Church at Magheragall. Rev William Rowan (1751–83) was dis-annexed from the church for

Reverend James Morgan

JAMES MORGAN was born on 15 June 1799 in Cookstown, the second son of Thomas Morgan, a bleacher. Thomas left the Church of Ireland and joined the local Presbyterian Church. James graduated from Glasgow University in 1815 and was ordained at Carlow on 21 June 1820. He was installed in Lisburn on 23 June 1824. In the previous year he married a daughter of John Gayer, a former Clerk in the Irish Parliament. He was installed as first minister of Fisherwick Place on 4 November 1828 where he served until his death on 5 August 1873. He quickly built up this church to be the premier congregation in Belfast and in doing so established his own reputation as a very capable preacher and pastor. James Morgan also played a leading role with Irish Presbyterianism in establishing new congregations around the ever expanding town of Belfast. Rev Morgan was Moderator of the General Assembly in 1846 and a distinguished Convenor of Foreign Mission from 1840 until 1873. In this capacity, it was James Morgan who introduced Revs Alexander Kerr and James Glasgow to the first General Assembly as its first missionaries. He was a close friend of Rev Henry Cooke and delivered the main address at the latter's funeral in 1868.

conducting clandestine marriages for individuals not under his care. The Church was united with Moira from 1929 until 2001, and thereafter has been a Stated Supply with Maze. Membership today stands at eighty-five families.

First Lisburn

was formed in the 1680s and the original Church was situated at the lower end of Bow Street. It was destroyed by fire in April 1707, as was much of Lisburn, and rebuilt on the current Market Square site. In the late 1740s, the Seceders seem to have gained their earliest Irish support in Lisburn, with some leaving this congregation. The current Church dates from 1768. Rev James Morgan (1824–28) was later to achieve fame as Convenor of the Foreign Mission (1840–47) and Moderator of the General Assembly (1846). The ministry of Rev John Rentoul (1872–86) was broken from 2 June until 20 December 1876, when he accepted, and then declined, a call to Perth, Australia. Rev William Boyd (1950–72) was elected Moderator of the General Assembly in

1967. It was during his ministry, in 1970, that the current frontage was added to the Church. Following serious damage in a bomb explosion on 5 August 1981, the church has been restored with several new stained glass windows. Membership stands today at 500 families.

Moira

was formed sometime before 1690 but details are unknown. Rev Samuel Harpur (1717–26) joined the Non-subscribing Presbytery of Antrim and the core of the people commenced to build a new church. This was completed by Rev Thomas Creighton but, when he died in 1741, the Seceders gained control of the church. The

Synod of Ulster and Secession Churches continued alongside until they united in 1830 under Rev William Moffatt. The church was united with Ballinderry from 1929 but this union was dissolved on 17 January 2001. New development in this locality has resulted in a near fourfold increase in membership over the past fifty years to currently total just above 300 families.

The 18th Century

Four new congregations were formed in this Presbytery in the 18th century: Dromara, Hillhall, Loughaghery and Magheragall. The first of these, in Dromara, grew out of Dromore for reasons of convenience for local Presbyterians attending worship. The others were all Seceder causes. It was in Lisburn that uneasiness first surfaced in relation to doctrinal orthodoxy and the congregation there divided over a candidate to succeed Rev Alexander McCracken after 1730. Unsurprisingly, enthusiasm for the new cause spread and led to the formation of the local Seceder congregations.

First Dromara

was originally part of Dromore but gained separate status in 1713. The first minister, Rev John Campbell, was ordained on 13

December 1715 and died on 3 June 1724. The third minister was Rev James Birch (1764–1820). He was assisted and then succeeded by his grandson, Rev James Black (1816–23), who was suspended for drunkenness on 13 May 1823 and died five months later, on 3 October. Famine and emigration decimated the local population and the church gallery has not been used since the mid 19th century. A succession of short ministries ended with Rev Franklin Jamison (1918–42). Extensive renovations took place in the early 1970s and in 1980 the gallery was adapted for display of historical artefacts. Membership today totals 200 families.

Hillhall

was called Lisburn for many years and Presbyterians in this locality were the first in Ireland to ask the Scottish Seceders to send a minister. Originally linked with Moira, the church became separate in 1753 and moved from Lisburn to the present location at Hillhall. The original church had an earthen floor and thatched roof. It was rebuilt during the ministry of Rev James Crawford (1866–81) and replaced again in 1902. A malicious fire destroyed the church hall on 15 November 1999 but a new hall was built and opened in September 2002. Membership stands at 450 families today.

Loughaghery

was formed in August 1750 when the Seceders conducted a service within Anahilt. The minister, Rev John Semple, was absent at a neighbouring Communion Service. The first settled minister here

17th century Irish Communionware

First Dromara History Gallery

FIRST DROMARA CHURCH can accommodate 700 people but the congregation reached its zenith during the ministry of Rev William Craig (1823–71). Subsequent local disruptions and emigration drained membership. Several new congregations were formed including a Reformed Presbyterian church in 1874. The church was refurbished in 1840 and the gallery has not been used in living memory. Rev Andrew McComb (1968–81) had the gallery refurbished for storage and display of historical artefacts. Communion ware, marriage and baptismal records and similar items are now arranged in display cabinets in this area. Descendents of former members of this congregation have regularly visited the gallery especially from USA and Australia and successfully traced their ancestry. The history gallery underwent extensive refurbishment in 2006 thereby ensuring its continued testimony to Presbyterian life in Dromara.

was Rev William Knox (1755–62). Rev Samuel Edgar (1771–86) conducted a Classical School here and was head of four generations of distinguished Presbyterian ministers. He was succeeded by Rev William Moorhead (1786–1829) and head of another dynasty of Irish Presbyterian ministers lasting 152 years. The present church is the third in this locality and was opened during the ministry of Rev Robert Moorhead (1829–77). It was extensively renovated in 1895. The congregation was united with Cargycreevy on 1 November 1971. Membership stands at about 165 families today.

Magheragall

was formed about 1763 and linked with Moira, which in that year was separated from Hillhall. Services were held in a barn for many years and the Magheragall section of the people became a separate

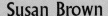

Susan Brown

SUSAN BROWN was born into ministerial circles. Her father was Rev John Brown (Magheragall 1829–77) and her mother, was the eldest daughter of Rev Samuel Edgar (Ballynahinch 1793–1826). Two brothers were ministers: Samuel in Ballywalter, Athlone and Clough, and Wallace, who was a missionary in India 1874–88. Susan Brown was the first Irish Presbyterian female missionary. She was commissioned on 26 October 1874 to work in India with the new Zenana Mission which was the brainchild of Rev Fleming Stevenson. This term refers to the part of a house reserved for women. Susan Brown developed the work which had been started by wives of missionaries. She established schools at Surat before moving to Borsad in 1877. She also improved the music in the missionary church. Susan Brown was supported by Irish Presbyterian women. Later, she assumed control of several orphanages in Surat. The Zenana Mission was very successful, often gaining more local support in Ireland than the Foreign Mission of the Church. A successful quarterly magazine changed in 1886 into 'Woman's Work'. Susan Brown served for ten years as a missionary in India before retiring in 1884.

congregation in 1809 under Rev Joseph Kelso (1809–29), who was suspended for intemperance and celebration of marriages in an irregular manner. The present church was built in 1840, during the ministry of Rev John Brown (1829–77). His daughter Susan was the first Zenana missionary to India of the Irish Presbyterian Church. Membership has risen by 35% over the past fifty years and stands at just over 200 families today.

The 19th Century

In most areas, the 19th century was the century of church extension and Dromore Presbytery was no exception. Nine new congregations were formed, including second churches for Dromore and Dromara and two more for Lisburn. Two Synod of Ulster causes (Drumlough and Hillsborough) and one Seceder cause (Banbridge Road, Dromore) were formed prior to the union of 1840. Following the union, new churches were formed at an unprecedented rate: three in the 1840s, one in the 1850s and another two in the 1860s.

Drumlough

was formed in 1818. The first minister was Rev Samuel Crory (1819–53) and membership was over 280 families. The second ministry was also of a respectable duration, Rev John McClelland (1855–92). Extensive renovations and new building was

Jean Shannon

JEAN SHANNON was born on 15 April 1937 and brought up in Drumlough Church. After Drumlough Primary School she pursued her education at Princess Gardens School and Queen's University, Belfast. Having graduated in Medicine in 1961 Jean undertook further study in Obstetrics. She then offered to serve as a medical missionary in India. Having completed Gujarati language study with distinction, in 1965 Jean started work in Hamilton McCleery Hospital in Dohad (now Dahod) where she quickly adapted to life, and another language variation, among the Bhil people. Jean Shannon founded a Community Health programme in the area and played a significant role in the local Church. Her home was often the location for Sunday School and Bible Study. She committed the bulk of her working life to India, retiring in 1990 after twenty-five years service, as the last Irish Presbyterian missionary in Gujarat. Not content to put her feet up, Jean enrolled on a part-time basis at Union Theological College in 1998 and graduated from Queen's University, Belfast, with a Bachelor of Divinity degree in December 2003.

Reverend James Rentoul

JAMES RENTOUL was born on 12 August 1839 into a famous Seceder ministerial family. His father and grandfather were ministers as were his two uncles, five cousins and brother! James was educated at Queen's and Assembly's Colleges and graduated from the Queen's University of Ireland. He was ordained in Clough, County Antrim on 14 March 1865 and ministered here for thirteen years before being installed in Banbridge Road, Dromore on 31 May 1878. There is no doubt that Rev Rentoul was 'a character'. A stickler for punctuality, on more than one occasion he repeated an opening praise and prayer if worshippers arrived late for Sunday Service. He resisted the installation of an inside toilet in the manse as 'unhygienic' yet, curiously, installed a two-seater outside toilet instead. When the church committee were slow to deal with a problem of damp in the manse, Rev Rentoul hired a tramp to cover the entire house in tar! It was more than fifty years before the last vestiges of this innovative damp proofing were removed. He often left packets of sweets in the pew for children who had experienced bereavement or who were returning to church after illness. Rev James Rentoul died on 2 January 1917.

235

undertaken in the 1930s and again in the 1950s. The first organ was used in services here in 1947. Dr Jean Shannon, medical missionary to India, was a member of Drumlough congregation. On 1 September 1974, the congregation was united with that of Anahilt. Membership totals about 130 families today.

Rentoul (1878–1917) exercised a long and worthy ministry here. He was succeeded by Rev William McMullan who died tragically in a car accident on 30 January 1920 aged twenty-eight years. A church hall was built in 1931 upon ground which had been purchased by Rev Rentoul. Recent new housing has transformed Dromore, and membership here has almost doubled over the past fifty years and standing today at just over 400 families.

Legacurry

Hillsborough

was formed in 1832; its first minister was Rev Henry Dobbin (1833–37). The second minister was Rev Samuel Dill (1837–53), who was later Moderator of the General Assembly (1860) and Professor of Theology at Magee College, Derry (1865–70). The shortest ministry was that of Rev Alexander Montgomery who was ordained on 28 March 1854 and resigned on 27 August in the same year. Rev Galbraith Johnston (1857–88) had earlier been an agent with the Belfast Town Mission prior to his ordination in 1855 and service as an Army Chaplain during the Crimean War. The longest ministry was that of Rev Herbert Orr (1915–62). Rev James Irvine exercised a significant ministry from 1963 until 1985, which saw congregation and town develop. Membership stands today at almost 550 families.

Banbridge Road, Dromore

was formed as a Seceder congregation in 1836. Early services were held in the Court House until this was denied by the local bishop whereupon the new congregation was granted use of the Reformed Presbyterian Church. A new church building was completed in 1843. The first minister, Rev John Allen, left in that year. Rev James

was formed in 1841, when Sunday afternoon services in a local school house had grown successfully following their commencement in the previous year. The first minister was Rev Phineas Whiteside (1841–65) and initially services were held in the open air until the church was completed in 1844. The building was extensively renovated in 1909. Rev Thomas Rankin (1910–49) played an active role in education policy throughout his ministry here. Rev John McCaughan (1949–83) saw real growth in the

congregation during his ministry. Membership has increased dramatically over the past fifty years, rising from 125 families to over 300 families today.

Second Dromara

was formed in 1844 to meet the needs of local Presbyterians who lived at some distance from First. The first minister, Rev John Murdoch (1844–52), was suspended and dis-annexed from his congregation for intemperance. Rev William Patton (1853–95) exercised a long and evangelical ministry, and published two books: *Pardon and Assurance* and *How to Live the Christian Life*. Rev Samuel McConnell (1921–33) continued the work of his father in producing a *fasti* of the Irish Presbyterian Church 1613–1840. Membership stands at 180 families today.

Cargycreevy

was formed in response to local requests in 1845 for a church near at hand. The first minister was Rev Robert Erwin (1846–87) and

his installation service took place in a field near the church which was opened in 1847. The longest ministry here was that of Rev Samuel Murray who was ordained on 9 May 1894 and died on 4 February 1926. A church hall was opened in September 1955 and the fifth minister, Rev Tom Reid (1958–64), was later Professor of Practical Theology and Principal of Union Theological College. The congregation was united with Loughaghery on 1 November 1971. Membership totals just over sixty families today.

Maze

was formed by Rev Edward Stevenson while he was a licentiate of Dromore Presbytery. He organised services in a barn about 1842 and, because of local Presbytery opposition, received help from Belfast Presbytery. He was ordained here on 20 June 1855. The church was opened on 1 July 1859 and Rev Stevenson continued as minister until his death on 12 December 1890. Two other lengthy ministries were those of Rev Thomas Dunn (1900–40) who wrote a short history of the congregation (1949) and Rev Thomas Parker (1940–81). Ballinderry has been a Stated Supply with Maze since June 2001. A new hall was opened in February 1995 and, in 2004, major renovations linked the hall with enlarged seating capacity in the church. Membership has risen by about 80% over the past fifty years and stands at 200 families today.

Railway Street

originated in services conducted in a hay loft in Castle Street in 1860. Although the early services were conducted by Rev John Powell, in 1861, the congregation called David Clarke to be their first minister and he served until his death on 23 November 1878, aged forty-four years. The church in Railway Street was opened on

237

2 March 1864. Two ministers of this congregation have served as Moderator of the General Assembly: Rev Robert Hamilton in 1924 and Rev Howard Cromie in 1984. Two ministers have gone on to Professorships in Magee College: Rev James Bigger (1879–85) lectured in Hebrew and Biblical Criticism and Rev Thomas Robinson (1930–38) lectured in Philosophy. In 1965, a new St. Columba's church was created from the Railway Street parish area and again, in 1976, Elmwood Church was similarly carved. Membership today stands at about 470 families.

Sloan Street

originated in the services conducted by Rev John Powell in Castle Street in 1860. A majority of the people formed Railway Street church with another minister but the minority remained loyal to Rev Powell and formed Sloan Street Church. The church is built upon a site given in 1863 by a Mr Sloan, and Rev Powell remained as minister until ill health forced him to retire in 1880. In 1887, the

congregation was received into the General Assembly. Extensive renovations were carried out in the 1950s, including the provision of a hall. Further renovations were completed in 2001 and these included the construction of a new hall. Membership stands at 190 families today.

The 20th Century

The Dromore Presbytery area has witnessed significant new housing development in the second half of the 20th century. As a result of its expansion, Lisburn received city status in 2002, as part of Queen Elizabeth's Golden Jubilee celebrations. Other towns such as Hillsborough, Dromara, Dromore and Moira have also expanded greatly. Presbyterian families in the Presbytery have increased by over 30% in the past fifty years. All three of the new causes (Harmony Hill, St. Columba's and Elmwood) are strong and vibrant congregations today.

Harmony Hill

originated as a Church Extension cause with services in Lambeg Presbyterian Hall, which commenced on 21 February 1954. Rev David Watson was ordained on 20 September 1956 with additional

responsibility for Seymour Hill, Dunmurry, and this link continued until 1962. Rev Watson served as minister for eighteen years, resigning on 24 June 1975. The Lambeg congregation grew rapidly and a new church was opened on 29 May 1965. The bell in the tower is engraved with a crown, harp and shamrock and the date 1874. It came from Clogher Church in County Mayo. Full congregational status was granted on 18 February 1968. A new hall was opened on 5 September 1971. The second minister was Rev Harold Gray who served from 1976 until his retirement in 1991. Membership has risen dramatically over the past fifty years from fifty-seven to the current total of 536 families.

St. Columba's

commenced in 1964 as a Church Extension cause with services held in a wooden hall on the Moira Road. The first minister, Rev Malcolm Scot, was installed on 2 June 1965. From 1967 the church operated under a Joint Methodist-Presbyterian Ministry Scheme. A new church was opened on 5 September 1969 and a Hall in March 1970. Rev Scott retired in 1998 and the second minister, Rev John Honeyford was installed on 1 September 1999. Membership currently stands at just over 300 families.

Elmwood

started in 1976 as a Church Extension cause in the Antrim-Glenavy area of Ballymacash. The first minister, Rev Robert Lockhart, was installed on 2 May 1976 and served here for twenty-seven years until his retirement in April 2003. The church was opened on

22 January 1977 and a suite of halls on 26 September 1981. Several items of furnishings were provided from the closure of Elmwood Church in Belfast and so the new congregation adopted the name 'Elmwood'. Full congregational status was achieved on 15 January 1984. The second minister, Rev Andrew Thompson, was installed on 14 June 2004. Membership currently stands at about 425 families.

Reverend Desmond Maxwell

JAMES DESMOND MAXWELL was born on 25 August 1952. He graduated with a BA in History from the University of Ulster in 1975 and then studied Theology at Westminster Theological Seminary in America where he graduated M.Div in 1978. This was followed by another year of study and a Th.M. degree from Princeton Seminary. He was ordained in 1979 in Sunny Corner, in New Brunswick, Canada and ministered there for three years. In 1982 he returned to Northern Ireland and was installed as assistant minister in Richview congregation with Rev Jack Kelly. On 2 November 1983 he was installed as minister of Berry Street Church in Belfast. This church was located in the heart of Belfast city centre and Rev Maxwell pioneered lunchtime services and other initiatives in city centre ministry. On 31 July 1987 he resigned from Berry Street and was appointed as a full-time lecturer in Belfast Bible College. Rev Maxwell has a special interest in exploring the Jewish roots of Christianity and has carved out a reputation as a dynamic teacher who reinforces his teaching with meticulously prepared powerpoint illustrations. Rev Desmond Maxwell has a vision for Christianity in Ireland which transcends denominationalism and willingly accepts teaching invitations from all quarters. He is a member of Elmwood Church.

Conclusion

The Dromore Presbytery contains twenty-two churches served by nineteen ministers. There are sixteen single charges, two joint charges and one charge linked to a Stated Supply. It is indicative of this locality that all but five of the churches are growing. The largest church is Hillsborough with 545 families and the average church size is 290 families.

The Lagan Towpath
SCENIC IRELAND

Introduction

The present Dublin and Munster Presbytery was created on 1 January 1963 by a union of these two previously separate Presbyteries. Six congregations from the former Donegal Presbytery were also added on that date. Currently the Presbytery contains thirty-seven congregations, served by twenty-four ministers. Geographically, this is by far the largest Irish Presbytery. Yet the total number of families is relatively small at about 2,000, providing an average congregational size of fifty-five families.

The 17th Century

There was an early Presbyterian presence, often linked with Puritanism, in the south and west of Ireland and, unsurprisingly, it was limited to the larger centres of population. Congregations were formed in Dublin, Waterford, Cork, Limerick, Galway and Sligo; in towns that were virtually independent in the earliest days with power in the hands of a few wealthy families. Several ministers in Cork in 1657 and Dublin in 1658 formed Associations in which they agreed to organise their activities according to the Westminster Assembly documents. Despite the re-establishment of the Church of Ireland in January 1661, Presbyterians flourished and by the close of the 17th century it was clear that 'second class' Dissenters, of whom the majority were Presbyterian, were to be a longstanding feature of Irish society.

Dublin & Munster Presbytery

Psalm twenty-three set in Gaelic

Twelve Pins, Connemara

SCENIC IRELAND

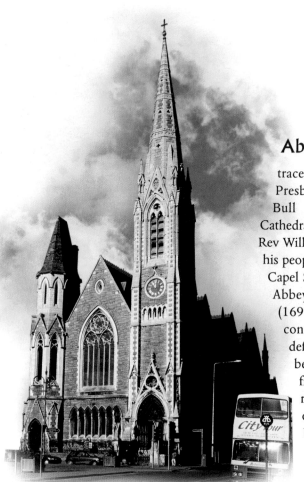

Abbey

traces its lineage from a Presbyterian congregation in Bull Alley, near St Patrick's Cathedral, about 1660. In 1667, Rev William Jacque and a section of his people formed a new church in Capel Street on the site of Mary's Abbey. Rev Francis Iredell (1699–1738) was called by the congregation in 1696 but defied Synod for three years before coming to Dublin from Donegore. Despite his relative inexperience, being ordained in 1688, he had been chosen as one of two ministers who represented Irish Presbyterians to the Duke of Schomberg and King William's army in 1689. In 1777, the church was rebuilt on the same site without access from Capel Street and was known as Mary's Abbey. The congregation dwindled to a handful of families but subsequently grew to over 2,000 individuals under the collegiate ministries of Revs Benjamin McDowell (1778–1813), James Horner (1791–1828), and James Carlile (1813–44). Dr Horner was largely responsible for the first Presbyterian Code of Discipline in 1825. In November 1864, the congregation moved to its present location in Parnell Square (then Rutland Square), into a building provided totally at the expense of Alexander Findlater, a wealthy Dublin wine merchant and member of Kingstown (now Dun Laoghaire) Church. In 1916, Union Chapel joined with Abbey. Membership stands at 100 families today.

Christ Church, Limerick

can trace its origins to the 1650s when the Puritan, Rev Claudius Gilbert, ministered here. Early records are scant but a new Church was built during the ministry of Rev Abraham Seawright (1760–1804). This in turn was replaced by another new church that was built in Upper Glenworth Street during the ministry of Rev John Pinkerton (1810–28). In 1853, another congregation was spawned in Ennis during the ministry of Rev David Wilson (1844–94) who served as Moderator of the General Assembly for two consecutive years, 1865 and 1866. Twenty-one ministers applied to succeed him! The Church was united with Ennis from

12 April 1951 until the latter was dissolved in 1972. In 1973, the Presbyterians and Methodists in Limerick united in one congregation, Christ Church, Limerick, operating a five year Alternating Ministry Scheme. Membership currently stands at 110 families .

Cork

was formed about 1675 but early records are scanty. A church was built in Princes Street. However, in the early 19th century, a significant section of the congregation was troubled by the Arian views of successive ministers. A second church, Trinity, was formed in 1830 under the control of the Synod of Ulster. It worshipped in Queen Street (now Father Matthew Street) before moving to a new building in 1861. A third congregation was formed in 1862 in the old Queen Street building. Numbers peaked in 1912 and the Queen Street and Trinity congregations amalgamated in 1928 under the name Trinity,

Cork; the original Princes Street congregation died out after 1990. Trinity, Cork was united with Aghada from 1 August 1973. Membership stands at thirty-five families today.

St. Patrick's, Waterford

was formed in the 1670s and the earliest known minister was Rev William Liston (1673–76). Rev Alexander Sinclair (1686–89) was persecuted and left Ireland for a time before returning to help establish the Plunket Street Church in Dublin (1692–1722). In 1854, the Church joined the General Assembly during the ministry of Rev William McCance (1826–64). McCance retired on 11 October 1864 to facilitate a union with the local Scots Church, a predominantly Scottish congregation which had been formed in 1847. On 8 November 1888, Portlaw was added to this cause but services there discontinued in 1931 due to diminished numbers. A particular focus of ministry at that time was to the crews of Scottish fishing boats which harboured at Waterford. A new Church in Lady Lane was opened in 1912, replacing the former building which had been known locally as 'The Hole in the Wall'. In 1961, the Church was partially destroyed by a gas explosion. St. Patrick's Church of Ireland closed and the Presbyterians were given the former Anglican building for their continued use. Kilkenny was added to Waterford as a Stated Supply from 1 August 1937, but this link was dissolved on 20 May 1984. Bandon was amalgamated with Cork in 1961. In 1984, the congregation united with the local Methodists to form a single Church within an eight year Alternating Ministry Scheme. Membership currently stands at fifty-three families.

Corboy

was also known as Longford and had a minister as early as 1675 but his name is unknown. The second minister, Rev John Mairs (1697–1706) complained of the greatness of the charge with two preaching places over five miles apart. In 1833, a section of the congregation was dissatisfied with the obvious Unitarian tendencies of Rev Thomas Kennedy (1817–39) and formed a separate Church at Longford. The Church was linked with Tully from 1881–86 and again, from 1894, with Longford making a triple charge from 1920. Longford was dissolved in the 1940s and Tully in the 1960s. In the latter half of the 20th century Corboy has been in various unions with other congregations but most recently, since 24 October 1979, with Mullingar. Membership stands at eleven families.

Killala

was linked with Sligo until 1698. It was originally known as Moywater. The first minister, Rev Samuel Henry was ordained in

1695. Emigration adversely affected numbers in the 18th century and a new church was opened in the 1820s. Rev Hamilton Magee served here from 1849 until 1854 when he became Superintendent of the Dublin Mission. The potato famine halved congregational membership to about thirty families in the late 1850s. In 1924, the church was united with Ballinglen and Dromore West. The church has been united with Ballina since 1942 and Ballymote since 1979. Membership currently totals seven families.

Sligo

was formed about 1695 and linked with Killala until 1698. The church was also linked with Ballymote from 1760 until 1823. Membership peaked at sixty families during the ministry of Rev James Heron (1824–60) who also organised services at Drum. Rev Moffatt Jackson (1855–60) was the first of a line of four generations of Irish Presbyterian ministers. From 1 July 1959 the minister here was also Stated Supply in Boyle and Ballymote though only with Boyle since 1979. Attendance has been boosted by a recent influx of immigrants in the city and membership stands at thirty-five families.

Galway

was formed in 1698 by Rev William Biggar of Limerick who was imprisoned by the local Episcopal bishop on a charge of 'dividing the Protestant interest'. The cause lapsed in the 1720s but was revived in 1835 when Rev Joseph Fisher was ordained. Rev John Clarke (1882–1917) had a very significant ministry, being a member of the first governing body of University College, Galway,

Reverend Hamilton Magee

HAMILTON MAGEE was born in Belfast in 1824. He graduated from the Belfast Institution in 1845 and was ordained in Killala on 8 August 1849. At College he was one of eleven students who vowed to pray for each other and most worked in Connaught. Rev Magee was Superintendent of the Dublin Mission for forty-three years, from 1854 until 1897. In Dublin he instructed candidate colporteurs and directed a network of such activity throughout Ireland. He insisted that all his workers should have a thorough knowledge of Roman Catholicism and Irish history. In addition they had to be familiar with the Maynooth Catechism and the Douay Testament. Rev Magee was editor of *Plain Words* a Presbyterian magazine which started initially as a vehicle of communication with Roman Catholics, in August 1859. This magazine was superseded by *Christian Irishman* which began in January 1883 and Rev Magee acted as editor until his retirement in 1894. In all his publications, Rev Magee had a single motto, 'speaking the truth in love'. He died on 11 October 1902.

and a Commissioner of National Education as well as Convenor of several Assembly Committees. He was Moderator of the General Assembly in 1909. In 1980, the congregation became joint Presbyterian-Methodist within an Alternating Ministry Scheme. Membership now stands at thirty-six families.

The 18th Century

Four new congregations were formed in the 18th century: Ervey, Drogheda, Athy and Ballymote. While the penal legislation of this century was primarily aimed at nullifying Roman Catholic influence, Presbyterians suffered also. Their chief complaint was possibly that their marriages were not recognised in law and numbers of Presbyterians emigrating to America reached 12,000 annually by the middle of this century. It was Dublin Presbyterians who, in 1750, founded a Widows Fund for alleviating hardship in ministers' families. One of the original trustees was Alexander Stewart, grandfather of Lord Castlereagh.

Ervey

was formed about 1700 and was linked with Corvally until 1832, when Rev Robert Winning resigned from Corvally and retained Ervey. He left in 1842 when he conformed to the Established Church. Rev Samuel Bennett was minister on two occasions, 1893–1906 and 1910–1912. The congregation was united with

Kells from 1939 until 1979 and then with Drogheda from 1979 until 2003. The union with Kells was resumed in February 2003. Membership currently stands at fourteen families.

Drogheda

was formed when Cromwellian soldiers occupied the town though the cause lapsed in the late 1680s. Ulster ministers who came to preach in the early 1700s were persecuted by the local Church of Ireland bishop, and were occasionally imprisoned. Following the appointment of several Non-subscribing ministers, the cause died in the 1760s. A congregation was formed again when Rev Josias Wilson was installed on 6 August 1822. A new church was opened in 1827. The longest ministry here was that of Rev Alexander Hall who served from 1889 until 1937. The church was united with Ervey from 24 October 1979 until 18 February 2003. Sunday attendance has risen lately to over 100, in no small part due to immigration, with Korean, Chinese and African Christians joining. Membership currently stands at sixty families.

Athy

was founded sometime before 1720 but ceased to exist after 1770. A new congregation was formed in 1851 and the minister was Rev John Hall (1852–61). A congregation was opened in 1855 and a gallery added in the 1860s. The church was united with Carlow from 1937. Rev Archibald Dodds (1937–59) refurbished the church at his own expense as a memorial to his parents. Naas was

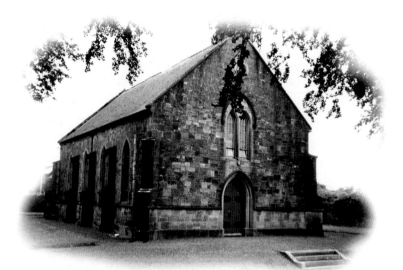

added to the union in 1978 and Carlow removed in 1993. Membership currently stands at fourteen families.

Ballymote

Ballymote was formed in 1795 and was supplied by Sligo ministers before gaining single congregation status in 1823. The church was in serious financial straits in the 1850s, requiring a new building and unable to secure a lease in perpetuity. Mr Jennet Duke of Newpark eventually offered a site with lease and a new church was built on his land. Numbers were never large and the congregation was united with Boyle on 1 July 1929. Both congregations became a Stated Supply to the minister of Sligo on 1 July 1959. From 1979 the church has been united with Ballina and Killala. Membership currently stands at eight families.

The 19th Century

This century witnessed the greatest expansion in Southern Presbyterianism with the formation of an incredible fifty-one new congregations, twenty-four of which are still functioning. Church extension and missionary enterprise, especially in the south and west of Ireland became very popular by the 1840s. At that time the Presbytery of Dublin was the only one in connection with the Synod of Ulster and effectively covered the provinces of Leinster, Munster and Connaught. The famine of 1846 ravaged the whole country and sparked new philanthropic and evangelistic endeavours, especially in Connaught, but the Roman Catholic Church responded with charges of proselytism. Presbyterian hopes of real gains in the 19th century were ultimately dashed.

Carlow

existed as a Presbyterian congregation for a time in the 17th century but ceased about 1750. Rev Henry Cooke provided the impetus for a new start when he conducted services here in 1818.

The first minister was Rev James Morgan (1820–24). Short ministries followed, and the first twelve ministers covered a period of only seventy-five years. The church underwent major refurbishment in 1900 between the 'double ministry' of Rev Robert Bailey, from 1887 until 1891 and from 19 May 1914 until 3 November 1914. The church was united with Athy from 1937 until 1993. From that year it has been designated a Home Mission Development Scheme. Membership is now about forty families.

disagreements with members of the congregation. A new church was opened in June 1863. Rev Francis Gardiner (1890–1927) had a notable ministry here. He successfully introduced an organ in 1896 and saw the Methodist congregation join his own in 1919. Rev Samuel Park (1942–71) was elected Moderator of the General Assembly in 1965. In June 1963, the church name was changed from Kingstown to Dun Laoghaire. Membership stands at about 160 families today.

Mullingar

was organised in 1821 due to the efforts of Rev James Horner of Mary's Abbey in Dublin. The first minister was Rev Alexander Gibson, who was ordained on 19 March 1823, suspended on 8 February 1838, and died on 13 June 1838. The church was united with Moyvore in 1915 and Killucan in 1930 with amalgamation arriving in 1961. In 1973, the church was united with Cavan and Corboy and from 1979 with Kells and Corboy. From 2002, the congregation was united with Corboy under the Board of Mission in Ireland. Membership stands at twenty-seven families today.

Bray

was formed through the initiative of the Irish Evangelical Society, which organised student-led services here from 1816. A church was

Dun Laoghaire

originated in 1828 as a Church for Scottish engineers who extended the railway in the Kingstown (now Dun Laoghaire) area. It was originally known as Scots church. The first minister, Rev William Freeland, was ordained on 1 June 1827. However, in 1838, he was advised to leave by Synod when he had serious

248

built in Main Street in 1817. Rev David Creighton and his congregation joined the Secession Synod on 24 May 1834 and the General Assembly in 1840. Numbers increased and the present church in Quinsboro' Road was opened on 12 September 1858. A harmonium was used in worship from 1878 despite the disapproval of the General Assembly and Dublin Presbytery. Rev Hugh Glenn (1892–1923) was Moderator of the General Assembly in 1920. In 1925, the congregation adopted the name St Andrew's, Bray, and was united with Greystones and Arklow from 1980 until 1989. From then the church has been linked with St. Andrew's, Blackrock. Membership stands at about thirty families today.

Clontarf and Scots

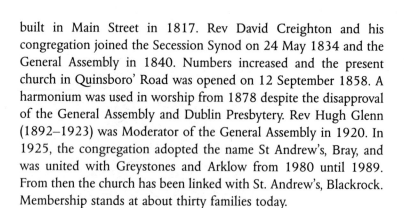

Fermoy

was formed in September 1837 though Rev Thomas Hincks had preached regularly in the town while a teacher at Fermoy Academy from 1815–22. The longest ministry here was that of Rev William Little (1919–1940) who also served Lismore. The congregation was amalgamated with Lismore and united with Cahir on 1 August 1967. This union was dissolved on 20 May 1984 but renewed in September 1997 when Rev Dr Sam Mawhinney was installed in what was designated a Home Mission 'experimental' ministry situation. The church was extensively refurbished in 1998. Membership currently stands at thirteen families.

Kilkenny

was formed in 1838 and the first minister was Rev Joshua Collins (1841–47). He was succeeded by Rev James Porter (ordained on 20

can trace its origin to a number of earlier Dublin churches. The Clontarf church was opened in 1888 though the congregation had previously worshipped in Gloucester Street (now Sean McDermott Street) and D'Olier Street, having been formed in 1836 as a Seceder congregation in Poolbeg Street. Rev John Morrow (1884–1940) had a very significant ministry, being editor of the *Presbyterian Churchman* for many years and Moderator of the General Assembly in 1929. During the ministry of Rev John Wynne, on 21 September 1973, the church was united with Ormond Quay/Scots. Membership stands at about 100 families today.

June 1848), who underwent Episcopalian ordination in some secrecy on 25 February 1877 by the bishop of Kilmore. When this came to light some weeks later he was obliged to resign on 3 April 1877. The church was added as Stated Supply to Waterford from 1 August 1937 until 20 May 1984 when it was united with Cahir. Numbers increased very significantly during the ministry of Rev John Woodside (1984–2002). From 1993 an experimental ministry was launched with Rev Stephen Johnston based in Kilkenny but ministering in Carlow, Fermoy and Cahir. The union with Cahir was dissolved in 1997 and a new church, capable of seating 350 people, was opened on 20 June 1992. Membership stands at almost 100 families.

Adelaide Road

was founded in 1840 as a new Presbyterian church on the south side of a rapidly growing city. Extra seating was necessary in the early 20th century to accommodate the growing congregation but this was reversed in the unrest surrounding war and independence. Thirty-one members of this church died on active service in World War One. Rev Robert Hanna (1914–47) was elected Moderator of the General Assembly in 1926. Numbers declined from the 1950s and the church was united with Donore in 1981. Rev Frank Sellar was installed on 5 December 1990 and the congregation undertook a major redevelopment scheme in which the church building has been replaced while retaining the original façade. The first services were held in the new premises on 9 June 2002. Membership stands at 120 families today.

Adelaide Road

ADELAIDE ROAD congregation has occupied its present site since its inception in 1840. The original building was demolished in 2001, while retaining the Victorian Palladian façade, with a new multifunctional five level building appropriate for city centre ministry in the 21st century. While the germ of the idea to re-develop goes back as far as 1979, it was in the ministry of Rev Frank Sellar that the bulldozers and builders moved in. The cost amounted to 4.9 million Euro. The congregation had decided that they were slowly sinking in their traditional expression of church life; most people travelled in on Sunday for worship and various activities took place throughout the week. In a deliberate attempt to become relevant to their immediate surroundings they opened an Unemployment Resource Centre and held courses in adult literacy and computer skills – a new form of ministry! The new building provides a worship centre, playgroup facilities, community level and residential floor. It was officially opened on 21 September 2002 by the Moderator of the General Assembly, Rev Dr Russell Birney.

Wexford

was formed in 1840 though there had been a Presbyterian cause here in the 17th century. The second minister, Rev John Bond

(1846–49) had come from and returned to the Church of Ireland. The church was united with Enniscorthy in 1927 and became part of a three point union with Gorey in June 1977 within an alternating Presbyterian-Methodist scheme. This arrangement ceased in June 2005 with Gorey reverting to the local Methodist circuit and Wexford and Enniscorthy becoming a joint Presbyterian Home Mission charge. Membership is now about twenty families.

for only two years. The cause lapsed but revived in 1843, when more Presbyterians came to the area. The church building was opened on 27 August 1854, however, numbers were never large. The church was amalgamated with Ballacolla on 1 January 1965 and linked with Tullamore from 1 April 1970. Membership is currently seven families.

Tullamore

Ballina

originated as a mission station attached to Killala. Under the leadership of Rev Thomas Armstrong (1846–68) the church opened in July 1851 and became a headquarters for famine relief and the establishment of a local network of Scripture and Irish schools. The church was united with Killala and Dromore West on 1 April 1942 and Rev Matthew Bailie (1942–46) also had pastoral oversight for Ballinglen, Castlebar, Westport and Newport. Dromore West closed in 1965 and the congregation became part of a new triple union with Killala and Ballymote in 1980. Membership stands at seventeen families.

Mountmellick

origins are unknown but Presbyterian activity in the early 18th century died out around 1798 with the closure of about seven local congregations and loss of their lands and assets. The Seceders established a mission here in 1820 and Rev Thomas Clarke was ordained to the congregation on 25 September 1829 but he stayed

was formed in 1856 as the second Presbyterian congregation in King's County (now Offaly). The first minister, Rev Samuel Kelly, was ordained on 3 December 1856 but left to undertake missionary work in Australia in April 1858. The church building was opened in 1866 by Rev Dr John Edgar, one of his last public acts. In 1937, the church was united with Birr but the latter closed in 1969. The congregation has been linked with Mountmellick since 1 April 1970. Membership currently stands at thirteen families.

Boyle

was formed as a result of fortnightly services conducted in Boyle Wesleyan Church. The Presbyterian Church was founded in 1857 and the church building was opened in May 1859. The church was united with Clogher in 1911, but the latter cause dissolved in 1930. The church was united with Ballymote on 1 July 1929 and from 1 July 1959 both congregations became a Stated Supply to the minister of Sligo. The congregation formed a new union with Sligo in 1980. Membership is currently four families.

Naas

was formed in 1857 and the first minister was Rev James Shannon (1858–79). In 1937, the church was united with Lucan and Summerhill and the latter was amalgamated with Lucan in 1903. The union with Lucan was dissolved in 1972 and the church was united with Athy and Carlow in 1978 though Carlow was removed in 1993. Membership is now twenty-two families.

Birr

The history of BIRR PRESBYTERIAN CHURCH is unique among all Irish Presbyterian congregations. In 1839 Father William Crotty and a majority of his congregation left the Roman Catholic Church and requested to be recognised as a Presbyterian congregation. The Synod agreed and Mary's Abbey and Usher's Quay churches in Dublin undertook to help the new cause in Birr. Rev Dr James Carlile of Mary's Abbey moved to Birr and worked there as missionary of his Dublin congregation for fourteen years. Dr Carlile's colleague in Mary's Abbey, Rev Dr William Kirkpatrick, carried on the ministerial duties in Dublin. Rev Crotty married in 1841 and served as a missionary in Birr, Roundstone, Galway and Connemara. He died on 25 July 1856, leaving a widow and ten children. A succession of short ministries followed Dr Carlile's death in 1854 and a church was opened in 1886. Numbers declined in the early 20th century and the church was united with Tullamore in 1937. Services ceased in the church in 1969 and the building was used for a time as the Tourist Office in the town.

Reverend Fleming Stevenson

WILLIAM FLEMING STEVENSON was born in Strabane on 20 September 1832. He graduated form Glasgow University in 1851 and was ordained in Rathgar on 1 March 1860. He spent his entire ministry here, dying on 16 September 1861, aged fifty-four. With over 200 children in his Sunday School, Fleming Stevenson was one of the first ministers to adopt the practice of a *Children's Address* as part of his Sunday services. He was innovative in other ways. Thanksgiving Services after Communion were conducted early on a Monday morning and followed by a breakfast for all. His congregation became the leading contributor to Foreign Missions. In 1872 their target was £42 and they contributed £347. Rathgar church pioneered the use of hymns in public worship. Rev Stevenson had an abiding interest in hymns and built up a collection of over 500 hymnbooks in various languages. His collection was used to produce several hymnbooks throughout Great Britain and was donated to the library of Assembly's (now Union) Theological College in Belfast. In 1881 Rev Stevenson was elected Moderator of the General Assembly. His congregation successfully held on to him when important congregations in London and Glasgow sought to call him.

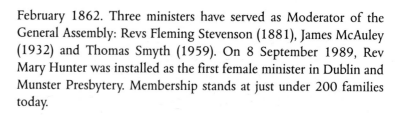

Christ Church, Sandymount

was formed in 1857 as Dublin expanded into new suburbs. Rev Thomas Lyttle (1857–80) was editor of the *Presbyterian Churchman* for many years. He was succeeded by Rev Alexander Rentoul (1881–89) whose father and three brothers were all Presbyterian ministers. On 1 June 1975, the congregation united with the local Methodist congregation under an Alternating Ministry Scheme and with a new name, Christ Church, Sandymount. Membership currently stands at eighty families.

February 1862. Three ministers have served as Moderator of the General Assembly: Revs Fleming Stevenson (1881), James McAuley (1932) and Thomas Smyth (1959). On 8 September 1989, Rev Mary Hunter was installed as the first female minister in Dublin and Munster Presbytery. Membership stands at just under 200 families today.

Enniscorthy

was formed in 1865 although Presbyterians had previously been active in this locality in the late 17th and early 18th centuries. The first minister, Rev William Arnold, was ordained on 26 March 1867 and served here for forty-seven years until his death on 24 October 1916. The church was united with Wexford on 23 June 1927 and became part of a three point union with Gorey in 1977 within an alternating Presbyterian-Methodist Scheme. This arrangement ceased in June 2005 with Gorey reverting to the local Methodist circuit and Wexford and Enniscorthy becoming a joint Presbyterian Home Mission charge. Membership is now twenty-five families.

Rathgar

was formed in 1859 as a result of enthusiasm from Rev John Hall of Mary's Abbey. The famous Rev Fleming Stevenson was ordained as the first minister on 1 May 1860 and the Church was opened in

Aghada

is the most southerly Presbyterian congregation in Ireland and originated as a Home Mission station in 1863. In 1869 the congregation was evicted from their church, which belonged to the Church of Ireland. They worshipped successively in a private home and small corrugated iron church before purchasing a Church of Ireland building in 1925. The church was amalgamated with

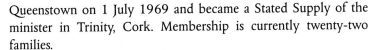

Queenstown on 1 July 1969 and became a Stated Supply of the minister in Trinity, Cork. Membership is currently twenty-two families.

Lucan

was formed in December 1876 and the first minister was Rev William White (1876–87). In February 1903, the church was amalgamated with Summerhill. Rev Dr James Irwin (1935–54) was an active supporter of the Irish Republican Movement and friend of Mr Eamon de Valera. Dr Irwin was offered the Irish Presidency by Fianna Fail in 1936 but would not run against a Fine Gael candidate. The Fianna Fail executive met monthly in Dr Irwin's manse during his time in Lucan. The church was united with Naas from 1937 until 1972 and with Donore from 1972 until 1980. Rev David Henderson (1968–72) resigned for security reasons in 1972. He had formerly been an Assistant Chaplain General in the British Army. Rev Henderson moved to Glamis in Scotland where he served as Chaplain to the Queen Mother. Rev

Kells

was formed in 1869 by Scottish families from the Headfort estate comprising the bulk of the congregation. Opened in 1871, the church was served by a series of ministers who provided short ministries, nine in the first sixty-five years. The longest serving minister here was Rev James Mitchell who ministered from 1904 until 1929. The Church was united with Ervey from 1939–79 and with Corboy and Mullingar 1979–2003. Union with Ervey was resumed in February 2003. Membership stands at twelve families.

Reverend Trevor Morrow

TREVOR WILLIAM JOHN MORROW was born in 1948 and brought up in Lisburn. He attended Magee College, Londonderry and graduated in Arts from Trinity College, Dublin and Theology from New College, Edinburgh. Following an assistantship in Hamilton Road, Bangor, with Rev Dr David Burke, Trevor was installed in Lucan on 18 March 1983 and has pioneered a new approach to Presbyterian ministry in Ireland. Membership in Lucan church has risen from thirty to 240 families. Dr Morrow has challenged the common view of many Presbyterians in Northern Ireland that churches in the south can only shrink. His ministry speaks to the current situation in Ireland where Irishness is coming of age in the 21st century. Rev Morrow articulates the view that that many Ulster Christians add cultural baggage to the simple gospel. Too often we give major emphasis to how we vote or dress, or how we socialise and make judgements accordingly. He believes that there is an urgent need for our churches to communicate effectively in language that ordinary people can understand. In 2000 Rev Morrow was elected Moderator of the General Assembly, one of the youngest ministers to hold this office in recent years.

Dr Trevor Morrow was installed here on 18 March 1983 and numbers increased significantly. He was elected Moderator of the General Assembly in 2000. Membership currently stands at 240 families.

Cahir

was formed in 1881 when the Presbyterians took over an existing Quaker meeting house. The church was united with Fermoy on 1 August 1967. This union was dissolved on 20 May 1984 but renewed in September 1997 when Rev Dr Sam Mawhinney was installed in what was designated a Home Mission 'experimental' ministry situation. Membership today consists of five families.

Greystones

originated in 1885 with evening services in the Episcopal school. A church was opened in July 1887 and a congregation formed in June

1889. The first minister was Rev Samuel Lundie (1890–1911). Rev Robert Lyle (1927–52) had won two international rugby caps in 1910; He exercised a significant ministry here. Until the 1970s the town had a majority Protestant population, though mostly Church of Ireland. The church has been united with Arklow from 1 July 1969 with Bray added to the union from 1980 until 1989. Membership is currently seventy-two families.

Howth and Malahide

was formed in Howth in 1893 though from 1850 Free Church of Scotland ministers had been conducting services for increasing numbers of Scottish fishermen using the harbour. Initially, Malahide members worshipped at 2 Killeen Terrace and Howth members in the Mariner's Hall, East Pier. The Howth church was opened on 12 August 1900. Thanks to a gift of land by the Kirker family, a church was also built at Malahide and opened on 25 November 1956. This was the first Presbyterian Church to be built in the Irish Republic after independence. Despite having two church buildings, there is only one Kirk Session and Committee. The current Clerk of Session is also father of The Edge of U2 who was brought up in Malahide congregation. Membership has risen to about 130 families and there is real pressure upon space in Malahide.

St. Andrew's, Blackrock

was formed in 1895 and the first minister, Rev James Snowdon was ordained on 10 October 1895. He spent his entire ministry of forty-one years here, dying on 21 January 1936. The church building was opened on 5 February 1899. It is octagonal in shape

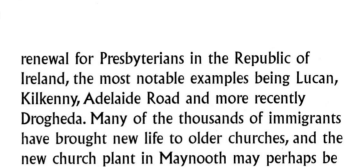

renewal for Presbyterians in the Republic of Ireland, the most notable examples being Lucan, Kilkenny, Adelaide Road and more recently Drogheda. Many of the thousands of immigrants have brought new life to older churches, and the new church plant in Maynooth may perhaps be forerunner of good things to come.

Arklow

with a tower at the front. A memorial plaque records the names of six members who lost their lives during the Great War, five on the field of battle, and one, St. John Ambulance Brigader Holden Stodart, who was killed by crossfire in Dublin in 1916. A much needed hall was added in 1959, being opened by Mrs Scott McLeod, wife of the then US Ambassador to Ireland. From 1989 the church has been linked with Bray. Membership stands at just under eighty families today.

was formed in 1913 and the church building was opened on 29 January 1915. The first ministry was that of Rev Dr Robert Wylie (1915–19) who had retired from Terrace Row, Coleraine. Numbers were never large and from 1 July 1969 the church was united with Greystones under a new Home Mission Scheme. Winter attendance was about thirty but a hall overflow was common in summer due to holiday visitors. Membership currently stands at thirty-three families.

The 20th Century

The earliest years of the 20th century were dominated by the political crisis surrounding Home Rule and Civil War. Partition left Presbyterians in the new Irish State as a very small minority. Presbyterian statistics indicate that numbers fell dramatically in all southern Presbyteries in the 1916–22 period: Cork down 45%, Munster down 44%, Connaught down 36%, Athlone down 30% and Dublin down 16%. Some were forced to leave and some chose to leave. A consequence of falling numbers was congregational unions and these abounded throughout the 20th century. One new feature was the emergence of an Alternating Ministry Scheme in which local Presbyterians and Methodists united to form a single more viable congregation and such schemes operate in several areas including Waterford and Galway. There have been signs of recovery and

Conclusion

Ireland is changing rapidly. Since 1973 the economy has prospered and a new confidence is growing in Irish society. The majority of southern citizens no longer live on farms but in urban areas. The Roman Catholic Church is in serious decline and a new pluralist society is emerging. In these days of openness, the Presbyterian Church in Ireland must surely seize the opportunity to speak and act in love, embracing this new society and presenting the Gospel in relevant terms.

Foyle Presbytery

Introduction

Foyle Presbytery was created on 1 January 1962 with the amalgamation of Glendermott and Limavady Presbyteries. The former contained eight churches (Banagher, Cumber, Upper Cumber, Donagheady, Donemana, Faughanvale, Glendermott and Gortnessey) and the latter eleven churches (Ballykelly, Balteagh, Bovevagh, Derramore, Drumachose, Dungiven, Largy, First Limavady, Second Limavady, Magilligan and Myroe). All of these congregations continue to comprise Foyle Presbytery. Only seven of the nineteen congregations in this Presbytery are single charges, the others are all joint charges.

The 17th Century

Four churches were formed in this area in the 17th century: Glendermott, Drumachose, Donagheady and Ballykelly. All of the early ministers suffered persecution under Episcopalian and Commonwealth authorities. Many of the other congregations in this Presbytery were formed out of these, especially Glendermott which spawned twelve new causes.

Binevenagh

Glendermott

is a very old congregation and the earliest known minister was Rev John Wool (1654–79). It was the third minister, Rev James Gordon (1683–92) who advised the apprentice boys in Derry to shut the gates in December 1688. The present church was built in 1696 in a traditional T-shape. In all, twelve other congregations were born out of this early congregation. A Second Glendermott church was formed in 1743 as a result of arguments during a six year vacancy. Rev Joseph Corkey was ordained in Second on 27 September 1860 and served as minister until his death on 25 January 1910. His eight sons were all ministers and his three daughters were all missionaries. The two congregations were united again in 1910. This is the largest church in Foyle Presbytery with membership of 475 families today.

Drumachose

was formed sometime in the 1650s and the earliest minister of whom there is any record is Rev Thomas Fulton (1655–88). The

Reverend Joseph Corkey

JOSEPH CORKEY was born in 1834 in Ballylane, Markethill. He graduated from Queen's University Ireland MA in 1857 and LLB. in 1859. He was ordained in Second Glendermott on 27 September 1860 and spent his entire ministry of fifty years there. Rev Corkey wrote several books and pamphlets in defence of his strong views in support of total abstinence. He was also a strong opponent of the use of instrumental music in worship. All eight of his sons became ministers: William (Windsor), Robert (Assembly's College), Marshall (Culnady & Swatragh), Joseph (USA), James (USA), Alexander (USA), John (Clonaneese) and David (Dundrod). All three of his daughters, Annie, Isabella and Mary, became missionaries. In addition, Revs Vernon Corkey (Finvoy) and Colin Corkey (Hydepark) were grandsons. Rev Corkey was Clerk of Glendermott Presbytery from 1863 until 1910. He was awarded a LLD. from the Royal University of Ireland in 1882, and edited the *Christian Banner* from 1877 until 1883. Rev Joseph Corkey died on 25 January 1910, in his 76th year.

Joseph Corkey and sons

Reverend Nathaniel Brown

NATHANIEL MCAULEY BROWN was born at Burren, near Ballynahinch, on 20 August 1820. He graduated with the General Certificate of the Old College, Belfast (Belfast Institute) in 1843 and was ordained in Drumachose on 25 November 1845. He served his entire ministry of almost sixty-two years here, resigning on 19 June 1907. He travelled by night mail coach to preach on trial here, having only preached on six previous occasions in his life. Congregational membership had recently fallen from 500 to 200 families but Rev Brown built up a sizable congregation and restored the church building to its original cross shape. A new church was opened in 1876 and the debt finally cleared in 1899. In 1885 he was awarded a DD by the Presbyterian Theological Faculty, Ireland and in 1891 he was elected Moderator of the General Assembly. His lasting legacy was in speaking out for the rights of tenant farmers. He is credited as the originator of the '3Fs' – fixity of tenure, free sale and fair rents – which were incorporated into Gladstone's Land Act of 1881. In addition, Rev Brown was Clerk of Presbytery for forty-six years. Rev Nathaniel Brown died 22 June 1910, aged ninety.

first church was built after 1661 at the east end of Main Street in Limavady. A new church was built in the early 1700s. Rev Henry Erskine was ordained on 4 May 1742 but a minority of the congregation retained the deeds of the church and ordained Rev Joseph Osborne in 1742 under the auspices of the Non-subscribing Presbytery of Antrim. This latter church became First Limavady. Rev Erskine built a new cross-shaped church in Church Street. An

extension was added during the ministry of Rev Richard Dill (1812–23). Second Limavady grew out of the congregation in 1839. Rev Nathaniel Brown (1845–1907) had an extraordinarily influential ministry here. In 1876 the present T-shaped church was built upon the foundations of the original 1743 church. The congregation was united with Derramore on 1 January 1925. Membership stands today at just over 300 families.

Princetown on 5 November 1776. When Route Presbytery refused to sustain a congregational call to Rev Richard Dill in 1823, the congregation reverted to the Derry Presbytery and Rev Dill was duly installed on 1 November 1823. The current church was built in 1828 at the expense of the Fishmongers Company. Three ministers were later elected Moderator of the General Assembly: Revs James Paton (1931), William McAdam (1958), and Tom Simpson (1983). Membership stands at just over 240 families today.

Donagheady

was formed in the 1650s. The first minister, Rev John Hamilton, was ordained in 1658 and is thought to have died in Derry during the siege. The choice of Rev William Armstrong (1741–61) did not please a minority of the congregation who formed a Second Donagheady congregation within Letterkenny Presbytery and called Rev William Wirling (1741–65) as their minister. Second church was replaced in 1856 and the two congregations were united in 1933 using Second church and First manse. The first minister of the united congregation was Rev Alfred Martin (1933–35) who was elected Moderator of the General Assembly in 1966. Membership currently stands at 150 families.

Ballykelly

was formed in the 1660s and the first minister of whom records survive was Rev William Crooks (1665–99) who was present in Derry during the siege. Rev John Haslett (1752–57) afterwards emigrated to America and fought as a Colonel in a Delaware Regiment in the War of Independence, dying in the battle of

The 18th Century

Five new congregations were formed in this area in the 18th century: Bovevagh, Cumber, Faughanvale, First Limavady and Banagher. The arrival of the Seceders stirred up local passions here as elsewhere. First Limavady was formed because of a serious dispute in Drumachose over a call to a new minister in 1742. Interestingly, the majority moved to a new site and formed a new church and the minority retained possession of the original building. Sciggan was formed in 1773 by disaffected members of Bovevagh.

Bovevagh

was formed in 1701 and the first minister was Rev Hans Stewart (1701–37) but earlier records refer to a previous Presbyterian congregation in this locality which seems to have dissolved. Dissatisfaction over the ordination of Rev Samuel Patton here on 20 August 1773 led to the formation of a new congregation, Scriggan, in the following year. A T-shaped church was built in the late 1770s to replace the original thatched church. The longest ministry here was that of Rev Adam Magill who was ordained on 8 March 1843 and died on 7 April 1898, a ministry of fifty-five years. During his ministry, the church was extensively renovated in 1879–80. A proposed union with Scriggan in 1901 came to nothing but the congregation was united with Balteagh on 28 November 1974. Membership stands at ninety families today.

Cumber

was formed in 1717, one of several congregations which was formed out of Glendermott. The first minister was Rev Major

Murray (1718–51) and the original T-shaped church was thatched and later slated. There have been only twelve ministers here since the formation of the church. The present church is constructed of natural stone and was opened in 1884. Unusually, it comprises two storeys with a hall on the ground floor and the church on the first floor. It is adjacent to the ruin of Brackfield Bawn which was built by Sir Edward Dodington who designed the walls of Derry. The church is also known as Lower Cumber and was united with Upper Cumber on 1 March 1976. Membership currently totals about 125 families.

Faughanvale

was originally called Muff and formed part of Glendermott in 1696. In 1731 this cause was recognised as a separate church, and Rev James Smyth was ordained here on 27 July 1731. He served as minister until his death on 13 February 1770. Rev Francis Petticrew (1859–86) became Professor of Theology in Magee College. The present church was opened in August 1894. The church developed strong links with the Royal Naval Air Station, Eglinton, between 1943 and 1959 and the church halls were for a time requisitioned as sleeping accommodation for military personnel. A new hall complex was built in 1975. The congregation was united with Gortnessey from 1 August 1979 until 18 February 2003. Membership stands today at a healthy 325 families.

First Limavady

was born out of strife within Drumachose congregation in 1742. A minority disapproved of Rev Henry Erskine and, having obtained the deeds of the church building, they ordained Rev Joseph Osborne under the auspices of the Non-subscribing Presbytery of Antrim. Under the ministry of Rev Alexander Stewart (1750–97)

result of a fall from a stack of hay. Rev James Heney (1905–46) came here after serving three years as Getty missionary at Larne. Rev Norman Houston (1946–76) maintained a successful ministry despite suffering a serious disability. He was also Convenor of the General Assembly's Student Committee. Membership totals just over 100 families today.

the church joined the Antiburgher Seceders and a new Irish Seceder Synod was formed on 12 April 1750. Rev John Wilson was ordained on 20 November 1828 in succession to his father, Rev William Wilson who had ministered here for thirty-two years. Sadly Rev Wilson senior died on the following day. A distinctive black stone church was built in 1857. In 1904 the General Assembly declared that, due to falling membership, the church should be dissolved or united with Second but this was successfully resisted. Rev David Armstrong (1981–85) resigned in dispute with elders and others over the propriety of his ecumenical relationship with father Kevin Mullan of the neighbouring Roman Catholic church. The church was united with Magilligan in 1987 and membership currently totals 250 families.

The 19th Century

As in most areas, the 19th century witnessed the greatest increase in new congregations in the Foyle area. Ten current congregations trace their origins to this period. The Seceders continued to make their presence felt with Donemana, Myroe, Derramore and Dungiven. Relations with the Synod of Ulster were not always co-operative as evidenced by competition in Donemana, Myroe and Dungiven. The new congregations and the 1840 union necessitated new Presbytery boundaries and the Presbytery of Newtownlimavady was created in 1834 (the 'Newtown' was dropped in 1876). The 1859 Revival also impacted upon several congregations, most notably in Largy and Myroe were extensions were added to the churches.

Banagher

was originally part of Cumber but separated about 1755. The first minister was Rev John Law (1756–1810). Rev Thomas Ellison was ordained here on 5 March 1822 and died on 6 January 1847 as a

Binevenagh
GORDON GRAY

Donemana

traces its origin to a Seceder Society which drew support from Presbyterians in Donemana and Badoney. Rev Robert Reid was ordained on 9 June 1800. The Donemana section declined and in 1833 the Synod of Ulster formed a congregation here known as First Donemana. A new church was built during the ministry of Rev John McMath (1873–1906). Rev Robert Coffey (1967–72) was also appointed Stated Supply in Strathfoyle Church Extension in Londonderry. Membership stands today at about 300 families.

Balteagh

was formed in 1823 by families who had previously worshipped at Drumachose. The first minister was Rev Samuel Templeton (1824–66). Rev Richard Macky (1872–83) left to become a missionary in Australia but returned in the following year when the congregation sent a telegram asking him to return as their minister. He served again from 1884 until 1891. Scriggan was dissolved in 1905 with the rump of members joining Balteagh. The congregation was united with Bovevagh on 28 November 1974. Membership stands today at 150 families.

Magilligan

was formed in 1813 and the first minister was Rev Samuel Butler (1814–51). He published a book of sermons, *Death and Life*. He was succeeded by his nephew Rev Hugh Butler (1851–1916), who died at age 103. The church was built in 1863. This church had only four ministers in its first 160 years; the latter being Revs Samuel Kennedy (1918–55) and Rev Rex Rutherford (1955–80). The church was united with First Limavady in 1987 and membership currently stands at fifty families. This is the smallest church in Foyle Presbytery.

Myroe

was formed in 1825 as a joint Seceder cause with Bolay (Derramore). The first minister, Rev David Lynch (1825–36) joined the Synod of Ulster with the Derramore church. Myroe did not join the General Assembly until 19 May 1843. Rev Robert Kennedy was ordained here on 30 March 1853 and retired in 1904 after serving as minister for fifty-one years. Numbers declined in the mid 20th century and the congregation was united with Second Limavady on

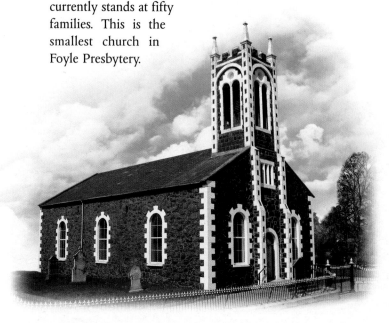

1 April 1974. In 1988–89 the roof and gallery of the church was replaced and new ancillary rooms and pews were added to the property. Membership stands today at almost 110 families.

Lower Cumber on 1 March 1976. Membership stands at just over 110 families today.

Derramore

was formed in 1825 as a Seceder cause and the first minister was Scotsman Rev David Lynch (1825–50). Rev John Orr was ordained here on 15 December 1881 and retired in order to facilitate a union with Drumachose which took place on 1 January 1925. Rev Orr was awarded a LLD. degree by the Royal University of Ireland in 1889. Membership stands at just over 110 families today.

Upper Cumber

was formed in 1828 for Presbyterians living in Claudy, some distance from any church. The designation Cumber Presbyterian Church over the door of the new building created friction with the older church of that name. The first minister was Rev William Brown (1834–74) and he is buried near the entrance to the church. A manse was built during the ministry of his successor, Rev James Smyth (1874–1907), and a hall was built during the ministry of Rev Andrew Scott (1910–18). The congregation was united with

Largy

was formed in 1830 in response to a petition signed by 127 heads of families. The foundation stone of the church was laid in 1831 but the building was not completed until on 26 August 1834 when the first minister and local man, Rev James Irvine, was installed. The congregation did not prosper. Rev Irvine resigned on 6 August 1846, being owed £145 and the congregation was only able to raise £40. Rev Thomas Kennedy (1848–80) had a successful ministry here and a new extension was added to the church in 1861 to accommodate a much larger congregation. Rev James Gallagher (1881–1919) was also Clerk of Presbytery. Upon his retirement the congregation successfully resisted Presbytery pressure to unite with another church. Extensive renovations were undertaken prior to the

Reverend James Irvine

JAMES FERGUS IRVINE was born in 1793, the second son of James Irvine, a farmer from Tamlaghtfinlagan, near Ballykelly. He graduated MA from Glasgow University in 1814 and was licensed by Route Presbytery in 1817. He was ordained in Pennsylvania and graduated MD from Pennsylvania University. Although called by Largy in 1833, his installation did not take place until 26 August 1834. The congregation did not flourish during his ministry and families dropped to thirty by 1842. In July 1846 Dr Irvine declared his intention to resign and stated that he was owed £145. 1. 7½. Largy promised to raise £40 and the Presbytery thought £52 a fair figure. Presbytery believed Dr Irvine had been slack in his duties and warned him not to use the civil courts to recoup his money otherwise they would not give him credentials. Dr Irvine obtained a solicitor's letter demanding his credentials and threatening legal action against the Presbytery. He later demanded £100 as a fair compromise but settled eventually for a payment of £52.

Dr James Irvine returned to America and became President of various Colleges, including New Brighton College, Pennsylvania. He retired in 1865 and died on 4 May 1872 in Ohio.

First Irish Seceder Synod

When Alexander Stewart was ordained in First Limavady on 11 April 1750 he was the third Secession minister in Ireland. The other two were Rev Isaac Patton (ordained in Lylehill on 9 July 1746) and Rev David Arrot (ordained at Markethill on 22 June 1749). All three men were Anti-Burghers. Three ministers was considered a sufficient number to merit the formation of an Irish Synod and, under instruction from the Anti-Burgher Associate Synod in Scotland, they met on the day following Rev Stewart's ordination, at Arkilly, and constituted the Associate Synod in Ireland. Revs Stewart and Arott were Scotsmen and Rev Patton was an Ulsterman, born in the vicinity of Myroe. They laboured together in the Seceder cause for almost half a century. Links between these men were close: Rev Isaac Patton married Magdalen, a sister of Rev David Arott and Rev Arott married a sister of Rev Patton! The Irish Seceders expanded and on 19 August 1788 they met in Berry Street church in Belfast. They organised themselves into a General Synod with four Presbyteries. Rev Stewart was absent on this occasion but Rev Arott presided and preached, and Rev Patton was elected as the first Moderator.

Dungiven

was founded as a Seceder church in 1835 and the first minister was Rev William McHinch (1835–48). The congregation was financially weak and a church building was only completed after a number of years. A Synod of Ulster church was also formed, Second Dungiven, and the first minister was Rev Alexander Gilmour (1839–48). At the union in 1840 both churches remained distinct but they united in 1849 when both fell vacant. The Second church was used for worship and the First church became a salt store and factory but was bought by the church again in 1890 for use as a hall. Some families from Scriggan joined in 1905. The civil disturbances in the 1970s resulted in bomb damage to the church on several occasions. Nine members of this church have become ministers. On 1 January 1995 the congregation was united with Largy. Membership currently stands at just under ninety families.

Second Limavady

was formed in 1840 from a desire to bring the original Drumachose church into the town of Limavady. A site was obtained in Irish Green Street. Rev George Steen could not persuade all of his people

sesquicentenary celebrations in 1981. On 1 January 1995 the congregation was united with Dungiven. Membership totals about 140 families today.

to abandon their old site but he served in Second from March 1845 until his retirement in 1882. The congregation wished to be known as Second Drumachose but this request was denied by the General Assembly. Mr William Ferguson Masey, Prime Minister of New Zealand (1912–25) was brought up in this congregation. A proposal for First and Second to unite in 1906 was resisted by both churches. The congregation was united with Myroe on 1 April 1974. Membership currently stands at almost 340 families.

was Strathfoyle in Londonderry and it failed due to population movement as a direct result of civil disturbances.

Strathfoyle

was a Church Extension cause which started in Londonderry in 1978 under the leadership of Rev John McWhirter of Glendermott. The cause did not prosper due to population movement in consequence to prolonged civil disturbances in Londonderry from 1969. Rev McWhirter continued to lead activities until his retirement in 1991. Strathfoyle remains a Church Extension cause and has never attained full congregational status. More recently the church site was sold and services are held on a three-way rota with Church of Ireland and Methodist ministers in Church of Ireland premises. Membership has fallen to thirty-five families.

Gortnessy

was formed about 1841 and the first minister, Rev John McConnell, was ordained on 9 November 1841. The church was opened in 1842 and services had previously been held for two years in the Grocers Company School. Rev McConnell served his entire ministry here, retiring in 1880. This was the longest ministry in this congregation and Rev McConnell had a record attendance of 230 persons present at Communion in June 1843. The congregation was united with Faughanvale on 1 February 1981 but this union was dissolved on 18 February 2003. Presently the congregation is a Stated Supply within Foyle Presbytery. Membership stands today at about seventy-five families.

Conclusion

Membership of this Presbytery has risen by 40% over the past fifty years (from 2,528 families to 3,598 families). It is one of the smallest Presbyteries, with an average congregation size of 190 families. A majority of the churches are linked in joint charges. As in other areas, the challenge of this century will be to maintain a relevant and sustainable gospel witness in this north-western area of County Londonderry.

The 20th Century

While Scriggan was dissolved due to declining numbers in 1905, the most notable trait in this century has been the union of the majority of the churches into joint charges. Drumachose and Derramore united in 1925, and a further five unions took place from 1974 onwards. The only attempt at a new Church Extension congregation

Iveagh Presbytery

Introduction

Iveagh Presbytery was created on 1 January 1962 by combining the former Presbyteries of Banbridge and Rathfriland. It consists today of twenty-eight congregations, served by eighteen ministers. There are eight single charges and ten double charges. The Presbytery extends across a swathe of South Down, from Newcastle on the eastern coast in a north westerly direction to Newmills and Tandragee in the west.

The 17th Century

Four churches within Iveagh Presbytery were formed during the earliest period of Presbyterian settlement in Ulster in the 17th century: Magherally, First Rathfriland, Tullylish and Loughbrickland. These were well spread across the present Presbytery area. All the early ministers here suffered persecution from the authorities, yet these congregations prospered and between them testify to many years of Presbyterian worship.

Newcastle and the Mourne Mountains

Magherally

was formed in the 1650s and the first minister, Rev Andrew MacCormick was ordained here in 1655, deposed in 1660, and fled to Scotland where he was killed at the Battle of Rullion Green on 28 November 1666. Rev John Martin (1883–1937) had a long and successful ministry here. He was active in politics and instrumental in having a Bill passed through Parliament to protect hand-loom weavers. When he died on 4 December 1946 he was the 'father of the General Assembly'. Rev John Orr (1937–46) was elected Moderator of the General Assembly in 1973. Membership currently stands at about 200 families.

First Rathfriland

was formed about 1657 when Rev Robert Hueston arrived from Scotland to minister among Presbyterians in this area. He stayed only two years and was succeeded by Rev James Campbell, though he was persecuted by the authorities in 1660. The first church was built in 1679. In 1708 a 'daughter church' was formed at

Ballyroney. Rev Samuel Barber (1763–1811) was active in the Volunteer Movement and was arrested in 1798. The present church was built in 1775 and John Wesley preached here in 1787. During the early 1800s there were over 1,300 families in membership. A manse and hall were built during the long ministry of Rev James Wilson (1863–1910). Membership stands today at 225 families.

Reverend Samuel Barber

SAMUEL BARBER was born in 1738 near Killead in County Antrim. His father, John, was a farmer. He graduated from Glasgow University in 1759 and was ordained in Rathfriland on 3 May 1763. In 1771 he married Elizabeth, daughter of Rev Andrew Kennedy of Mourne. Samuel Barber played an active role in the Volunteer Movement, as Colonel in the Rathfriland Regiment. In 1790 he was elected Moderator of the Synod of Ulster. In this same year he played an active role in securing the election to Parliament of Robert Stewart, later Viscount Castlereagh. He came under government suspicion and his house was searched in March 1797 for illegal arms – none were found. Rev Samuel Barber was eventually arrested in June 1798 for his criticism of the authorities and imprisoned at Downpatrick jail until January 1799. Upon his release he immediately resumed his ministerial oversight in Rathfriland. When the Synod of Ulster met in August 1798 an acknowledgement was made of those ministers and licentiates who had been implicated in the recent Rebellion but no mention was made of Rev Samuel Barber. He continued as minister in Rathfriland until his death at Tullyquilly on 6 September 1811.

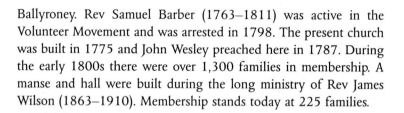

Reverend Samuel Morrell

Samuel Morrell was born in Ballyquin near Dungiven, the second son of James Morrell. He graduated from Glasgow University in 1762 and was licensed by Route Presbytery in 1768. The church at Tullylish had been vacant for two years when Mr Morrell accepted a call in 1770 and he was ordained there on 6 March that year. Rev Morrell preached against many local superstitions such as belief in fairies and that bad luck would follow the cutting of a hawthorn bush. His arrival at Tullylish coincided with an outburst of serious agitation among small farmers in the area over severe rent increases. Secret societies such as the 'Whiteboys', 'Oakboys' and 'Steelboys' operated a campaign of intimidation against local landlords in an attempt to reduce rents. Property was attacked and cattle maimed. Sir Richard Johnston of Gilford Castle was the object of much of the local indignation. On 6 March 1772 Rev Morrell heard of an imminent attack upon the Castle and hurried there to warn Sir Richard. In the ensuing skirmish this minister was shot and killed. He died on the second anniversary of his ordination in Tullylish. In gratitude to Rev Morrell's action, Sir Richard Johnston paid for a memorial tablet in the vestibule of the church.

longest serving minister was Rev John Smyth of Taughboyne who was ordained here on 31 October 1757 and died on 27 May 1804. Rev Robert Crawford (1857–69) was Clerk of Presbytery but also played a leading role in writing on and defending the doctrine of Assurance in 1865, clashing with Rev Dobbin of Anaghlone. The congregation was united with Scarva on 1 February 1927 under the ministry or Rev Thomas Reid (1911–48). Rev Patricia McBride was installed here on 15 October 2004, the first woman minister within Iveagh Presbytery. Membership totals 150 families today.

Tullylish

was formed in 1670 in the aftermath of the Cromwellian wars. Rev Gilbert Kennedy (1703–45) had an influential ministry in building up this cause. Rev Samuel Morrell (1770–72) has the dubious distinction of being the only Irish Presbyterian minister who died from a gunshot wound. Rev John Johnston (1811–62) was a noted evangelical and open-air preacher. Elected Moderator of the General Assembly in 1858, he was instrumental in igniting the 1859 Revival throughout the Presbyterian Church. The church was extensively renovated in 1877. In 1954 another minister was honoured with election to the office of Moderator of the General Assembly, Rev John Knowles (1922–57) who served in 1954. The church was united with Gilford on 1 December 1986. Membership stands today at about 110 families.

Loughbrickland

Rev John Mairs (1687–97) is the earliest known minister to have served here but it is known that others ministered before him. The

The 18th Century

Ten congregations within Iveagh Presbytery trace their origins to the 18th century. It is very significant that seven of these churches were Seceder causes. The Burgher Seceders were very active in this area, chiefly through the labours of Rev Thomas Mayne of Drumgooland. The Seceder churches often served local Presbyterian communities which formerly had to travel some distance to a Synod of Ulster church. There is also evidence that some Synod of Ulster ministers were cool and aloof in their theological opinions whereas the Seceders were warn and earnest.

Donaghmore

was formed as a separate cause in 1705 although Presbyterians in this locality had for some time worshipped in Newry. There were early disputes with Drumbanagher and Glen but the congregation survived and flourished under the lengthy ministry of Rev James Johnston (1707–65). The church was enlarged in 1762 and under the ministry of Rev Moses Finlay (1804–37) membership rose to 2,894 persons. Rev John Elliott (1862–75) was called in 1862 in unusual circumstances. He chaired a congregational meeting at which the original candidates were unsuccessful and he then, at the same meeting, received a unanimous call from the assembled voters. The church was extensively refurbished in 1895 and was united with Glascar on 1 December 1973. This congregation maintains

the custom of sitting at tables in the aisles to celebrate Communion. Membership totals eighty-five families today.

Ballyroney

was formed by Armagh Presbytery in 1708 out of First Rathfriland church. Many local Presbyterians emigrated to America during the early decades of the 18th century. A site for the church was only secured in June 1733. Rev Alexander Neilson (1751–82) was father of Samuel Neilson, a founder member of the United Irishmen. Rev Neilson supervised the building of a new church in 1759. The church was extended in 1832, becoming T-shaped and catering for a membership of 600 families. The present church was opened on 26 January 1929 and the congregation was united with Drumlee on 1 September 1976. The church underwent extensive renovation in 2003. Membership stands today at 175 families.

Samuel Neilson
United Irishman

SAMUEL NEILSON was born on 17 September 1761, the third son of Rev Alexander Neilson of Ballyroney. Following an apprenticeship as a woollen draper in Belfast with his older brother John, Samuel married and launched his own successful career in the woollen trade. Samuel Neilson became active in politics, enthusiastically campaigning in the 1790 General Election on behalf of Robert Stewart, later Viscount Castlereagh. Disappointed by the progress of the Northern Whig Club in pressing for political reform, Samuel Neilson was a founder member of a more radical Society, the United Irishmen, which was formed in Belfast on 14 October 1791. On 4 January 1792 Samuel Neilson founded the Society's newspaper, *The Northern Star*, which praised the triumph of the French revolution and highlighted the many injustices in Irish society. The military authorities smashed the presses in May 1797 and Neilson was imprisoned in Dublin for one year and five months. At the time of the 1798 rebellion he was arrested again and imprisoned at Fort George in Scotland for four years without trial. He was released in June 1802 upon condition that he emigrated to America, which he did. Samuel Neilson died on 29 August 1803 at Poughkeepsie, a small town on the Hudson River.

Reverend Joseph Dickie

JOSEPH DICKIE was born at Killen, near Dundalk, on 27 September 1809. He was the seventh child of James Dickie. Joseph was educated at Trinity College, Dublin where he graduated with a BA degree in 1829 and was licensed by Armagh Presbytery on 1 November 1831. He was ordained in Third Rathfriland on 17 June 1834. He spent his entire ministry here, retiring on 3 August 1880 after forty-six years service. The soirée following his ordination was a 'dry affair', it having been determined 'that no ardent spirits whatever shall be provided for the members of Presbytery, or those who may dine with them, at the expense of the congregation, as we consider that it would be highly impudent of us to expend the money of the public in thus supporting what we believe to be a vice'. In what is surely a unique event in Irish Presbyterian history, Rev Dickie was shot and seriously wounded by a person unknown, while conducting an evening service in his own pulpit on 26 February 1843. No one was ever charged for this crime and thankfully the minister made a full recovery. Evening services were lit by candles at that time and the resultant poor light, coupled with general panic, may explain why no one could identify the attacker. Many suspected the recently deposed Rev John Carey of Brookvale but legal proceedings failed through lack of evidence. Rev Dickie died on 6 April 1883, aged seventy-five years.

Scarva Street

was formed in 1716 to cater for Presbyterians in the growing town of Banbridge who had previously worshipped at Magherally. The first minister was Rev Archibald Maclaine (1720–40). Rev Henry Jackson (1743–90) was said to be a relative of American President, General Jackson. Trouble erupted when Rev James Davis (1814–30)

271

joined the Non-subscribing Synod in 1830. The orthodox section of the congregation continued under Rev Robert Anderson (1830–72) and he was ordained in the partially completed new church. The church grew noticeably throughout the 20th century. Membership stands at about 550 families today, making this the largest congregation in Iveagh Presbytery.

Donacloney

was the first Seceder cause in this locality and was formed abut 1748. Rev Thomas Mayne co-ordinated Seceder activities here and in several outposts in County Down in the mid 18th century. Rev John Thompson (1763–69) was the first minister here. Rev John Riddell was ordained on 3 November 1786 but deposed on 16 March 1790 on the grounds that his marriage was 'illegal and clandestine'. The original mud-walled and thatched church was replaced in 1798 and a gallery was added in 1840. The present church was opened on 17 October 1900. Membership currently totals 210 families.

Drumgooland

was formed from a Seceder Society which arose due to a lengthy vacancy in Ballyroney. Rev Thomas Mayne was ordained here at an open air service on 20 June 1749, the first Burgher minister to settle in Ireland. He ministered here until his death on 1 June 1806 and was succeeded by his grandson, Rev Thomas Mayne Reid (1800–52), who in turn was succeeded by his son, Rev John Reid

(1852–64). The current church was opened on 16 July 1835. The church was united with Kilkinamurry on 1 December 1937. Membership stands at 150 families today.

The Drumgooland Burghers

The church at Drumgooland figures largely in the establishment of Burgher Seceders in Ireland. Rev Thomas Mayne was ordained here on 20 June 1749 as the first Burgher minister to settle in Ireland. On this same day the Anti-Burghers ordained David Arott in Markethill as the second Anti-Burgher minister in Ireland, after Rev Isaac Patton in Lylehill. Thomas Mayne had fought in the Royal Army as a volunteer at the battle of Falkirk in 1746. He presided at the first meeting of the Irish Burgher Synod at Monaghan on 20 October 1779 and died on 1 June 1806. Rev Mayne was succeeded in 1808 in Drumgooland by his grandson, Rev Thomas Mayne Reid who had been educated at Glasgow University and Cahans in County Monaghan. Rev Reid was Clerk of the Secession Synod (1826–40) and Joint Clerk of the General Assembly (1840–68). He built a new church at Drumgooland, which opened on 16 July 1835. He retired from congregational duties in 1852 and died on 9 July 1868. Rev Reid was followed in Drumgooland by his son, Rev John Reid, who was ordained on 12 October 1852 and died on 5 June 1864.

Scarva

was built in 1753 by the Reilly family, landlords, as part of the new village of Scarva which was founded in 1746. This Seceder cause was initially under the care of Rev Thomas Mayne of Drumgooland. The church was linked with Glascar for many years in the late 18th century. Rev William Reid (1810–58) was succeeded by his nephew Rev John Reid (1859–93). The church was then linked for a time with Poyntzpass. The congregation was united with Loughbrickland on 1 February 1927 under the ministry or Rev Thomas Reid who served until 1948. Rev Patricia McBride was installed on 15 October 2004, the first woman minister in Iveagh Presbytery. Membership is currently eighty-four families.

Glascar

was formed about 1756 as a Seceder church was initially under the care of Rev Thomas Mayne (Drumgooland). The first church was built in 1769 but the first minister, Rev Alexander Moore, was not

ordained until 26 May 1778. He was Moderator of Synod in 1787 and emigrated to America in 1796. Rev John Rogers (1798–1834) farmed extensively in this area in addition to his ministerial duties and was followed by his son, Rev James Rogers (1834–84). The longest ministry here was that of Rev John Lusk who was ordained on 19 March 1889. He retired after fifty years service on 30 May 1939 and died two days later. The church was united with Donaghmore on 1 December 1973. Membership currently stands at just over ninety families.

Ballydown

was formed in 1796 as a Seceder congregation (Burgher) of twenty-two persons. Plans for a church building were organised within a year. The first minister, Rev John Rutherford (1800–46), was succeeded by his son, also Rev John Rutherford (1848–74), who resigned in 1874 in order to emigrate to America. Another father and son succession occurred in the 20th century. Rev Buick Knox (1909–42) witnessed the union of the church with Katesbridge in 1938. He was succeeded by his son, also Rev Buick Knox, on 19 November 1942. Rev Knox junior served here until 31 December 1957 when he resigned upon his appointment as Professor of Church History at Aberystwyth. He was later to serve in a similar position at Westminster College, Cambridge. Membership stands today at about 165 families.

Castlewellan

was formed as a Seceder cause in 1796 for the convenience of Presbyterians living in the parish of Kilmegan who previously

belonged to Clough. Although a free site for a church was granted immediately by Lord Annesley, it was not completed until 1809. The first minister was Rev Thomas McKee (1806–44) and initially he conducted services in the local Market House. The longest ministry here was that of Rev Hugh Watson (1851–95). The congregation was united with Leitrim on 1 May 1973, and the first minister of the united charge was Rev James Johnston who was installed on 14 March 1974. Membership stands at just over ninety families today.

Newmills

was formed as a Seceder cause in 1796 following services which commenced here in 1792. The first minister, Rev William Agnew, spent his entire ministry here, being ordained in 1796 and dying on

5 December 1836. Rev Joseph Nimmons was installed on 6 January 1932 after serving for eight years as a missionary to China. He ministered here for twenty-three years before resigning on 21 September 1955. The church was destroyed in an arson attack on Tuesday 5 June 2001. Plans were immediately commenced to clear the site and rebuild and the new church was opened on Tuesday 13 May 2003. Membership currently totals 230 families.

The 19th Century

Fourteen churches within this Presbytery claim their origin in the 19th century. The Seceders continued their prolific local expansion and formed another six churches. Iveagh Presbytery is no exception to the general rule that the 19th century witnessed the greatest profusion of new churches within Irish Presbyterianism. The union of First and Second Anaghlone in 1890 was a sign of future trends among smaller churches throughout this area.

First Anaghlone

Anaghlone

was formed as a Seceder cause about 1800 and briefly united with the Seceder church in Rathfriland. The first minister, Rev David McKee (1804–67) founded a Classical School in Anaghlone and was a noted advocate of Total Abstinence. In 1819 a Synod of

Second Rathfriland

Ulster congregation (Second Anaghlone) was also formed although the first two ministers here, Rev Samuel Crawford (1821–22) and Alexander Orr (1824–38) both became Unitarians. During the ministry of Rev David Macky (1876–90) in First, the capacity of the church was reduced from a square shape to a smaller rectangular shape in order to more appropriately accommodate the congregation. The ministry of the Rev William Dobbin (1839–90) in Second was long and distinguished. He was a strong supporter of Tenant Rights and deeply involved in a post 1859 Revival controversy with Rev Crawford of Loughbrickland concerning the doctrine of Assurance. Both congregations united in 1890. The congregation was united with Garvaghy on 28 March 1983. Membership stands at sixty-seven families.

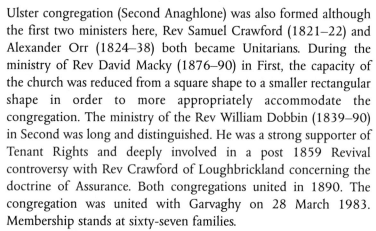

Second Anaghlone

Third Rathfriland

Second & Third Rathfriland

currently operate as a single charge in all but name. Second was formed as a Seceder cause in 1802 and the first minister was Rev Thomas Tate (1804–42). Prior to 1840 it was known as Rathfriland Secession. Third was formed as a Synod of Ulster cause in 1833 because First was full. The Third church was opened on 26 August 1836 by Rev Henry Cooke (though, confusingly, it was known as Second prior to 1840 because it was the second Synod of Ulster church in the town). In 1843 Rev Joseph Dickie (1834–80) of Third was shot while conducting worship. No one was identified as the attacker and Rev Dickie made a full recovery. In 1884 both congregations agreed to unite but disagreements arose and each chose their own minister. In 1927 they formed a joint charge under the new ministry of Rev Hugh Scott (1927–32). For eighty years the congregations have acted in unison and currently they worship

James McKnight

JAMES McKNIGHT was the son of a farmer and was born on 27 February 1801 near Rathfriland. In November 1825 he entered the Collegiate Department of the Academical Institution, Belfast where he excelled in languages and metaphysics. He commenced studies with the intention of entering the Presbyterian ministry but, in 1827 he left to become editor of *The Belfast Newsletter*. His Liberal political views clashed with the Conservative views of the Newsletter owner and, in 1846 he left Belfast to become editor of *The Londonderry Standard*. James McKnight was fluent in Greek, Latin, Hebrew, German, French and Irish. He was a powerful advocate for Tenant Rights and often shared platforms with southern spokespersons. One of his most influential pamphlets was entitled, *The Ulster Tenant's Claim of Right* which was published in 1848. Mr McKnight came to occupy the place of leading lay person in the Presbyterian Church. His articles and reviews were eagerly read, and helped shape public opinion. James McKnight was utterly orthodox in his theological views but he was, equally, implacably opposed to the General Assembly's insistence upon unqualified subscription to the Westminster Confession. James McKnight died on 8 June 1876.

275

as a single congregation, using each church building on alternate Sundays. The two Kirk Sessions meet as one and there are single organisations for both congregations. Closer amalgamation would appear to be a logical development in the near future. Membership of Second stands at sixty families and membership of Third at 110 families.

Garvaghy

was formed as a Seceder cause in 1803 by Presbyterians who had worshipped at Magherally. From 1713 they worshipped at Dromara but resolved to organise their own church in 1799. Their first

Rev David Neely (1939–76) was awarded an MBE for services in connection with National Savings. The church was linked with Clonduff from 1942 until 1965. On 1 September 1976 a new union was formed with Ballyroney. The original school beside the church was used as a church hall but a new hall was opened in 2004. Membership stands at fifty-five families.

Kilkinamurry

was formed as a Burgher Seceder cause in 1821 following initial tent meetings in the previous year. The first minister, Rev George Legate, served here for forty-eight years, from his ordination in 1824 until his retirement in 1875. The church was united with Katesbridge from 1 May 1927 until 1 July 1937. A new union was formed with Drumgooland on 1 December 1937 and the current church was opened on 4 August 1955. Membership stands at sixty families.

minister was Rev Isaac Allen (1803–44). He survived opposition from his elders in 1809 who charged him 'with marrying a couple on one day's proclamation, going to a play that was acted in the neighbourhood, and with being too much given to farming'. He was succeeded by Rev Robert Moorhead (1844–87). The congregation was united with Anaghlone on 28 March 1983. Membership stands at sixty-five families today.

Drumlee

was founded in 1808 as a separate Seceder cause by a minority of families from Drumgooland who objected to the settlement there of Rev Thomas Mayne Reid. The first minister, Rev James Porter was ordained on 3 April 1808 and died as a result of a fall from his horse on 20 February 1851. The original church was demolished about 1828 and the present church was built upon the same site.

Tandragee

was formed in 1825. The church was built at a cost of £689. 7s. 6d. and was opened by Rev Henry Cooke on 22 March 1829. The first minister was Rev Richard Dill. He was ordained on 17 December 1829 and resigned in May 1835 upon accepting a call to Usher's Quay, Dublin. Rev William McMordie (1882–86) had been a missionary in India, from 1867–81. He was the main driving force behind the Twentieth Century Thanksgiving Fund which funded the building of Church House in Belfast and he was elected Moderator of the General Assembly in 1905. A major refurbishment of the church halls was completed in 2004. Membership currently stands at 245 families.

Hilltown

was formed in 1826 and the first minister, Rev Edward Allen, was ordained on 5 June 1827 but deposed the following year for

immorality. He was succeeded by Rev Robert Lochart (1829–84). An attempt to unite the congregation with Third Rathfriland in 1921 was successfully resisted. Rev James Brolly (1956–64) had previously served as a missionary in India for thirty-three years. The church was united with Clonduff on 1 July 1965 and membership now stands at fifty-five families.

Leitrim

was formed as a Seceder cause in 1835 following services commenced in the previous year by Rev James Porter of Drumlee. The first minister, Rev John Henry, was ordained on 29 March 1836 and served as minister for one day less than fifty years, dying on 28 March 1886. The church was built shortly after Rev Henry arrived and was sometimes known as Benraw. Rev Samuel Boyce (1888–98) resigned in order to emigrate to Canada. Rev James Hagan served here for almost thirty years, from 13 September 1898 until 13 March 1928. The congregation was united with Castlewellan on 1 May 1973, and the first minister of the united charge was Rev James Johnston who was installed on 14 March 1974. Membership is currently forty-two families.

Clonduff

was formed in 1840 and the church built in 1840 on a site granted by the Marquis of Downshire. The first minister stayed for less than one year; from 6 July 1840 until 22 June 1841. He was followed by Rev James Steen (1842–81) who had previously been a Reformed Presbyterian minister. The church was united with Drumlee from 1942 until 1965 and a new union was formed with Hilltown. The first minister of the new united charge was Rev Charles McCurdy

the original building in 1909. It was a gift from Mrs Murray whose husband was associated with the tobacco firm, Murray & Co., Sandy Row. This work was completed during the ministry of Rev James Keers (1889–1936) who also built many of the houses in the growing town. Rev Andrew Anderson (1936–65) was a gifted author and historian. In 1965 he was awarded a Doctor of Divinity degree by the Presbyterian Theological Faculty, Ireland but died on 23 May that year, a few days before the ceremony. The church organ was installed in 1976 as a memorial to Rev Anderson. Membership currently stands at about 360 families.

(1966–73). Rev Clifford Wright (1979–88) was the first married minister here in over sixty-five years, and his wife Dale founded a Girl's Brigade Company and acted as first captain. Membership stands at about seventy-five families.

Newcastle

was formed in 1840 and the first minister, Rev Samuel Smith (1840–81), was ordained on 23 June 1840 in the Methodist church building, a mere seventeen days before the formation of the General Assembly of the Presbyterian Church in Ireland. The new congregation continued to use the Methodist church until their own was completed in 1842. The present Scrabo stone church replaced

Gilford

was formed on 13 June 1843 as a result of services conducted in the old Corn Mill from April that year. Seventy families joined immediately and the first minister was Rev James Hume (1844–54). The church was opened on 11 October 1846. Rev Hume was an eccentric and some families withdrew from his ministry; for example reading Joshua chapter two on one occasion and illustrating it by covering the Bible with a handkerchief, holding out a bunch of keys and lowering string from the pulpit! The church was extensively refurbished for centenary celebrations in 1843. Rev Samuel Hutchinson (1966–85) later served as Clerk of Assembly and was elected Moderator of the General Assembly in 1997. The congregation was united with Tullylish on 1 December 1986. Membership stands at eighty families today.

Newcastle
SCENIC IRELAND

Katesbridge

was formed in 1866 to relieve pressure for Presbyterians in the Banbridge area. The first minister was Rev John Barnet (1866–1901) who had previously been a student-sponsered missionary in Connaught. Rev Samuel Hopkins acted as Stated Supply from 1922 until 1927 and, following his departure, the church was united with Kilkinamurry. This union was dissolved in 1937 and a new union was formed with Ballydown in 1938. Rev

Buick Knox, who had been minister in Ballydown since 1909, was now installed on 20 October 1938. Membership is currently fifty families.

Bannside

was formed in 1867 as a second congregation in Banbridge due to increased membership in Scarva Street following the Revival in

1859. The first minister, Rev George Wilson (1867–80), later became Literary Superintendent of the British and Foreign Bible Society (1889–97). Rev John Anderson (1918–60) maintained a lengthy and useful ministry despite a physical handicap. Rev Ernest Rea (1974–79) later became head of Religious Programming with the BBC. Rev Uel Matthews was installed on 1 June 1979 and was awarded a Doctor of Divinity degree by the Presbyterian Theological Faculty, Ireland in 2006. Membership currently stands at 440 families, the largest in Iveagh Presbytery.

The 20th Century

No new congregations were formed in Iveagh Presbytery during the 20th century. Rather there have been ten unions between congregations: the earliest in 1927 and the most recent in 1983. The most interesting union is that of Second and Third Rathfriland who became a joint charge in 1927, continuing to worship in each church building on alternate Sundays, sharing single organisations, yet maintaining separate finances and statistics.

Conclusion

Iveagh Presbytery is typical of several within the Presbyterian Church in Ireland. Overall numbers are rising, showing an increase of 21% over the past fifty years. As a result of recent congregational unions, the number of ministers in the same period has fallen from twenty-two to eighteen. The average size of congregations is 158 families but most are smaller. This is a stable area and several churches have experienced very healthy growth while others are small and getting smaller. Fourteen congregations comprise less than 100 families and some of these may experience future difficulties.

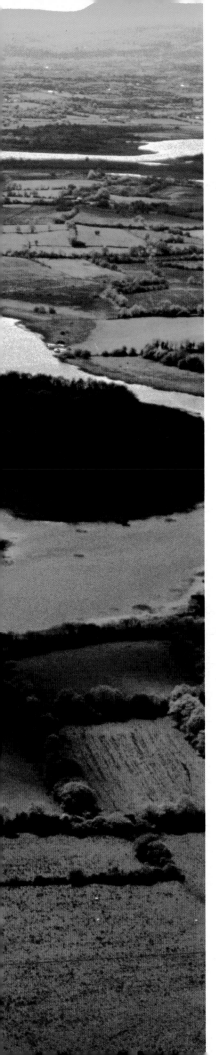

Introduction

Monaghan Presbytery consists of twenty-seven congregations, served by nine ministers. Currently there is one single charge (Clontibret), two double charges, two triple charges and four quadruple charges. The Presbytery area is a large tear shape and covers Counties Monaghan and Cavan. The churches are widespread from Glennan in the north to Bellasis in the south, and from Frankford in the east to Drumkeeran in the west.

The 17th Century

There are five Presbyterian churches in Monaghan Presbytery which trace their formation to the 17th century: Glennan (1650), Drum pre 1675), Killeshandra (1688), First Monaghan (1697) and First Ballybay (1698). These five form an arc from Glennan in the north to Killeshandra in the south and west. The second half of the century was troubled and early ministers suffered opposition, ejection, and several had an ability to preach in Irish.

Monaghan Presbytery

Upper Lough Erne

SCENIC IRELAND

282

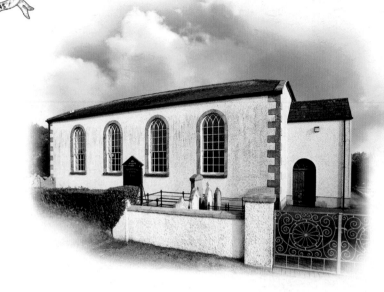

1994 the congregation was united with Cootehill and Kilmount. Membership currrently totals sixty-three families.

Glennan

was also known as Glasslough and was formed in the 1650s under the ministry of Scotsman Rev Thomas Gowan (1658–66) who continued to preach here after being deposed in 1661. For a time the cause was united with Kinnaird (Minterburn). Rev John Davidson (1862–1913) had a long and successful ministry and was elected Moderator of the General Assembly in 1907. A new church was built in 1874. The congregation was united with Middleton on 1 October 1922 during the ministry of Rev John Ritchie (1913–38). Rev Ronald Craig (1944-48) exercised his early ministry here and was elected Moderator of the General Assembly in 1980. The union with Middletown was dissolved on 1 November 1959 and Glennan became a Stated Supply of Ballyalbany. Membership today stands at twenty-nine families.

Drum

was originally known as 'Dartry' or 'Drumdartry' and was formed sometime before 1675. The cause was weak and suffered through the formation of new congregations at Cootehill in 1715 and Longford in 1717. Second Drum was formed in the period 1750–54 as a Seceder church (Burgher) and both churches were united in March 1881, albeit in the face of some stern local opposition. Matters settled under the lengthy ministry of Rev William Armstrong (1886–1932). The church was united with Cootehill and Kilmount on 1 August 1957 and Rev William Hook (1958–62) was the first minister of this triple charge. From 1 May 1972 Drum became a Stated Supply of First Monaghan and in

Killeshandra

was formed in the 1670s and was originally known as 'Croghan'. The first minister, Rev Samuel Kelso, was ordained before 1680 but left in 1689. Rev Joseph Denham (1799–1834) was father of Rev Dr James Denham of Londonderry. Rev William Sweeney (1841–67) sought and received assistance from the General Assembly to halt 'various violent interruptions given to him while officiating at the burial of the dead'. The church was united with Carrigallen and Belturbet on 1 June 1930 and Drumkeeran was added on 1 November 1935. A major reorganisation took place on 1 June 1980 with the creation of a new union: Killeshandra, Drumkeeran, Cavan and Bellasis (with Carrigallen amalgamated with Killeshandra and Ballyjamesduff amalgamated with Bellasis). Rev Jean Mackarel, the first woman minister in Monaghan Presbytery, was installed to this quadruple charge on 27 January 1986. Membership totals fourteen families today.

First Monaghan

was formed about 1697 when Scotsman Rev Robert Darragh was ordained. Presbyterians had previously worshipped at Rock Wallace. Rev Darragh was deposed in 1712 for intemperance and other irregular conduct. A section of the congregation separated in 1728 to form First Clontibret. Rev David Hutcheson (1744–57) was one of the first Presbyterian ministers to be paid monthly. Rev John Bleckley (1821–73) conducted a successful Classical School in Monaghan for many years and among his pupils were several future ministers, for example: Hope Waddell (missionary) and Thomas Armstrong (Home Mission). Rev Bleckley was elected Moderator of the General Assembly in 1852. Rev Robert Corkey (1910–17) was later Professor of Christian Ethics in Assembly's College, Belfast, a Stormont MP and Cabinet Minister. In 2003 Smithborough was added as a Stated Supply. This church is the largest in Monaghan Presbytery with membership standing at 125 families today.

First Ballybay

was formed in the 1690s and the first minister, Rev Humphrey Thompson (1698–44), is said to have preached in Irish and English on alternate Sundays. The ordination of Rev James Morell on 6 August 1799 led to a schism and formation of Derryvalley church. Rev Morell died in 1831 and another split occurred with a minority forming Second Ballybay and ordaining Rev John Morell, son of the aforementioned minister, on 2 January 1834. First Ballybay congregation was united with Derryvalley on 21 November 1909, and from 1937–45 was a Stated Supply under the care of Rev James Kilgore of Clontibret. A new union with Cahans and Derryvalley came into effect on 1 December 1945. On 1 June 1972 these three

Hope Masterton Waddell

HOPE MASTERTON WADDELL was born in Monaghan on 14 November 1804, the fifth child of James and Susanna Waddell. His mother's maiden name had been Hope. He was raised in Cahans Secession Church and wanted to study for ministry but was persuaded instead to follow a career in business in Dublin because he had a speech defect. He returned to Monaghan in 1822 and studied Greek and Hebrew before theological courses at the United Secession Hall in Edinburgh. He was ordained in Edinburgh in 1829 and travelled to Jamaica as the first Presbyterian missionary, and there he worked for sixteen years. Rev Thomas Leslie of Kilraughts followed him to Jamaica in 1835 but he died on 18 August of that year, after only three months in the Caribbean. Slavery ended on the island shortly after Rev Waddell arrived and in 1845 he sailed with some former Jamaican slaves on a new missionary expedition to Nigeria. He established a new mission in Calabar over a twelve year period. Returning to Dublin in 1859 Hope Waddell became one of four members of Kirk Session in the new United Presbyterian Church of Scotland congregation in Lower Abbey Street. Rev Hope Waddell died on 18 April 1895 aged ninety-one.

David Bell,

Reverend David Bell

DAVID BELL was a son of Rev Thomas Bell, minister of Mosside (1794–1841), and native of Radrum in County Monaghan. David studied for the ministry in Old College, Belfast, and was ordained as the third minister of Derryvalley on Tuesday 1 October 1839, only three miles from where his father had been born. The Presbytery of Ballybay was formed in 1841 and David Bell was Clerk from 1847 until 1853. In addition, he served as Moderator of Synod in 1851. Due to the Famine, membership in Derryvalley fell significantly; from 165 families in 1846 to 85 families in 1856. Rev Bell supported the anti-landlord attitudes of many of his congregation and became a strong advocate of Tenant Rights. The Tenant League was formed in 1850 and Rev Bell gave several public lectures to vast crowds in support of the movement. The Tory section of his congregation and the local community disapproved and, Bell claimed, due to persecution he resigned his pastoral charge on 27 November 1853. David Bell continued to advance his liberal political views and in the spring of 1864 he was sworn into the Irish Republican Brotherhood and served as one of seven men on the Executive Council. In 1865 he emigrated to America and appears to have become minister of a church in Brooklyn. He died there on 14 November 1889.

Stonebridge

was formed in 1700 and the first minister was Rev Patrick Dunlop (1700–04) though he left because of a number of grievances, including money arrears. The most troublesome ministry here was that of Rev Archibald Meharg (1804–20). On three separate occasions he was suspended by Presbytery for three months for various misconducts, including the celebration of irregular marriages and encouraging elopement. He was finally dismissed on 1 August 1820. Rev William White served here for 53 years (1820–74) and was succeeded briefly by his son, also Rev William

congregations amalgamated under the name 'First Ballybay' and the latter two churches closed. Drumkeen was united with these congregations in February 1957. The latest union took place on 2 April 2006 when Rev David Nesbitt, minister of First Ballybay and Drumkeen since 1970, was installed in the additional congregations of Second Ballybay and Rockcorry. Two buildings are used each Sunday on an alternating basis. Membership is fairly stable at eighty families today.

The 18th Century

There are eleven churches today within Monaghan Presbytery which were formed in the 18th century. The dominant feature of this period was the arrival of the Seceders. Early activists included Revs David Telfair and John Jervey but the minister who made the biggest impact locally was Rev Thomas Clark who established Cahans as the earliest Seceder cause in this area. In all eight Seceder churches were founded though Cahans, Second Drum and Braddox (Second Clontibret) have all since united with other congregations. The Synod of Ulster formed five new churches between 1700 and 1720 and the Seceders formed eight between 1749 and 1770.

White (1874–75). Another son, Rev James White, served here from 1884–86. In 1889 the church was placed on the Weak Congregation Fund. On 1 November 1914 it was united with Newbliss and Drumkeen was added from 1 April 1927 until 1 July 1937. In 1961 the church was united, initially with Clones and Ballyhobridge, and, in 1965, Newbliss was added as a Stated Supply. Membership stands at eleven families today.

Corvally

was formed around 1700 and originally known as 'Carrickmacklin'. The new cause was linked with Ervey for more than a century. The first minister was Rev John Lee (1703–10) but there was a constant shortfall in maintenance. There was an eleven year gap until a second minister, Rev William Patton, was ordained on 7 December 1721 and he served for fifteen years. The congregations separated in 1832 and a new church was built at Corvally in 1839. The name

of the church officially changed from Carrickmacklin to Corvally in 1880. On 22 April 1958 the church was united with Corlea and this arrangement continued until 2000 when the church became a

The White Family

WILLIAM WHITE was a farmer in Pottle, Bailieborough, and his family contributed significantly to the Presbyterian Church in Ireland. Two of his sons, Patrick and William, became ministers as did eight of his grandsons and one great-grandson. A third son, James, died before his ordination. Rev Patrick White was born on St Patrick's Day 1785 at Pottle, Bailieborough. He was ordained in Corglass (First Bailieborough) on 28 August 1810 and married a daughter of Rev William Moore of Corvally. He was elected Moderator of Synod in 1828 and died on 17 January 1862. He had seven sons who became Presbyterian ministers. Rev William White served in Killeshandra (1835–39) and Downpatrick (1839–87). Rev James White served in First Carrickfergus (1838–89). Rev Verner White served in Donaghmore, County Down (1840–44), Islington, Liverpool (1844–73) and South Kensington, London (1874–?). Rev Patrick White served in Scotstown (1848–51), Donaghmore, County Down (1851–62), First Bailieborough (1862–73) and Islington, London (1873–86). Rev Thomas White served in Loughmourne, Monaghan (1862–65), Athy (1865–74), First Bailieborough (1874–1906). Rev Vere White served in Second Newtownhamilton (1863–84), Corvally (1864–69). In addition a grandson, Rev Patrick White, served in Kells (1872–77), Strangford (1878-81), Middletown (1881–86) and Stonebridge (1886–1914).

Rev William White served his entire ministry in Stonebridge (1820–74) where he also conducted a successful Classical School. He had two sons who were ministers: Rev James White served in Stonebridge (1884-86) and Hollymount (1907–11) and Rev William White served in Fethard (1854–57), New Brunswick, Canada (1857–59), Westport (1859–74), Stonebridge (1874–75) and Lucan (1876–87).

Stated Supply with First Castleblaney and Frankford under Rev Nancy Cubitt. A monthly service is held in Carrickmacross in a former Methodist church which came into Presbyterian possession in 1920. Membership currently stands at fifteen families.

First Bailieborough

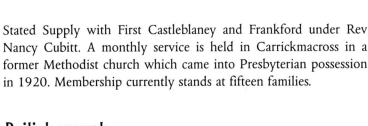

was formed in the early 18th century and the first minister settled here was Rev David Sim (1714–24). A church was built at Corglass, two miles from Bailieborough on the Cootehill Road but poverty threatened to obliterate the new cause. The third minister, Rev Hugh Mulligan Wilson (1742–57), was only paid £12 in 1753 and the Synod asked each congregation to forward 13d (5p) to Bailieborough. The current church was built in 1795. The eighth minister was Rev Patrick White (1810–62) who served as Moderator of Synod in 1828 when the Arian issue was settled. He was elected Moderator of the General Assembly in 1854 but declined the honour. He was succeeded by his son, also Patrick (1862–73). Rev Thomas Byers (1921–24) was later Moderator of the General Assembly (1946). Glassleck was united with this congregation on 1 August 1938 and Corraneary was added on 29 October 1957. On 28 February 1974 a new union was formed: First Bailieborough, Corraneary and Trinity, Bailieborough. The latter two causes had both formed from First Bailieborough; Corraneary in 1763 and Trinity in 1770. On 1 July 2000 Glassleck amalgamated with First Bailieborough. Membership today stands at forty-five families.

1946–52. The congregation of Broomfield was amalgamated with First Castleblaney in July 1973. Rev Nancy Cubitt was installed on 3 June 1994 and Corvally was added to this union in 2000. In 2003 Rev Cubitt became the first female Clerk of Presbytery in the Presbyterian Church in Ireland. Membership stands at fifty families.

Cootehill

was formed in 1717 when a new Presbytery of Longford was created from that of Monaghan, and the first minister was Rev Andrew Dean (1721–60). A Second Cootehill congregation, a Burgher Seceder cause, was formed in 1789 and membership peaked at about eighty families in the 1860s. Rev John Johnston (1808–11) of First Cootehill was later Moderator of the General Assembly (1858) and a leading figure in the 1859 Revival. On 27 September 1870 First and Second Cootehill churches were united under the ministry of Rev John McCleary (1870–80). A new church was built during his ministry. From 1 August 1958 until 1 April 1972 the church was united with Drum and Kilmount. On this latter date the union was dissolved and Cootehill became a Stated Supply with First Ballybay and Drumkeen. At this time a new hall was built. A union with Drum and Kilmount was again formed in June 1994. Membership stands today at about thirty-five families.

First Castleblaney

was formed in 1718 when the Synod of Ulster responded positively to a suggestion from Lord Blaney to assist his Dissenter tenants build a church. The first minister was Rev Samuel Hempill (1718–41) who played a prominent role in support of compulsory subscription to the Westminster Confession of Faith. A division occurred within the congregation during the ministry of Rev James Gordon (1744–51) and the minority party formed Second Castleblaney (Frankford) as a Seceder cause. The congregation was united with Frankford on 1 November 1929 and the first minister of the united charge was Rev James Collins (1930–33). Rev William Haslett (1937–52) was also Clerk of Monaghan Presbytery from

Clontibret

was formed about 1725 and was also known as Legnacreeve. The first minister was Rev William Sloan (1728–32) and the church operated very closely with First Monaghan. A dispute arose in 1778 when the church was transferred to Dromore Presbytery and a Seceder cause was established. It was known as Second Clontibret (also Braddox) and aroused objections from some neighbouring Seceder congregations. The shortest ministry in either congregation was that of Rev Joseph Leitch who was ordained in Braddox on 16 March 1864 and resigned on 23 May 1864. The two congregations

united in 1902 under the name First and Second Clontibret but the people could not agree on a minister. Eventually the church adopted the name Clontibret and the first minister of the united charge was Rev John Thompson (1906–34). The congregation is the only single charge within Monaghan Presbytery and continues to maintain two buildings for worship on alternate Sundays. Membership is now ninety families.

Ballyalbany

was formed about 1751 as a Seceder cause, an offshoot from Cahans. The first minister was Rev Dr Thomas Clark (1751–64) who was ordained in the open air on 23 July 1751. The second minister, Rev Felix Quinn (1771–91), was a convert from Roman Catholicism. During his ministry the first church was demolished by members of First Ballybay who were opposed to this new cause and a new church was built at Ballyalbany. Rev James Rankin (1794–1831) was succeeded by his son, Rev John Rankin (1831–79). A hall was built in 1881. Major renovations were undertaken in the church building in 1886. The three small galleries were replaced by one large gallery and the pulpit was

moved from the west to the south wall. Rev Samuel Orr (1889–1906) moved to Scotland and was elected Moderator of the Free Church Assembly in 1915. On 1 November 1959 Glennan became a Stated Supply of Ballyalbany. Membership now stands at eighty families.

Frankford

was formed about 1750 when the non-evangelical Rev James Gordon of First Castleblaney (1744–51) argued with his

Reverend Dr Thomas Clark

THOMAS CLARK was born in Paisley, Scotland in 1720. In 1744 he matriculated at Glasgow University and in the following year fought against the Young Pretender before resuming his studies. He was ordained in the open air at Cahans on 23 July 1751. He exercised a very energetic and aggressive ministry over a wide area being described as a tall, dark, gaunt man, who wore a highland bonnet and spoke with a broad Scotch accent. He was called Dr because of his medical experience and ability. Rev Clark helped spread Seceder influence in several centres including Castleblayney, Newbliss, Monaghan, Emyvale, Cootehill, Bailieborough and Corraneary. He had strong scruples about taking oaths in court and in 1752 he was imprisoned for two months for his views. In publications he attacked what he believed to be the doctrinal error and lax discipline of the Synod of Ulster ministers, thereby justifying the intrusion of the Seceders. On 10 May 1864 he led a party of 300 Presbyterians, many from his own congregation, in emigrating to New York – the Cahans Exodus. He preached for a time at Salem, Washington (1764-82), and from 1782 at Cedar Spring, Little Rum and Long Cane in South Carolina. He died on 26 December 1792 at Long Cane, sitting in a chair while composing a *Pastoral Letter* to his congregation at Cahans.

congregation, the Presbytery, Lord Blaney and the widow of his evangelical predecessor. A division occurred within the congregation and the minority party formed Second Castleblayney (Frankford) as a Seceder cause, linked with Derrynoose (Drumhillery) and Keady (Tassagh). Rev John McAuley (1755–63) had been the first Irish student at the Burgher Divinity Hall under the leadership of Rev Ebenezer Erskine of Stirling. The ordination of Rev David Longmoor (1820–32) caused a split in the congregation and led to the formation of a new church at Garmany's Grove. The name of the congregation was changed from Second Castleblayney to Frankford in 1913, during the ministry of Rev Samuel Lewis (1896–1929). In this same year Garmany's Grove was accepted into the General Assembly and united with Frankford. This union was dissolved in 1929 and the congregation was then united with First Castleblayney from 1 November 1929. Corvally was added as a Stated Supply in 2000. Membership is twenty-four families.

Corraneary

was formed in 1763 as a Seceder church, one of four which branched out of First Bailieborough. The first minister, Rev John Craig (1763–93), was also responsible from 1770 for services at Urcher every third Sunday. This union lasted until 1812 when Urcher (Trinity, Bailieborough) became a separate charge. Rev Samuel Croookshanks (1813–64) was one of eight Seceders who did not join the General Assembly. The church was not received into the General Assembly until 7 June 1955 when they were united with Kilmount in Cavan Presbytery. On 29 October the church was united with Glassleck and First Bailieborough. On 28 February 1974 the church was united with First Bailieborough and Trinity, Bailieborough. Membership stands at forty-seven families.

Newbliss

was formed in 1754 amidst some controversy. Local Presbyterians desired a new church but neighbouring congregations in Stonebridge, Drum and Cootehill objected. The Seceders, at the instigation of Rev Thomas Clark of Cahans, established a Burgher cause here in union with a similar cause at Drum. The congregation became a single charge about 1801 and built a new church in 1842. The church was united with Stonebridge on 1 November 1914 and Drumkeen was added from 1 April 1927 until 1 July 1937. In 1965 the church was added as a Stated Supply to the union of Stonebridge, Clones and Ballyhobridge. Membership today stands at about thirty families.

Trinity, Bailieborough

was formed as a Seceder congregation about 1770 and known as Urcher. It was initially linked with Coraneary and services were held every third Sunday. Rev William Bell (1814–62) served here as a single charge and, from 1827, had additional responsibility for a mission station at Seafin. In 1888 the church name was changed to Trinity, Bailieborough. Rev Thomas Killen spent his entire ministry here, from his ordination on 18 February 1891 until his death on 15 December 1938. On 1 July 1925 Seafin was united with the church. Bellasis was added to the union on 1 March 1953. This triple union was dissolved on 1 July 1973 and Seafin was amalgamated with the church on this date. On 28 February 1974 the church was united with First Bailieborough and Coraneary. Membership currently totals about fifty-five families.

The 19th Century

There are ten churches in Monaghan Presbytery which can trace their origin to the 19th century. The century began as the previous one had ended, with the Seceders actively planting new churches: Drumkeen (1806), Smithborough (pre 1812) and Rockcorry (1815). From about the time of the famine (1840–50) Presbyterians in Cavan and Monaghan were in steady decline. The excitement of church planting gave way to the beginnings of a policy of amalgamation. The exception to this general decline was at the time of the revival in 1859 which greatly affected a swathe of congregations in both counties. By 1865, however, the general decline in numbers was continuing.

Drumkeen

was formed as a Seceder cause (Burgher) in 1807 with a core of people who belonged to Cahans but desired a more local place of worship. The first minister was Rev David Maxwell (1808–12). An original church was built in 1803 but the current building dates from 1828. Sir Thomas Crawford (1824–95) is commemorated in a marble memorial in the church. He was brought up in this congregation and became Director General of the Army Medical Department and honorary Surgeon to Queen Victoria. Three sons, John, Thomas and Hugh all were all awarded the Military Cross for service during World War I. The church was united with Cahans on 1 October 1924 with the Sunday service here fixed at 3pm but the union was short-lived, being dissolved on 1 April 1927. On this same date a new union was forged with Newbliss and Stonebridge. Drumkeen was united with First Ballybay, Derryvalley and Cahans from February 1957. A new union with Second Ballybay and Rockcorry was formed in April 2006. Membership stands today at about twenty families.

Smithborough

joined the Burgher Seceder Presbytery in 1812 but had been formed some years earlier by a Rev William Gunn under the auspices of the Ulster Evangelical Society. Rev William Smith was ordained here on 30 August 1814 but died of fever on 21 July in the following year. Rev John Elliott (1817–68) gained many

members from Stonebridge congregation where there was much dissatisfaction and he also ran a Classical School in Smithborough. Rev John Martin (1910–36) had three sons in the ministry and all three served for a time in New Zealand. For most of the 20th century the church was in union with or a Stated Supply link with various neighbouring congregations. The church was Stated Supply with Clontibret from 1984–2003 and with First Monaghan since 2003. Membership stands at twenty-four families.

Bellasis

was formed about 1833 under the leadership of Rev John King (1833–76). The building of the first church was halted by local Church of Ireland opposition. During the ministry of Rev Richard McFarland (1906–41), in 1925, the church was united with Ballyjamesduff. From 1 March 1953 the church was united with Trinity Bailieborough and Seafin. This union was dissolved on 1 July 1973 after which the church became a Stated Supply with Kells and Ervy, with services taking place on the first, third and fifth Sunday of each month. Bellasis is the only PCI church in East Cavan. A major reorganisation took place on 1 June 1980 with the creation of a new union: Killeshandra, Drumkeeran, Cavan and Bellasis (with Carrigallen amalgamated with Killeshandra and Ballyjamesduff amalgamated with Bellasis). Membership is now twenty-four families.

Rockcorry

was formed as a Seceder congregation in 1815 and the first minister was Rev Samuel Moore (1815–60) who also practised medicine in this area. Rev Moore disapproved of the union in 1840 and remained with the original Seceders. He was assisted and succeeded by his son Rev David Moore who emigrated to Australia in 1861. The congregation joined the General Assembly in 1860. From 30 October 1921 the church became a Stated Supply to the minister of Drumkeen, and from 1 January 1925 a Stated Supply to the minister of Second Ballybay. The church was united with Second Ballybay on 1 March 1947. Corlea was amalgamated with Rockcorry from 1 July 2005. The joint charge was united with First Ballybay and Drumkeen in a new quadruple charge in April 2006. Membership stands today at about thirty-five families.

Samuel Oliver – Precentor

SAMUEL OLIVER died in Corvally on 27 October 1917, aged seventy-four. He had been precentor in Cahans church for the previous forty-nine years and three months. He had also taught in the Sunday School for an even longer period of time. Amazingly, Mr Oliver lived over five miles from the church and he walked to and from services all his life. By training, he was a tailor and he lived at Ardaghy with his wife Mary and their four children, John, William, James Samuel and Sarah. In Presbyterian churches, precentors predated the introduction of musical instruments and choirs. His responsibility was to read or sing each line of a psalm before the congregation sang it. Irish Presbyterians used the Scottish Psalter which had been issued in 1650 until an Irish Psalter was issued in 1880. It was reported in the *Monaghan Presbyterian* of Mr Oliver, 'The late Mr Samuel Oliver possessed a good leading voice. His enthusiasm in singing, expressed with bodily energy, had an old time fervour about it which contrasted strongly with the deadly dignity of some of our modern artists. It had a contagious effect filling some of his followers with a splendid recklessness in attacking the tune to the fascinating interest of musical spectators.'

Cavan

was formed in 1833. The first minister, Rev James McClatchy, was ordained on 3 April 1834 and died of consumption on 21 November 1836. The congregation experienced serious debt during the ministry of Rev Robert Fleming (1837–51) and the Synod of Ulster appealed for funds from other churches in order to prevent the sale of the church here. The longest ministry in the history of this church is that of Rev William McDowell who served for sixty-three years (1890–1953) and was Clerk of Presbytery for forty-four years. The church was united with Ballyjamesduff on 1 October 1962. On 1 June 1980 a new quadruple union was formed: Killeshandra, Drumkeeran, Cavan and Bellasis (with Carrigallen amalgamated with Killeshandra and Ballyjamesduff amalgamated with Bellasis). Membership stands at eight families.

Second Ballybay

was formed as a result of a dispute in First Ballybay upon the death of Rev James Morell in 1831. A minority of people wanted Rev John Morell to succeed his father James as minister but could not obtain a majority agreement. Rev John Morell was ordained as minister of Second Ballybay on 2 January 1834 and he ministered here until his retirement on 5 August 1884. He was succeeded by his son, Rev James Morrell who served as minister for thirty years until his death on 17 December 1914. The church was united with Rockcorry on 1 March 1947 under the ministry of Rev John Barkley, who later became Principal of Union Theological College, Belfast. The joint charge was united with First Ballybay and Drumkeen in April 2006. Membership is now eighty families.

Drumkeeran

was formed in 1835 and the first minister was Rev John Carmichael (1835–44). The church building opened on 27 October 1839 and in 1881 the congregation was united with Carrigallen for eight years. Killeshandra was united with Carrigallen and Belturbet on 1 June 1930 and Drumkeeran was added on 1 November 1935. A further reorganisation took place on 1 June 1980 with the creation of a new union: Killeshandra, Drumkeeran, Cavan and Bellasis (with Carrigallen amalgamated with Killeshandra and Ballyjamesduff amalgamated with Bellasis). Membership currently stands at eleven families.

Ballyhobridge

was formed as a Seceder congregation in 1836 following mission work by probationer Frederick Buick. The first minister was Rev Matthew Clarke (1836–45), and the third minister was a son, Rev Robert Clarke (1852–63). The seventh minister, Rev Robert Kennedy, was ordained here on 4 March 1879, thirty-three years after his licensing. He served for twenty-two years. Despite efforts in the early 20th century to unite the church with others, the cause survived as a single charge when it was realised that property would revert to the landlord if the congregation ceased to have its own

Reverend Dr John Dixon

SAMUEL JOHN DIXON was born on 30 March 1943, the only son of Matchett and Lily Dixon. His father was Clerk of Session in Ballyhobridge during the ministries of Revs William Young (1925–52), Robert Crawford (1953–56) and Andrew Rogers (1957–65). John was converted as a young teenager and entered Magee University College, Londonderry in 1961. He graduated BA in 1964 and pursued theological studies at New College, Edinburgh and Assembly's College, Belfast. He was ordained as assistant minister in Carnmoney on 4 January 1968 before serving in First Rathfriland from 1970 until 1980. Rev Dixon was installed in First Antrim on 15 May 1980 in succession to Rev Tom Blackstock. He led the congregation into innovative evangelistic outreach and established a system of prayer triplets and prayer chains. Under his ministry ten members have become ministers within Irish Presbyterianism. Rev Dixon's interest in missionary work saw him serve on the Irish Council of OMF International, and to chair this committee from 1986. From 1992–2000 he was Convenor of the Eastern Committee of the PCI Overseas Board. Rev Dixon was elected Moderator of the General Assembly in 1998. From 2000 he served as Convenor of The Board of Mission Overseas.

minister. The church was united with Clones in May 1921. Rev John Dixon, Moderator of the General Assembly in 1998, was raised in this congregation. In 1961 the church was united with Stonebridge and Clones with Newbliss added to this union in 1965. Membership now stands at nine families.

Clones

was formed as a Seceder cause in 1854. Early services were held in the courthouse and the church building was opened By Rev Dr Henry Cooke in 1858. A schoolroom was added during the ministry of Rev John Gass (1859–96) and developed into Clones High School. The church was united with Ballyhobridge in May 1921 under the ministry of Rev Samuel Currie. Rev William Young had a distinguished ministry here from 1925 until his retirement in 1952. In 1961 the church was united with Stonebridge and

Ballyhobridge with Newbliss added to this union in 1965. Membership now stands at eighteen families.

Kilmount

was formed in 1861 and is the youngest church in Monaghan Presbytery. The church struggled financially in early years with the first four ministers serving for a total of seven years. The first substantial ministry was that of Rev John Greer (1869–93). Rev Foster McClelland was minister on two occasions, 1893–1915 and 1919-48. In 1956 the church was united with Corraneary and on

1 August 1958 it was united with Cootehill and Drum. For some time Kilmount was a Stated Supply with Corlea and Corvally. In 1994 the congregation was united once more with Drum and Cootehill. Membership stands at thirty-four families.

The 20th Century

This century witnessed further contraction in the Presbyterians living in Counties Cavan and Monaghan and resultant unions and closures. In 1955 there were 5,275 Presbyterians in thirty-eight congregations within two Presbyteries. By 2005 these figures had fallen to 2,952 Presbyterians in twenty-seven congregations and one Presbytery. The Monaghan closures were: Cahans, Broomfield, Loughmourne, Crieve, Corlea, Derryvalley and Scotstown. The Cavan closures were: Glasleck, Seafin, Ballyjamesduff, Belturbet and Carigallen.

Conclusion

The congregations in Monaghan Presbytery range in membership from 125 families (First Monaghan) to eight families (Cavan). Unions, amalgamations, closures of buildings and lengthy vacancies are all emotive issues for the Presbyterian family in Monaghan. The reduction in the number of congregations has certainly reflected a wiser use of manpower and buildings and perhaps each congregation today is more viable than would otherwise have been the case. Certainly this area, in common with much of Ireland, is changing rapidly at the beginning of the 21st century. These are days of opportunity in which the Presbyterian community can seize the moment and testify to the Gospel of Jesus Christ and the faith of their fathers.

Lough MacNean
COLM CONNAUGHTON

Newry Presbytery

Introduction

The name Newry derives from the Gaelic word for yew tree. Newry Presbytery consists of twenty-six congregations under the care of fifteen ministers. The Presbytery covers much of South Armagh, South Down and North Louth and is dominated by the city of Newry. City status was conferred in 2002 as part of Queen Elizabeth's Golden Jubilee celebrations.

The 17th Century

Five congregations within Newry Presbytery trace their origins to the 17th century. These are: First Newry (1642), Dundalk (1650), Warrenpoint (1688), Markethill (1693) and Mourne (1696). Presbyterians were active here from the earliest years of the 17th century and Rev James Simpson of First Newry provides a very direct link with the original Army Presbytery, being a chaplain in Major-General Robert Munro's Scottish Army which introduced Presbyterian structures to Ireland. The earliest churches are evenly spread throughout the area and indicate that Presbyterians were numerous here.

Cloughmore Stone overlooking Carlingford Lough

SCENIC IRELAND

present church building is the third used by this congregation. Carlingford was added to the union in May 1940. Membership now stands at fifty families.

First Newry

is the oldest congregation in this Presbytery and the first minister, Rev James Simpson (1642–50), was a chaplain in Munro's Scottish army which formed the first Presbytery at Carrickfergus on 10 June 1642. The original church was burned down during the troubles of 1689-91. Rev James Moody served here for thirty-nine years (1740–79) but was never officially installed. Rev John Michel (1823–29) was a professed Arian and left the Synod of Ulster in 1829. On 13 May 1812 a section of the church was formed as a separate congregation. Their new church in Sandys' Street was opened on 22 September 1830. The settlement of Rev Todd Martin here on 19 November 1862 caused a schism and the formation of Third Newry congregation. Rev Martin was later Professor of Ethics in Assembly's College and Moderator of the General Assembly in 1893 and 1894. Three other ministers were later elected Moderator of the General Assembly: Rev James Thompson (1891–99) in 1927, Rev William Gordon Strachan (1900–31) in 1922 and Rev William McAdam (1931–61) in 1958. Membership today totals 145 families.

Dundalk

was formed in 1650 and the first minister was Rev Joseph Bowersfield. Initially the congregation was Independent but became Presbyterian after the time of William III. The church was served by a series of Scottish ministers, and several of them could preach in Irish. Rev William Neilson (1796–1818) was a distinguished linguist and published a famous Irish Grammar in 1808. Rev Robert Black (1860–79) was an able Convenor of the Soldiers' and Sailors' Mission. On 17 November 1926 the church was united with Castlebellingham. Rev Temple Lundie (1940–49) was later elected Moderator of the General Assembly (1974). The

Warrenpoint

was formed sometime prior to 1688 for in that year it was linked to Newry. The church was originally known as 'Narrow-water'. Rev John Wilson, a Scotsman who could preach in Gaelic, served here from 1701 and a church was built in 1707. The cause was linked with Carlingford from 1701 until 1820. In 1830 Rev Samuel Arnold and part of the congregation left the General Synod and joined the Remonstrants. The remainder of the congregation stayed with the Synod and built a new church in 1831, calling Rev Thomas Logan (1831–42) as minister. The church became known as Warrenpoint about 1880. The longest ministry here was that of Rev James Morrow (1931–59). The church was united with Rostrevor on 1 February 1982. Membership now stands at about sixty-five families.

297

Reverend Dr John Dunlop

JOHN DUNLOP was born in Newry, County Down, in 1939, the third of four children. He attended the local Model and Grammar School and was brought up in membership of Sandys' Street congregation. He was also educated at the Royal Belfast Academical Institution, Queen's University Belfast and New College, Edinburgh and Assembly's College, Belfast. He was ordained on 7 December 1966 as assistant minister in Fitzroy. From 1968–78 John Dunlop served as a PCI missionary in Jamaica. On 1 November 1978 Rev Dunlop was installed as minister of Rosemary congregation and he served here until his retirement on 30 September 2004. John Dunlop was elected Moderator of the General Assembly in 1992. He is a regular contributor to radio and television broadcasts and is recognised as perhaps the leading minister most comfortable in commentating upon the current religious and sectarian scene in Ireland. He has given lectures in America and throughout the United Kingdom to appreciative audiences – marked by his clarity of thought, honesty and harmony with biblical Christianity.

Reverend William Neilson

WILLIAM NEILSON was born on 12 September 1774, the fourth son of Rev Moses Neilson of Kilmore (1767–1810). He attended his father's academy at Rademon and entered Glasgow University, aged fifteen, in 1782. He was ordained in Dundalk on 21 December 1796 and noted for his expertise in Gaelic. He was arrested in his father's church at Rademon in 1798 for addressing the congregation in Irish but freed when his manuscript was found to be harmless. William established a Classical School in Clanbrassil Street in Dundalk and taught Latin, Greek, Hebrew and Irish. In March 1806 he completed *An Introduction to the Irish Language*, a work said to have been started by his father in 1769. Glasgow University had conferred a DD degree upon him in the previous year for his *Greek Exercises* and *Key to the Greek Exercises*, published in Dundalk in 1804. Other academic publications followed. Rev Neilson resigned from Dundalk in 1818 upon his appointment as Head of Classics at Belfast Academical Institution. He was also, from 1818, Professor of Greek in the Old College Belfast. In April 1821 William Neilson contracted rheumatic fever and he died on 26th or 27th of that month. On his death-bed he learnt that he had been appointed Professor of Greek at Glasgow University in succession to his former lecturer, John Young.

First Markethill

Presbyterian minister in Ireland to be prosecuted in the Episcopal Church courts for performing Presbyterian marriages. A second congregation in Markethill was formed in 1739. Rev George Ferguson (1741–82) survived several challenges and quarrels but Rev William Charlton (1794–1808) was deposed for 'a long series of scandalous and reprehensible practices'. The Second church became a Seceder cause and their first minister was Rev David Arrot (1749–1807) who started four other churches: Moira, Sheepbridge (Second Newry), Tyrone's Ditches and Ahorey. On 1 November 1919 the two congregations were united though continued to use both buildings. Membership currently stands at about 250 families.

Second Markethill

Mourne

was formed about 1696 and the first church was situated at Ballymageough. The earliest known minister was Rev Charles Wallace (1696–1736). In 1751 a church was built upon the present site. Rev James Canning (1839–48) incurred serious debt in feeding hungry people during the Famine. Rev William McMordie

Markethill

was formed about 1693 when the 'Scots Church' appears on a local map. It is likely that several of the earlier 17th century ministers in this area were Presbyterian as far back as 1604. The first known minister, Rev Archibald Maclaine (1700–1734), was the first

(1886–1914) had been a missionary in India (1867–81) and was elected Moderator of the General Assembly in 1905. The church was refurbished and a new suite of halls built during the ministry of Rev Alan Flavelle (1956–72). Rev David McCaughey had a significant ministry here (1973–2003) and was elected Moderator of the General Assembly in 1994. Mourne is the largest church in Newry Presbytery. Membership currently totals 730 families.

The 18th Century

Ten churches in Newry Presbytery can trace their formation to the 18th century. Five of these new churches were Seceder causes with three Burgher: Tullyallen (1742), Kingsmills (1788) and Clarkesbridge (1791) and two Anti-Burgher; Tyrone's Ditches (1762) and Downshire Road, Newry (1772). Unsurprisingly, there was animosity among these various groupings. The opening of the Newry Canal in March 1742 brought new prosperity to this region providing straightforward access for cargoes such as linen cloth, coal, grain and farm produce.

Carlingford

was formed in 1700 by several Scottish families who had moved to this area, having previously been connected with Dundalk. The first minister, Rev John Wilson (1700–29) developed a cause at Narrow-water and was one of eight ministers appointed to preach in Irish. Several ministers here were Non-subscribers: Rev Robert Dickson (1765–1804), Rev Samuel Arnold (1805–20) and Rev James Lunn (1821–30) who took the congregation into the Remonstrant Synod in 1830. Rev Robert Mears of Jonesboro started afternoon services here under the auspices of the Synod of Ulster. Carlingford was united with Dundalk in May 1940. There are six families in membership today.

Creggan

was formed in the early 1730s and the first minister was Rev Alexander McComb (1733–95). The original church, also known as Freeduff, was destroyed by fire in 1746 and not rebuilt for eight years. Rev McComb also started a new cause at Newtownhamilton in 1781 and the two congregations were linked until 1835. In the 1790s a new church was built in Altnamackin, beside Clarkesbridge Secession Church. On 1 March 1926 the church was united with Second Newtownhamilton under the ministry of Rev George Shaw (1926–33). Membership currently totals twenty-three families.

First Drumbanagher & Jerrettspass

was formed in 1902 by the amalgamation of First Drumbanagher (founded in 1740) and Jerrettspass (founded in 1800 as a Burgher Seceder cause). The latter church was founded by members of the former who were unhappy under the ministry of Rev Alexander Patterson (1796–1805). The united congregation prospered under the ministry of Rev James Mulligan (1903–40). On 1 January 1978 the church was united with Kingsmills and the first minister in this new arrangement was Rev Victor Patterson (1979–85). Membership stands at fifty-three families today.

Mountnorris. Presbytery declared that Rev Francis Turrettin (1778–1804) should conduct worship at Mountnorris. The first ordination here was that of Rev Willaim McGowan (1804–47) a native of Mountnorris. Rev William Lowe (1884–89) was later Moderator (1921) and an outstanding Clerk of the General Assembly (1909–31). The church was united with Tullyallen on 1 July 1921. Membership stands at ninety families.

Tyrone's Ditches

Tullyallen

was formed in 1742 by local Presbyterians who had formally worshipped at Markethill, Clare and Drumbanagher. The church was also known as Portnorris. The first minister was Rev John Mulligan (1742–76). A division occurred in the 1780s when the church was rebuilt. One section wanted to rebuild on the same location and another section wanted to build at Moutnorris, three-quarters of a mile away. Both parties built a church and Rev Francis Turrettin conducted services in a bleach mill midway between both buildings. Tullyallen continued as a separate church though a further division led to the formation of Kingsmills congregation in 1788. The church was united with Mountnorris on 1 July 1921. Membership totals about ninety families.

was formed about 1762 and was an Anti-Burgher cause, also known as Drumbanagher. The first minister was Rev Samuel King. He was ordained here on 24 July 1765 and retired after fifty-three years in 1818. Tyrone's Ditches did not join the General Assembly in 1840 but remained as an Original Secession congregation. Rev William McMahon (1853–60) had been a licentiate of the General Assembly. The church joined the General Assembly and was united with Cremore from 1 June 1919 until 1 March 2000. From this later date the church became a Stated Supply with Bessbrook church. Membership stands at thirty-seven families.

Mountnorris

was formed in 1791 when a division occurred in Tullyallen congregation over the location of a new church building. Two new buildings were started, one on the original site and one at nearby

Downshire Road, Newry

was formed from an earlier congregation which met at Sheepbridge, one mile from Newry, from about 1761. This congregation moved into Newry in 1782 under the ministry of Rev William Laing (1780–1806) and was known as Second Newry. The present church dates from 1843, during the ministry of Rev John Weir (1834–44) and in 1888 the church name was changed to Downshire Road. Rev Phineas McKee (1913–43) was elected Moderator of the

General Assembly in 1943 but died on 9 November 1943, during his moderatorial year. Membership totals 220 families.

Clarkesbridge and First Newtownhamilton

was formed in September 1887 by the union of First Newtownhamilton (formed in 1781) and Clarkesbridge (formed in 1791). From its foundation the Newtownhamilton Church was linked with Creggan but a schism occurred in 1835. It became a

separate cause and was known locally as 'the hill meeting'. Clarkesbridge was a Burgher Seceder church. Rev William McAllister (1826–50) took Clarkesbridge into the General Assembly in 1843 but did not inform his people and several families left and formed Tullyvallen Original Secession Church (the bog meeting). The first minister of the united charge was Rev Robert Tweed (1888–1928). Garmany's Grove and McKelvey's Grove

congregations were briefly joined to this union from 1931–38. On 5 June 1957 the congregation was united with Garmany's Grove, and McKelvey's Grove was a Stated Supply. The First Newtownhamilton church building was closed in the 1980s. From 1 January 1999 Clarkesbridge and First Newtownhamilton was united with Garmany's Grove and McKelvey's Grove. Membership currently stands at about fifty families.

Kingsmills

was formed in 1788 by members of Mountnorris who met in the loft of a corn mill owned by a Mr Alexander King. The original church with thatched roof and earthen floor was built in 1788. The first minister was Rev William Beatty (1792–1825). The current church was opened in 1837, during the ministry of Rev Alexander Henry (1826–63). Rev James Meeke (1884–1933) was Clerk of Newry Presbytery for many years. Trouble arose in the church in the 1950s and a Special Commission of Assembly was appointed to investigate. Eventually, Rev Ronald Adams (1949–58) resigned. Harmony was restored under the ministry of Mr. D. Thompson (1958–65), a Lay Agent of the General Assembly. In 1965 Kingsmills became a Stated Supply linked to First Drumbanagher and Jerrettspass. A new union of these congregations was formed on 1 January 1978. Membership stands at ninety families.

The 19th Century

As with most Presbyteries, the 19th century represents the century of greatest expansion within Newry Presbytery. Thirteen churches today can trace their formation to the 19th century. Six of these churches were Seceder congregations. Another, Tullyvallen church, was formed in 1851 and had links with Garmany's Grove and Tyrone's Ditches before finally joining the Reformed Presbyterian Church. The Subscription controversy was notable, perhaps especially in Carlingford church.

Cremore

was formed in 1802 as a Burgher Secession cause and the first minister was a Monaghan man, Rev John Caldwell (1802–06). Cremore was one of several Seceder churches which did not join the General Assembly in 1840 but did join in the following year upon receiving assurances about the continuing use of Psalms in worship. The church was united with Tyrone's Ditches on 1 January 1919 and this union lasted until 2000. From 1 March 2000 the church was united with Fourtowns and Poyntzpass. Membership totals forty-five families.

Fourtowns

was formed in 1810 as an Anti-Burgher Secession church. Within two years it had become a Burgher cause. The first minister, Rev Thomas Heron (1813–16) died when he fell from his horse on 25 October 1816. He was followed by Rev Alexander Bryson (1817–55) who was in turn followed by his son, Rev John Bryson (1855–98). In 1927 the church was united with with Poyntzpass under the ministry of Rev David McCausland (1927–52). A new three-point union was formed on 1 March 2000 when Cremore was added. Membership totals forty-one families.

Second Newtownhamilton

was formed in 1814 by the Anti-Burgher Seceders who exploited a weakness in the congregations of Creggan and First

Newtownhamilton. A church was built during the ministry of Rev Robert Clarke (1818–22) and the congregation grew during the longer ministry of Rev John West (1823–64). The church was united with Creggan on 1 March 1926. A series of short ministries followed including those of two brothers: Rev Robert Logue (1944–49) who was succeeded by his brother, Rev Charles Logue (1950–61). Membership stands at seventy-three families.

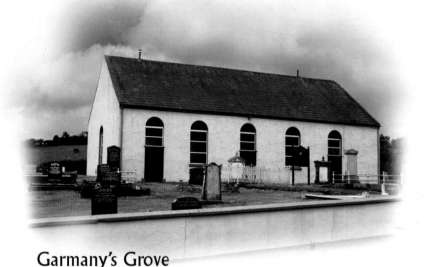

Garmany's Grove

was formed as a Secession cause in 1820 out of a dispute when Rev David Longmoor was ordained in Frankford (Second Castleblayney) Church. The church was built on a site given by a Mr Garmany and the first minister was Rev Samuel Dunlop (1822–47). In 1833 there were 160 families (700 individuals) in membership. The church did not join the General Assembly in 1840 but helped form the Original Secession Synod. In 1903 the congregation was united with Tullyvallen Original Secession church under the ministry of Rev George McMahon (1903–12) who died on 26 July 1912, aged eighty-six, following an accident in which he was thrown from his trap. In 1913 the church joined the General Assembly and was united in turn with several congregations: Frankford (1914–29), Clarkesbridge (from 1931) and McKelvey's Grove (from 1938). A new union was formed on 1 January 1999 between Clarkesbridge & First Newtownhamilton, Garmany's Grove and McKelvey's Grove. Membership currently totals twenty-four families.

Kilkeel

was initially formed in 1822 as a Seceder church but was unable to secure the services of a minister until 1827 when Rev John Allen was installed here. He hired a house capable of accommodating worship services and the church was opened in 1829. The

congregation flourished despite local hostility under the ministry of Rev George Nesbitt (1831–74). Rev Robert White (1875–1910) was installed as his successor on 15 February 1875, accepted a call to Second Stewartstown on 15 February 1882, changed his mind, and was re-installed in Kilkeel on 5 May 1882. The current church was opened in August 1897 and extended in 1986 during the ministry of Rev Ian McNie (1980–91) when the stones of the front wall were numbered, dismantled and reassembled thirty feet nearer the main road. Membership currently stands at about 260 families.

Brookvale

was formed in 1833 as a Seceder cause, originally known as Grallagh or Ballymogra. The first minister was a Scotsman, Rev James Patterson (1834–37). He was succeeded by Rev John Carey (1840–42). The church was united with First Rathfriland from 1933 until 1969. It was united with Ryans on 31 July 1970, and continued under the ministry of Rev Carson McCullough (1970–85). Membership currently totals about fifty families.

Ryans

was formed as an Original Burgher Seceder church in 1834 and the first minister was Rev William Stevenson (1835–50). The church joined the Synod of Ulster in 1837 and resisted efforts by the Original Burghers to re-establish their authority. The longest ministry in the history of this congregation was that of Rev Dr Hugh McIlroy who was ordained here on 6 April 1915 and retired, after forty-four years, on 31 December 1959. He was elected Moderator of the General Assembly in 1951. The congregation has been united with Brookvale since 31 July 1970. Membership currently stands at about seventy families.

Poyntzpass

was formed in 1836 and the foundation stone of the new church laid in the following year. The first minister was Rev Samuel Priestly (1838–63). Rev Priestly's services commenced at 12 noon and concluded at 3 pm. The church was united with Scarva from 1892 until 1927. From 1927 a new union was formed with Fourtowns under the ministry of Rev David McCausland (1927–52). A new three point union was formed on 1 March 2000 when Cremore was added. The first minister of this new united charge was Rev Robert Mattison who was installed on 22 September 2000. Membership stands today at about fifty families.

Annalong

was formed from Mourne church in 1839. The earliest services were held at the Corn Mill until the church opened in 1842. The first minister was Rev Samuel Burnside (1840–87). A gallery was added to the church building in 1861 and further renovations in 1891. The present tower was added in 1963 as a memorial to Rev Edwin Pyper (1910–45). During much of the 1930s Rev Pyper had a famous 'war of words' with one member, Mr James Pierce, who thought there was a serious lack of evangelical fervour in the church. Rev James Adair (1945–81) was the General Assembly's Temperance Convenor for a number of years. Rev Stuart Finlay was installed here on 21 April 1982 has been Clerk of Newry Presbytery since 1989. Membership totals about 280 families.

Reverend John Carey

JOHN CAREY was born on 15 June 1800. In 1822, he commenced theological studies in the Old College, Belfast. He was ordained on 2 April 1839 as the first minister of the new church of Albany in County Tyrone. Following disagreement over financial matters and the provision of regular services, Rev Carey resigned on 15 April 1840. He was installed as minister of Brookvale on 19 May 1840 but suspended by Presbytery on 5 July 1842 for attempting to obtain money for his congregation by using a forged document. Carey was deposed from the ministry by the General Assembly. Sensationally, John Carey was arrested on suspicion of shooting Rev Joseph Dickie of Rathfriland on Sunday 26 February while that gentleman prayed during evening service. Carey was released for lack of conclusive proof. He inherited a substantial fortune from his mother and retired to 'Rarity Cottage' in Toome. He acquired a reputation as a wealthy eccentric, known for many philanthropic enterprises. He constructed the 'Temple of Liberty', a public hall capable of accommodating 1,500 people for lectures and musical events. In 1879 he founded lectureship for the promotion of theological studies. John Carey died of acute bronchitis on Sunday 23 August 1891, aged ninety-one.

McKelvey's Grove

was formed in 1847 and the first minister, Rev Matthew Macauley (1847 and 1848–86), was ordained in a barn belonging to a Mr McKelvey. The second minister, Rev Samuel Lundie (1887–90) was one of three brothers who all served as Presbyterian ministers. The church was united with Garmany's Grove on 1 July 1938. From 1952 until 1958 the church was a Stated Supply linked with Clontibret. From 1957 the church was a Stated Supply linked with Clarkesbridge & First Newtownhamilton. On 1 January 1999 Clarkesbridge & First Newtownhamilton, Garmany's Grove and McKelvey's Grove were united. Membership today totals thirty-three families.

Rostrevor

was formed about 1849 by a number of Presbyterians connected with Warrenpoint when they commenced to hold services in the local dispensary. The first minister was Rev Thomas Morgan (1850–1909), son of Rev James Morgan of Fisherwick. Three other sons of ministers also served here for a time: Rev Alexander Harrison (1909–14), Rev James Rentoul (1914–18) and Rev William McNeill (1924–30). Rev Rentoul died on 29 September 1918 on active service with the Royal Army Medical Corps. The church was united with Warrenpoint on 1 February 1982. Membership now stands at thirty-seven families.

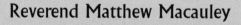

Reverend Matthew Macauley

MATTHEW MACAULEY was born at Drumgooland, between Banbridge and Castlewellan, on 15 October 1815. He entered the Old College, Belfast in 1837 where he studied Theology for three years, taking a final year in Edinburgh University. He was ordained on 18 January 1847 by Ballybay Presbytery in the newly formed Seceder congregation of McKelvey's Grove. This service was held in a barn and a new church was built soon afterwards. The congregation was extremely poor, contributing only thirty shilling towards the building costs, and Rev Macauley's ministry commenced at the height of the famine. Before the end of 1847 he resigned and accepted a call to Boveedy but he was never installed there as that congregation split over his candidature. In 1848 Rev Macauley accepted a second call to McKelvey's Grove and was again installed as minister there. He was a life-long abstainer and supporter of the Temperance Movement. In addition he supported the tenant farmers. Controversially, Rev Macauley was the sole voice in support of Home Rule at the 1886 General Assembly. Matthew Macauley retired on 16 November 1886 and was appointed as a JP in Banbridge. He died on 5 January 1907, aged ninety-one.

Reverend Alexander Stuart

ALEXANDER STUART was one of five sons of Rev Joseph Stuart of Clare who became ministers. He was ordained in Bessbrook on 21 May 1913 and four of his brothers were also ordained as Presbyterian ministers; Thomas (Carryduff), Robert (Stranraer), Samuel (Drumgooland) and Henry (Donaghmore). Alexander Stuart was a gifted evangelist and was one of seven ministers set aside by the General Assembly for such work. Following work with the YMCA in Egypt and Malta, he received a commission as an Army Chaplain in October 1917 and was posted to France. He was killed after only ten days, on 24 October 1917, by an exploding shell. He was thirty-eight years old and the first minister of the Presbyterian Church in Ireland to die in active service. It is interesting to note that his Presbytery colleague, Rev James Rentoul of Rostrevor, also joined the army and was killed in the following year, on 30 September 1918. Alexander Stuart was one of eighteen members of Bessbrook congregation who died on active service during World War I. Rev Alexander Stuart is buried in Ruyaulcourt Military Cemetery, nineteen kilometres east of Bapaume in the Pas de Calais.

Bessbrook

was formed in 1853 and a church was built in that same year. This is the youngest church in Newry Presbytery and the first minister was Rev Thomas Cromie (1854–1906). Rev Alexander Stuart (1913–17) was killed in action while serving as an Army Chaplain on 24 October 1917. Rev Hugh Sydney Carser (1936–71) served in the Belfast City Mission before coming to Bessbrook where he spent his entire ministry. The congregation lived through dark times in 'The Troubles' and experienced personal loss, most notably in January 1976 when five members were murdered by terrorists. Rev Robert Nixon (1972–98) served faithfully here through the worst times of danger and unemployment. A hall was built in 1975 and the church building underwent major renovations during 1978–80, it re-opened on Sunday 7 December 1980. Membership today stands at 121 families.

The Kingsmills Massacre

ON THE EVENING OF 5 JANUARY 1976 a group of about twelve Republican gunmen stopped a minibus carrying workmen travelling from Glennane Mill to Bessbrook. Ten men were killed and one, Alan Black (32), survived despite suffering eighteen gunshot wounds. Five of those who were murdered belonged to Bessbrook congregation. Reggie Chapman (25) was married and a father of two young children. He was a Sunday School teacher, choir member and youth leader in the church. His brother Walter (23) was also killed. Joseph Lemmon (46), also a choir member, was married with three daughters. John McConville (20) was preparing to go to Bible College in Scotland to become a missionary. James McWhirter (58) was a hard-working devoted family man. The one Roman Catholic man on the bus, Richard Hughes, was singled out by the gunmen and ordered to run from the scene. The five other victims were: Kenneth Worton (24) married with two children, Robert Chambers (19), John Bryans (46), Robert Freeburn (50) and Robert Walker (46). A congregation of 2,000 people gathered for the funeral services in the Presbyterian and Church of Ireland churches. This atrocity struck at the heart of the local community and to date no-one has been brought to justice for these murders.

Mr Robert Freeburn

Conclusion

No new congregations were formed in this area in the 20th century and the locality has suffered more than most in Northern Ireland from 'The Troubles'. As a direct consequence of the civil unrest there has been a discernable move by many Presbyterians out of this area. Naturally, this has had a detrimental affect upon many congregations. Presbyterian families in the area have fallen by about 500 (15%) in this period. Congregational size ranges from the largest, Mourne, with 730 families, to the smallest, Carlingford, with 6 families. The average size is 110 families. As in may other areas, churches in Newry Presbytery face the challenge of nourishing God's people in their locality and also presenting the Gospel which alone can bring meaning and purpose for people's lives.

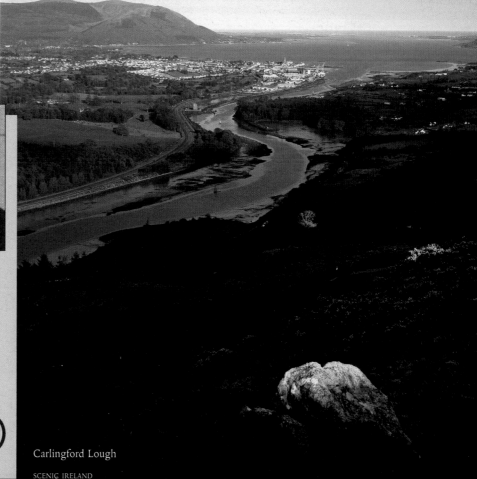

Carlingford Lough

SCENIC IRELAND

Introduction

Omagh is the largest town in County Tyrone (population 21,000) and was founded in 1610 on a site where the rivers Camowen and Drumragh meet to form the River Strule, in the foothills of the Sperrin Mountains. The town dominates Omagh Presbytery which extends over much of County Fermanagh and a portion of County Tyrone. In its present form, this Presbytery was created on 1 January 1963 by an amalgamation of the previously existing Presbyteries of Clogher and Omagh. Today the Presbytery contains twenty-nine congregations under the care of fifteen ministers. Presbyterianism has never been strong in County Fermanagh and this is reflected in the fact that the average size of these congregations is ninety-six families.

The 17th Century

Eight congregations in Omagh Presbytery trace their origins back to the 17th century: Clogherney, Clogher, Drumquin, First Omagh, Enniskillen, Cavanaleck, Fintona and Aughnacloy. Omagh itself comprised about 150 homes in 1670. Anglicans always outnumbered Presbyterians in this area and the infant Presbyterian congregations often faced persecution from the Anglican aristocracy. Individual ministers often had responsibility for services in several locations, for example Rev Robert Wilson in Termon McGurk (Clogherney) and The Omry (Omagh), Longfield (Drumquin) and Pettigo. In 1657 the Presbytery of Down covered this area but in 1659 the Presbytery of Tyrone was carved out of Down. The town of Enniskillen successfully resisted James II and his forces in 1689 though Omagh was burned.

Omagh Presbytery

Devenish Island, Lower Lough Erne

SCENIC IRELAND

Clogher

was formed in the 1650s and the earliest known minister was Rev Robert Auld (1657–59). The longest ministry here was that of Rev Andrew Millar (1773–1831). He also founded a boys' boarding school at Lungs and was succeeded by his son-in-law, Rev John Hanna (1829–57), who in turn was succeeded by his son-in-law, Rev James Robb (1858–74). Rev Rupert Gibson (1935–38) became Moderator of the General Assembly in 1971 and died in his moderatorial year. A history of the congregation was published in 1958 by Rev Brian Murphy (1956–63). The church was united with Glenhoy on 1 December 1973 and the first minister of the united churches was Rev William McKeown (1976–84). Membership today stands at eighty-one families.

Clogherney

was formed about 1655 and the first minister, Rev Robert Wilson (1655–60) died later in Derry during the siege. The cause was originally known as Termon McGurk and in the 17th century often shared a ministry with Cappagh, Pettigo and Omagh. The church became a single cause in 1747, upon separation from Pettigo. Rev Joseph Scot (1752–80) played a leading role in the Volunteer Movement and died in mysterious circumstances at Seskinore on 2 January 1780. His demise was as a result of a dispute with a local gentleman who desired the hand of his daughter in marriage. The present church was opened in 1902 during the ministry of Rev Thomas Martin (1897–1904) who was followed sometime later by his nephew, Rev William Herbert Martin (1933–40). Rev John Lockington was installed here on 23 May 2003 having been elected Moderator of the general Assembly in 1999. Membership today stands at 140 families.

Drumquin

was formed about 1675 and was originally known as Longfield and was linked with Termon McGurk (Clogherney) and Cappagh. In 1793 the church was separated from Castlederg and united with Pettigo under the ministry of Rev Thomas Anderson (1794–1812). The church became a separate charge in 1827 and the present church was built between 1860 and 1863. During the ministry of Rev Joseph Davison (1939–77) the church building was divided by a wall in order to provide a hall within the same structure. The church was united with Dromore on 1 December 1978. Membership today stands at seventy-four families.

First Omagh

was formed in 1676, though Rev Robert Wilson of Termon McGurk (Clogherney) preached here as early as 1655, and the first church building was opened at Crevenagh. This church was replaced by a new building in Omagh during the ministry of Rev James Maxwell (1699–1750). Rev Hugh Dunlap (1751–87) was succeeded by his son, also Rev Hugh Dunlap (1790–1805), but this led to division and the formation of Second Omagh (Trinity) and a Burgher Seceder church at Ballinahatty. The present church was built at a cost of £6,000 and was opened on 30 May 1897 during the ministry of Rev Andrew Macafee (1893–1925). First Omagh is the largest church within Omagh Presbytery and has a current membership of 329 families.

Enniskillen

was formed in 1676 and the earliest minister appears to have been Rev James Trailzeur (1677–80). Initially the cause was linked with Monea and Derryvullen. Mr David Young was installed here on 8 June 1772 at a service with only one minister present, Rev David Hamilton, who could not perform an act of ordination alone. David Young was ordained at a later service, on 8 August and served for three years. On 8 March 1861, during the ministry of Rev Alexander McClatchy (1837–82), Enniskillen became the first Irish Presbyterian congregation to use an organ in public worship. This action sparked a church-wide debate and severe opposition from many quarters but minister and people remained united in their action and eventually most churches followed suit. One piece of this original harmonium still survives. Rev Lawrence Wynne was minister here on two occasions, 1947–54 and 1985–86. Six members of this church lost their lives in a bomb blast at the town

Cenotaph on Remembrance Day 1987. The eyes of the world watched those events in horror and a stained glass window and explanatory plaque in the church offers a full explanation for visitors. This is the only single charge Presbyterian congregation in County Fermanagh and membership today stands at 195 families.

Remembrance Day 1987

Ted Armstrong *Kit Johnston* *Jessie Johnston* *Johnny Megaw* *William Mullan* *Nessie Mullan*

ON REMEMBRANCE DAY, 8 November 1987, the people of Enniskillen gathered at the Cenotaph in the town to pay a customary tribute to the dead of two world wars. A bomb exploded without warning, killing eleven people and injuring sixty-three others, including thirteen children. Six members of Enniskillen church died in that incident: Edward Armstrong (52), John Megaw (68), Kitchener Johnston (70) and his wife Jessie (70), William Mullan (72) and his wife Nessie (70). Mr Johnston and Mr Mullan were elders in the church and a choir member, Mr Jim Dixon, was also seriously injured in this incident. The others who died were: Wesley Armstrong (62) and his wife Bertha (53), Edward Armstrong (52), Georgina Quinton (72), Samuel Gault (49) and Marie Wilson (20). Rev David Cupples, who conducted so many funerals and gave pastoral care to so many at that time, had only been installed as minister a few weeks earlier, on 1 September 1987. The Christian response of Gordon Wilson whose daughter Marie died was reported around the world, 'I have lost my daughter, and we shall miss her. But I bear no ill will … (and in reference to those who had planted the bomb) … I shall pray for those people tonight and every night.'

Cavanaleck

was formed sometime during the ministry of Rev James Trailzeur (1677–80) who also preached at Enniskillen. The congregation struggled until the arrival of Rev Josiah Cornwall (1704–28). A surviving pewter communion set here dates from 1710. The church was originally known as Aghalurcher. Rev William Johnston (1781–1824) was followed some years later by his nephew, Rev Galbraith Johnston (1856–7) as Stated Supply at a time of conflict between congregation and Presbytery. Rev David Greer (1864–84) was the first person to be buried in the graveyard adjoining the church. The present church was opened in 1921, during the ministry of Rev Thomas Edwards (1907–26). In addition, a hall was built at Loughermore and services commenced. The church was united with Aughentaine on 1 December 1955 and the first minister of the new union was Rev George Eagleson (1956–62). Services at Loughermore ceased in 1975. Membership today totals eighty-four families.

Fintona

was formed in the 1690s and was originally known as Goulan or Golan. The earliest known minister was Rev Robert Colthart

(1697–1730). The church was united with Dromore until 1834. The present church was built during the ministry of Rev George McKay (1874–1915). Rev Arthur O'Neill was installed on 23 February 1966 and led the church into a new union with Ballinahatty and Creevan on 12 November 1969. Rev O'Neill retired on 31 July 2000. Membership today stands at 118 families.

Aughnacloy

was formed in 1743 but grew out of an older congregation, Aghalow, which had been formed in 1697. Rev Baptist Boyd, who had been minister in Aghalow, continued as minister with the Aughnacloy people until his death on 25 November 1749. The church was united with Ballygawley from 1787 until 1829. The original church floor was bare earth, and occasionally a portion of ceiling fell among worshippers. A storm removed most of the roof in December 1848 and the present church was then built. It was opened on 1 August 1849. Rev William Forbes Marshall, a native of Sixmilecross, was ordained here on 26 June 1913 and served as minister until 11 April 1916. On 1 December 1926 the church was united with Ballymagrane and the first minister of the new union was Rev Andrew Fullerton (1927–32). Rev George Dickson served twice as minister, 1973–76 and 1977–95. Membership today stands at eighty families.

The 18th Century

Nine congregations can trace their origins to the 18th century and five of them were formed by the Seceders. All of these Seceder congregations belonged to the Burghers, generally thought to be more liberal and tolerant than the Anti-Burgher Seceders. Instrumental in the formation of all these Seceder churches was Rev Thomas Dickson who was ordained in Ballymagrane in 1767 and initiated services in Aughentaine. After seven years, he was installed as minister in Aughentaine where he ministered for two years. He was then installed in Sixmilecross and Ardstraw (Drumlegagh) in 1776, serving eight years in the former and eleven years in the latter. He also established the work in Glenhoy.

Pettigo

was formed sometime before 1703, probably from a Mission Station. The earliest known minister was Rev Joseph Hemphill (1721–47) who also served in Clogherney (Termon McGurk). In 1792 the church was united with Drumquin. Rev Samuel Armour was ordained to the joint charge on 7 December 1812 but resigned

from Pettigo and retained Drumquin on 7 February 1827. A series of short ministries did not help the church here prosper. Rev Simon Nelson (1844-47) established a local network of Irish speaking schools. The original church building at New Park was replaced by the current church in June 1852. A chestnut, still flourishing, was planted beside the church and bears the following inscription; 'This tree was planted by FW Barton in commemoration of the taking of Sebastopol AD. 1856 parapet by his son H Barton.' The church was united with Irvinestown on 10 August 1908 and Tempo was added to the union on 1 July 2002. Membership today stands at forty-nine families.

Dromore

was formed about 1704 and operated in union with Fintona, with each church holding services on alternate Sundays. This arrangement ended in 1834. The present church was constructed in 1846, during the ministry of Rev James Reid Dill (1835–87). Rev William McFarland (1897–1905) resigned to become a missionary in Syria. The shortest ministry here was that of Rev William McConnell who was ordained on 25 November 1909 and resigned on 25 April 1910. The church was united with Drumquin on 1 December 1978 and the first minister of the new union was Rev William Craig (1981–90). Membership today stands at fifty-two families.

Trinity, Omagh

was formed in 1754 as a result of a division in First Omagh, following the arrival there of Rev Hugh Delap. The first minister here was Rev Robert Nelson (1754–1801) and the church was

Reverend James Reid Dill

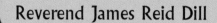

JAMES REID DILL was born on 14 August 1814 at Springfield in County Donegal. This family contributed a dozen ministers to the Presbyterian Church over three generations. It was said at one time that the General Assembly was composed of ministers, elders and Dills. James father, Rev Richard Dill was minister in Knowhead, County Donegal from 1793 until 1846 and his brothers; Rev Richard Dill, was minister of Tandragee (1829–35) and Usher's Quay (1835–48), later Ormond Quay, and Rev Edward Marcus Dill was minister successively of Coagh (1835–38), Cork (1838–46) and Clonakilty (1860–62). James was ordained in Dromore, County Tyrone on 10 November 1835 and spent his entire ministry here, retiring on 10 May 1887. The present church was built in 1846. A year after his retirement, in 1888, he published a history of his family, *The Dill Worthies*, in which he detailed events in the lives of his ministerial relatives. In the same year, 'partly for amusement and partly to fill a vacant hour' he published his own *Autobiography of a Country Parson* in which he reviews his own ministry. Rev James Reid Dill died on 1 September 1896 and was buried beside Dromore church.

known as Second Omagh. Three ministers have later been elected Moderator of the General Assembly: Rev Thomas Hamill (1879–84) in 1915, Rev George Thompson (1898–1903) in 1923 and Rev Joseph Gibson (1927–42) in 1950. The name of the church was changed to Trinity, Omagh, in 1905. The present church was opened in 1856, extended in 1901 and renovated again in 1969 when the pews were painted grey. On 1 October 1970 the church was united with Gillygooley. The bell tower was empty for 118 years until 1974, when the bell from Stranooden parish Church in County Monaghan was donated by the Church of Ireland. Membership today stands at 325 families.

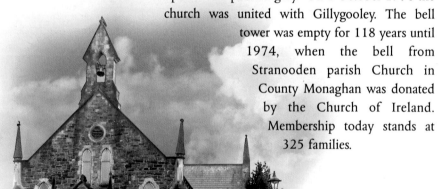

Sixmilecross

was formed as a Seceder cause in 1764 and was initially linked with Clogher. In May 1776 Rev Thomas Dickson was installed as minister of Sixmilecross and Drumlegagh but in 1784 he resigned from the Sixmilecross portion. Rev Lewis Brown (1792–1840) was

a founder member of the Irish Evangelical Society in 1798. The longest ministry here was that of Rev Thomas Junk (1845–1895). Rev William Forbes Marshall (1916–28) made a notable contribution in historical and literary circles far beyond this congregation. Rev John Eakins (1931–68) and Rev Hugh Pattison (1944–80) gave significant service in the 20th century. Membership today stands at 116 families.

Ballymagrane

was formed as a Burgher Seceder cause about 1766 and the first minister was Rev Thomas Dickson (1766–74). For twenty-four years the church was united with Derryfubble (Eglish) under the ministry or Rev David Holmes (1776–1800) who was a founder member of the Irish Evangelical Society. Rev John Stinson was ordained here on 18 November 1851 but the General Assembly ordered a new vote. Rev Stinson again topped the poll and was then settled in Ballymagrane for a second time, on 21 September 1852. He served here until his death on 17 July 1885 and was succeeded by his son, Rev Thomas Stinson (1887–1901). On 1 December

313

1926 the church was united with Aughnacloy and the first minister of the new union was Rev Andrew Fullerton (1927–32). There are fifty-three families in membership today.

Aughentaine

was formed in 1774 as a Secession cause and the first minister was Rev Thomas Dickson (1774–82). For some years afterwards the church was united with Glenhoy. Rev Hugh Stokes (1798–1832) preached in each place on alternate Sundays. The church became a

single charge in 1833. The present church was built in 1844 during the ministry of Rev James Malcolmson (1836–86). A series of short ministries was ended by Rev John McDowell (1902–50). The church was united with Cavanaleck on 1 December 1955 and the next minister was Rev George Eagleson (1956–62). A new hall was constructed in 1994 and membership today totals forty-four families.

Drumlegagh

was formed as a Seceder cause in Ardstraw in 1782 and Rev Thomas Dickson of Aughentaine was given this extra responsibility which he carried until 1787. Originally the church was known as Second Ardstraw. Rev Andrew Maxwell (1788–1816) was succeeded by his son, also Rev Andrew Maxwell (1815–1866). Interestingly, father and son both died on 2 February, exactly fifty

Reverend WF Marshall

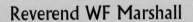

WILLIAM FORBES MARSHALL was born at Drumreagh, Omagh, on 8 May 1888. He was educated at Dungannon Royal School and Queen's College, Galway, graduating in Arts in 1908 and Law in 1910. He then studied Theology at Assembly's College, Belfast. Rev Marshall was ordained in Aughnacloy on 26 June 1913. He served in Sixmilecross (1916–28) and Castlerock (1928–54). Rev Marshall became an outstanding figure in Irish literature, specialising in colloquial language, prose and historical research. In 1942 he was elected as a member of the Royal Irish Academy. His publications include a novel, *Planted by a River* and *Ulster Sails West* (a history of 18th century emigration to America). He also published four books of poems, all of which feature *Tyrone* in the title. He became known as 'the Bard of Tyrone'. In addition, he wrote a dialect version of *A Midsummer Night's Dream*, which was broadcast by the BBC. Rev Marshall spent many years compiling a dictionary of Ulster dialect but unfortunately the only manuscript was torn to pieces by his dog! His brother was Professor of English and History at Magee University College, Derry, and his son, Charles, was Presbyterian minister at Ballyshannon (1948–84). William Forbes Marshall died on 25 January 1959, aged seventy.

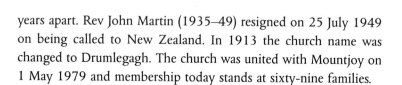

years apart. Rev John Martin (1935–49) resigned on 25 July 1949 on being called to New Zealand. In 1913 the church name was changed to Drumlegagh. The church was united with Mountjoy on 1 May 1979 and membership today stands at sixty-nine families.

Glenhoy

was probably formed in the 1780s. It was a Seceder cause and initially linked in some measure with Aughentaine. The original church was built at Longridge and served as a school on weekdays.

Mountjoy in 1878 during the ministry of Rev John Gilmour (1862–89). The fifth minister was Rev James Croskery (1897–1903) and he died suddenly on 5 June 1903 on the eve of a Professorship of Theology in the Presbyterian College of Halifax in Nova Scotia. Rev John Moore (1939–79) was Convenor of the General Assembly's Public Worship Committee from 1969–75. The church was united with Drumlegagh on 1 May 1979 and membership stands today at 233 families.

Rev Hugh Stokes (1798–1832) preached in each location on alternate Sundays. The current church was built in 1843 during the ministry of Rev James Dales (1840–74) and at the opening service the preacher was the celebrated Rev Dr Henry Cooke. Edward Cooney, founder of the Cooneyite movement, came to this area in 1909 and six or seven families followed him. The church was united with Clogher on 1 December 1973 and a new hall was opened on 29 January 1979. Membership now totals sixty families.

Mountjoy

was formed about 1789 and known as Cappagh or Crossroads. There had been an earlier church in Cappagh in the 17th century but it appears to have lapsed. The first minister was Rev James McClintock (1791–1821). The church name was changed to

The Cooneyites

EDWARD COONEY was born on 11 February 1867 at 4 High Street in Enniskillen. He was the third of eight children in a wealthy merchant family who attended the local Church of Ireland. At fourteen years of age, and after education at Portora Royal School, Edward was sent to an apprenticeship in Armagh. He was converted in 1884 at the age of seventeen and worked for a time in the family business. In 1901 he abandoned his business and gave £1,300 to religious causes before embarking upon a career as an itinerant preacher. Along with Scotsman and ex-Faith Mission pilgrim William Irving, he formed the 'Cooneyites' a breakaway group from the Faith Mission. They believed in old-time religion, with emphasis upon a second blessing for personal holiness, and were anti-organised churches. Some Presbyterians were attracted for a time, notably in County Fermanagh. Edward Cooney himself was expelled from the sect in 1928 but continued to lead a smaller group of followers. Cooney travelled all over Ireland by bike and on foot preaching where people would listen, refusing all gifts, and starting house groups. He died in Australia in 1960.

The 19th Century

As in most Presbyteries, the 19th century bears witness to a profusion of new congregations, eleven in all. The Seceders, who united in 1818, formed five: Gillygooley, Ballynahatty, Lisbellaw, Newtownparry (Seskinore) and Ballyreagh. None of these churches operates as a single charge and only Seskinore has a family membership in excess of 100 families.

Ballynahatty & Creevan

was formed in 1928 by an amalgamation of Ballynahatty (a Seceder cause formed in 1805) and Creevan (a Synod of Ulster cause formed in 1834). Ballynahatty was formed by members of Omagh who disapproved of Rev Hugh Delap. The church was united with Gillygooley under Rev John Watson though support in Ballynahatty dwindled considerably. Creevan was originally known as Second Ballynahatty and the first minister here was Rev John Porter (1837–68). The name was changed to Creevan in 1900. Ballynahatty and Creevan were amalgamated on 1 May 1928. Rev William Cochrane exercised a lengthy ministry here from 18 July 1929 until 19 July 1969. Ballynahatty and Creevan was then united with Fintona on 12 November 1969. Membership today stands at sixty-seven families.

Gillygooley

was formed in 1806 as a Burgher Seceder cause and united with Ballinahatty. A church was built in 1807 and the first minister, Rev John Watson (1807–34), also preached in Ballynahatty. The church was seriously damaged on 'the night of the big wind', on 6 January 1839. Rev Samuel Paul (1869–1904) also ran a successful school in Castle Street in Omagh. In September 1928 the congregation was made a Stated Supply with Trinity, Omagh and the two churches were united on 1 October 1970. The first minister of the united charge was Rev Robert Clarke (1971–92). Membership today stands at seventy-two families.

Lisbellaw

was formed in 1821 as a Seceder cause and the earliest church here was built in 1822. The first minister, Rev James Green (1822–28),

315

was deposed from the ministry for conducting irregular marriages and he was followed by a series of short ministries. A manse was built in 1861 and the present church was opened in 1910. From 1918 until 1957 the church was united with Tempo and for the next eight years the church was united with Enniskillen. Rev Kenneth Gregg (1967–78) ministered in the new four-point Home Mission charge of Lisbellaw, Maguiresbridge, Lisnaskea and Newtownbutler which had been created on 1 July 1965. There are now fifty-four families in membership.

church in 1827 but his health was affected by the stress of attempting to recoup funds by public subscription. In 1898 the church name was changed to Seskinore. The longest ministry was that of Rev William James McAskie who was ordained on 31 July 1894 and died here on 18 May 1937. The church was united with Edenderry on 1 January 1982. The church property has recently been augmented by the addition of a new manse and hall extension. Membership stands at 110 families.

Maguiresbridge

was formed in 1821 by members of Enniskillen who lived here, seven miles from that church. The first minister was Rev James McWilliams (1822–60), a native of Aughnacloy. The introduction of hymns here in 1867 incurred the displeasure of Presbytery. Rev Ewing Gilfillan (1885–87) also took services in a new cause at Lisnaskea. Rev James Stoops (1915–39) also had responsibility for Newtownbutler from 1922. From 1 July 1965 Maguiresbridge was united with Lisbellaw and Newtownbutler and Lisnaskea to form a Home Mission four-point charge. Membership today stands at twenty families.

Ballygawley

was formed in 1829 after separation from Aughnacloy. The first minister was Rev David Cochrane (1830–40). The present church was opened on 27 March 1887 during the ministry of Rev David Smyth (1872–98). He gifted the Smyth Memorial Hall to the

Seskinore

was initially known as Newtownparry and originated as a Mission Station in 1824. The first minister was Rev Andrew Graham (1825–53) and, at his own expense, he commenced building a

Reverend Robert Corkey

ROBERT CORKEY was born in Glendermott manse on 20 March 1881, the seventh son and ninth child of Rev Dr Joseph Corkey. Eventually, all eight sons became ministers and all three daughters became missionaries. He entered Magee College in 1898 and graduated in 1902 with First Class Honours in Mental and Moral Science. He studied Theology at Edinburgh University and Magee College before adding a Doctor of Philosophy degree from the Royal University of Ireland in 1908. Robert Corkey was ordained in Ballygawley on 11 December 1906 where he served for four years. He then ministered in First Monaghan (1910–17) before his appointment as Professor of Christian Ethics in Assembly's College Belfast where he served for thirty-four years before his retirement in 1951. Robert Corkey was elected as Member of the Northern Ireland Parliament in 1929 for Queen's University and he sat in Parliament and Senate for thirty-one years. He was appointed Minister of Education in the Northern Ireland Government in 1943. Dr Corkey was elected Moderator of the General Assembly in 1945. He was also a strong supporter of the League of Nations and Temperance Reform. He died on 26 January 1966.

317

Painting by Frank McKelvey

was formed by the Secession Synod in 1835 and a church was built by 1839. The first minister, Rev James McKee, was ordained here on 9 August 1840 but resigned on 21 December that year upon his appointment as a missionary in India. The second minister was Rev Hugh Alexander and he stayed considerably longer, being ordained on 30 May 1843 and resigning in 1874 to emigrate to New Zealand. From 1928 until 1948 the church was united with Ballygawley. They were united again on 1 August 1973. The first minister of the united charge was Rev Samuel Conkey (1975–84). Membership today stands at fifty-eight families.

congregation and it was opened on 13 September 1913. Rev Robert Corkey (1906–10) was later elected Moderator of the General Assembly (1945) and also served as a MP for Queen's University, Belfast. From 1928 until 1948 the church was united with Ballyreagh. Following a period as a single charge, the church was once again united with Ballyreagh, from 1 August 1973. There are seventy-seven families in membership today.

Ballyreagh

Edenderry

was formed in the late 1830s following worship services which were held in a local barn. The first minister was Rev William Hamilton (1840–74). Rev William Sinclair (1935–64) also served as an RAF Chaplain during the Second World War. Dr Hugo Hezlett (1965–69) had previously served as a medical missionary in India (1934–64). New church seating and a hall were completed during the ministry of Rev Harold Pinkerton (1970–83). The church was united with Seskinore on 1 January 1982. A new hall was opened on 9 September 2006. There are seventy-eight families in membership today.

Hugo Hezlett

HUGH ALEXANDER HEZLETT (Hugo) was born in Coleraine in 1904. From Coleraine Academical Institution he progressed to Queen's University, Belfast, where he studied medicine. After some work experience in Sheffield and Belfast he was accepted as a medical missionary with the Jungle Tribes Mission. Founded in 1889, this Mission pioneered medical work in Dohad with Mr JH Neill. Hugo Hezlett was ordained as a missionary-elder for service in India on 15 November 1934. With his wife Mave, a nurse who had lived in India, Hugo supervised the building of Hamilton McCleery hospital at Dohad which opened on 5 January 1939. In 1953 he was honoured when asked to serve as Moderator of the Presbytery of Gujarat and Kathiawar and completed twenty-seven years service in India in 1962. Upon his return to Ireland he was ordained in Edenderry congregation on 29 June 1965. He served there for four years and then from 1969–73 in Greystones and Arklow. He retired to Drumbo and later to Newtownbreda where he gave additional assistance to the minister. The family moved to England in 1987 and Dr Hazlett died on 24 November 2002, aged 95 years.

Irvinestown

was originally known as Lowtherstown and was formed as a result of services conducted in the local Courthouse which commenced in 1836. The first minister was Rev William Guy (1846–73). The church name was changed to Irvinestown in 1885. On 10 August 1908 the church was united with Pettigo. Rev John Multree (1941–45) also served as Chaplain to several Air and Military Bases around Lough Erne. On I July 2002 a new triple union was formed between Irvinestown, Pettigo and Tempo. Membership today stands at eighty-four families.

Tempo

was formed in 1841 and the church building was opened in January 1845. The first minister was Rev Thomas Holmes (1842–49) who resigned to go as a missionary to Canada. He was succeeded by Rev David Clements (1849–97) who also served as Clerk of Clogher Presbytery for forty-nine years. On 6 May 1918 the church was united with Lisbellaw. From 1957–73 the church was linked with Clogher and from 1973–77 it was linked with Dromore. After 1977 the church became a Stated Supply linked to Pettigo and Irvinestown. On 1 July 2002 Tempo was united with Pettigo and Irvingstown. Membership today stands at thirty-two families.

Lisnaskea

had its origins in 1886 when Rev Ewing Gilfillan of Maguiresbridge commenced evening services. The church building was opened on 13 May 1900 on a site granted by Lord Erne. For many years this cause was a Mission Station linked with

Maguiresbridge and from 1 July 1965 it was united with Lisbellaw and Newtownbutler also in a new four-point Home Mission charge. Membership today totals twenty families.

The 20th Century

One new church, at Newtownbutler, was formed in the 20th century. The hallmark of Presbyterianism in Omagh Presbytery in this century has been congregational unions. There are only four single charges: First Omagh, Enniskillen, Clogherney and Sixmilecross. Eighteen of the twenty-nine churches in the Presbytery are part of a double charge. In addition, the first PCI four-point charge was created on 1 July 1965 with the union of Lisbellaw, Lisnaskea, Maguiresbridge and Newtownbutler. The local community was shocked by a terrorist bomb attack in Omagh on Saturday 15 August 1998 in which twenty-nine people, and two unborn babies, were killed and many more injured. Local ministers led the whole community in an Act of Prayerful Reflection in the town on Saturday 22 August.

Newtownbutler

was formed by local Presbyterians who met for worship once a month in the village Parish hall from 1922–36. Permission to hold fortnightly services was denied so they built their own church which was opened on 26 July 1937. Successive ministers of Maguiresbridge have been responsible for Newtownbutler also. The first minister was Rev James Stoops (1922–39). From 1 July 1965 Newtownbutler, Maguiresbridge and Lisbellaw and Lisnaskea were united in a new four-point charge. Membership today stands at sixteen families.

Conclusion

Presbyterianism in this area has shown a slight increase, about 2%, in numbers over the past fifty years. Communities tend to be settled and the local network of congregations long established. The Troubles have of course left their mark in this locality but the majority of people live and work together, respecting the basic Nationalist and Unionist opinions which are sincerely held. The challenge here, as elsewhere, is for the churches to proclaim the Gospel in power and simplicity, living in a manner that demonstrates the attractiveness of God's new society.

Route Presbytery

Introduction

The name Route is derived from Dalriada, the territory of the descendents of Riada, a third century chieftain. This area was under the control of the Macdonnells from the mid 16th century. The Route Presbytery contains twenty-two congregations under the pastoral oversight of seventeen ministers. It extends across much of North Antrim from Dunloy in the South to Croaghmore in the North. The area is dominated by the town of Ballymoney which contains the three largest congregations within Route Presbytery.

The 17th Century

In 1654, as a result of expanding numbers, the original Army Presbytery was divided into three Presbyteries: Antrim, Down and Route. Three years later Laggan Presbytery, comprising much of County Donegal, was carved out of Route. Six churches within Route Presbytery trace their origins to the 17th century: First Ballymoney (1646), Bushmills (1646), Dervock (1646), Ramoan (1646), Kilraughts (1660) and Finvoy (1688). Presbyterians have been resident in this area from about 1610, mainly Scots from Argyllshire and Wigtownshire. The Presbyterian settlers survived the Uprising in 1641 and the Commonwealth period only to suffer again with the renewed strict adherence to Episcopalianism after 1660. It is in the latter part of this century that early Presbyterian meeting-houses (churches) were constructed.

Dunluce

First Ballymoney

was formed in 1646 and the first minister, Rev James Ker was ordained here in that year but deposed for Non-conformity by Bishop Jeremy Taylor in 1661. Rev Hugh Kirkpatrick (1693–1712) was father of Dr James Kirkpatrick, later minister of Templepatrick and Belfast. Rev Robert McBride (1716–59) was a staunch supporter of subscription to the Westminster Confession. The current church was built in 1777 during the ministry of Rev Alexander Marshall (1772–99). Membership rose to 1,000 families during the ministry of Rev Robert Park (1817–66) who was a noted evangelical. He served as Clerk of the General Synod (1830–40) and General Assembly (1840–76). Both St. James' (in 1835) and Drumreagh (in 1838) were formed out of this congregation. A dispute with one individual over non-payment of pew rent erupted in 1870 and lasted ten years. Tactics included six committee members occupying the pew for a month and thereafter it was boarded up until the offending member eventually paid. A hall was built in 1897 and major refurbishment to the church, including installation of electric lighting, a war memorial organ, and relocation of the pulpit took place in 1921. During the ministry of Rev Noble McNeely (1984–97) a new hall was built beside the church and opened in May 1993. Membership today stands at almost 400 families.

Bushmills

was originally known as Billy and was formed in 1646. The first minister, Rev Jeremiah O'Quin (1642–58), was one of the earliest native Irishmen to become a Presbyterian minister. Following the death of Rev John Porter (1713–38) the congregation argued over various potential successors for eight years. The original thatched Presbyterian church stood on the site of the present Dunluce church but moved to the current site in 1753, during the ministry of Rev John Logue (1746–56). A minority remained and formed Dunluce church. The present church was opened on 27 June 1829. Rev Francis Paul (1902–11) left to become Professor of Church History

Reverend Robert McBride

ROBERT McBRIDE was born in 1687 to Rev John McBride of Clare (later Belfast). He graduated from Glasgow University in 1702 and undertook further study at Leyden University in Holland. While still a Probationer for the ministry he was asked to preach to the Belfast Independent Company of Volunteers on 26 May 1716, on the occasion of the anniversary of the birth of George I. The sermon was subsequently published. He was ordained in Ballymoney on 26 September that same year, in succession to Rev Hugh Kirkpatrick. Rev McBride made a name for himself in several clashes with the Non-subscribers, most notably Revs Haliday, Abernethy and Kirkpatrick. He defended both the Westminster Confession and subscription to it. In 1725 he clashed publicly with Rev Robert Higinbothem of Coleraine who published a pamphlet in criticism of the Synod Overtures which attempted to limit the influence of the Non-subscribers. Rev McBride produced an answering pamphlet, *The Overtures set in a Fair Light*, on behalf of the Subscribers. The Non-subscribers replied with three pamphlets but Rev McBride made no further comments in this controversy. Robert McBride was elected Moderator of the General Synod on 18 July 1728 and continued as minister in Ballymoney until his death at his home in Main Street on Sunday 2 September 1759, aged seventy-three.

Reverend Francis Paul

FRANCIS JAMES PAUL was born in 1878 at Glarryford, County Antrim. He was brought up in Killymurris congregation and was educated at Ballymoney High School and Methodist College, Belfast. He graduated with Honours from the Royal University of Ireland and studied Theology at Assembly's College and New College, Edinburgh. He was ordained at Bushmills on 5 November 1902 and combined this pastorate with further theological studies at Leipzig, Madrid and Geneva. He was fluent in German, French, Spanish and Italian. From 1911–22 he served as Professor of Church History and Pastoral Theology in Magee University College, Londonderry. From 1922–41 he was Professor of Church History and Symbolics at Assembly's College, Belfast, with additional responsibilities as College President (1923–24) and Principal (1924–41). Rev Paul had honorary DD degrees conferred upon him by both Queen's and Glasgow Universities. He was, in 1938, the first Irish Presbyterian minister to deliver the Cunningham Lectures and they were in turn published as *Romanism and Evangelical Christianity*. In his latter years Principal Paul suffered serious illness but he continued with his work, dying suddenly on 3 July 1941, aged sixty-three years.

at Magee College, Londonderry. Stained glass windows were added to the church building between 1929 and 1937. A new organ was presented to the church on 16 June 1991 by Rev Samuel Eaton who had been minister here from 1950–59. Major renovations were undertaken in 2005 providing a larger entrance vestibule and space

at the front of the church. Prior to these renovations, the organ top was used as a communion table. Membership today stands at 270 families.

Dervock

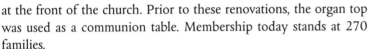

was originally known as Derrykeighan and the first minister, Rev John Baird, was installed here in 1646. He had preached the sermon at the formation of the Army Presbytery in Carrickfergus on 10 June 1642. The original church was in the Strahan valley then moved to a site opposite the present church during the ministry of Rev Thomas Stirling (1703–18). He had succeeded his father, Rev Robert Stirling, as minister. The third church building, and first on the present site, was opened during the ministry of Rev Joseph Douglass (1751–90). The current church was built during the ministry of Rev Joseph Bellis (1827–57). Major renovations were undertaken in 1883 and a hall was added in 1887. Rev Professor Richard Smyth, MP for Londonderry and Moderator of the General Assembly in 1869 and 1870 was raised in Dervock congregation. The longest ministry here was that of Rev Robert McBride (1926–70). Membership today stands at 140 families.

Ramoan

was formed in 1646 and the first minister was Rev David McNeil (1646–61) but he conformed to the Episcopal Church in 1661. The next known minister was Rev John Mairs (1704–23). Membership peaked at 400 families during the ministry of Rev Robert Brown (1738–67). A school was opened in 1827, during the long ministry of Rev John Simms (1805–66), and the present church was completed in 1856. The second longest ministry in Ramoan was that of Rev Silas Johnston (1890–1944). Miss Sarah Hunter retired in 1956 after serving here as a Sunday School teacher for sixty-four years. On 16 January 1996 the church was united with Armoy. Membership today stands at 126 families.

First Kilraughts

was formed in 1660 and the first minister, Rev William Cuming (1660–71) was ejected in 1661 for Non-conformity. The first

Presbyterian church was built here during the 1690s and replaced by another during the ministry of Rev John Cochrane (1716–48). Rev Thomas Leslie (1830–35) left to undertake missionary work in Jamaica but died only a few months after arriving there. Rev Robert Love (1836–49) had been raised in the congregation. At the union in 1840 the church was named First Kilraughts. During the ministry of Rev FA Robinson (1930–70) a hall was built (in 1933). An organ and hymn singing were introduced in Kilraughts. On 4 April 1971 the church was destroyed by a fire caused by an electrical fault. The current octagonal shaped church was opened on 31 May 1975. Membership today stands at 183 families.

Finvoy

was formed in 1688 and the first known minister was Rev Robert Henry. The earliest church was built about 1690 and was very primitive with a thatched roof and mud floor. The congregation leaned against the walls or sat on stones. Rev James Elder (1780–1843) was widely acclaimed for his evangelical preaching. The present church was opened during the ministry of Rev Andrew Todd (1843–91) on 6 January 1847 and a lecture hall was added in 1875. A new hall was opened in 1963 during the ministry of Rev Vernon Corkey (1934–74) who was the fifth of the eight sons of Rev Dr Joseph Corkey of Glendermott who entered the ministry. Three neighbouring congregations have grown from Finvoy: Rasharkin (in 1830), Drumreagh (in 1834) and Dunloy (in 1840). Membership today stands at 200 families.

Reverend James Elder

JAMES ELDER was born in Garvagh on 25 December 1757, the first son of John Elder, a farmer at Ballury. He studied Theology at Glasgow University from 1771 and was ordained in Finvoy on 13 June 1780. James Elder developed a distinctive preaching style. He was known for his evangelical views and his passionate and powerful preaching. Such was his reputation that he was called 'the gun of the gospel'. In 1840 Rev Elder was elected Moderator of the Synod of Ulster and therefore, on 10 July 1840, had the honour of leading that Synod in procession from May Street Church to Rosemary Street Church, where the General Assembly of the Presbyterian Church in Ireland was formed. Rev Elder read from John 17 and led in prayer before the Act of Union was read. In 1841 James Elder suffered a serious fall at home and thereafter preached from his pew beside the pulpit. Having spent his entire ministry of sixty-five years in Finvoy, he died on 4 November 1843, aged eighty-five. Rev Samuel Elder of Ballyeaston (1813–21) was his son.

Reverend John Cameron

JOHN CAMERON was born near Edinburgh in 1724. He served as an apprentice in a bookshop before studying at Edinburgh University. About 1752 he came to Ireland as a probationer of the Reformed Presbytery and engaged in open-air preaching. When a division occurred in Bushmills in 1754 the minority formed a new congregation (Dunluce) and invited John Cameron to be their minister if he would join the General Synod. He agreed and was ordained in Dunluce on 3 June 1755. Throughout his forty-four year ministry in Dunluce Rev Cameron wrote several books. The first, published in 1767, was *The Policy of Satan to Destroy the Christian Religion* and the last, published posthumously in 1828, was *The Doctrine of the Holy Scriptures concerning the True God*. These works are evidence that John Cameron was an Arian in his theology, denying the full divinity of Jesus Christ. This is most evident in *Theophilis and Philander, a Dialogue* (published in 1772), in which a New Light character triumphs over an orthodox character. Rev Cameron was elected Moderator of the Synod of Ulster in 1768, the year in which the Synod received a report from the Non-subscribing Presbytery of Antrim for the first time since 1726. Rev John Cameron died on 31 December 1799, aged seventy-five.

The 18th Century

Five congregations were founded in this locality during the 18th century: Roseyards (1748), Bushvale (1748), Dunluce (1755), Armoy (1768), and Mosside (in 1794). Three of these churches were Seceder causes, both Burgher and Anti-Burgher. The Seceder missionaries in Ireland brought a simple gospel to people, when several Synod of Ulster ministers were peddling 'New Light' doctrines and the church at large was infected with a more secular atmosphere. Emigration to America was rife, mainly due to religious intolerance and economic hardship, and several congregations struggled to survive. Much of Ballymoney was burned by Government forces in 1798 as punishment for perceived support for the rebellion of the United Irishmen.

Roseyards

was formed as a Seceder church about 1748 and, in union with Derrykeighan and Carnabuoy (now Ballywatt), ordained Rev John Tennnet on 16 May 1751 as the first minister. In the early 1770s

poverty was so extensive in this area that Rev Tennent was granted permission to emigrate to Nova Scotia, but he stayed with his congregation and died on 13 May 1808. Rev Tennent and his successor, Rev William Munnis (1812–60), cover a period of 109 years. The present church was opened on 7 April 1907, during the ministry of Rev Alexander Crothers (1889–1939). Rev William James Watson (1956–96) was renowned for his ability to paint and carve horses. Membership today stands at about 190 families.

Dunluce

was formed in the late 1740s by a substantial minority of Billy congregation (Bushmills) who refused to move to a new site on the east side of the River Bush. They built a new church and called Rev John Cameron (1755–99) as their first minister. He was a prolific author. The present church, which was designed by Charles Lanyon, was opened on 27 July 1847, during the ministry of Rev William Oliver (1836–65) who was chosen as an early missionary to India but was unable to go due to failing eyesight. He published two books: *Family Piety* and *Ministerial Support*. Rev James Kirkpatrick (1865-96) was a bachelor and left £8,000 in his will which was used to build Kirkpatrick Memorial Church in Belfast in 1924. Major alterations within the church and an extension to ancillary property were undertaken in 1994-5. Membership today stands at 220 families.

Armoy

was formed in 1768 for local Presbyterians who previously travelled to Ramoan, Dervock or Kilraughts. The first minister was Rev Hugh McClelland (1771–1813). The present church was opened in 1842, during the ministry of Rev Jackson Graham (1814-68). A manse was built in 1888. The long ministry of Rev Albert Crawford (1895–1939) was recognised by the Presbyterian Theological Faculty, Ireland, by the offer of a DD degree. Unfortunately the letter arrived at the manse on 13 March 1939, about thirty minutes after Rev Crawford died. In 1973 a former school was renovated for use as a church hall. The church was united with Ramoan on 16 January 1996 and membership currently totals 130 families.

Bushvale

was formed as a Burgher Seceder church in 1793, though a Society existed here from as early as 1748. The church was originally

known as Magheraboy, then as Second Kilraughts at the union of Synods in 1840, and from 1905 as Bushvale. The first two ministers, Rev Moses Kerr (1793–1816) and Rev James Moore (1819–29) both emigrated to America. The longest ministry here was that of Rev Thomas Caldwell who was ordained on 2 December 1879 and died on 23 October 1932. A hall was built in 1957. Membership today stands at just over 200 families.

Mosside

was formed in 1794 as a Burgher Seceder church and Rev Thomas Bell (1794–1841) was ordained as the first minister, several years before the first church was built. This early building had a clay floor and the high-backed pews were fastened to posts which were driven into the floor. A new church was constructed in 1848 during the ministry of Rev Robert Maconachie (1842–79), who was ordained on 26 April 1842 at an open-air service. Following the 1859 Revival it was necessary to add two side galleries to the church to accommodate increased attendances. The long ministry of Rev Thomas Heney (1890–1930) was noteworthy both for his effective preaching and pastoral care. Major renovation to the church was completed in 1967 and a new hall was opened in September 1981. The church was united with Toberdoney on 1 June 2002 and membership today stands at 180 families.

The 19th Century

As in most localities, the 19th century witnessed the greatest expansion in churches in what is now Route Presbytery. Eleven churches can trace their formation to this century, four of which were Seceder causes. The schism within the Synod of Ulster, which ultimately led to the formation of the Non-subscribing Presbyterian Church, was presided over in 1829 by Rev Robert Park of First Ballymoney. In 1834 Route Presbytery was divided into two, with several churches now within Coleraine Presbytery. Finvoy was detached from Route in this year but returned in 1874. The Route Tenants' Defence Association was formed in 1869 and, with strong Presbyterian membership, pushed for tenants to be able to buy their farms.

congregation joined the new Synod of Protestors in Scotland. The first minister, Rev John Millar, was ordained on 13 July 1828 by Ayr Presbytery. In 1852 the United Original Secession Synod and Free Church of Scotland united and a division arose in Toberdoney. A lawsuit in 1855 found against Rev Millar and a minority of the congregation who then formed a new church, Benvarden. Rev Francis Davidson (1909–21) was later to become Principal of the Bible Training Institute, Glasgow. The church joined the General Assembly in 1956 during the ministry of Rev James Beggs (1948–85), the first Irishman to minister here. The church was united with Croaghmore from 30 September 1957 until 19 February 2002. A new union with Mosside was formed on 1 June 2002. Membership today stands at 90 families.

Toberdoney

was formed by about sixty families in 1810 as a Seceder church in connection with Associate Presbytery. This Seceder Presbytery was formed by Seceders who did not agree with *regium donum* payments to their ministers. The church was built by 1813 and in 1821 the

Trinity, Ballymoney

was formed in 1814 as a Burgher Seceder church though a Seceder Society had been meeting in Charlotte Street in Ballymoney since 1748. The first minister, Rev Robert Lougheed (1815–35), was deposed for intemperance and conducting irregular marriages. He

later founded Garryduff church. Rev John Rentoul (1837–69) came from a famous ministerial dynasty and a church was built in 1854. The current church was opened on 4 September 1885, during the ministry of Rev James Brown Armour (1869–1925). The spire and sloped and rounded seating were innovative, and for some, controversial, in the 1880s. The church had been known as Second Ballymoney since 1840 but Third Ballymoney had also been known by that name prior to 1840. In 1905 both churches changed their name, with Second adopting the new name, Trinity. The original manse which had been built in 1854 was demolished and replaced with a modern house in 1970. The ministry of Rev Derek Poots (1964–1990) was significant for congregational growth. A new suite of halls was opened on 16 September 2004. Membership today stands at 420 families.

Ballycastle

was formed in 1827 and the first minister was Rev Samuel Lyle (1829–67). Interestingly, he received a call on 14 October 1828, prior to completing his theological studies. The church building was enlarged during the ministry of Rev George McFarland (1867–82) who left to become Mission Secretary of the General Assembly. The church was again extended during the ministry of Rev John Jackson (1882–1929) and a hall opened in 1901. Rev Godfrey Brown exercised an influential ministry here from 1964 until 2001. He was

Reverend James Brown Armour

JAMES BROWN ARMOUR was born on 20 January 1841 in the townland of Lisboy, near Ballymoney. He was the youngest of six children, and the family attended Kilraughts Church. Armour graduated with a BA degree from Queen's College, Cork in 1864. He spent his entire ministry in Trinity, Ballymoney, from his ordination on 19 July 1869 until his retirement on 2 September 1925. As a young man, Armour was known as 'wolf man' with his distinctive black hair and beard. He supported a more generous treatment of Irish Roman Catholics and was extremely hostile towards the Church of Ireland which he identified with the conservative landlord ascendancy. It was his political activities which brought him to public fame. An enthusiastic Liberal supporter, from 1892 Armour was known as a supporter of Home Rule. He received considerable public and private criticism for his views. He consistently protested that the majority of Presbyterians were foolish in aligning themselves with Conservatives against Home Rule because, as a denomination, they would not receive adequate public appointments or parliamentary candidates. Rev Armour caught a chill at a luncheon in honour of Prime Minister Sir James Craig in 1928. Pneumonia developed and James Armour died at the Trinity manse, Ballymoney on 25 January 1928.

Reverend Dr Godfrey Brown

ANDREW WILLIAM GODFREY BROWN was born in 1936 and brought up as a member of Newcastle congregation. Living in a Christian home, he was converted at a very young age and never doubted the authenticity of that experience. He graduated with a BA degree from Queen's University, Belfast, in 1957, studied Theology in Assembly's College and graduated BD from London University in 1961. On 9 December 1960 he was ordained as Assistant Minister in Fitzroy Avenue and served there under Rev Robert Alexander. Rev Brown was installed as the fifth minister of Ballycastle on 20 May 1964. Throughout his ministry there, he maintained leadership of the CSSM team in Portrush and also pioneered outreach work in Ballycastle at the annual Auld Lammas Fair. In 1977 Rev Brown was awarded a PhD degree for a thesis on *Irish Presbyterian Theology in the Early Eighteenth Century*.

Dr Brown served on numerous Committees and Boards of the General Assembly, perhaps most notably as Convenor of the Memorial Record (1976–83) and the Board of Studies (1997–2004). He was elected Moderator of the General Assembly in 1988. Always a devoted churchman with a courteous and efficient manner, he retired on 31 October 2001 having served in Ballycastle for thirty-seven years.

elected Moderator of the General Assembly in 1988. The church was united with Croaghmore on 1 June 2002 and membership stands today at 220 families.

Croaghmore

was formed in 1829 and the church building was opened in 1830. The first minister was Rev Robert Kennedy (1830–51) but some families disapproved of his selection and helped form Toberkeigh Secession church. The second minister, Rev William Richie (1852–1915), spent his entire ministry here. Alterations were made to the interior of the church during the ministry of Rev Hamilton Henderson (1893–1930); they included the installation of a new pulpit which he made himself. The church was united with Toberkeigh from 1930 until 1945 and with Toberdoney from 1957 until 2002. A new octagonal oak pulpit was installed in 1952, a gift of Mr David McConaghy, Clerk of Session. A new union with Ballycastle was formed on 1 June 2002. Membership stands today at 50 families.

Toberkeigh

was formed as a Seceder church in 1830. The first minister was Rev John Simpson (1830–69) and his wife was from Croaghmore. Early services were conducted in private houses until a church was built. A larger church was soon required. The present church, which was opened on 23 March 1889, was largely built with funds raised by Rev James Moore (1869–88) when he engaged in a lecture tour in America. The church was united with Croaghmore from 1930 until 1945 during the ministry of Rev James McFarland. Five young men

became students for the ministry during Rev McFarland's time here. Two members of Toberkeigh have become Moderator of the General Assembly: Rev William Currie (1938) and Rev John Thompson (1986). Membership currently stands at 150 families.

St James', Ballymoney

was formed in 1834 and initially known as Second Ballymoney. At the union in 1840 the name was changed to Third Ballymoney and the older Seceder church became known as Second Ballymoney. In 1905 the church name was changed to St. James'. The first minister was Rev James Ussher (1835–74) who died in Portrush only a few months after his retirement. The church building was opened on 20 March 1836 and a gallery, which raised the capacity of the building to 700, was added in 1858. A manse was built in 1875 and a hall in 1889. Rev Robert Hugh Wilson (1912–45) brought stability to

330

the church following a series of shorter ministries. A new hall was opened in 1958 and a new manse built upon the site of the previous one in 1971. Five Irish Presbyterian ministers have come from this congregation in addition to two ministers of the American and one of the Scottish Presbyterian Church. Membership today stands at almost 550 families, making this the largest church in Route Presbytery.

(1840–52), left to become a missionary in New South Wales. Rev Thomas Forsythe was ordained here on 31 March 1862 but died on 16 September 1866, aged only thirty. The church was enlarged in 1891 during the ministry of Rev Thomas Gregg (1867–1907). The sixth minister, Rev George Cromie (1939–78), was an Irish rugby international, who spent his entire ministry here and saw the church renovated in 1953 and a hall built in 1955. Another major church renovation and extension was completed in August 2004 during the ministry of Rev Maurice Barr, who was installed here in 1986. Membership today stands at 182 families.

Drumreagh

was formed in 1834 and the first minister was Rev Thomas Beare (1838–77). Early services were held in Bendooragh School and a church was completed in 1839. A gallery was added in 1859, the year of the Revival. Rev Samuel Wallace (1883–1930) also served as Clerk of Presbytery for forty-one years. The church was united with First Ballymoney from 1930 until 1935. Rev John Barkley (1935–39) was later Principal of Union Theological College, Belfast. A church hall was completed in 1956, during the ministry of Rev John Forbes (1951–72) and the church was united with Dromore on 1 October 1957. The church underwent major refurbishment prior to re-opening on 20 June 1970 and a new suite of rooms was added at that time. A major hall extension was completed in 1980 and membership today stands at 315 families.

Garryduff

was formed in 1840 by Rev Robert Loughead (1840–44), who had been deposed as minister of Second Ballymoney (now Trinity) in 1835 for intemperance and irregular marriages. A Mission Station had previously been operating here under Ahoghill Presbytery. The

Ballyweaney

was formed in 1835 and the first minister was Rev Thomas Craig (1840–52). The church was opened on Friday 30 September 1842 by Rev Dr Henry Cooke. The first minister, Rev Thomas Craig

church building was completed in 1847 during the ministry of Rev James Gamble (1846–53). The church roof was blown off in February 1857. The sixth minister, Rev Robert Millar (1906–12), resigned to continue his ministry in New Brunswick, Canada. He was succeeded by Rev Samuel Reid, who was installed on 23 October 1912 and died of blood poisoning on 26 May 1916. In 1929 the church succeeded in maintaining its independence despite Presbytery pressure to unite with Drumreagh. The church was united with Dunloy on 1 July 1995. Membership today stands at 175 families.

membership of the Free Church of Scotland. They worshipped in various buildings until a new church was built in 1856–7. The church operated as a member of the Original Secession Church and the first minister was Rev Andrew Anderson (1852–60). Rev Edward White (1889–1929) had formerly been a missionary in India but returned due to his wife's poor health. The Original Secession Church ceased to exist in 1956 when its congregations joined the Church of Scotland. In that year Dromore was received into the General Assembly (along with Toberdoney). Dromore is the youngest church in Route Presbytery. It was united with Drumreagh on 1 October 1957 and membership today stands at twenty-three families.

Dunloy

was formed in 1840 and the church building was opened on 21 August 1842. The first minister was Rev William Orr (1841–65). The church was remodelled in the 1880s, during the long ministry of Rev James Mairs (1866–1913). Rev John Corkey (1913–25) was one of eight sons of Rev Dr Joseph Corkey of Glendermott who entered the ministry. The Communion Table here was a gift in 1950 in memory of Rev Joseph Magill (1925–44). The fifth minister was Rev Herman Brown (1944–89) and a hall was built in 1954. On 1 July 1995 the church was united with Garryduff and congregational membership currently stands at sixty-five families.

Dromore

was formed in 1852 as a Seceder church when a majority of Ballylintagh congregation (belonging to the Original Secession Church of Scotland) refused to follow their minister into

Conclusion

The Route Presbytery is a stable area for Presbyterianism. While there have been no new congregations formed here in the 20th century, both Dromore and Toberdoney churches only joined the General Assembly in June 1956, when the Original Secession Church in Scotland, to which they belonged, ceased to exist. As with other Presbyteries, congregational unions have been a noticeable feature of church life in Route in the 20th century. Over the past fifty years membership within the Presbytery has risen by about 25% from 3,596 to 4,459 families. Most of this growth is centred upon the town of Ballymoney which dominates the area. There has also been significant growth in Ballycastle and Bushmills.

Templepatrick Presbytery

Introduction

The Presbytery of Templepatrick was formed in 1725 from sections of the Presbyteries of Antrim and Belfast. It consists today of twenty congregations served by seventeen ministers. The three joint charges are: Hydepark & Lylehill, First Randalstown & Duneane, and Killead & Loanends. The Presbytery covers an area to the north and east of Lough Neagh with Antrim town as its focus.

The 17th Century

There are at present eight churches within Templepatrick Presbytery which can trace their origins to the 17th century, though First Randalstown and Old Congregation Randalstown developed from a division in one congregation in the 1830s. Presbyterians were numerous in this locality from the earliest years of this century and the 1625 Revival and *Antrim Meeting* are evidence of their spiritual influence prior to the formation of the Army Presbytery at Carrickfergus on 10 July 1642. Several of the early ministers were persecuted by State and Anglican authorities but Presbyterianism survived and flourished.

Lough Neagh
SCENIC IRELAND

First Antrim

was formed about 1645 and the first minister, Rev Archibald Ferguson (1645–54), was imprisoned for a time at Carrickfergus in June 1650. Rev Thomas Gowan (1672–83) conducted a Classical and Divinity School at Antrim which enabled ministerial students to receive their higher education locally. The original church was situated on the Steeple Road and this was replaced in 1701 by a new church in the Scotch Quarter (now Church Street). Rev John Abernethy (1703–26) was a leading Non-subscriber and in 1726 a split occurred in the church. The orthodox party built a new church in Millrow in 1728 and called Rev William Holmes (1730–50). The present church was opened on 9 June 1837 and in 1860 the name was changed from *Millrow* to *First Antrim*. The church building was severely damaged by fire on 10 January 1862 but repaired within a

matter of months. The longest ministry here was that of Rev Thomas West (1867–1919) who was elected Moderator of the General Assembly in 1916. An extensive suite of halls was opened in 1969 during the ministry of Rev Tomas Blackstock (1962–79). Rev John Dixon was installed here on 1 November 1980 and was elected Moderator of the General Assembly in 1998. First Antrim is the largest congregation in Templepatrick Presbytery and membership totals 827 families.

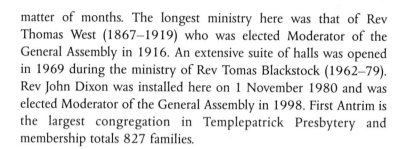

Reverend Thomas Gowan

THOMAS GOWAN was born at Caldermuir, Scotland in 1631. He graduated MA in 1655 from Edinburgh University and was ordained in 1658 at Glasslough, County Monaghan, where he preached in the parish church for nine years. In 1657 he moved to Connor, County Antrim, where he taught languages and philosophy. He was deposed in 1661 for Non-conformity but acted as 'constant supply' in Connor from 1666–71. He resisted a call to Antrim in early 1672 but was eventually installed there in August of that year. Through the influence of Lord Massereene he was granted permission to preach in Antrim parish church. With the help of Rev John Howe (a notable Non-conformist minister and chaplain to Lord Massereene), Rev Gown established a school of Philosophy and Divinity in Antrim. The General Synod recognised these courses for ministry students. Following the defeat of the Scottish Covenanters in 1679, Rev Gown was one of two Irish Presbyterian ministers who were nominated to represent their fellow Presbyterians in Dublin and give proof of their loyalty to the Government. Rev Gowan eventually obtained permission to build a Presbyterian church at a site on Steeple Road in the town but he never preached in it. He died on 15 September 1683 and was buried at Antrim. The church, which was a simple barn-like structure with a thatched roof, was completed in 1684.

Templepatrick

was formed about 1646 and the first minister was Rev Anthony Kennedy (1646–97). Presbyterians had previously been under the ministry of Rev Josias Welsh (1626–34), grandson of the celebrated Scottish Reformer John Knox. Rev John Abernethy (1774–96) was described as 'fond of money, addicted to manual labour, able in argument and acquainted with various branches of science.' Rev Robert Campbell (1796–1829) held strong anti-Trinitarian views and withdrew, with a part of the congregation, from the Synod of Ulster on 3 November 1829. The remainder of the congregation stayed under the authority of the Synod and called Rev John Carson (1831–59) as their minister. The people worshipped in a barn at Kirkhill until 1834 when they built a new church in the village (now a Church of Ireland hall). The present church was built two miles from the village and opened on 26 October 1845. A church hall was opened on 14 September 1974, during the ministry of Rev David Clarke (1974–80) who was elected Moderator of the General Assembly in 2006. Membership today stands at 305 families.

Old Congregation,
Randalstown

First Randalstown

was formed in the 1830s as the minority party in the earlier
Randalstown congregation which had been founded in 1655. The
first minister, Rev John Couthart, was ordained on 21 May 1656
but nothing is known of him beyond 1658. The second minister
was Rev Richard Wilson (1671–85) who was succeeded by his son,
Rev John Wilson (1688–94), but there were serious disputes among
the congregation concerning a plan to build a new church. The
seventh minister, Rev Thomas Henry (1786–1823), was father of
Rev Dr Pooley Shuldham Henry, the first President of Queen's
College, Belfast (1846–79). The congregation permanently divided
after the death of Rev Archibald Jamieson (1826–35) with the
minority party retaining the title *First Randalstown*, building a new
church and, from 1840, operating within Templepatrick Presbytery.
The new church was opened on 29 August 1841. The church was
united with Second Randalstown from 1922 until 1930. The
present union with Duneane was formed in 1932 and membership
today stands at 140 families.

Old Congregation, Randalstown

was formed in the 1830s as the majority party in the earlier
Randalstown congregation – called simply Randalstown at the
time, and shared a common history with First Randalstown until
1835. The current oval church was built in 1790 on a site granted
by the only daughter of Sir Henry O'Neill of Shane's Castle. The
church adopted the name 'Old Congregation' and, from 1840,
operated within Ballymena Presbytery. During the ministry of Rev
Frederick Bell (1922–40) the church walls were raised and the
distinctive oculus gallery windows added. A large suite of halls was
built in 1969, during the ministry of Rev Alan McAloney
(1950–90). Membership today stands at 414 families.

First Donegore

was formed in the 1650s though Presbyterians had earlier
worshipped in the parish church under the ministry of Presbyterian
Rev Andrew Stewart (1627–34). He was succeeded by his son-in-
law, Rev Thomas Crawford (1655–70). Rev Francis Iredell
(1688–99) was later minister in Capel Street, Dublin, and a very
prominent minister in the Synod of Ulster. The famous Rev Henry
Cooke (1811–18) was succeeded by another famous minister, Rev

James Reid (1819–23) who was later appointed Professor of
Church History in Glasgow University. Rev William Gillespie
(1854–67) emigrated to Australia and became Moderator of the
Presbyterian Church there. The longest ministry here was that of
Rev Alexander McKinney who was ordained on 4 March 1884 and
retired after forty-eight years, in September 1932. Membership
today stands at 250 families.

Killead

was formed about 1660. The first minister, Rev Robert Hamilton (1660–73), was deposed in 1661 and imprisoned in 1663 through alleged implication in Blood's Plot. The 1625 Revival at nearby Oldstone is testimony to earlier Presbyterian influences in this locality. The earliest church was probably built in the 1670s and the present church dates from 1750. It is a T-plan building with three entrances. Killead has produced two famous ministers from its

membership: Rev Samuel Barber of Rathfriland (1763–1811) was a noted supporter of the United Irishmen and Rev Henry Montgomery of Dunmurry (1809–65) was leader of the Non-subscribing Party in the Synod of Ulster. Rev Dr John Irwin (1903–26) was a controversial figure, supporting Home Rule and while on a preaching tour of America, he appeared on platforms with Eamon de Valera. Several families left the church in protest and Rev Irwin resigned on 19 October 1926. On 1 January 1976 the church was united with Loanends, during the significant ministry of Rev Derek Weir (1966–2004), who was appointed Clerk of Templepatrick Presbytery in 1972. A new suite of halls was opened on 17 June 2006 and membership today stands at 162 families.

Duneane

was formed as a single charge with Grange in the 1660s. The first minister was Rev Joseph Hamilton (1670–86). Rev John Henderson (1713–53) joined the Presbytery of Antrim about 1725 and was one of the last survivors of the Belfast Society. Rev Henry Cooke was ordained here on 10 November 1808 before moving to

Reverend John McConnell

VIRTUALLY NOTHING IS KNOWN about the life of Rev John McConnell of Killead, but he has spoken clearly in his death! He was a native of Connor in County Antrim and was licensed by Templepatrick Presbytery in 1734. Rev McClelland was ordained in Killead on 3 May 1737 and served as minister there for over forty years. Pewter communion vessels were obtained in 1745 and there were disagreements among some of the congregation who helped form the Seceder church at Lylehill in 1746. Rev McConnell was not an advocate of Subscription and remained a bachelor all his life. When he died, on 8 June 1770, he was buried beneath the floor of the church, immediately in front of the pulpit, with a flat stone marking the spot. He is reported to have left instructions regarding his burial with the remark, 'The congregation tramped on me while I was alive so they might as well continue to do so after my death.' This stone was uncovered in 1993 during major refurbishment of the church.

BELFAST TELEGRAPH

Rev Derek Weir examines the headstone of his predecessor Rev John McConnell

Reverend Henry Montgomery

HENRY MONTGOMERY was born on 16 January 1788 at Boltnaconnell, Killead, the fifth son and youngest child of Archibald and Sarah Montgomery. He was educated at Crumlin Academy and by Rev Isaac Paton of Lylehill, then Glasgow University (1804–08). He was ordained in Dunmurry on 14 September 1809. In 1812 he married Elizabeth Swan of Summerhill, Antrim. In addition to his ministerial responsibilities, Rev Montgomery served as headmaster of the English School in the Belfast Academical Institution for twenty-two years (1817–39). He was Moderator of the General Synod in 1818, aged only thirty, and leader of the Non-subscription Party. He clashed with Rev Henry Cooke on several occasions in Synod, perhaps most notably in 1827 and 1828 and eventually withdrew from the Synod with his congregation in 1830 and formed the Remonstrant Synod. In theology, politics and personality Montgomery was at loggerheads with Cooke. He served as Professor of Church History and Pastoral Theology to the Non-subscribing Association from 1838 until 1865. He was tall, at six feet four inches, and renowned for his gift of eloquent oratory. In his latter years he was opposed by radicals among his own students and was scorned for adding some theological questions to the Remonstrant Synod's new Code of Discipline. Henry Montgomery died on 18 December 1865 and was buried at Dunmurry in a ceremony attended by his old rival Rev Henry Cooke.

Donegore in 1811. Rev John McClure (1883–96) emigrated to Capetown, South Africa and was later elected Moderator of the Presbyterian Church in South Africa. The present church was donated to the congregation during the ministry of Rev Robert Elliott (1903–44). The donation was made by Mr James Kerr Fulton of Johannesburg in memory of his parents. The church was united with First Randalstown in 1932. Duneane is the smallest church in Templepatrick Presbytery with membership currently standing at ninety families.

First Ballyeaston

was formed in the interval 1676–81 and the first minister was Rev William Adair (1681–90) who was regarded as a leading minister within Irish Presbyterianism. The church suffered lengthy vacancies

of eight, five and nine years between the earliest ministers. The present church, which is the third upon this site, was opened in 1834 during the ministry of Rev William Raphael (1821–65). Rev Raphael also guided the church through the union of Synods, the potato famine and the 1859 Revival. The use of funds raised at a Bazaar in 1902 became the subject of a bitter dispute which involved legal proceedings and the lodging of money in Chancery. It was eventually used to build a lecture hall in 1937. A new church hall was opened on 4 September 1976 and a further extension opened on 8 April 1995. Membership today stands at 350 families.

The 18th Century

There are currently five congregations within Templepatrick Presbytery which were formed in the 18th century: Crumlin, Lylehill, Second Ballyeaston, Second Randalstown and Second Donegore. Four of these five churches were Seceder causes and Lylehill has the distinction of being the first Irish Seceder church, with Rev Isaac Patton ordained there on 9 July 1746. Significant numbers of Presbyterians in this area were sympathetic to the cause of the United Irishmen and several thousand participated in the ill-fated Battle of Antrim on 7 June 1798.

Reverend William John McCracken

WILLIAM McCRACKEN was born in Glascar, County Down, on 6 January 1836. Following studies at Queen's College and Assembly's College in Belfast he was ordained in Loughmourne, Monaghan, on 5 December 1865. He was installed in First Ballyeaston on 19 April 1878. Services each Sunday were at 12noon and 5pm. Income from a manse farm was being used to augment congregational funds and Rev McCracken took the church trustees to the High Court in Dublin where he won his case and obtained possession of the farm. Further legal action emerged in 1915 over how to use money raised at a Bazaar held in June 1902. Essentially this dispute was over the choice of building stables or a hall and Rev McCracken was not directly involved. Interestingly, in 1904 Rev McCracken asked the Committee to consider installing a bathroom in the manse but his request was denied! Rev McCracken's health started to deteriorate in 1911 but he continued as minister in First Ballyeaston until 2 May 1916 when he announced his retirement after thirty-eight years in the congregation. He died only six days later, aged eighty. He was buried in the church graveyard.

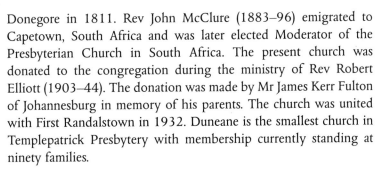

Crumlin

was formed in 1715 from an earlier cause at Glenavy. The first minister, Rev Thomas Crawford (1724–82), served here for fifty-eight years. Rev Nathaniel Alexander (1799–30) was a man of

Mission. Rev Thomas Patterson (1941–52) was elected Moderator of the General Assembly in 1977. On 1 December 1976 the church was united with Hydepark. A major refurbishment and extension to the church, and the provision of a new manse, have taken place during the ministry of Rev Paul Dalzell who was installed here on 6 January 1996. Membership today stands at 105 families.

Second Ballyeaston

much ability and conducted a successful school at Antrim. He was elected Moderator of Synod in 1817 but joined the Non-subscribing Presbyterians in 1830. The orthodox party in the congregation then called Rev Alexander Canning (1838–88) who was succeeded by his son, Rev John Canning (1889–1929). Rev Robert Brown (1964–71) resigned to become Lecturer in Biblical Studies at Stranmillis College, Belfast. Membership currently stands at 130 families.

Lylehill

was formed in 1746 as the first Seceder congregation in Ireland. The church was originally known as Templepatrick. The first minister, Rev Isaac Patton (1746–99), was also the first Moderator of the Associate Synod which was formed in 1788. The church joined the General Assembly in 1840 during the ministry of Rev John McMillan (1830–56). The fifth minister, Rev James Black (1860–81), had previously been an agent for the Belfast Town

was formed in 1758 as an Anti-Burgher Seceder church at the Five Corners in the townland of Rashee. Rev William Holmes (1768–1813) was inadequately paid and undertook preaching duties in Larne and Islandmagee. He played a prominent part in the Volunteers and, in 1798, formed and trained the Ballyeaston Yeomanry. The name *Second Ballyeaston* was adopted at the time of the 1840 union, during the ministry of Rev John Wright (1813–42). The church was renovated in 1901–03 and a manse built in 1907. More recent renovations were undertaken during the ministries of Rev Robin Boyd (1966–88) and Rev Purvis Campbell (1990–2005). Membership today stands at 395 families.

Second Randalstown

was formed as a Seceder church in 1774 and was initially supplied by Rev William Holmes of Ballyeaston. The first minister was Rev Thomas Smith (1780–98) and he had to emigrate to America due to his political activities prior to 1798. A gallery was added to the church in 1867, during the ministry of Rev Henry Stewart (1850–78). The church was briefly united with First Randalstown from 1922 until 1930 and known as *Randalstown United*. Lord O'Neill granted a site for a hall in 1958, during the ministry of Rev Wilfred Martin (1947–59). The hall was built by voluntary labour and finally opened on 20 October 1973, during the ministry of Rev Robert Coffey (1972–75), who resigned and joined the Baptist Church. Membership today stands at 200 families.

Second Donegore

was formed as a Burgher Seceder church in 1788 by local Presbyterians who disapproved of the Unitarian sympathies of Rev John Wright (1755–1807) in First Donegore. The first minister, Rev Josias Wilson (1794–1804), had a medical qualification from Glasgow University and emigrated to America. The original church was built in 1788 and was thatched with heather. Rev William Windell (1848–50) was later appointed a missionary to Canada.

The Rev Joseph McKee (1852–90) had a significant ministry during which a manse and farm were purchased. The longest ministry here was that of Rev David Craig who was ordained on 17 November 1891 and retired on 4 November 1941. The current church was opened on 14 June 1908 and the old church was demolished in 1962. Membership currently stands at 186 families.

The 19th Century

While most Presbyteries witnessed prolific expansion during the 19th century, this was not so in the Templepatrick Presbytery area. Only six churches within the Presbytery trace their origin to this century, most probably because Presbyterianism was already long established here. The six new churches were: Loanends, Dundrod, Muckamore, Kilbride, High Street, and Hydepark. These new churches represented a desire on the part of Presbyterians to have local churches.

340

Loanends

was formed in 1816 in connection with the Associate Presbytery of the Original Seceders in Ireland. This group maintained opposition to ministers receiving *regium donum* payments from Government. The first minister was Rev Hugh McIntyre (1816–68) who lived for several years at Craigmore and was also responsible for services at Loanends and Knockloughrim. The church was built in 1830 and from 1832 Rev McIntyre was only responsible for Loanends. In 1858 the church became part of the United Presbyterian Church of Scotland and from 1900–1922 was a member of the United Free Church of Scotland. Loanends joined the General Assembly of the Irish Presbyterian Church in June 1922, during the ministry of Rev William Salmond (1879–1922). A hall was opened on 3 June 1967 and named after Rev Salmond. The church was united with Killead on 1 January 1976 and membership currently totals 156 families.

Dundrod

was formed in 1827 and the first minister, Rev William Loughridge (1829–38), emigrated to America and was minister in Fourth Philadephia church. The fourth minister, Rev John McConnell (1880–84), emigrated to Australia and was minister in Footscray Church, Melbourne. Rev James Little (1900–10) was later Westminster MP for County Down (1939–46). The longest ministry here was that of Rev David McKinney who was ordained on 5 March 1925 and retired on 31 December 1967. An impressive new suite of halls was opened in May 2003 and the church underwent extensive renovations in 2006. Membership today stands at 238 families.

Stuart Graham

STUART GRAHAM was born on 21 July 1945 and joined Muckamore church in 1989. He travelled with a container lorry to Croatia in January 1993 with humanitarian aid organised by Muckamore. He stayed in Croatia for three months that year and made important contacts with local Christians. In the following year, Stuart and his wife Ann established a charitable organisation *Church Growth Croatia and Bosnia*. Their aim is to respond to the needs of the local Christians with practical help. Several individuals have been brought to Belfast for theological training and Redzo Trako is completing doctoral studies at Queen's University in Bosnian Church History. Since 2002 *Church Growth Croatia and Bosnia* has been funding a major project: a new translation of the Bible in Bosniak. The work is being undertaken by Islamic scholars in Sarajevo, and Wycliffe Bible Translators are providing consultant support. Half of the translation was completed in 2006 and the entire project will be finished in 2008, at a cost of £140,000. This new translation will make the Bible accessible to three million Muslims living in Bosnia. One hundred percent of all donations to *Church Growth Croatia and Bosnia* go directly to the mission.

Muckamore

was formed in 1840 and the first minister, Rev Thomas Morrow (1840–61), appears not to have approved of elders and eventually joined the Church of England. Rev Thomas Lyle (1873–93) was later Superintendent of the Irish Mission. The congregation has nurtured three theological professors: Rev James Heron (1861–69) was Professor of Church History in Assembly's College (1889–1917) and Moderator of the General Assembly in 1901. Rev Cecil McCullough (1969–75) was Professor of New Testament in Union College (1988–) and Rev Laurence Kirkpatrick (1984–96) was appointed Professor of Church History in Union College in 1996. The present church is the second on this site and was opened in October 2006. Membership currently stands at 230 families.

High Street, Antrim

was formed in 1850 by about sixty people who withdrew from First Antrim church. Services were held in the Primitive Methodist Chapel, then the Court House, before their own church was opened in Main Street on 29 May 1853. The first minister, Rev John Orr (1851–95), also served as Clerk of the General Assembly from 1869 and was elected Moderator in 1887. The third minister, Rev William Mitchell (1924–52), was also Secretary of the Widows of Ministers Fund. Accommodation was cramped in the church and the congregation moved to a new site in October 1974, during the ministry of Rev Lawrence Henry (1971–92). Membership today stands at 450 families.

Hydepark

was formed in 1861 and early services were held in the *Brown Room* of the Hydepark Bleach Works. The church was opened on 7

Kilbride

was formed in 1847 following earlier unsuccessful attempts to form a congregation at Doagh. Early services were conducted by a licentiate, Alexander Barklie, in Kilbride schoolhouse, and the first minister was Rev William Orr (1847–79). Full congregational status was granted on 14 March 1848 and the church building was opened on 13 March 1849. The second minister, Rev Robert Allison (1879–1923), was Clerk of Carrickfergus Presbytery for thirty-two years, a post which was also occupied by three following ministers: Rev John Armstrong (1924-48), Rev James Armour (1949–56) and Rev Frederick Neill (1956–65). A gallery was added to the church in 1860 and a new vestibule in 1895. A major refurbishment was undertaken in 1983 during the ministry of Rev Sam McClintock (1979–96). A new suite of halls including a Youth Centre was opened in September 2005. Membership has risen very significantly in recent years and stands today at 480 families.

ARDENS SED VIRENS

342

December 1862 and the first minister was Rev Alexander Bell (1863–67). After three short ministries Rev James Houston served here for almost fifty years, being ordained on 22 September 1874 and retiring on 31 December 1923. Another long ministry followed, that of Rev Andrew Mulholland who was ordained on 29 May 1924 and retired on 30 June 1964. Rev Colin Corkey (1965–76) was the last minister to serve here in a single charge. A new hall was built in 1970 and on 1 December 1976 the church was united with Lylehill. Membership today stands at 160 families.

The 20th Century

The first union of congregations, First Randalstown and Duneane, took place in 1932 and this was followed in 1976 by two others: Killead and Loanends, and Hydepark and Lylehill. Greystone Road church, the third Presbyterian congregation in Antrim and the only new church in this century, was formed in 1969. The Presbytery of Templepatrick remained unaltered for much of this century until 1 January 1962 when the following six

congregations were added: High Street, Antrim, and Old Congregation, Randalstown from Ballymena; Hydepark from Belfast; and First Ballyeaston, Second Ballyeaston and Kilbride from Carrickfergus.

Greystone Road

Reverend Colin Corkey

COLIN CORKEY was born at Drumhillery, County Armagh, on 21 May 1911. His brother Vernon was minister in Finvoy (1934–74) and his father, Rev Vernon Corkey, had seven brothers who were all ministers and his grandfather, Rev Dr Joseph Corkey, was also a Presbyterian minister. His father Vernon was minister in Drumhillery (1906–12) and Culnady (1912–40). Colin Corkey, known to his family as Tony, was ordained on 21 July 1936 and served as a missionary in Manchuria, China from 1936 until 1941. He undertook responsibilities for a time as YMCA Secretary in Moukden and ministry in Liaoyang. Much to his disappointment, Rev Corkey was brought home with other missionaries in 1941 as the political situation in Manchuria deteriorated. He spent the rest of the war years as an RAF Chaplain. Rev Corkey served as minister in three Irish Presbyterian churches. He was installed in First Castlederg on 6 August 1947 and remained there for five years. He started a Boys' Brigade Company before resigning on 16 December 1952. His second church was Albert Street in Belfast. He was installed there on 17 December 1952 and served for over twelve years, resigning on 15 May 1965. Rev Corkey's final ministry was in Hydepark where he was installed on 19 May 1965, serving until his retirement on 31 July 1976. Rev Colin Corkey lived a long and fulfilled life, dying on 26 May 2004, aged ninety-three.

Rev Colin Corkey with members of the Boys Brigade in Manchuria

Greystone Road, Antrim

was formed in 1969 as a third Presbyterian church in Antrim where the population was expanding rapidly. Initial services were held in a prefabricated building, and Rev Derek Weir of Killead served for two years as Stated Supply (1969–71). The present church was opened on 9 September 1972. Full congregational status was gained on 16 January 1977, during the ministry of Rev George Cunningham (1971–83). Major renovations took place in 2006 and membership currently stands at 456 families.

Conclusion

The Templepatrick Presbytery has grown significantly over the past fifty years. Presbyterian families have increased by 44% from 3,971 families in 1955 to 5,734 families in 2005. Average congregational size is 286 families and fifteen of the twenty churches in this Presbytery are growing.

Lough Neagh
SCENIC IRELAND

Introduction

Tyrone Presbytery contains thirty-three congregations and extends over a large area of County Tyrone on the western side of Lough Neagh, stretching from Swatragh in the north to Clonaneese in the south, from Albany near the shore of Lough Neagh in the east to Pomeroy in the west. As currently constituted, the Tyrone Presbytery was formed on 1 January 1963 when eleven congregations (Bellaghy, Knockloughrim, Castledawson and Curran, Culnady and Swatragh, Draperstown, Maghera, First Magherafelt, Saltersland, Tobermore) were added from the former Presbytery of Magherahoghill. Currently there are two triple charges (Coagh, Ballygoney, Saltersland and First Stewartstown, Brigh, Albany), ten double charges and seven single charges within the Presbytery.

The 17th Century

Following the formation of the first Presbytery on 10 June 1642, seven congregations were formed in this locality in the 17th century: Carland, Brigh, Maghera, Dungannon, First Moneymore, First Cookstown and Castledawson. In 1659 the Presbytery of Tyrone (sometimes known as Dungannon) was the fifth to be formed, indicating the spread of Presbyterianism in mid-Ulster. Prior to this date congregations belonged to Down Presbytery.

Tyrone Presbytery

Gortin Lakes

Carland

was originally known as Donaghmore and was formed about 1646. The first minister, Rev Thomas Kennedy (1646–89) had been a chaplain in Munro's army. From 1714 a section of the congregation formed Dungannon church. The third minister, Rev William Kennedy (1754–94), was a grandson of the first minister. A new church was built during his ministry, in 1767. The present church was opened in 1859, during the ministry of Rev Stuart Carse (1846–90). The seventh minister was Rev Gilbert Kennedy (1888–90), a great grandson of the first minister. The church was united with Castlecaulfield from 1949 until 1960. A new union was formed with Newmills in 1960 and continues at present. Membership today stands at around 100 families.

Brigh

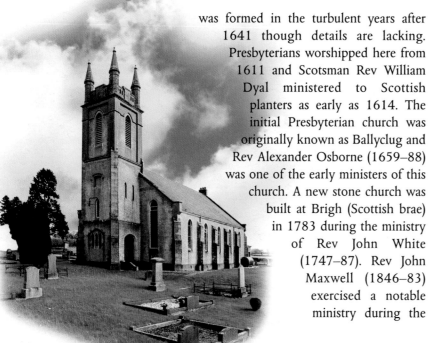

was formed in the turbulent years after 1641 though details are lacking. Presbyterians worshipped here from 1611 and Scotsman Rev William Dyal ministered to Scottish planters as early as 1614. The initial Presbyterian church was originally known as Ballyclug and Rev Alexander Osborne (1659–88) was one of the early ministers of this church. A new stone church was built at Brigh (Scottish brae) in 1783 during the ministry of Rev John White (1747–87). Rev John Maxwell (1846–83) exercised a notable ministry during the

years of revival and also took a public stand for tenant farmers against oppressive landlords. He also gifted the church a manse and a farm, and is commemorated in a memorial window. Rev James McFeeters (1888–93) left to become headmaster of Rainey Endowed School, Magherafelt. The present church building was opened on 26 September 1909, during the ministry of Rev William McIlhatton (1907–21). The church was united with Albany on

Reverend Thomas Kennedy

THOMAS KENNEDY was born in 1625 in Ayrshire, Scotland and graduated from Glasgow University in 1643. He served as a chaplain in Munro's Army which was defeated by Owen Roe O'Neill at Benburb in 1646. Shortly afterwards he was installed in Donaghmore (Carland) Episcopal church. He was ejected in 1661 for maintaining Presbyterian practices and continued to preach in a log house. His actions were not tolerated by the authorities and he was imprisoned in Dungannon for several years, being denied visits from his wife. Upon gaining his freedom, Rev Kennedy took refuge in Derry during the siege and afterwards returned to Scotland. Following a short ministry in Glasgow, Thomas Kennedy returned to Carland in 1693 and helped build a new church on the site of the present church. Two sons also served as Presbyterian ministers: Thomas in Brigh (1700–46) and John in Benburb (1714–61). Rev Thomas Kennedy of Carland was elected Moderator of the Synod of Ulster in 1697. He died on 9 February 1716, aged eighty-nine. He was interred within the Old Church of Donaghmore and a tombstone erected to his memory. A later rector removed Rev Kennedy's remains from the church but replaced them when threatened by Rev Thomas Kennedy junior and a number of local Presbyterians. The tombstone was rediscovered in the early 1990s.

Reverend John Glendy

JOHN GLENDY was born at Faughanvale, near Londonderry, on 24 January 1755. His father, Samuel, was a prosperous farmer. John graduated from Glasgow University and was ordained in Maghera on 16 December 1778. A new church was built in 1785 soon after his arrival and he had the distinction of baptising Henry Cooke, who was to become the most famous Irish Presbyterian minister of the 19th century. Rev Glandy served as Captain and Chaplain in the local Volunteers and sympathised with the aims of the United Irishmen. When the Rebellion in 1798 failed, Glendy was a marked man. His house in Maghera was burned and he was on the run from the authorities. He was eventually captured and tried and permitted to leave Ireland. He and his wife sailed from Derry to America where, in 1803, he became the first minister of Second Baltimore, where he ministered until his retirement in 1826. Rev Glendy was appointed Chaplain to the House of Representatives in 1806 and also to the Senate in Washington in 1815–6. He died at Philadelphia on 4 October 1832, aged seventy-seven, and was buried in Baltimore.

1 November 1923 and Stewartstown was added on 1 May 1980 thereby forming a triple charge. Membership today stands at about ninety families.

William Reid had a long and influential ministry in First from 1876 until 1919. The two congregations were united on 15 October 1919 and worshipped together as one congregation, with services being held on alternative Sundays in each building. Membership today stands at 115 families in First and eighty families in Second.

Maghera

was formed about 1655 and the first known minister was Rev Robert Rowan (1658–61). The church was linked with Dawson's Bridge (Castledawson) for some years prior to 1700. The present church was built in 1785 during the ministry of Rev John Glendy (1778–98). Rev Thomas Witherow (1845–65) resigned upon his appointment as Professor of Church History in Magee College, Londonderry. He was followed by Rev Matthew Leitch (1866–79) who became Principal of Assembly's College, Belfast. The professorial connections continued with the ministry of Rev James Haire (1940–44) who also became Principal of Assembly's College, and Moderator of the General Assembly in 1970. A new hall was built during the ministry of Rev Dennis Clarke (1960–70) and also the interior of the church was extensively refurbished by constructing new interior walls and installing new pews. Membership today stands at 250 families.

First Moneymore

was formed in 1660 and the first minister was Rev John Abernethy (1660–75 and 1684–91). Rev John Barnett (1827–72) was Moderator of the General Assembly in 1849. A Seceder congregation, 'Second Moneymore', was formed about 1824 during the ministry of Rev William Moore (1782–1826). Rev

First Cookstown

was originally known as Derriloran and formed in 1673. The first minister, Rev John McKenzie (1673–96), was in Derry during the siege and wrote a famous account of it. The original church at Oldtown was demolished by the local Rector in 1701, though the communion table has survived. A second church was built at

348

Killymoon and was used until 1764. The third church building, in Main Street, was completed on 4 January 1764, during the vacancy between Rev James Hull (1752–63) and Rev George Murray 1765–95). It was at the Synod meeting in this church in 1828 that Henry Cooke and Henry Montgomery clashed so spectacularly over the question of subscription to the Westminster Confession. A Seceder congregation, 'Second Cookstown', was formed in the town in 1801. During the ministry of Rev Alexander Fleming (1837–46) in First, a minority party formed 'Third Cookstown' (Molesworth). The present church building, on the same site in Main Street, was completed in 1841. Membership today stands at 390 families.

The 18th Century

Eleven congregations within Tyrone Presbytery can trace their origins to the 18th century. Only four were connected to the Synod of Ulster, the others being organised by the Seceders, who were very active in this area. Six of the seven Seceder congregations were organised by the Burghers, often through the activities of licentiate Thomas Clark. Many Presbyterians emigrated to America in this century and contributed significantly to settlement expansion in New England.

Castledawson

was originally known as Dawson's Bridge and was formed in 1694 when the church was linked with Maghera. Rev John Tomb (1694–1718) resigned the Maghera connection in 1700 and a link was then formed with Magherafelt. Rev James Glasgow (1835–40) left to become a missionary in India and translator of the Gujarati Bible. Rev Robert Henderson (1888–89) also served for over thirty years as a missionary in India. He drowned at Portstewart Strand on 11 August 1921. Rev Robert Charlton (1890–98) was later Moderator of the South African Church (1920) and Rev Robert Johnston (1899–1904) was later Moderator of the Canadian Church (1932). The church was united with Curran in 1906 during the ministry of Rev Pattison Black (1905–14). Rev David McGaughey (1968–73) was later Moderator of the General Assembly (1994). Membership today stands at 210 families.

Coagh

was formed in 1708 in the face of strong Presbytery opposition on the grounds that the churches at Moneymore and Ballyclug (Brigh) would be weakened. The first minister was Rev David Tomb (1711–26). He was succeeded by local man Rev Hugh Sharp (1732–53). The location of the first church is unknown but the present square church was built during the ministry of Rev John McClelland (1755–98), who was buried in the earliest grave in the adjoining graveyard. Rev Edward Dill (1835–38) was a member of a famous ministerial dynasty. The church was united with Albany from April 1917 until July 1923. Rev George Faris (1924–25) died after only twenty months and his widow became headmistress of Victoria College, Belfast. Both church and hall were extensively renovated during the long ministry of Rev William Mercer (1951–85). The church was united with Ballygoney in 1931, and Saltersland was added to the union on 1 March 1986. Membership today stands at seventy-five families.

Tobermore

was formed in 1737 despite opposition from Maghera. The first minister, Rev James Turrentine (1744–48), returned for a second term as minister (1750–54) before the vacancy could be filled. Rev Alexander Carson (1798–1805) resigned from the church and Synod and formed an independent church which later became a Baptist congregation. He was succeeded by Rev William Brown (1810–60), who published a work on baptism. A new church was opened in 1897 during the ministry of Rev Marcus Stevenson (1884–1905), who resigned to become headmaster of Tralee Intermediate School. The church was united with Knockloughrim from 1915 until 1928. Following the ministry of Rev Robert Nixon (1965–72), the church was united with Draperstown on 1 March 1973. Rev Robert Dickenson (1973–89) was elected Moderator of the General Assembly in 1985. Membership today stands at seventy-seven families.

Dungannon

was formed in 1716 though Rev George Keith (1659–61) and Rev Thomas Kennedy of Carland both preached in Dunganon in earlier times. The first church was built about 1723 during the ministry of Rev Nathaniel Cochrane (1718–35). The Irish Volunteers held notable meetings in this church in 1782, 1783 and again in 1793. In 1803 a Seceder congregation, 'Second Dungannon', was formed in the town but it was united with 'First Dungannon' in 1928. The church was remodelled by the addition of transepts and a tower during the influential ministry of Rev Charles Morell (1844–82), who was elected Moderator of the General Assembly in 1868. The church continued to grow in the 20th century under the successive ministries of Rev Stanley Thompson (1915–64) and Rev Andrew Rodgers (1965–96), the latter being elected Moderator of the General Assembly in 1993. This is the largest church in Tyrone Presbytery and membership today stands at almost 600 families.

First Magherafelt

was formed as a separate congregation in 1738 having previously been in union with Moneymore prior to 1692 and then with

350

Castledawson. The first minister was Rev Hugh Wallace (1738–61), who had preached here and in Castledawson for the previous sixteen years. Both Rev Wallace (in 1741) and his successor Rev William Wilson (in 1783) were elected Moderator of the General Synod. Two long and noteworthy ministries here were those of Rev James Wilson (1813–54) and Rev Alexander Montgomery (1854–89). In more recent times Rev James Johnston was minister here for thirty-eight years, from 1926 until 1964. He was awarded a Doctor of Divinity degree by the Theological Faculty, Ireland. Membership today stands at 305 families.

(1771–98), was court martialled for high treason in 1798 but acquitted. He emigrated to America. He was succeeded briefly by his son, also Rev James Harper (1800–01) who also emigrated to America, where he again succeeded his father, as minister in Abingdon. The church joined the Associate Presbytery of Ireland and was united with Boveedy in the 1840s. Following the ministry of Rev Hugh McIntyre (1881–1912) the church joined the General Assembly and became a joint charge with Tobermore from 1915 until 1928. On 1 October 1928 the church was united with Bellaghy. Membership today stands at seventy families.

Upper Clonaneese

was formed as a Burgher Seceder cause in the early 1750s under the ministry of licentiate Thomas Clark. Occasional preaching in the area by Synod of Ulster ministers had ceased some time earlier. An early 'clabber' church was built in 1755 and the first minister was Rev Hugh McGill (1753–71) but he was deposed after a bitter public dispute with a licentiate, Mr Felix Quinn. The congregation split in 1788 over a proposal to build a new church on a different site. The minority remained, became an Anti-Burgher cause, and assumed the name Lower Clonaneese. The majority moved to higher ground, remained with the Burghers, and assumed the name Upper Clonaneese. Rev John Lowry (1794–1846) of Upper was briefly suspended in 1830 for publishing a pamphlet expressing approval of hymn singing in worship. Both congregations were united in 1907 and the first minister of the united charge was Rev Thomas Bole (1907–24). Membership today stands at 125 families.

Ballygoney

was formed as a Burgher Seceder cause in 1762 due to the pioneering work of licentiate Thomas Clark. Rev Joseph Kerr (1762–85) was the first minister here and initially the church was united with a cause at Moree (which later divided into Sandholes and Pomeroy). Rev Thomas Heron (1815–61) had the honour of proposing the election of Rev Samuel Hanna as Moderator of the first General Assembly on 10 July 1840. His successor, Rev George

Knockloughrim

was formed about 1761 as a Burgher Seceder congregation in the Presbytery of Down. The first minister, Rev James Harper

McCloskie (1860–73), was appointed Professor of Natural History in Princeton University in 1874. Rev George Wilson (1912–19) had previously served as a missionary in India, and he resigned in 1919 to return to India. For ten years the church was supplied by Rev John Entrican of Molesworth before it was united with Coagh in 1931. The present church, built upon the site of the former, was opened on 8 October 1955. Saltersland was added to the union on 1 March 1986. Membership today stands at thirty families.

Eglish

was formed as a Burgher Seceder cause in the 1760s by Presbyterians who were unhappy with the ministry of Rev Andrew Johnston of Benburb. In the early years the church was known as Derryfubble and united with Ballymagrane. The first minister, Rev David Holmes (1778–1802), supervised the building of a new church at Eglish, but had to retire when he became mentally unstable. The church became a separate charge under the ministry of Rev Hugh Bell (1803–48). Rev William Latimer (1872–1911) oversaw the rebuilding of the church in 1882 and made a reputation as a capable historian. From the late 1920s Eglish became a Stated Supply with Benburb. The church was united with Castlecaulfield on 1 November 1962. Membership today stands at eighty families.

Sandholes

was formed as a Burgher Seceder cause in the 1750s, arising out of preaching activities of licentiate Thomas Clark at Moree, north of Carland. The first mention of Sandholes is 15 July 1767 when Rev John Beatty (1767–73) appears to have been installed here. The original primitive church was replaced by the present church in 1798, during the ministry of Rev Thomas Dickson (1787–1816). Trouble erupted during the ministry of Rev William Harkness (1816–32) who was eventually suspended and defrocked. Legal proceedings started over ownership of the church building. His successor, Rev John Edmonds (1834–44), experienced difficulties through his strong support of Temperance and also by the innovation of asking the congregation to stand for singing. The church was extended in 1862 and underwent a major renovation in 1931 with the installation of a new pulpit and pews. A new hall was built in 1962 and the church re-roofed in 1978, during the ministry of Rev Edwin Barr (1952–88). The church was united with Pomeroy on 1 January 1992. Membership today stands at 112 families.

Reverend William Latimer

WILLIAM THOMAS LATIMER was born in 1842, the only son of Rev John Latimer of First Ballynahatty. He graduated BA from Queen's College, Belfast, in 1870 and studied Theology at Assembly's College. He was ordained in Eglish on 7 October 1872 and he spent his entire ministry here, retiring on 1 November 1911. Rev Latimer built up Eglish congregation from sixty-nine to 100 families at a time when emigration from the area was rife. He maintained an interest in history and published several important works, most notably *A History of the Irish Presbyterians* which ran to three editions (first published in 1893). Other notable works included, *Ulster Biographies* (1897) and *History of the Life and Times of Henry Cooke*. In addition Rev Latimer published over 200 articles and congregational histories. He obtained an MA from Queen's University in 1910 and was awarded a DD degree from the Presbyterian Theological Faculty, Ireland in 1915. His son, also Rev William Latimer, declined a call by Eglish congregation in 1911 to succeed his father, choosing to remain in Carnone. Rev Dr Latimer died on 19 July 1919, aged seventy-six.

First Stewartstown

was formed in 1788 by members of Brigh who lived in Stewartstown and wanted to worship locally. The first minister was Rev William Henry (1790–91). The longest ministry in the history of this congregation was that of the fourth minister, Rev Robert Allen (1814–48), who later became Superintendent of the Connaught Mission (1848–65). A Burgher congregation was formed in Stewartstown about 1815 but it did not prosper and was finally dissolved in 1904. Rev Isaiah Harkness (1865–85) was Convenor of the Temperance Committee and produced several tracts in this cause. On 1 May 1980 the church was united in a new three-point charge with Albany and Brigh. Membership currently stands at seventy-seven families.

Lower Clonaneese

was formed in 1788 when a majority of the Clonaneese congregation voted to relocate on higher ground. The minority remained, became an Anti-Burgher cause, and assumed the name Lower Clonaneese. The first minister, Rev William Wilson (1789–99), was deposed for unspecified reasons. In 1809 Lower left the Anti-Burgher Presbytery of Markethill and joined the Burgher Presbytery of Lower Tyrone, despite opposition from Upper Clonaneese. Rev James Kinnear (1811–64) was father of Rev Dr John Kinnear, MP of Letterkenny. The last minister of this single charge was Rev Robert Gill (1865–1906) and Upper and Lower Clonaneese were united in 1907. Major renovations were undertaken in 1990 during the ministry of Rev Ian Fleck (installed in 1989). Membership today stands at about thirty families.

Lecumpher

was formed as a Burgher Seceder church in the 1790s and the first minister was Rev John Wilson (1796–1821). The congregation

Reverend Robert Allen

Ballina Orphanage,
County Mayo

ROBERT ALLEN was born on 1 October 1789, the youngest son of Robert Allen, a merchant in Cookstown, County Tyrone. He was educated at Glasgow University and ordained in First Stewartstown on 7 June 1814. In November 1834 Rev Allen applied to the Irish Mission Directors for permission to establish Irish Schools in the mountain areas of Tyrone and Derry. Thirty schools were formed within a year, teaching literacy in Irish through the use of the Bible. This school system grew rapidly and was then extended to the South and West of Ireland. In 1848 Rev Allen resigned from First Stewartstown and was appointed Superintendent of the Connaught Mission, a position he filled for seventeen years. He was based in Ballina. This network of Irish Schools was integral to a concentrated Irish Presbyterian outreach throughout Connaught in the mid-nineteenth century. In 1854 Rev Allen opened an orphanage in Ballina which fulfilled a valuable role in the Mission for nearly fifty years. He was elected Moderator of the General Assembly in 1855. Rev Allen was also a regular contributor to local journals and newspapers and the *Missionary Herald*. At its height there were over 200 teachers in these Irish Schools catering for over 10,000 pupils. Robert Allen died in Ballina on 1 April 1865 and was buried in Donaghendry graveyard at Stewartstown.

waited four years before calling his son, Rev James Wilson (1825–74), as their second minister. The third minister, Rev Thomas Wilson (1874–84), was a son of Rev James Wilson and grandson of Rev John Wilson. The fourth minister, Rev John Wilson (1884–90) was a brother of Rev Thomas Wilson. The church was united with Union Road, Magherafelt, on 1 May 1926 during the ministry of Rev Robert McCammon (1890–1935). Rev Rodney Sterritt (1965–71) was later elected Moderator of the General Assembly (1991). Membership today stands at ninety-two families.

The 19th Century

As in most Presbyteries, the 19th century in Tyrone witnessed the greatest church growth with fourteen local congregations founded in this period. Six of these churches were Seceder. Not all Presbyterian ministers and congregations approved of the union in 1840 and Culnady only joined the General Assembly in 1878. Several churches experienced growth at the time of the 1859 Revival.

Castlecaulfield

was formed as a Burgher Seceder cause in 1800 and was linked with Ballygawley. The first minister was Rev John Bridge

(1800–28), and the people worshipped in a stable belonging to the Castle. Rev Bridge resigned when a substantial majority of his congregation barred him from the church because they believed he had not done enough to help the case of a member of the congregation, Mr George Richey, who was convicted of murder. The present church was opened in 1842, during the ministry of Rev Joseph Acheson (1833–76), who also conducted a school in Dungannon. Rev Robert McClean had a long and influential ministry of fifty-five years here from 1877 until 1932. Rev Thomas Eakins (1941–62) resigned in order to work with Parkanaur House Rehabilitation Centre. The church was united with Eglish on 1 November 1962 and membership today stands at 126 families.

Molesworth

was formed in December 1928 by an amalgamation of a Second Cookstown (founded in 1801 as a Burgher Seceder church and known as Second from 1840) and Molesworth (founded in 1835 in connection with the General Synod and known as Second before the union in 1840 and Third post-1840). The first minister of Second was Rev Thomas Millar (1804–52), who gained a high reputation for a Classical School he organised in this locality from 1806. The church building was situated in Loy Street. The second minister here was Rev John Wilson (1853–93): he died one month short of forty years service. The first minister of Third was Rev John Leslie (1835–93) and the church building was opened on 19 March 1837. This church was formed by members of First who were

354

disappointed that Rev Leslie could not secure a call to that church. The name Molesworth first came into use in 1894. In December 1928 the two congregations were to form a single charge under the ministry of Rev John Enrican (1893–1944) and adopted the name Molesworth Street. The united congregation worshipped in Molesworth and the Seceder building became the hall for First Cookstown. Membership today stands at 310 families.

Culnady

was formed as a Burgher Seceder congregation about 1805 and the first known minister was Rev Alexander Mulligan (1805–49). The church disapproved of the union in 1840 but joined the General Assembly in 1878 during the ministry of Rev John Forsythe (1875–81). A manse was built in 1890. The church was united with Swatragh in 1902 and the first minister of this two point charge was Rev John Heney (1902–07). Rev Vernon Corkey (1912–40) was one of eight sons of Rev Dr Joseph Corkey of Glendermott who were all ordained. A hall was built here during the ministry of Rev Leslie Casement (1969–72). Membership today stands at 165 families.

Pomeroy

was formed about 1810 as a Burgher Seceder church. The people had earlier worshipped at Moree, north of Carland. The church building was completed in 1802. The first two ministers were both suspended and subsequently resigned from the ministry: Rev

William McIlree (1810–14) and Rev David Evans (1815–37). The relatively long ministries of Rev David McKinney (1839–68) and Rev Robert Evans (1868–94) saw the congregation grow but a series of short ministries in the 20th century weakened the cause again. Rev James Kane (1951–75) was Clerk of Dungannon Presbytery and later, Tyrone Presbytery. The congregation suffered several losses due to terrorist attacks during the more recent 'Troubles'. The church was united with Sandholes on 1 January 1992 and membership currently stands at 118 families.

Second Moneymore

was formed as a Seceder church about 1824 and its first minister was Rev Samuel Mitchell (1826–31). The second minister, Rev George Thompson (1832–45) experienced considerable difficulties. Two long ministries followed: Rev Robert Sinclair (1844–72) and Rev John Sharpe (1873–1919). The church was united with First

Reverend George Thompson

GEORGE ROBERT THOMPSON was ordained in Moneymore Secession church on 24 July 1832. His was a troubled ministry. His neighbour, Rev John Barnett in First Moneymore, wrote to Presbytery about Rev Thompson's lack of tact and wisdom. A special Presbytery Visitation took place on 1 July 1834 and five elders asked that Rev Thompson be removed. At a subsequent meeting he was further accused of 'neglect of visiting and catechising families'. He was also said to have made pointed remarks from the pulpit, conducted baptisms without informing the elders, and sung Psalms 'of an annoying kind'. Presbytery advised him to resign but he refused to do so. Rev Thompson produced a petition with seventy-one names asking that he stay. The Presbytery retired to a nearby inn to discuss the matter and decided to suspend Rev Thompson, but he was restored on 1 April 1835. He was later removed from the congregation but restored for a second time in February 1836. In 1842–3 he was again suspended, disannexed, restored and suspended again. He appealed to the General Assembly in 1845 and was again restored to ministry and placed under the care of the Tyrone Presbytery.

Moneymore on 15 October 1919 and they still worship together as one congregation with services being held on alternative Sundays in each building. Membership today stands at eighty families.

Rev John Simpson (1826–30). The church was in financial difficulties in the early years and Rev Robert Fleming (1835–37) led the church into membership of the General Synod on 25 August 1836. A new Synod church was founded in Bellaghy in 1833–4 and they amalgamated on 5 February 1850. The longest ministry here was that of Rev Thomas McCrea (1877–1928). On 1 October 1928 the church was united with Knockloughrim. Membership today stands at 107 families.

Orritor

was formed in 1824 and the first minister was local man Rev John McGowan (1825–55). A manse was built in 1861, the pulpit moved from a central position on the long north wall to a short wall and the pews rearranged accordingly. Rev George McCahon (1929–57) had previously been a missionary in China with the English Presbyterian Church. During his ministry a new floor, ceiling, pews and pulpit were added to the church. The church was united with Claggan on 23 December 1957. Another major renovation was undertaken in 1968 during the ministry of Rev John McWhirter (1965–74). Membership today stands at 155 families.

Bellaghy

was formed as a Seceder church in 1826 and the first church building was on the present site. The first minister was a local man,

Swatragh

was formed in the 1820s. The church building opened in 1827 at a cost of £260 of which the Mercer's Company contributed £150. The earliest known minister was Rev Samuel Sloan (1831–50). The shortest ministry here was that of Rev James Graham who was ordained on 12 March 1857 and died on 24 November 1858. He was succeeded by Rev Thomas Turner (1859–98). The church was united with Culnady in 1902. Membership today stands at eighteen families.

the united charge was Rev Robert Dickinson (1973–89) who was elected Moderator of the General Assembly in 1985. Membership today stands at 46 families.

Newmills

was formed as a Seceder cause in 1835 and a church was built in 1837 with considerable assistance from the Earl of Castlestuart. The first minister was Rev William Brown (1839–41) who later emigrated to Canada. Rev James Foster (1850–90) had previously worked for the Belfast Town Mission and published an account of the 1859 Revival in this locality. His daughter, Lydia, published several books about Irish Presbyterian life including *The Bush that Burned*. Another long ministry was that of Rev David Macky (1890–1927). A new union was formed with Carland on 1 June 1960, during the ministry of Rev Harold Gray (1956–69). Membership today stands at 152 families.

Draperstown

was formed in October 1835 and the first minister was Rev Samuel Smith (1837–76). The second minister, Rev William Macky (1876–86) emigrated to New South Wales, Australia, where he became minister of the Scots Church in Sydney. The longest ministry here was that of Rev Charles Dickey who was ordained on 1 February 1887 and retired after fifty-two years, on 1 February 1939. His son, Rev Dr RS Dickey, was a missionary in India (1918–57). Rev John Brown (1940–47) was followed here by his cousin, Rev William Robert Brown (1948–49). The church was united with Tobermore on 1 March 1973 and the first minister of

Curran

was formed in 1837 and the first minister was Rev James McKee (1840–68). The second minister, Rev James Mitchell (1869–73), emigrated to California after four years service. The sixth minister, Rev Robert Smyth (1896–1906), organised a major refurbishment of the church and emigrated to Canada in 1906. In the ensuing months the church was united with Castledawson. Further refurbishment took place in 1936–7 during the ministry of Rev Walter Gaston (1932–67). Membership today stands at 71 families.

Saltersland

was formed in 1838 and the first minister was Rev Robert Campbell (1839–47). Early services were held in Ballynenagh Schoolhouse. The church was opened on 21 August 1842 and called Saltersland in honour of the Salters Company which gave the site. The longest ministry here was that of Rev Alexander Minnis who was ordained on 27 September 1854 and retired in 1900. Both Rev Robert McLean (1902–08) and Rev Thomas McKinney (1941–54) emigrated to Canada. The church was united with Coagh and Ballygoney on 1 March 1986. Membership today stands at twenty-eight families.

Albany

was formed in 1838 on the initiative of local ministers and Lord Castlestewart for the convenience of local Presbyterians who had previously worshipped at Brigh. The name Albany honours the Castlestewart family whose ancestors were Dukes of Albany. The first minister was Rev John Carey (1839–40) who later became an eccentric philanthropist in Toome. The second minister, Rev David Macky (1841–91), firmly established the congregation in times of famine; he built the manse in 1864 and partly paid for it himself. On his retirement, he left the property to the congregation. From 1 April 1917 the church was united with Coagh for six years. From 1 November 1923 it was united with Brigh, and Stewartstown was added on 1 May 1980. Membership today stands at twenty-eight families.

Claggan

was formed in February 1846 following the formation of a Sunday School here in 1836. The church building was opened in April 1846 and the first minister was Rev Henry McCaw (1846–87). Evening services commenced in 1859, a manse was built in 1862 and the church was extended in 1872. One controversial aspect of this extension was the addition of a church bell. One member, Miss Lydia Elizabeth Ramsey served for forty-two years as a missionary in Chuan Chow, Amoy in China with the English Presbyterian Church. The use of hymns and an organ at services were introduced in 1936, during the ministry of Rev John McCay (1929–38). Rev Charles Eadie (1951–57) emigrated to Canada. The church was united with Orritor on 23 December 1957 and membership today stands at eighty-seven families.

Reverend Andrew Weir

ANDREW WEIR was born on 16 August 1873 at Derrygennard in County Londonderry. He was brought up in Claggan congregation where his father was a Sunday School teacher. Educated at Queen's and Assembly's Colleges in Belfast, he was ordained in Claggan on 23 August 1899 and designated for missionary service in Manchuria where he spent his entire ministry. Based initially at Kwanchengtze, Rev Weir witnessed the brutality of the Boxer Rebellion in 1900 in which 332 Manchurian Christians were martyred. During his first five years as a missionary, his salary was paid by his colleagues on the mission field. From 1906 Rev Weir served for twenty-seven years as Irish Joint Secretary of Mission Conference. He witnessed revival in 1908 and actively participated in the development of a strong Chinese Church which would ultimately thrive under Chinese leadership. After serving for a time in Chaoyang in the southwest of Manchuria, Andrew Weir was appointed to Kuyushu in the north where he worked for twenty-two years. His headquarters were at Changchun. His first wife, Dr Eva Simms, died in Manchuria in 1915. On 10 May 1917 he married Margaret Grills, who had been a missionary for twelve years in Changchun. Their son, Andrew John (Jack) was to make a mark upon Irish Presbyterianism as a renowned Clerk of Assembly (1964–85) and Moderator in 1976. Andrew Weir contracted typhoid and died on 10 October 1933. He was buried at Mukden in Manchuria.

Union Road, Magherafelt

was formed in 1868 and the first minister, Rev John Hemphill (1868–69), resigned to minister in Calvary, San Fransisco. None of the first six ministers stayed more than four years until Rev Samuel McCune (1887–1905). The church was united with Lecumpher on 1 May 1926 and Rev Robert McCammon, who had been ordained in Lecumpher in 1890, was installed in Union Road on 25 May 1926. He retired on 5 March 1935. Rev John Maddock (1955–64) was followed by Rev Rodney Sterritt (1965–71) who was elected Moderator of the General Assembly in 1991. Membership today stands at 143 families.

Conclusion

The Tyrone Presbytery is a fairly stable area for Presbyterianism. Family membership in these thirty-three churches has fallen by 11% over the past fifty years, from 4,501 to 4,031 families. There have been no new congregations formed here in the 20th century and, as with other Presbyteries, congregational unions have been a noticeable feature of church life in Tyrone over the past decades. A system of two-point and three-point charges has served Tyrone Presbytery well. Eighteen ministers here serve a widespread and loyal Presbyterian community in which the average congregational size is currently 136 families.

Near Donaghmore, County Tyrone
SCENIC IRELAND

Acknowledgements

A large number of people have enabled this publication to speak so eloquently for the Presbyterian Church in Ireland.

We are truly grateful to our main photographers, Rev Dr Gordon Gray and Christopher Hill, who have provided an outstanding visual contribution, and to Robert Lyons, without whom the project would not have started; to the author, Professor Laurence Kirkpatrick; to the proof-readers, Rev Ronnie Hetherington and Professor Bill Addley; to Tom Fulton and Stewart Moore, for their efficient promotion of the book; to Dale Wright from Union College, Lorna Anderson, Ed Connolly from Church House, Gladys Elliott, Alan McMillan of the Presbyterian Historical Society, Patricia Crossley, Wesley Weir from Belfast Central Mission, for their administrative skills and practical assistance; to Rosalind Gillespie, encaustic artist from Portrush Presbyterian Congregation, for her painting; also to Leanne Higginson from Graphic Base. We express our thanks to the numerous ministers who have prepared and sent individual contributions to the Presbyteries Section.

We would like to thank contributions from photographers: Rodney Cameron, Des Clinton, Peter Collins, Colm Connaughton, Esler Crawford, Patricia Crossley, Trevor Geary, James Hamill, John Hanna, Raymond Hughes, David Irvine, Maureen Irvine, MA Kelly, Alan Lyons, Stephen Lynas, Frank Malthouse, Jim McCaughan, John Rushton, Lloyd Toal, Kieran O'Loughlin, Lillian Webb.

We are particularly indebted to Wendy Dunbar, designer and picture editor, who, with the help of Dermott Dunbar, has worked tirelessly to ensure the quality of this book's production.

Finally, this project would not have been completed without the unreserved and practical support of Very Rev Dr Finlay Holmes, Very Rev Dr Harry Uprichard – both former Moderator of the General Assembly – and Rev Dr Donald Watts, General Secretary. A special word of thanks to Sephen Lynas, Information Officer, from Church House, for his invaluable advice and encouragement.

Every effort has been made to trace and contact copyright holders before publication. If notified the publisher will rectify any errors or omissions at the earliest opportunity.

DR CLAUDE COSTECALDE

Published by Booklink, Ireland
Publisher: Dr Claude Costecalde

ISBN 0-9554097-1-3

© Text, 2006, Laurence Kirkpatrick
© Photographs: Chris Hill/Scenic Ireland, Gordon Gray and various contributors

Design by Dunbar Design, Ireland © Design Booklink

Printed in Ireland by Universities Press

Bluebells, Murlough, Co Antrim
SCENIC IRELAND